Balibar and the Citizen Subject

Critical Connections

A series of edited collections forging new connections between contemporary critical theorists and a wide range of research areas, such as critical and cultural theory, gender studies, film, literature, music, philosophy and politics.

Series Editors
Ian Buchanan, University of Wollongong
James Williams, Deakin University

Editorial Advisory Board

Nick Hewlett
Gregg Lambert
Todd May
John Mullarkey
Paul Patton
Marc Rölli
Alison Ross
Kathrin Thiele
Frédéric Worms

Titles available in the series
Badiou and Philosophy, edited by Sean Bowden and Simon Duffy
Agamben and Colonialism, edited by Marcelo Svirsky and Simone Bignall
Laruelle and Non-Philosophy, edited by John Mullarkey and Anthony Paul Smith
Virilio and Visual Culture, edited by John Armitage and Ryan Bishop
Rancière and Film, edited by Paul Bowman
Stiegler and Technics, edited by Christina Howells and Gerald Moore
Badiou and the Political Condition, edited by Marios Constantinou
Nancy and the Political, edited by Sanja Dejanovic
Butler and Ethics, edited by Moya Lloyd
Latour and the Passage of Law, edited by Kyle McGee
Nancy and Visual Culture, edited by Carrie Giunta and Adrienne Janus
Rancière and Literature, edited by Grace Hellyer and Julian Murphet
Agamben and Radical Politics, edited by Daniel McLoughlin
Balibar and the Citizen Subject, edited by Warren Montag and Hanan Elsayed

Visit the Critical Connections website at
edinburghuniversitypress.com/series-critical-connections.html

Balibar and the Citizen Subject

Edited by Warren Montag and Hanan Elsayed

Edinburgh University Press is one of the leading university presses in the UK. We publish academic books and journals in our selected subject areas across the humanities and social sciences, combining cutting-edge scholarship with high editorial and production values to produce academic works of lasting importance. For more information visit our website: edinburghuniversitypress.com

© editorial matter and organisation Warren Montag and Hanan Elsayed, 2017
© the chapters their several authors, 2017

Edinburgh University Press Ltd
The Tun – Holyrood Road, 12(2f) Jackson's Entry, Edinburgh EH8 8PJ

Typeset in 11/13 Adobe Sabon by
Servis Filmsetting Ltd, Stockport, Cheshire

A CIP record for this book is available from the British Library

ISBN 978 1 4744 0421 1 (hardback)
ISBN 978 1 4744 0422 8 (webready PDF)
ISBN 978 1 4744 0424 2 (epub)

The right of Warren Montag and Hanan Elsayed to be identified as the editors of this work has been asserted in accordance with the Copyright, Designs and Patents Act 1988, and the Copyright and Related Rights Regulations 2003 (SI No. 2498).

Note on Transliteration
We have used a simplified version of the *International Journal of Middle East Studies* (*IJMES*) conventions for the transliteration of Arabic terms.

Contents

Introduction: Balibar and the Citizen Subject   1
Warren Montag and Hanan Elsayed

Part I: Balibar Reading Schmitt Reading Hobbes: Equality or Similitude?

1. Schmitt's Hobbes, Hobbes's Schmitt   37
   Etienne Balibar, Translated by Warren Montag

2. The Mortal God and his Faithful Subjects: Hobbes, Schmitt and the Antinomies of Secularism   94
   Etienne Balibar, Translated by Warren Montag

Part II: Transindividual/Universal

3. The "Other Scene" of Political Anthropology: Between Transindividuality and Equaliberty   111
   Jason Read

4. Intersubjectivity or Transindividuality: The Leibniz–Spinoza Alternative   132
   Vittorio Morfino, Translated by Dave Mesing

5. A Parallelism of Consciousness and Property: Balibar's Reading of Locke   157
   Warren Montag

6. Figures of Universalism: Notes on Philosophy and Politics in Etienne Balibar   182
   Mohamed Moulfi, Translated by Vanessa Brutsche

7. Balibar and the Philosophy of Science: The Question
   of the "Epistemological Break" 203
   Giorgos Fourtounis

   Part III: Inequality, Violence and the Possibility of Citizenship

8. *La Haine:* Falling in Slow Motion 235
   Hanan Elsayed

9. Morbid Perseverance: The Internal Border and
   White Supremacy 253
   James Edward Ford III

10. Just like a Woman: Balibar on the Politics of
    Reproduction 284
    Nancy Armstrong

11. Another "Neo-Racism": Balibar and the Everywhere
    War 309
    Mike Hill

    Notes on Contributors 333
    Index 335

Introduction: Balibar and the Citizen Subject
Warren Montag and Hanan Elsayed

There are many pathways in contemporary thought that commence, or recommence after appearing to have broken off, in the work of Etienne Balibar. Some of these pathways begin at the point of his collaboration with Louis Althusser, while others only appear after, in certain cases long after, this collaboration had come to an end. It would be a mistake, however, to read Balibar's work in relation to an imaginary "Althusserianism," whether as its continuation or as a radical break from it. The collective project in which both Althusser and Balibar participated during the 1960s and 1970s was anything but a closed theoretical totality; on the contrary, it was a movement able to persist as a singular, but composite, body of thought only through a process of internal differentiation that impelled it outside of itself in search of what would preserve its existence, exposing it to various aleatory encounters. Althusser once referred to himself, as well as to his so-called disciples, as so many distinct effects of this collective project, itself part of a specific historical conjuncture:

> if we are here, it is as the effects of a theoretical conjuncture. The person who is addressing you is, like all the rest of us, merely a particular structural effect of this conjuncture, an effect that, like each and every one of us, has a proper name. The theoretical conjuncture that dominates us has produced an Althusser-effect, as it has produced a Rancière-effect, a Balibar-effect . . . and so on.

He added "this effect exhibits variations" that "do not coincide."[1]

What Althusser termed the "Balibar-effect," even in its specificity, cannot be understood as a linear, progressive development that would lead from *Reading Capital* to Balibar's most recent work, nor as two distinct developments separated by a chronological break that would allow us to speak of a "before" and an "after." If we can say that Balibar's work is marked by constant innovation that prevents us from understanding it as a continuous development (that would be another way of speaking of the famous theoretical "detours" or deviations that, for Althusser, finally constituted the sole way forward), we must also recognize that it constitutes a line of thought that is compelled to make a detour through its own past. This is not the past understood as the foundation of the present, a series of theoretical acquisitions that would serve as the basis for future inquiry, but a past composed of unresolved problems, unfinished theses and irreducible conflicts, some of which become visible as such only later. The pathway we wish to trace in this collection is one such detour: it circles back upon itself, its own past, to comprehend the present and open the way to a possible future. It may best be identified and made visible through the application of Balibar's own title: "citizen subject."

Without attempting to construct a genealogy of Balibar's own genealogy of the subject or the citizen subject, we can begin by noting that both terms recall (without reproducing or imitating) Althusser's theory of the interpellated subject, or, to use the lexicon of Althusser's first attempt to formulate its basic concepts, the theory of the individual to whom agency is imputed so that he may be held accountable for the actions ascribed to him.[2] To formulate it in this way is to emphasize the most decisive and least understood aspect of Althusser's intervention: his insistence on the necessary and unbreakable tie between subjectivity (understood as consciousness or agency) and subjection. He reminds us that the term "subject" has two antithetical meanings:

> a free subjectivity, a centre of initiatives, author of and responsible for its actions; (2) a subjected being, who submits to a higher authority, and is therefore stripped of all freedom except that of freely accepting his submission. This last note gives us the meaning of this ambiguity, which is merely a reflection of the effect which produces it: the individual *is interpellated as a (free) subject in order that he shall submit freely to the commandments of the Subject, i.e. in order that he shall (freely) accept his subjection*, i.e. in order that he shall make the gestures and actions of his subjection "all by himself". *There are no subjects except by and for their subjection.*[3]

What Althusser here calls an "ambiguity" (but that is in fact a paradox or a contradiction) was already present in Locke and Kant, both of whom admitted in so many words that the notion that the individual is the free or undetermined cause of his actions, while finally unverifiable, was absolutely necessary (for the operation of law and for the coherence of any moral doctrine): we must act "as if" the notion that the individual was the origin and author of his actions was indisputably true. It was enough that this freedom could plausibly be imputed to an individual by a superior instance (God – to whom the imputation would have to be imputed – or the earthly sovereign) for it to be regarded as given in both senses of the term, that is, transferred or given over to the individual as the means of his inclusion in the realm of law, and an accurate representation of the actual state of affairs (it is true because we need it to be true). Thus, in an important sense, from this point of view the subject as agent, as "center of initiatives," is a subject on whom the supposition of freedom has been imposed: the individual is subjected to subjectivity.[4]

Althusser, however, actively and progressively suppressed the history in which the contradictory character of the subject was concretized in order to present the final version of his theory of the interpellation of the subject in the form of an allegory. The rhetorical force of Althusser's conceptual scheme depended on the abstraction of the drama of the subject from its historical and textual settings in order to emphasize the essential, that is, omnihistorical, character not only of ideology (the imaginary relation of individuals to their real conditions of existence – including and above all their own actions) but also of the process of interpellation in which the imaginary relation had its existence. Althusser succeeded in a spectacular way in recasting the notion of ideology by placing the figure of the interpellated subject at its center, but not without certain theoretical "*sous-produits*," as he liked to call them: the unintended byproducts or side effects necessary to the accomplishment of his objective that nevertheless often returned against it to compromise or decompose it. It appeared that the cost of the theory of interpellation was a functionalist account of social reproduction that could not explain revolt or resistance, as well as the ahistoricism of a "formal structure" composed of a "quadruple system" realized in its various historical expressions – the very model that he regarded as the idealist element that the great works of structuralism could not escape.[5] Thus, the ideological state apparatuses (ISAs) essay offers an apparent meaning that in fact eludes us the more closely we examine it. Not only did Althusser produce an allegorical figuration of the individual subject, but he allegorized problems rather than solutions, and advanced a critique camouflaged as a theory. Perhaps we must recognize that, despite its striking originality, the notion of the interpellation of the individual as subject is also a simplification, albeit a paradoxical simplification of a theory that did not (yet) exist, and therefore an anticipatory simplification that risked becoming (and to a certain extent did become) an obstacle to the very theory whose advent it announced.

Balibar has in a certain sense returned to the problem or problems indicated in the ISAs in the body of work referred to here, but his insistence on an approach that is historical, above all in its tracing of the movement of concepts in the materiality of their actual written existence, leads him to intervene in the multitude of questions and problems surrounding the theme of the subject (from subjection to agency) by writing the doublet Citizen Subject (that has served as the title of an essay published in 1988, as well as the title of a recent book) without a hyphen or virgule to connect its two terms.[6] In doing so, he has interposed an absence that, combined with the proximity and priority of "citizen" in relation to "subject," serves to make visible the contradictory meanings that have been attached to (or have from the beginning inhabited) the term "subject" against a historical tradition that has obscured the fact that subjection is inextricably bound up with every existing account of the subject as origin and agent from Descartes and Hobbes to Heidegger. Balibar reminds us that it is only by a retrospective projection that Heidegger is able to read in Descartes the origin of the modern notion of the subject as the substrate or substance (the ὑποκείμενον or subjectum) from which or upon which other existences may arise (its properties or attributes), a reading made possible only by a suppression of the fact that the term also designates that that is placed under, physically and/or legally. Further, the only subject found in Descartes' work (and we are speaking of the concept: the word itself is hardly to be found there) is the subject subjected to a divine sovereignty.[7] It is this subjection that alone precedes and makes possible the existence of a thinking thing capable of certain, that is, indubitable knowledge and that retains an identity through time. Only through this subjection can the individual achieve the mastery over himself that allows him to be thought of, or to think of himself, as free, a thought that presupposes an identification with the image of God. Balibar shows that Kant is the source of the retrospective reading of Descartes as the thinker of the nominalization of "I think" or "I am thinking" as "das: *Ich denke*," "the Cogito," as if in doing so Kant were fabricating the fictitious origins or foundation of his own thought.[8] But even Kant's use of "*Subjekt*" to describe "the I think" draws on the etymology of subjection (*Subjektion*), as if the semantic field of the sovereign subject were the site of a struggle against, or against revealing, a perpetually re-imposed subjection. Further, Kant grants to the concept of "*Subjekt*" its political significance: in order to consent to the sovereign's power, the subject must be deemed capable of consent and, even more, capable of having freedom imputed to him (by virtue of anthropological traits: adult, male, European, sane and so forth). It appears that the modern notion of the subject (and this applies equally to notions of agency, a term that shares the same moral and legal history) is caught in a circle of subjection: when it seeks the foundations of its freedom and self-determination within itself, the subject discovers the trace of the other who confers upon it its autonomy.

It is precisely to break open the circle of subjection that Balibar introduces the notion of "citizen." The Hobbesian conception of the sovereign as guarantor not simply of peace but of the equality between individuals (an equality rooted in nature but denied by "the children of pride," each of whom believes himself superior to his fellows – one of the causes of war in the state of nature), renders subjection the pre-condition of citizenship ("no peace without subjection"). As Roberto Esposito has shown, universal subjection to the sovereign suspends the fear and animosity that constitute the natural relation between individuals: citizenship becomes possible only when every individual is protected from every other and from himself (from the inclinations that would lead him into conflict with others: fear, envy, pride and so on).[9] For Locke, this protection is extended beyond the person to his property (without which, according to Locke, the living individual who is the necessary bearer of the juridical person cannot exist) and is consecrated as natural law, that is, God's law, which severely limits sovereign right, whether monarchial or popular. Rousseau's starting point is accordingly the rejection of the very notion of starting point or origin. While Hobbes and Locke claim to have gone in search of a pre-social world of solitary individuals and thus a condition prior to the constitution of society, neither "succeeded in arriving there." They "have transferred to the state of nature ideas taken from society. They spoke of savage man and described civil man."[10] They have in fact fabricated the origin that their own reason has rendered inaccessible to them out of the materials at hand, that is, their own social and political worlds. But even a philosopher capable of setting aside every assumption derived from civil existence will run up against the barrier of the absolute alterity of the state of pure nature; nothing we can know or think pertains to it because the routes "that must have led man to the civil state" have been "forgotten and lost."[11] If we by some chance can locate and follow some of these routes backward, we discover the signs of a progressive denaturation of which the means of the journey of discovery are a consequence until we come to the boundary imposed by our knowledge itself. It is the point at which we discover that reason and the knowledge impossible without it are the very means by which the forgetting of the origin has taken place: to reach this point is to discover not simply the inaccessibility of the state of pure nature, but in fact its radical absence. It "no longer exists except in what is other than itself, in its contrary."[12] The only true origin for Rousseau is that from which what followed cannot be deduced or derived, a nothingness from which nothing follows, a state of negation that must be negated for history to begin.[13]

Balibar argues that the voiding of the origin in Rousseau is the necessary theoretical precondition of his notions of popular sovereignty and the general will, themselves necessary to the movement from subject to citizen. Both the "artificialist" and "corporatist/organicist" foundations of subjection disappear: neither the definitive moment (real or implied) at which each separate individual consents to his or her own subjection on the basis of a calculation of self-interest, nor the "spontaneous" model of command and obedience according to which individuals are born into subjection in the family or household that are the natural or biological foundations of social and political life are conceivable in the state of pure nature. The so-called alternatives are composed of notions that belong to the civil state and are nothing more than attempts to justify one political form or another. It is here that the paradoxes of Rousseau's theory of the social contract take on their importance: if the individual is necessarily both citizen and subject, this necessity is inscribed in the fact that he is subject not to the will of another but to a law of which he as citizen is the maker. Because the sovereign is made up of all individuals in a condition of association, every one equal to every other one, equally "above" the law as its maker and under it as a legal subject, the citizen's relation to the law is one of immanence: the activity of the citizen (the making of law) is one and the same thing as the citizen's passivity (obedience to the law).[14] The immanence of this relation (or even this antimony) vanishes as soon as inequality appears, even if it applies only to the person of the sovereign who would then become the only citizen in a world of subjects.

Balibar insists here on the link between equality (that cannot be meaningful if it is merely "symbolic," the representation of equality in law without any necessary relation to the material conditions of equality) and the process of permanent insurrection or permanent revolution. Because equality is not synonymous with similitude, the struggle for equality is itself in a sense immanent in the processes of differentiation that characterize social existence. The struggle for equality is not a struggle to reduce difference or, failing that, to deny it by refusing to represent it. It is instead a struggle against the permanent tendency to assign a political meaning to these differences through a hierarchization that installs an unequal relation of forces. This is what Foucault described as the "underside" of the law that allows ever more elaborate declarations of equality by "guaranteeing the submission of bodies and forces."[15] This explains why Rousseau's contract cannot be an original moment or an origin at all: it is what Balibar, citing Derrida, calls the supplement of the origin, the contract that emerges only after the equality of association that it founds and what is more that exists only in the power to insure that "men are born and remain free and equal."[16]

Rousseau's paradoxes will be further developed in the contradictory character of the modern citizen as expressed in the Declaration of the Rights of Man and of the Citizen (1789). Balibar notes that the opening statement that "Men are born and remain free and equal in rights" contains the recognition that freedom and equality are not only granted to "men" upon birth (whether by nature or by virtue of the social and political condition into which they are born) but remain so (as if to identify as a problem the withering away even of the rights that cannot freely be alienated through exposure to tyranny or simply to the unequalizing tendencies of modern social and economic life). The gap between the rights we are born with and those that remain ours can be reformulated as the distinction between symbolic/formal and actual rights, between rights that exist by law or in principle (and that each inherits by virtue of being born) but that the individual does not have the ability to exercise given the effectivity of forces beyond the purview of the law, particularly those existing in the nominally free realm of civil society, and the rights the individual is capable of exercising. Against both the "left" position that the existence of the discrepancy between formal and real rights necessarily invalidates the notions of right and equality as such by reducing them to their "bourgeois" meaning, and the "rightist" position that any attempt to insure the actual exercise of legally guaranteed rights leads to a totalitarian expansion of the state, in particular into what is properly a "private" realm (of property), Balibar argues that this discrepancy marks the unrest or instability proper to the citizen, whose essential (and "hyperbolic") existence is realized in permanent insurrection against the barriers to the realization of merely formal rights.

But there is another, perhaps more unsettling, dimension of the citizen and citizenship. The very form of the universality of the citizen according to the Declaration is tied to its tendential identity with "man." As Balibar notes, the "man" (*l'homme*) of the "Rights of Man (*les droits de l'homme*)" is presumed to be a synonym of "human being," a "synecdoche of the universal in accordance with the classical definition of this trope: the substitution of the part for the whole."[17] The whole represented by the trope, however, is already itself a synecdoche, which both obscures (in the "universality" it proclaims) the absence of woman and assumes both the capacity of men to represent women, as well as the necessity that women be represented by men, politically as well as discursively. In this way, "man" became the signifier of humanity as such, while woman emerged from the crucible of the Revolution as something like "man minus," marked as different and, in a mimetic relation to child-bearing, condemned to carry the lack within herself that defines the female as (less than the) male. The exclusion of women from the realm of the political was therefore secured by means of the language of universalism; their exclusion could be said to be the effect of the mode of their inclusion: women were not pushed beyond the limits of citizenship, but inscribed within it in the form of "passive citizens," those who enjoy the protection of the law but who may play no part in making it (by electing law-makers).

Precisely because they, like servants and laborers, were understood to be dependent on a male property-owner and thus subject directly or indirectly, through force or consent, to his will, women could not, it was argued, think for themselves, as was required of an active citizen. In part, their dependence was a matter of social custom and to a certain extent civil law, but the passivity ascribed to them was also seen as the necessary consequence of their role in human reproduction. Women could thus enter the universal but only in the mediated form the synecdochic figure captures: they were citizens of the nation only insofar as they were represented by a man.

If every (active) citizen is a man, however, not every man is a citizen. If it is the case that "the citizen is unthinkable as an 'isolated' individual," the category of citizen nevertheless functions as a principle of exclusion, producing its counterpart, not only passive or partial citizens whose inability to possess and exercise civil rights by virtue of their dependence on another (the male slave or servant, the man without property), but also a mass of non-citizens, women as well as men, whose natality/nationality disqualifies them from the freedom and equality proper to the citizen.[18] Balibar reminds us that while Rousseau places sovereignty in the people (a profoundly ambiguous and unbounded notion as it is described in his work and thus open to universalization), the Declaration des Droits de L'Homme et du Citoyen places it in "the nation," rendering all those (male property-owners) residing in a circumscribed territory equal at the same moment that it excludes all those outside the nation.

Balibar has argued on a number of occasions that the demarcation of one nation from another in terms of spatial boundaries limits the universality of its notion of citizenship to those (born) within its borders, or increasingly today, those born within its territorial limits who must in addition be recognized or identified as belonging to or authentically of the nation understood as a biopolitical entity. Historically, the concept of citizen, the bearer of legal equality, has tended to produce the shadowy other of this equality: the never-ending search for a non-juridical, biological or cultural foundation for the specific universal codified in law and for the criteria by which a distinction can be made between what in France today is called the *Français de souche* and the *Français de papier* (those who have been French for many generations and those who are the descendants of recent immigrants). The effect of such distinctions, as Balibar reminds us, is the demarcation of an internal border between authentic and merely "paper" (legal) members of the national community. The internal borders may be based on language, ethnicity or religious identity so that even those who are both born in a given national territory and originally "belong" to its culture, may find themselves on the wrong side of an internal border that defines a natural community that precedes any social or legal ties.

Here, Balibar, drawing on the work of Georg Simmel and Alfred Schutz,[19] insists on the increasing relevance of the category of the stranger (the foreigner or alien, "legal" or "illegal," as well as the one who, although a "native," is identifiable through "anthropological" or phenotypical differences, or increasingly through "culture ... the new name under which the conception of the 'diversity of the human races' and their inequality is perpetuated and adapted to a new conjuncture") to any comprehension of the contradictions proper to the notion of the citizen, contradictions that have matured considerably since 1789.[20] The result is the production of the figure of the "internal stranger" determined as such by virtue of "inassimilable differences" whether cultural, political or religious, despite his natality. As Balibar shows, this is the "internal" consequence of an identification of nation and citizenship. In its insurrectionary moment the citizenry could imagine the nobility as a foreign race (enemies of the nation) whose physical expulsion alone would insure the nation's freedom, as if race war were the original form of class war, with implications that the latter could not escape. In opposition, it may be the nation itself, that is, the authentic nation, that had to be identified and recovered by a drawing of internal borders that are intensive rather than extensive, borders that separate cultures and languages. But the quest to distinguish the true national from the strangers (often not recognized as such) among which he is dispersed (a distinction that must precede any drawing of borders) is never ending: anthropological and cultural differences once regarded as insignificant, part of the nation's legitimate and natural diversity, may suddenly be invested with a decisive political significance that determines the very identity of the nation – that in turn then finds itself contracting as it divests itself of the foreign elements that are regarded as impurities or adulterates. At the extreme, the internal stranger becomes the internal enemy whose supposed identification with a hostile "other" outside the nation or whose unwillingness or inability to efface the marks of difference in order to assimilate, renders him an immediate threat, triggering what is in fact a social and political autoimmune reaction.

The power of Balibar's work here lies in the extent to which it has pushed the limits of visibility and legibility by insisting precisely on understanding the concepts of subject, subjection and subjectivity in the historicity (and materiality) of their discursive and textual existence. He insists that "only singular texts . . . state theses and pose *determinate* problems of interpretation," such that an author can "never write the same text twice." Restatements invariably diverge from those they claim to reformulate, often producing interpretations of preceding statements that add or subtract from them.[21] Thus, the "simple reconstruction of arguments" characteristic of Anglo-American Analytic philosophy cannot serve as "substitutes for texts," although these reconstructions become texts themselves to be analyzed as such.[22] His approach refuses in principle to treat these concepts as disembodied ideas, abstracted from the complexities not simply of language, that is, a specific language (whether Latin, French, English or German) but precisely of the mutual interaction or interference of multiple languages in the actual formation of concepts that are thus also products of the work of translation.

Balibar approaches Locke's invention of the concept of consciousness by examining the French translation, supervised by Locke himself, of *An Essay Concerning Human Understanding*. Such an approach allows him to determine the theoretical effects of "the materiality of writing":

> I am effectively convinced – as was the group that produced the *Vocabulaire européen des philosophies* – not only that the difficulties of translation (and in particular the case of untranslatability, which leads to terminological inventions and to strategies of paraphrase and periphrasis) constitute privileged indicators of the meaning of concepts, but that they form an important part of the conditions of possibility of philosophical thought (as important as logic or rhetoric) in that philosophers *think by means of writing* in a determinate conjuncture, and most often at the intersection of several languages.[23]

Thus, philosophy, even in its most insular forms, must knowingly or unknowingly engage constantly in "co-lingualism," attempting to naturalize words and concepts that may have been imported, but that just as often appear uninvited after having migrated unpredictably across linguistic borders (driven by sound as well as sense). Such words may on occasion provoke a semantic or lexical crisis by proving resistant to translation. What they resist is typically a reduction or subtraction of meaning and in their resistance make visible the line between what can and cannot be said within the host language: the impossible proper to it.

Balibar's insistence on the "materiality of writing" strictly speaking allows us to comprehend the untranslatability of the very concepts, phrases and texts that have nevertheless been translated, even if by "translation" we can no longer assume that a meaning can be separated from the words (and the order of those words) in which it was "expressed" (or better, immanent) without semantic additions or subtractions. Moreover, the history of the "adoption" or "loaning" of words and phrases between languages is littered with examples of failed migration, not only in the sense that words acquired new and different meanings, irreducible, if not opposed, to their original sense, but also that certain words simply didn't "take" and were rejected as if they were pathogenic foreign bodies whose presence within a linguistic system would threaten the proper functioning of its elements, as well as the conceptual regime coextensive with it. There are few examples of this history as salient as that of the "subject," whose history is the intensification of an overdetermined contradiction, a process of combined and uneven development that has imprinted opposing and apparently incompatible meanings on the word. Balibar has shown us that the concept cannot exist except on the basis of this contradiction, on the antagonism proper to it, the trace of subjection (itself necessarily a relation of unequal forces) against which every form of subjectivity (a concept that emerged from a process of mistranslation/transformation of an original meaning) attempts to immunize itself, as if it came into being through the work of compensation.

But there is another dimension to the problem of translation to which Balibar points but does not explore. In his discussion of the trans-lingual conversation/conversion that made possible the invention of consciousness (from which every notion of subjectivity is finally inseparable) as both word and concept he writes:

> The invention of consciousness extends its roots throughout the concatenation of events that inaugurate modernity. It concerns the entire

field of theology, politics, moral and philosophical thought, as well as literature. We may imagine it as a drama consisting of several episodes whose protagonists belong both to an insular and a Continental culture on both sides of the Channel. They speak Latin (also reading and sometimes reconstructing Greek, but not Arabic), Italian, Dutch, French (the language of the "Republic of Letters"), English and, beginning in the eighteenth century, German.[24]

"But not Arabic": Balibar's reference to the absence of Arabic from this drama (not only in relation to the invention of consciousness, but perhaps even more to the problem of the subject more generally) marks it as an active exclusion rather than a mere absence occasioned by ignorance or indifference, as if it were simply one of the many other languages that played no part in this drama. There is reason to suspect that its exclusion, in contrast to (or at least to a greater extent than) that of other languages, is *necessary* in certain respects to the "dialogue and a process of translinguistic reflection" out of which the modern notion of the subject emerged. What marks the specificity of this exclusion, however, was the fact that it was retroactive, an isolation and expulsion into exteriority of what was already profoundly internal. Only an active forgetting can conceal from us today the fact that it once appeared to a significant part of the Christian world that the Arabic of Alfarabi (Al-Farabi), Avicenna (Ibn Sina), and above all, Averroes (Ibn Rushd) may well be the medium most conducive to the discovery and expression of certain ideas, including ideas directly related to notions of individuality and conscience/consciousness.[25] The Medieval Church encouraged the translation of both scientific and philosophical works from Arabic (as well as Hebrew and Greek), notably by consolidating a school of translation in Toledo in the twelfth century and later establishing chairs of Arabic at the universities of Oxford, Paris and Salamanca.[26] While many of the translations, particularly of the works of Avicenna and Averroes, were justified on the grounds that they were in fact commentaries on Plato and Aristotle that could be trusted to explain these notoriously difficult texts without any reference to the Islamic faith, it became clear over time that certain of the commentaries had in fact overshadowed and perhaps even supplanted the Greek texts. And the fact that what was transmitted from Arabic to the Christian world was neither reducible to Aristotle nor to Islam but was instead a singular body of thought expressed in the

Arabic language whose every part challenged the defining and necessary elements of Christian theology whatever its form, provoked mounting opposition, which finally resulted in the Condemnations of 1270–7.[27] Of the 219 theses condemned by the Bishop of Paris, most of which derived not from Aristotle, but from Aristotle as read by Averroes, certain nodal points of controversy stand out. One of the most disturbing was identified by Bonaventure, among the most determined opponents of Averroes's philosophy, as one of the three fundamental errors afflicting the philosophy of his time: "That intellect is one in all (men), that is against the root of distinction and individuation." The consequence of such a doctrine, he argued, can only be that "there is no difference in merit and reward, if one (and the same) is the soul of Christ and of Judas the betrayer. The whole (of it) is heretical."[28] What is extraordinary here is that Bonaventure has in fact charged Averroes with restoring "conscientia" to its original meaning of a knowing and thinking in common with others and therefore with resisting the separation of consciences and, in a pre-emptive way, consciousnesses. Averroes's notion of a transindividual intellect (العقل/al-'aql) suggested that individuals do not and cannot think or feel alone, a condition that calls into question the possibility of each shall be judged according to what he alone has thought, said or done. In fact, Alain de Libera has argued that Averroes's doctrine of "monopsychism" (as Leibniz called it)[29] was what Hobbes and Locke had to reject and deny in order to develop their notions of the individual, the person and, in the case of the latter, consciousness. Further, Averroes constitutes one of the points of emergence of what de Libera calls the tradition of "*Es denkt*" (It thinks) associated above all with Freud and Lacan who tell us that

> in a sense I am not the subject of my thoughts. Of course, they do not say that it is a unique and separate intellect common to all men who thinks in me when I think. But there is a continuity between Averroisme and the tradition of *Es denkt in mir* [It thinks in me].[30]

The exclusion (that is finally the exclusion of philosophical texts written in Arabic), the action of drawing a line of demarcation, an action that continues today as the after-life or reactivation of the Paris condemnation, separates and protects the concepts of consciousness and the subject in their modern senses from all that they have rejected to become what they are.[31]

The different meanings of the term "subject" and the way in which the notions of subjectivity and subjection are frequently condensed and combined makes even its translation from one European language to another difficult.[32] This situation, according to Balibar, confers a distinct advantage on the English and French languages precisely because of the irreducible ambiguity of the terms "subject" and *"sujet"* in contrast to languages such as Latin and German that distinguish between, on the one hand, *subjectum* or *Subjekt* (the subject as agent) and *subjectus* or *Untertan* (with its emphasis on being under or subjected to something higher).[33] The unresolved ambiguity characteristic of English and French simultaneously evokes both the continuity and the mutations (and thus the progress) of the notion of subject.[34] To translate the term into other languages, and we refer specifically to the case of Arabic here, this equivocal unity is inevitably lost (but in a way very different from the cases of Latin and German) given the fact that the equivalent terms have emerged from their own specific semantic histories that do not correspond to that of "subject/sujet."

To translate the concepts of subject, subjectivity or subjection into Arabic requires the use of a number of different terms that do not share a common root since each is linked to a specific meaning. In the case of the notion of subjection expressed in the Latin *subjectus*, one would translate "subjet" as *raʿiyya* (رعيّة). But such a translation requires, in turn, an acknowledgment of the distinct trajectories and semantic particularities of each of the two terms. To treat them as if they were simply equivalent without registering their differences is to open the way to a series of problems and misunderstandings.[35] Foremost among them is the fact that the idea of "being placed under" (the meaning of the root of *subjectus*, the verb *"subicio"*) is completely absent from the Arabic word. At the etymological level the root ر ع ي signifies "to care for" or "to attend," implying the sense of responsibility or duty captured by one of its derivatives, *rāʿī* (راعي, keeper or shepherd). Moreover, these terms also have a religious dimension. The Prophet Muhammad declares in a Hadith:

> Each of you are *rāʿī* (guardian) and are responsible for your *raʿiyya*; the ruler (emir or imam) is *rāʿī* and is responsible for his *raʿiyya*; the man is *rāʿī* of his family and responsible for his *raʿiyya*; the woman is *rāʿiya* (fem.) of her husband's house and children and is responsible for her *raʿiyya*, a servant ("slave" in another version) is *rāʿī* of his

master's property (*māl*) and is responsible for his *ra'iyya*. So all of you are *rā'ī* and are responsible for your *ra'iyya*.³⁶

According to its seventh-century Islamic conception, *ra'iyya* (in the singular) is the object that must be protected by the *rā'ī*, and for which he is responsible; in this sense the *rā'ī* is virtually any member of society who is charged with an obligation, irrespective of his rank. Here every *rā'ī*, as *subditus*, exists in a relation of obedience: he must assume the duty that originates in a divine command transmitted to the Prophet. According to Mohamad Abid al-Jabiri, "This Hadith breaks completely with the concept of *shepherd and flock* as known in the thinking of the ancient orientals, in [P]haraonic, Babylonian, Hebrew and, later, Persian systems of thinking."³⁷ In place of the shepherd–flock relation, all *ru'āt* (رعاة, plural of *rā'ī*) are equal in the face of divine sovereignty. Subjected to God and accountable for his conduct, the *rā'ī* cannot claim absolute power.³⁸ Al-Jabiri explains that "the term al-raa'i (shepherd, keeper) is not considered in Islam an attribute of God Almighty. Muslims believe that God has 99 attributes, called His Beautiful Names (for example, the Merciful, the Omniscient, the Resurrector); *al-raa'i* is not one of these names." He concludes that "the concept of *sheperd/flock*, then, is foreign to Islam, and what is closer in meaning (in this regard) to Islam is the idea of the citizen."³⁹ Not only did Muhammad refuse the designation of "king" or "chief," but his supporters would not have considered themselves as being "led" or "ruled"; they designated themselves and were designated by the Arabs as "*Sahāba*" (صحابة, companions).⁴⁰ This relation in turn is based on the Islamic concept of *al-shūrā* (الشورى, mutual consultation) (Koran 42: 36–9), which is discussed with faith, prayer and charity.⁴¹ The practice of *al-shūrā* is specifically recommended to the Prophet in another verse.⁴² Muhammad's four successors, (الخلفاء الراشدون, *al-Khulafā' al-Rāshidūn*) – Abū Bakr, 'Umar, 'Uthmān and 'Alī – maintained this practice that would eventually become limited to a narrow circle of those closest to the sovereign. Historical sources confirm that each of the four Caliphs were on a number of occasions publicly questioned, confronted and contradicted by the common people, including women.

Within the theological framework, it is true that the obedience of the *ra'iyya* was the counterpart of the emir's responsibility, even when the former disagreed with the latter. This obedience, however, was neither total nor unconditional as numerous Hadiths attributed to the Prophet demonstrate:

> It is obligatory for one to listen to and obey the ruler – in what he likes and what he dislikes – as long as he is not ordered to commit an act of disobedience to God. If such an act of disobedience is imposed, then no listening nor obeying is required of him.[43]

But from the moment that impiety was no longer manifest or obvious, it was not easy to determine whether a given act would lead to disobedience. The fact that the common people possessed only a limited and somewhat vague knowledge of Islamic precepts meant that they were unable to make a determination about a given action. From this, however, followed not simply uncertainty and confusion, but also a tendency to question the judgments made by the authorities. While the degree of obedience expected of the people in this Hadith is considerable, the very conditions of obedience separate the case of the believer (or *subditus-subjectus*) from that of the slave (*servus*) and mark a distinction between the emir's sovereignty and despotism.[44] The "subject," that is, the believer, cannot be totally subjected to the sovereign, whose legitimacy remains relative and thus risks at any given moment being called into question. It is precisely the notion that true power can come only from God understood as *al-Malik* (المَلِك/the Sovereign), *al-Jabbār* (الجبّار/the Powerful), *al-ʿAzīz* (العزيز/the Self Sufficient) that prevents total subjection, even if the emir attempts to impose it through pre-emptive action, and opens a permanent space for disagreement and resistance. The instability and variability of the "ruler–ruled" relation here is structural and as such resists the imposition of a purely formal distribution of right and power.

According to Ibn Khaldun (1332–1406), the ability to retain power (المُلْك/*al-mulk*) depends on an entire apparatus of administrative and military power:

> It should be noted that, by himself, the ruler is weak, and he carries a heavy load. He must look for help from his fellow men. He needs their help for the necessities of life and for all his other requirements.[45]

The function of the government depends on a number of divisions, each of which occupies a particular domain that is itself subdivided. Among the "instruments" necessary to the functioning of government is the *wazirate* that Ibn Khaldun regards as "the mother of governmental functions and royal ranks." He writes that the "name itself simply means 'help.' *Wizârah* (wazirate) is derived either from *mu'âzarah* 'help,' or from *wizr* 'load,' as if the wazir were helping the person whom he supports to carry his burdens and charges."[46] More than a century before Machiavelli, Ibn Khaldun warned that the authority of the sovereign depended also on the support of the people, a fact that rendered him dependent on their collective disposition and numbers, as illustrated in one section that he subtitles "The greatness of a dynasty, the extent of its territory, and the length of its duration depend on the numerical strength of its supporters."[47]

With the formation and then the expansion of the Muslim empire from the end of the seventh century, the extent of political power increased considerably: the movement towards absolute sovereignty was accompanied by a growing gap between the emir and his subjects. Mu'āwiya Ibn Abī Sufyān (602–80), founder of the Umayyad dynasty in Damascus, was the first to establish a system of hereditary succession by naming his son, Yazīd, as his successor, putting an end to the practice of designating the successor by committee. The movement away from the original conception of the emir accelerated and was expressed in a marked tendency to luxury and ostentation. Here again it is useful to refer to Ibn Khaldun whose *al-Muqaddimah* (*Prolegomena*) provides an introduction to the scientific study of society, principally through the formation and decline of the state.[48] In his careful analysis of the transformation of power following its establishment, Ibn Khaldun emphasizes one of the key elements of this transformation – the inaccessibility of the sovereign.[49]

> Now, if a dynasty at the beginning of its rule is a Bedouin one, the ruler possesses austerity and the desert attitude. He is close to the people and easily accessible. Then, when his power is firmly established, he comes to claim all the glory for himself. He needs to keep away from the people and to remain aloof with his friends ... Therefore, he seeks to keep away from the common people as much as possible. He employs someone at his door to admit (only) those of his friends and of the people of the dynasty whom he cannot avoid, and to prevent people (in general) from having access to him.[50]

Henceforth, the term *ra'iyya* will be employed in the plural (*ra'āyā*) and will acquire a purely political dimension implying submission and dependence. It is this term that Ibn Khaldun employs in his œuvre to designate the ruler's subjects, whose prosperity or misfortune is closely linked to the nature of the sovereign's reign:

> Their [subjects'] interest in him [the ruler] lies in his relation to them. Royal and governmental authority is something relative, a relationship between two things (ruler and subjects). Government becomes a reality when (there is a ruler who) rules over subjects and handles their affairs. A ruler is he who has subjects (*ra'āyā*), and subjects are persons who have a ruler.[51]

If it happens that the ruler should lead the people to ruin, he will eventually suffer the consequences in the form of either rebellion or the loss of the people's loyalty and conspiracy against him. According to Ibn Khaldun, the subjects' obedience can become a kind of unquestioned and unquestionable habit that takes root after power has been established and endures for generations, even if, at the beginning, it is not easy to bring about their submission to a new regime.[52] The habit or custom of obedience works to prevent criticisms of the sovereign power or neutralize them if they take shape, and thus protects the regime from active protest. Therefore, the definition of sovereign power as absolute is not merely theoretical: it benefits from a temporal continuity that is not easily disrupted and disobedience occurs only when the old habits of obedience begin to lose their force. Despite its advantages, however, earthly power is by its nature ephemeral: like a human being, it is destined to senility and death. Accordingly, the cyclical theory of history developed by Ibn Khaldun is based on the key concept of *al-'asabiyya* (العصبية, rendered as "group feeling" by Franz Rosenthal), which refers to the cohesive force or the solidarity of tribal origin necessary to the growth of a centralized power capable of extending itself to larger populations. Such a power is able to subdue any resistance and establish its authority by means of its military prowess. But Ibn Khaldun explains also that *al-'asabiyya* in which power originated is progressively weakened by contact with the urban world where tribal structures are disrupted, martial ability diminished and where luxury generates laziness and incompetence. From this arises another *'asabiyya* that had remained up to this point stifled that generates a new cycle of power. For Ibn Khaldun, power (*al-mulk*) is a natural and necessary development that prevents inter-individual aggression by regulating social conflict.

To avoid a reign marked by excess, Ibn Khaldun argues that the position of the sultan must require certain conditions: "knowledge [علم/*'ilm*], probity [العدالة/*'adāla*], competence [كفاية/*kifāya*] and freedom of the senses and limbs from any defect that might affect judgment and action."[53] In his analysis of the social and political structures of the Maghreb, which in his time was in a phase of stagnation, Ibn Khaldun insisted on the importance of justice as the essential character of sovereign power and declared injustice (in all its forms) destructive of civilization.[54] For Ibn Khaldun, injustice and aggressivity represent the return of an animal nature in man that could bring about the extinction of the human species through perpetual war and anarchy. He singles out two forms that this animalization has historically taken. The first is the infringement of the right of property by the state to despoil its own people; the insecurity that the necessary consequence of such an action will lead to ruin:

> It should be known that attacks on people's property remove the incentive to acquire and gain property. People, then, become of the opinion that the purpose and ultimate destiny of (acquiring property) is to have it taken away from them ... The extent and degree to which property rights are infringed upon determines the extent and degree to which the efforts of the subjects to acquire property slacken ...
>
> Civilization and its well-being as well as business prosperity depend on productivity and people's efforts in all directions in their own interest and profit. When people no longer do business in order to make a living, and when they cease all gainful activity, the business of civilization slumps, and everything decays. People scatter everywhere in search of sustenance, to places outside the jurisdiction of their present government.[55]

The second is the use of violence and coercion as the primary means of governing. In such a case, not only do the means prevent the realization of the end through a constant disturbance of the social order, but compel the common people to conceal what they have and develop habits of deceit and distrust simply to survive.

If the ruler uses force and is ready to mete out punishment and eager to expose the faults of people and to count their sins, (his subjects) become fearful and depressed and seek to protect themselves against him through lies, ruses, and deceit. This becomes a character trait of theirs. Their mind and character become corrupted.[56]

The vices of the subjects, the essential cause of which is the sovereign himself, become an instrument by which the failure of a regime can be measured and analyzed. To counteract the effect of the sovereign's character and to attempt to dissociate himself from the baseness of his subjects, he will take on a majestic and transcendental aura that will produce infatuation and fascination. This, however, only excludes the possibility of a genuine connection with the mass of people.

More recently, the term *ra'āyā* has taken on the meaning of "citizens," a title increasingly rejected in favor of *muwāten* (مواطن ; plural: *Muwātenūn* or *muwātenīn*). *Muwāten* (citizen) and *muwātana* (citizenry) are modern terms that became current in Arabic political discourse only in the last few decades of the postcolonial era (before European colonization most Arab countries were under Ottoman administration). The first to have employed "citizenry" in its modern sense was the Egyptian Rifa'a Rafi' al-Tahtawi (1801–73) using the formulas *ibn al-watan, al-watani* or *al-wataniyya*.[57] It is still the case that most of the relatively recent publications in Arabic are concerned with citizenship and civic activities in their normative or ideal form; as a consequence, the notion of the citizen remains all but absent and seems in most cases to concern the virtual citizen, the citizen to come. The result is the tone that is paradoxically pessimistic, didactic and optimistic at the same time that characterizes many of these discussions.

At the linguistic level and as we saw previously with the term *ra'iyya*, the root of a word denotes a general meaning (in this case, it is "caring for" and "attending"). The term *Muwāten* is a derivative of *watan*, which today means "nation" or "*patrie*" while originally, in medieval texts, it designated the place where one was raised or lived, one's homeland or native land. An important linguistic aspect pertaining to *muwāten* (citizen) and *muwātana* (citizenry) concerns their form (or, more exactly, pattern, وزن/*wazn*). In Arabic morphology, the patterns of words can, for instance, express reflexivity, participation, intransitivity and so forth. The pattern of *muwātana* is *mufā'ala*, which carries the meaning of "participation" and "involvement." In this sense *"muwātana"* reflects the notion of the active citizen. This perfect correspondence, however, is limited to the linguistic level, since there is no question in practice of full citizenship. There is thus a discrepancy between the meaning conferred on the term in language and the lived experience of the *"muwāten."* Undoubtedly, the true *muwāten* cannot coexist with the multiple modalities of subjection: "what distinguishes [the citizen] from the subject of the Prince is his participation in the formation and implementation of the decision, the fact that he is both legislator and magistrate."[58] *"Muwāten"* nevertheless has the merit of capturing the full meaning of citizen even as it is simultaneously, and curiously, the equivalent of the citizen in fact absent from the Arab world.[59] It is clear that equality, the fundamental principle in the absence of which subjection flourishes, abolishes hierarchization and privilege and renders sovereign and subject equal, thereby calling sovereignty perpetually into question. By insisting on the relation of freedom and equality, Balibar very pertinently poses the question "Who is the citizen?" and not "Who is a citizen?" His answer: "The citizen is a man enjoying all his 'natural' rights, fully realizing his humanity as a man who is free simply because he is equal to all others."[60] In the Arab context today it appears that only the question "Who is a citizen?" is possible; and the response would be any person bearing the nationality of a country. In fact, the term "citizenship" is often employed in the language of everyday life, as well as that of the media, as a synonym of "nationality." We can see that there is no apparent resistance to adopting these modern notions as long as their actual meanings are amended and adjusted according to the local political dynamic.

Thus, the very notion of subject, even when it is understood as a unity of opposites, that is, when it designates the subjugated individual who is submitted to the power of another and simultaneously the free individual who is endowed with both the right and the ability to determine his own actions, is in an important sense foreign to the primary concepts that govern the history of political thought in Arabic. Not only do they resist the individualization characteristic of both Roman law and its appropriation by Christianity (through the Islamic concept of *al-Shūrā*, or consultation, and Ibn Khaldun's notion of *al-ʿasabiyya* – the group feeling, solidarity, which keeps the collective bound together), these notions carry within them a sense of the singularity of social and political formations that in turn demands a permanent recognition at the level of theory itself of the concatenation of unpredictable events and forms into what we call history. These are the qualities that have necessitated the forgetting of philosophy and political thought in Arabic either by means of translations that transmute it in its difference into an inferior version of itself, or by denouncing it as the absence of political thought masquerading as its presence, a void in which neither rationality nor justice is to be found and where force decides all. In his book on Montesquieu (*Montesquieu. La politique et l'histoire*), published at the height of the Algerian War, Althusser could not refrain from pointing out that this denunciation of the Arab and Islamic world was the West's projection of its own violence. It was perhaps the only way that Europe could acknowledge what it otherwise had to deny, the unprecedented savagery of the violence it continued to inflict upon the world, itself included, without regard to the very law and rationality it held up as its defining characteristic. To reintroduce Arabic into the conversation is not only to make visible the cruelty that attends every form of subjection and the punishment that awaits the subject who alone is responsible for his actions, it is also to illuminate those other forms of both individual and collective existence confined to the darkness of exclusion both within and beyond the borders of the West.

We are very pleased to introduce here two previously untranslated essays by Etienne Balibar both focused on the relation between Thomas Hobbes and Carl Schmitt. In neither of the essays is Balibar content to remain within the limits of a chronology that would compel him to assess the degree of influence of the earlier on the later or, in contrast, the criticisms addressed by the later to the earlier. Instead, he begins by proposing a more complex conception of historical time that would allow for the possibility that Hobbes may have anticipated and formulated a critique of some of Schmitt's most essential ideas. In this way, we can reconstruct, on the basis of Hobbes's own texts, a reading of Schmitt. Balibar's essay "Schmitt's Hobbes, Hobbes's Schmitt" – originally the preface to the French translation of Schmitt's book on Hobbes and the Leviathan – provoked a lively debate over the legitimacy of Schmitt's œuvre and by extension the analyses devoted to it that, critics argued, only served to rehabilitate a Nazi philosopher who, above all in his book on Hobbes, articulated a theory of the

Jew as the permanent threat to the European order. Balibar argues in response that just as Nazism was not an exception to an otherwise rational and law-abiding European order, but thoroughly rooted in a history of racism and colonialism, so Schmitt's work, even that composed during the period of his direct engagement with National Socialism, is in no way extrinsic to European political thought and practice, but in fact dramatizes its most enduring antagonisms. Thus, at the heart of Schmitt's confrontation with Hobbes is the notion of *Gleichheit*, one meaning of which is equality, a decisive concept for Hobbes both in his explanation of the state of nature as a state of war and as a means of securing absolute sovereignty in the civil state. But the term also means "similarity" in German, allowing Schmitt to assert the need to distinguish between those who are equal in their sameness from those who because of their irreducible otherness or foreignness have no place in the community of equals.

In "The Mortal God and his Faithful Subjects: Hobbes, Schmitt and the Antinomies of Secularism," written some years after the previous essay and published here for the first time, Balibar notes the unavoidability of a political theology even in Hobbes, one of the first thinkers of secularism, by virtue of the absoluteness of absolute sovereignty that is in turn necessary to the absolute secularity that will put an end to religious conflict and its perpetual order. This leads Hobbes, commonly regarded as a methodological and political individualist, to theorize the existence of groups or "systems" based on religious differences. For Schmitt these collectivities represent the internal enemy that the state must hold back though permanent counter-revolution. It is from the Hobbes–Schmitt encounter that the theory of the modern secular state and its permanent offensive against the marks of religious difference were born.

The contributors' essays are organized around a set of themes. Jason Read argues that transindividuality and equaliberty frame much of Balibar's thought on questions of politics, citizenship, race and philosophy. Tracing what he calls a "lineage of transindividual thinkers," he shows that Spinoza and Marx are the two major thinkers of Balibar's conception of transindividuality and that they both "represent twin assaults on the most commonplace nature of a philosophical anthropology, of a human essence that is both universal, a shared essence, and transcendent, existing prior to and outside of its relations." In his discussion of the relation and of the conceptual overlap between transindividuality and equaliberty, Read demonstrates the mutual irreducibility of the individual to the collective and of the collective to the individual.

Vittorio Morfino's "Intersubjectivity or Transindividuality: The Leibniz–Spinoza Alternative" takes as its starting point Balibar's reading of the concept of transindividuality. Morfino draws a line of demarcation within the philosophical accounts of community and sociality since the seventeenth century and finds that the two opposing tendencies made visible by this demarcation can be understood as organized around one of two alternatives: intersubjectivity (Leibniz) or transindividuality (Spinoza). The first starts with the individual in its search for an other who must be discovered within before it is sought without. The second seeks to determine how individuation takes place and what forms of individuality are possible. From the perspective of transindividuality, relations and encounters precede the individual whose separateness can only be the temporary effect of an interconnectedness.

In "A Parallelism of Consciousness and Property: Balibar's Reading of Locke," Warren Montag develops the implications of Balibar's reading of Locke's philosophy as a parallelism. Following Balibar's account of "the invention of consciousness," Montag notes that Locke's invention has the effect of sealing off the individual from the thoughts and feelings of others, while restoring to him the perceptions that are his and his alone. But this same individual precisely by virtue of being separated from all others serves as the foundation of absolute property right. Property is no longer understood merely as a relation between persons and things, it becomes a prosthetic extension of the body from which the individual as consciousness cannot be separated. The complicity between consciousness and property, however, does not unify Locke's project, but instead outlines the terrain on which all the contradictions of his thought will develop.

Mohamed Moulfi's essay outlines an overview of the significant conjuncture of the problematic of universalisms and anthropological difference in the work of Balibar. Moulfi's focus on the concept of anthropological difference, whose first articulation appeared in 2010, stems from his belief that it is key to Balibar's interpretation of the "*continuum/reversal of modernities.*" He shows that Balibar's proposition of equaliberty serves as the "antidote" to the arbitrariness of political power and to the anthropological difference that promoted privileges while restricting access to citizenship. Moulfi points to the important distinction that Balibar made between *extensive* and *intensive* universalism, which proved crucial to determination of citizenship.

In "Balibar and the Philosophy of Science: The Question of the 'Epistemological Break'" Giorgos Fourtounis examines another aspect of Balibar's notion of the paradoxes of the universal. His focus is on the very concept of science understood as the concrete existence of a knowledge whose truth is universal. Fourtounis turns to Balibar's substantial but relatively unknown work on the philosophy of science or epistemology since the late 1970s, much of which represents a reconsideration, but not a rejection, of Althusser's reflections on the scientificity of Marxism. Balibar, according to Fourtounis's reading, proposes in relation to science a universal that simultaneously unfolds within the true (to use Canguilhem's expression) and embodies a plurality of singular sciences.

In "*La Haine*: Falling in Slow Motion," Hanan Elsayed uses Balibar's reflections in "Uprisings in the *Banlieues*" on the events of November 2005 as a starting point to examine the ways in which the three principal characters in Mathieu Kassovitz's film, *La Haine*, are stigmatized. She analyzes the ways that discursive mechanisms reproduce and maintain subjection through modes of address, such as the use of the informal *tu*. Elsayed shows how the film both displays and interrogates Althusser's concept of interpellation by de-universalizing the individual being interpellated, the form that subjection takes and movements of interpellation.

Drawing on Balibar's work on both the citizen subject and the exclusions that accompany the political form of universalism, James Ford looks at the process by which slaves were freed by their own initially successful attempts to destroy the old order in the South in the context of Reconstruction, rather than by the rhetorical force of the Emancipation Proclamation. Ford shows the ways in which both W. E. B. Dubois and Martin Luther King understood this struggle as a structural feature of US society; each gain won by Black people will be met with opposition. This is a reconceptualization of "backlash" as the violence that in a certain way precedes and attempts to pre-empt the exercise of civil rights, and that cannot be understood simply as a reaction to disruption or protest.

Nancy Armstrong's essay sheds light on a paradox in political philosophy that consists in acknowledging the role of women and novels within modern political societies while undermining the political significance of that role. Balibar, according to Armstrong, "creates the conditions of possibility for thinking about women and novels outside the binaries that inevitably oppose women to men and fiction to political philosophy." She sees this in his original reading of Locke's proposition concerning the relation between the individual and property, including "property in oneself." Armstrong demonstrates that the simultaneous importance and marginalization of women point to the need for both the philosopher and the theoretician of the novel to move beyond the limits set by their respective traditions.

Using Etienne Balibar's remark "we are all *in* war" as a starting point, Mike Hill provides an in-depth examination of new types of war and their applications both internally in national security strategy and externally within counterinsurgency doctrine. He demonstrates that Balibar's work on citizenship, war, multitudes and neo-liberalism bears on "some of the key manifestations of how we are *in* war today." Hill shows how communication, technology and modes of representation complement the current "war machine" whose "soft" violence has moved into civil society and has impacted identity, community and communication. Two key questions structure Hill's essay: "to what extent is this war an adherent of neo-racism?" and how does the human become terrain – "the unmanning of man"?

Notes

1. Louis Althusser, "The Philosophical Conjuncture and Marxist Theoretical Research," in *Humanist Controversy and Other Writings*, trans. G. M. Goshgarian (London: Verso, 2003), 17.
2. For the theory of interpellation, see the texts written from 1969 to 1976, collected in Louis Althusser, *On The Reproduction of Capitalism*, trans. G. M. Goshgarian (London: Verso, 2014). Althusser's first outline of this theory appears in *Psychoanalysis and the Human Sciences*, trans. Steven Rendall (New York: Columbia University Press, 2016). This text is a transcript of two lectures that Althusser gave in 1964.
3. Althusser, "Ideology and the Ideological State Apparatuses," in *On the Reproduction*, 269; emphasis in the original.
4. Althusser, "Ideology," 269.
5. Althusser, "Ideology," 268–9.

6. Etienne Balibar, "Citizen Subject," in *Who Comes after the Subject?* (London: Routledge, 1991), 33–57; Etienne Balibar, *Citoyen Sujet: et autres essais d'anthropologie philosophique* (Paris: Presses Universitaires de France, 2011).
7. Balibar, "Citizen Subject," 38.
8. Balibar, *Citoyen Sujet*, 77; Immanuel Kant, *Critique of Pure Reason*, trans. Norman Kemp Smith (New York: St Martin's Press, 1965), 169.
9. Roberto Esposito, *Communitas*, trans. Timothy Campbell (Stanford: Stanford University Press, 2010).
10. Jean-Jacques Rousseau, "Discourse on the Origin and Foundations of Inequality," in *The First and Second Discourses*, ed. Roger D. Masters (New York: St. Martin's Press, 1964), 102 (translation modified).
11. Rousseau, "Discourse," 178.
12. Louis Althusser, *Cours sur Rousseau* (Paris: Le Temps des Cerises, 2012), 69.
13. G. W. F. Hegel, *The Science of Logic*, trans. George Di Giovanni (Cambridge: Cambridge University Press, 2010), 51.
14. Balibar, *Citoyen Sujet*, 56–7.
15. Michel Foucault, *Discipline and Punish* (New York: Vintage, 1977), 222.
16. Balibar, *Citoyen Sujet*, 51.
17. Balibar, *Citoyen Sujet*, 480.
18. Balibar, *Citoyen Sujet*, 56–7.
19. Georg Simmel, "The Stranger," in *On Individuality and Social Forms*, ed. Donald Nathan Levine (Chicago: University of Chicago Press, 1971); Georg Simmel, *On Individuality and Social Forms*, ed. Donald Nathan Levine (Chicago: University of Chicago Press, 1971), 143–50; Alfred Schuetz, "The Stranger: An Essay in Social Psychology," *The American Journal of Sociology*, 49.6 (May 1944): 499–507.
20. Balibar, *Citoyen Sujet*, 485–6.
21. Balibar, *Citoyen Sujet*, 17.
22. Balibar, *Citoyen Sujet*, 17–18.
23. Etienne Balibar, *Identity and Difference, John Locke and the Invention of Consciousness* (London: Verso, 2013), IX; emphasis in the original.
24. Balibar, *Identity and Difference*, 17.
25. Philippe Büttgen, Alain de Libera, Marwan Rashed and Irène Rosier-Catach. eds. *Les Grecs, les Arabes et nous. Enquête sur l'islamophobie savante* (Paris: Fayard, 2009), 188.

26. Council of Vienne, 1311–12, Decree 24: "We desire earnestly that holy church should be well supplied with catholic scholars acquainted with the languages most in use by unbelievers. These scholars should know how to train unbelievers in the Christian way of life, and to make them members of the Christian body through instruction in the faith and reception of sacred baptism. In order, then, that skill in these languages be attained by suitable instruction, we have stipulated, with the approval of the sacred council, that schools be established for the following languages wherever the Roman curia happens to reside and also at Paris, Oxford, Bologna and Salamanca: that is, we decree that in each of these places there should be catholic scholars with adequate knowledge of Hebrew, Arabic and Chaldaic. There are to be two experts for each language in each place. They shall direct the schools, make faithful translations of books from these languages into Latin, and teach others those languages with all earnestness, passing on a skilful use of the language, so that after such instruction these others may, God inspiring, produce the harvest hoped for, propagating the saving faith among the heathen peoples." <http://www.papalencyclicals.net/Councils/ecum15.htm> (accessed May 23, 2016).
27. On the condemnations, see Etienne Gilson, *History of Christian Philosophy in the Middle Ages* (New York: Random House, 1955), 387–427, and Alain de Libera, *La philosophie médiévale* (Paris: Presses Universitaires de France, 1993), 413–17.
28. Bonaventure, *Collationes de septem donis Spiritus Sancti*. V. <https://franciscan-archive.org/bonaventura/index.html#COLLATIONES> (accessed May 28, 2016), 16–19.
29. G. W. Leibniz, "Preliminary Dissertation on the Conformity of Faith with Reason," in *Theodicy*, ed. Austin M. Farrer (Peru, IL: Open Court, 1985), 77–81 at 77.
30. Alain de Libera, "Entretien avec Alain de Libera: autour de l'Archéologie du sujet," *Actu philosophia* (January 4, 2009), <http://www.actu-philosophia.com/spip.php?article77>.
31. "In contrast, the misrecognition of the role played by Islamic thinkers in the history of philosophy becomes a powerful rhetorical tool in the hands of those who defend a purely Western history of reason" (Alain de Libera, *Penser au Moyen-Âge* (Paris: Éditions du Seuil, 1996), 104).
32. See Etienne Balibar, Barbara Cassin and Alain de Libera, "Subject," in *Dictionary of Untranslatables: A Philosophical Lexicon*, ed. Barbara Cassin (Princeton: Princeton University Press, 2004), 1,069–91.

33. Balibar, "Citizen Subject," 38.
34. "It is perhaps for lack of having paid attention to what such a continuity indicates that Heidegger proposed a fictive interpretation of the history of metaphysics in which the anteriority of the question of the subjectus/Untertan is 'forgotten' and covered over by a retrospective projection of the question of the Subjekt as subjectum" (Balibar, "Citizen Subject," 38).
35. Bernard Lewis ascribes a static and univocal meaning to *ra'iyya*: "The term *ra'iyya* occurs in literary and scribal writings as well as religious and legal writings, with the same meaning" (Bernard Lewis, *The Political Language of Islam* (Chicago: University of Chicago Press, 1988), 61).
36. *Sahih al-Bukhārī*, Hadith 849 (Elsayed's translation), Muhammad Al-Bukhārī, *Sahīh al-Bukhārī*, Islamweb. <http://library.islamweb.net/hadith/display_hbook.php?bk_no=146&hid=849&pid=98801> (accessed May 28, 2016).
37. Mohamad Ali al-Jabiri and Mohammad Mahmoud El-Imam, *Human Development in the Arab World: The Cultural and Societal Dimensions* (United Nations: Human Development Studies Series, No. 2, 1995), 49; emphasis in the original.
38. An extract of the first letter composed by the second caliph Umar and addressed to Abu Ubaydah, whom he placed in charge of the army, can serve as a concrete example about this: "I admonish you to fear God, who lasts while what is other than him perishes . . . God has tested you through me and has tested me through you" (Abū Ja'far Muhammad Al-Ṭabarī, *The History of al-Ṭabarī*, vol. 11, trans. Khalid Yahya Blankinship (Albany, NY: State University of New York Press, 1993), 158–9).
39. Al-Jabiri and El-Imam, 49, 50; this point contradicts Lewis's argument: "It [*ra'iyya*] expressed the pastoral metaphor of government common to Islam, Judaism, and Christianity, perceiving the ruler as the shepherd and the people as the flock which he tends and protects" (Lewis, *The Political Language of Islam*, 61).
40. Al-Jabiri and El-Imam, 50.
41. Al-Jabiri and El-Imam, 50.
42. "And take counsel with them in all matters of public concern" (Koran, 3:159, trans. Muhammad Asad).
43. *Sahih al-Bukhārī*, Hadith 2,750 (Elsayed's translation), Muhammad Al-Bukhārī, *Sahīh al-Bukhārī*, Islamweb. <http://library.islamweb.net/hadith/display_hbook.php?bk_no=146&hid=2750&pid=101417> (accessed May 28, 2016).

44. This point echoes the distinction made in the Christian context (see Balibar, *Citoyen Sujet*, 31–4).
45. Ibn Khaldûn. *The Muqaddimah. An Introduction to History*, trans. and ed. Franz Rosenthal (New York: Bollingen Foundation, 1958), (vol. 2), 3.
46. Ibn Khaldûn. *The Muqaddimah* (vol. 2), 6.
47. Ibn Khaldûn. *The Muqaddimah* (vol. 1), 330.
48. Franz Rosenthal writes: "Ibn Khaldûn's philosophy can be called secular, as scholars have occasionally described it. His secularism does not imply, however, any opposition to the supernatural order, let alone disavowel of it; to him its existence was as certain as anything observed by means of his senses" (Introduction, *The Muqaddimah*, vol. 1, lxxi–lxxv).
49. On luxury, see Ibn Khaldûn. *The Muqaddimah* (vol. 2), 48–53, 65–71.
50. Ibn Khaldûn. *The Muqaddimah* (vol. 2), 111–12; it was the duty of *al-hājib* (doorkeeper) to restrain access to the ruler (see vol. 2, 14–19).
51. Ibn Khaldûn. *The Muqaddimah* (vol. 1), 382–3.
52. Ibn Khaldûn. *The Muqaddimah* (vol. 1), 314.
53. Ibn Khaldûn. *The Muqaddimah* (vol. 1), 394.
54. Ibn Khaldûn. *The Muqaddimah* (vol. 1), 103; while religious law does not censor royal authority and does not ban its exercise, it condemns its excesses that can take the form of tyranny, injustice and pleasure-seeking (Ibn Khaldûn. *The Muqaddimah* (vol. 1), 391).
55. Ibn Khaldûn. *The Muqaddimah* (vol. 2), 103–4.
56. Ibn Khaldûn. *The Muqaddimah* (vol. 1), 383.
57. Abd al-Jalil Abū al-Majd, *Mafhūm al-muwāṭana fī al-fikr al-'Arabī al-Islāmī* (Casablanca: Afriqiya al-Sharq, 2010), 13, 56, 58.
58. Balibar, "Citizen Subject," p. 47.
59. The absence of "*muwāten*" is noticeable even in the national mottos of Arab states such as the Jordanian and Moroccan ones: "God, the Nation, the King."
60. Balibar, "Citizen Subject," 45.

Bibliography

Abū al-Majd, Abd al-Jalil. *Mafhūm al-muwātana fī al-fikr al-'Arabī al-Islāmī*. Casablanca: Afriqiya al-Sharq, 2010.

Althusser, Louis. *Montesquieu. La politique et l'histoire*. Paris: Presses Universitaires de France, 1959.

Althusser, Louis. "The Philosophical Conjuncture and Marxist Theoretical Research." In *Humanist Controversy and Other Writings*. Ed. François Matheron. Trans. G. M. Goshgarian. London: Verso, 2003. Pp. 1–18.

Althusser, Louis. *Cours sur Rousseau*. Paris: Le Temps des Cerises, 2012.

Althusser, Louis. "Ideology and the Ideological State Apparatuses." In *On the Reproduction of Capitalism*. Trans. G. M. Goshgarian. London: Verso, 2014. Pp. 232–72.

Althusser, Louis. *On The Reproduction of Capitalism*. Trans. G. M. Goshgarian. London: Verso, 2014.

Althusser, Louis. *Psychoanalysis and the Human Sciences*. Trans. Steven Rendall. New York: Columbia University Press, 2016.Balibar, Etienne. *Citoyen Sujet. Et autres Essais d'anthropologie philosophique*. Paris: Presses Universitaires de France, 2011.

Balibar, Etienne. *Identity and Difference, John Locke and the Invention of Consciousness*. London: Verso, 2013.

Etienne Balibar, Barbara Cassin and Alain de Libera. "Subject." In *Dictionary of Untranslatables: A Philosophical Lexicon*. Ed. Barbara Cassin. Princeton: Princeton University Press, 2004. Pp. 1,069–91.

Balibar, Etienne, Barbara Cassin and Alain de Libera. *Vocabulaire Européen des philosophes: Dictionnaire des intraduisibles*. Ed. Barbara Cassin. Paris: Le Robert/Seuil, 2004.

Bonaventure. *Collationes de septem donis Spiritus Sancti*. V. <https://franciscan-archive.org/bonaventura/index.html#COLLATIONES> (accessed May 28, 2016).

Al-Bukhārī, Muhammad. *Sahīh al-Bukhārī*, Islamweb. <http://library.islamweb.net/hadith> (accessed May 10, 2016).

Al-Bukhārī, Muhammad, *Sahīh al-Bukhārī*, Hadith 849, Islamweb. <http://library.islamweb.net/hadith/display_hbook.php?bk_no=146&hid=849&pid=98801> (accessed May 28, 2016).

Al-Bukhārī, Muhammad, *Sahīh al-Bukhārī*, Hadith 2,750, Islamweb. <http://library.islamweb.net/hadith/display_hbook.php?bk_no=146&hid=2750&pid=101417> (accessed May 28, 2016).

Büttgen, Philippe, Alain de Libera, Marwan Rashed and Irène Rosier-Catach, eds. *Les Grecs, les Arabes et nous: Enquête sur l'islamophobie savante*. Paris: Fayard, 2009.

Council of Vienne, 1311–12. *Decree 24*, Papal Encyclicals Online. <http://www.papalencyclicals.net/Councils/ecum15.htm> (accessed May 23, 2016).

De Libera, Alain. *La philosophie médiévale*. Paris: Presses Universitaires de France, 1993.

De Libera, Alain. *Penser au Moyen-Âge*. Paris: Éditions du Seuil, 1996.
De Libera, Alain. "Entretien avec Alain de Libera: autour de l'Archéologie du sujet." *Actu philosophia* (January 4, 2009). <http://www.actuphilosophia.com/spip.php?article77> (accessed May 1, 2016).
Esposito, Roberto. *Communitas*. Trans. Timothy Campbell. Stanford: Stanford University Press, 2010.
Foucault, Michel. *Discipline and Punish*. New York: Vintage, 1977.
Franz, Rosenthal, ed. and trans. *Ibn Khaldûn. The Muqaddimah. An Introduction to History*. 3 vols. New York: Bollingen Foundation, 1958.
Gilson, Etienne. *History of Christian Philosophy in the Middle Ages*. New York: Random House, 1955.
Hegel, G. W. F. *The Science of Logic*. Trans. George Di Giovanni. Cambridge: Cambridge University Press, 2010.
Al-Jabiri, Mohamad Ali and Mohammad Mahmoud El-Imam. *Human Development in the Arab World: The Cultural and Societal Dimensions*. United Nations: Human Development Studies Series, No. 2, 1995.
Kant, Immanuel. *Critique of Pure Reason*. Trans. Norman Kemp Smith. New York: St. Martin's Press, 1965.
Leibniz, G. W. "Preliminary Dissertation on the Conformity of Faith with Reason." In *Theodicy*. Ed. Austin M. Ferrer. Peru, IL: Open Court, 1985. Pp. 73–122.
Lewis, Bernard. *The Political Language of Islam*. Chicago: University of Chicago Press, 1988.
Al-Qur'an. The Message of the Qur'an. Trans. Muhammad Asad. Bristol: The Book Foundation, 2003.
Rousseau, Jean-Jacques. "Discourse on the Origin and Foundations of Inequality." In *The First and Second Discourses*. Ed. Roger D. Masters. New York: St. Martin's Press, 1964. Pp. 99–248.
Schuetz, Alfred. "The Stranger: An Essay in Social Psychology." *The American Journal of Sociology*, 49.6 (May 1944): 499–507.
Simmel, Georg, *On Individuality and Social Forms*. Ed. Donald Nathan Levine. Chicago: University of Chicago Press, 1971.
Simmel, Georg. "The Stranger." In *On Individuality and Social Forms*. Ed. Donald Nathan Levine. Chicago: University of Chicago Press, 1971. Pp. 143–9.
Al-Ṭabarī, Abū Jaʿfar Muhammad. *The History of al-Ṭabarī*. Vol. 11. Trans. Khalid Yahya Blankinship. Albany, NY: State University of New York Press, 1993.

I Balibar Reading Schmitt Reading Hobbes: Equality or Similitude?

I

Schmitt's Hobbes, Hobbes's Schmitt
Etienne Balibar
Translated by Warren Montag

To read, to study Schmitt?

There is a rumor going around the academic microcosm that a new and rather unsavory alliance has been concluded between a segment of left (or ultra-left or Marxist) intellectuals, and certain currents of the far right, more or less openly nostalgic for the "new European Order" of the 1940s. The intermediary of this regrettable encounter: Carl Schmitt, the German legal scholar of sinister repute who, or whose work, has been elevated retrospectively to the rank of "great political philosophy." And behind this body of work, the fascinating individual who presented himself before his judge at Nuremberg as an "intellectual adventurer," a man who took the risk of thinking.[1] It is this that has been called the Schmittian fashion, or the infatuation with Schmitt. The consequences? A neo-Romantic contestation of liberalism, rationalism and the principles of the rule of law: a sly rehabilitation of the totalitarian mode of thought, while the tragic experiences of the twentieth century are fading and the dark side of the liberal and democratic order is becoming apparent and finally (since it was impossible to begin there), a new outbreak of anti-Semitism in its intellectual forms (that prepared the way for its other forms or contributed in advance to their legitimation).

And the lessons of history sound the warning of the coming storm. Do they know what they are doing when they "intensively" translate Schmitt? When they comment on him, make their students read him, discuss his theses, seek in his philosophemes (decision, sovereignty, state of exception, friend–enemy distinction, the opposition between legality and legitimacy, and constituent power) the premises of a new elaboration of the political, do they do so with an intention opposed to his? Are they aware of the fact that Schmitt – even more than Heidegger (who prevailed on him to join the National Socialist Party (NSP)) and more effectively than he – was an enthusiastic adherent of the Nazi party and made himself an instrument of its legitimation in the legal sphere? Do they know that in his academic and administrative capacities he was a zealous advocate of purges? Do they know that after 1933 he justified some of the crimes committed by the state of the new regime in the name of law and of the superior capacity of the Fürher to distinguish between friend and enemy within the Reich itself?[2] Do they know that he wrote pages of openly anti-Semitic material not only *before* but *after* 1945 in what he presented as a meditation on the tragic in history, whose vicissitudes he experienced in both the spirit and the flesh?[3] Do they know that he was not simply a "conservative" or a "traditionalist," an admirer of counter-revolutionary thought, but set about constructing a spiritual and political legacy that consists of a half-century of efforts to bring democracy to ruin, or to destroy it, in relation to a neo-fascist tradition that runs from the Francoist state in Spain to Pinochet's Chile, from the ideologues of the French "*Nouvelle Droite*" to those of the *Vlaams Blok*, for whom he remains a master thinker?

We know. And from knowing this we do not draw, or in any case, *I* do not draw the conclusion that we must abstain from reading his texts, treat them as if they were contaminated or censor them. On the contrary, we should read and re-read, analyze and discuss them. Even the worst of them: the least equivocal and the most equivocal. For in question here is one of the most inventive, provocative and representative bodies of thought of the twentieth century. And this is precisely the issue. To run away from this problem, to devise protective incantations against it is to be condemned at best to stupidity and at worst to impotence in the face of the unfortunate events of a history that – it must be admitted – is not yet finished.

Against these attempts at intimidation, I might be content simply to oppose two classical arguments: that of freedom of inquiry and that of the importance of "knowing the enemy." I regard them, however, as insufficient.[4] There is no doubt that freedom of inquiry and in consequence the material conditions it requires (in which the publication of writing plays a singularly important role), as well as the specific risk that accompanies it (that of opening up to the influence of the enemy the freedom of the free spaces that they themselves would never surrender), forms a condition of the thought. I was about to say the intelligence, the misrecognition of which leads, as we can see only too clearly, to foolishness, conformism, intolerance and self-destruction. But it remains purely formal and does not favor any particular interest. To the retroactive "boycott" that weak minds take for an act of political morality, it can only oppose a kind of utopia of universal communication.

For its part, the necessity of knowing the enemy requires the application of a strategic rule to the intellectual field. It very usefully reminds us that theory or discourse are also forces acting in history, not only in their own conjuncture, but also retrospectively, which means that in a sense there can never be a "neutralization" of theory. But this position, too, when we carefully examine it, is formal in the sense that everyone at a given moment has an "enemy," unless we establish absolute criteria, simple, fixed lines of demarcation. These, in turn, cease to be obvious as soon as what is at stake in thought, beyond the level of propaganda, becomes apparent. It is then a matter of defining their configuration. The fundamental question is no longer that of knowing the enemy's ruses, his strong and weak points, but of knowing *who* is an enemy, *in what sense* and *why*. In brief, it is the very category of enemy, like that of "freedom" not so long ago, that poses a problem (and precisely from this point of view Schmitt is not a good teacher). It is not as an *enemy* that we read the divine Plato, although the antidemocratic critique that traverses his entire œuvre persisted in leading philosophers to a denunciation of "opinion" and "debate" that veered into violence and justified every kind of precaution in the sphere of education. Conversely, we read the writings of Hitler or Rosenberg as delusions of identity, as protocols of hatred and programs of extermination whose enduring toxicity expresses the paradoxical power of empty thought.[5] We read Heidegger or Schmitt as located at a certain point between Plato and Hitler, because their œuvres bear witness to the absolute uncertainty of the relations between theory, politics and ethics. But at what point?

Because the arguments based on the freedom of inquiry and knowing one's enemy are useful but fall short of what is needed in the case that concerns us here, we must give priority to two others, which are in fact closely linked. First, the coincidence of extremes and, second, the place of Nazism in European history.

That "the extremes meet" is an old idea, not as simple as it seems, that has conferred on the idea of totalitarianism both its force and its limits and applies directly to the case before us. It is well known that Schmitt himself offered several illustrations of this idea from his earliest texts, in which he postulates a relation between the revolutionary institution of the "dictatorship" of public safety and the necessity of the sovereign's "deciding the situation of exception" to preserve the state at the expense of positive law,[6] including, finally, his study of the guerilla wars of the twentieth century as symptoms of the emergence of a new international order of peace and war ("the nomos of the earth") following the foundering of the *jus publicum europaeum* based on the primacy of nation states[7] by way of an analysis of the analogies between the two great mass political "myths" of contemporary history: the proletarian myth (the Sorelian general strike, the revolution of the soviets or workers' councils) and the nationalist myth (the power proper to which was illustrated, in his eyes, by Mussolini's "march on Rome").[8]

It is important to take note of the fact that this idea, whether in the form of an exposition of the themes common to the "extremes" (for example, the critique of juridical formalism), or in the form of a study of the production of the effects of imitation between revolutionary and counter-revolutionary movements, is not the property of any ideology: it is in fact found as much in liberal authors as socialists or conservatives. Its force, it seems to me, does not come primarily from the symmetry that it establishes between adversaries, each of whom sees the other as a representative of "evil," which does not prevent them from borrowing political forms and methods of repression from each other, and, under certain conditions, temporarily collaborating. It comes instead from what such a conjunction of extremes reveals: the *repressed* element that affects from within the "moderate" republican constitution based on the division of powers, the liberal order, or what was not long ago called "bourgeois" democracy (that is, to understand the term etymologically, the democracy of *citizens*, the *politeia*). Clearly, if extreme doctrines both theorize and practice politics on the basis of the *state of exception*, necessarily seeking to make it permanent, as durable in any case as a total transformation of society, the liberal order must permanently include a *facet of exception*, whether acknowledged or concealed, that pertains to the fact that it is embodied in a state that guarantees both particular and communitarian interests. It is a legal or constitutional state (*État de droit*), but also a police state (*État de police*): a state devoted to the integration of individuals and groups into "the community of citizens," but also a state that excludes rebels, abnormals, deviants and foreigners; a "social" state, but also a class state organically linked to the capitalist market with its implacable "laws of population;" a democratic and civilized state, but also a state of power, of colonial and imperial conquest. In a latent and sometimes open way, extremism is not only found at the margins, but also exists *at the center*.[9] It is for this reason that the meeting of extremes, whether its basis is substantial or contingent, subjective or objective, not only expresses their common incompatibility with the existing order, or their calling into question the meaning of history (and sometimes its non-meaning) as it takes shape through the relations of hegemonic power, but also constitutes a reaction to the way that these power relations define a normality protected by an "armor" composed of constraints and security practices that neutralizes social, religious and moral conflicts and establishes the legal space of a *legitimate* pluralism. It is when it attempts to think its own extremism from within (that we should note is more commonly the case with counter-revolutionary than with revolutionary thought) or to conceptualize the intersection of apparent order and repressed disorder, of normality and latent conflict (that has been the case of revolutionary thought in the contemporary period, notably in the different discourses originating in Marxism) that the theory that moves to the extremes in order to "deconstruct" the dominant image of society and the state makes an essential contribution to our understanding of the political institution.

At the same time, we are confronted with another problem: the place that Nazism occupies in European history. There is no question here of resuming the complex discussion of the *causes* of the emergence and victory of Nazism in Germany or the question of the extent to which they are linked to individual and collective, moral and political, national and international responsibility. It is a matter of knowing if Nazism must be understood as external to this history in its social, political and cultural dimensions, as if a continuity of meaning or of transformation could be read by bracketing off the catastrophe of the collapse of democracy (just as, on a smaller scale, the French Republic believed that it was possible to declare the Vichy regime non-existent). Or if, on the contrary, Nazism, as an event that never should have happened,[10] and thus exceeding any explanation based solely on the development of structures or the rationality of actors, would give us the (unmeasurable) measure (*la mesure [démesurée]*) of the degree of antagonism between the interests and forces at play, of the depth at which there is an intersection, in the historical dialectic, of civilization and barbarism, the human and the inhuman that finally made the last century, to use Hobsbawm's excellent phrase, the "age of extremes."[11] As far as I am concerned, there can be no doubt about the response, given that I cannot see how in the uncertainty of the European and global present it is possible to sketch out the lines of progress and regression, to interpret the effects of repetition and measure the collective risks, without constantly returning to the question of knowing when and how the overdetermined effects of "ultra-nationalism" (the war of mutual extermination, institutional racism) and of economic crisis (the disappearance of social guarantees for the mass of small proprietors, employees and proletarians) have become uncontrollable for politics. And what follows from this: irreversible.

Concepts or positions?

But the question does not only concern social or institutional processes; it is just as relevant to intellectual movements. It is here that the Schmitt "case" is particularly revealing in the light of the very specific account he has given of his own intellectual formation and the sources of his legal and philosophical thought. The sources are, of course, contradictory in relation to each other and thus generate permanent tensions and differences in emphasis that, pushed to the limit, appear as pure and simple reversals of position – whether or not they are associated with political choices (thus the primacy of "legitimacy" or "legality" Schmitt alternately applied in his attempts to oppose a militarist and conservative dictatorship[12] to the "national socialist revolution," then in his effort to construct the Nazi regime itself as an "organic" *Rechtsordnung* that expressed the concentric unity of the People, the State and the Movement[13] and finally in retrospectively thinking the geo-historical conditions of the classical "right of war" based on the division of the world among the "civilized" states).[14] But these sources are profoundly rooted in the intellectual traditions of European juridico-philosophical thought, and it cannot be surprising under such conditions that the "dialogue" with Schmitt's ideas or formulas could not have been interrupted even by his compromise with Nazism. The ideological universes in which Schmitt's thought participated historically extended beyond Nazism, even as Nazism as a real political event exceeded and transformed them. There can be no question of exteriority between the two, but only a reciprocal envelopment.

Although there have been significant differences on this point among commentators, it seems to me that, thanks to a number of excellent works in different languages, it is possible to locate with accuracy the concurrent paradigms at work in Schmitt's writing (without distinguishing here between what pertains to law, politics and philosophy, since his discourse is characterized by the fact that it never separates these different perspectives).

Of these paradigms, one (rooted simultaneously in – Augustinian, Thomist – Catholicism and constantly tempted by a gnostic interpretation of its fundamental dogmas, notably that of original sin and its redemption by means of a temporal mediator, is organized around the theme of "political theology," that is, of *the reversibility of the statements* concerning the sacredness of power according to which it is the reflection of divine transcendence and of creation ex nihilo and those statements that express the juridical idea of the decision "in the last instance" subtracted from its own normality (*ab legibus solutus princeps*). This paradigm was no doubt sustained by references to the legists of the Middle Ages and the classical age. As Schmiitt himself showed, however, it was more fundamentally a retrospective construction carried out by modern counter-revolutionary thought (De Maistre, Bonald, Donoso Cortès) motivated by the necessity of countering another historical figure of the absolute one derived from the very origins of sovereign political authority: the revolutionary idea of the "constituent power" of the people.[15]

We observe precisely the inverse movement in the second paradigm, common to Schmitt and to the "conservative revolutionary" tendency in Germany in the 1920s (Moeller van den Bruck, Spengler, the Jünger brothers and Ernst Niekisch, as well as, to a certain extent, philosophers like Arnold Gehlen and Heidegger):[16] in this case, it was no longer a question of investing sovereign decision with the traditional *aura* from within an eschatological perspective, but rather of defining a "nationalist myth" capable of mobilizing the same energies as the revolutionary myth and of bringing about the "exceptional" fusion of legislative and executive powers, not to the advantage of a transition to democratic equality, but to the advantage of a restoration – or perhaps "creation" – of a hierarchical and communitarian order.

And to conclude, we must consider a third paradigm whose logic would also be based on a point by point opposition, but in an entirely different discursive space: that of a realist conception of law that renders it the expression of a "concrete political order." It proceeds, in part, from the historical conception established by Savigny in opposition to Kant and Hegel (even if he attempted later to recover a part of the Hegelian heritage).[17] In part, also, it proceeds from Italian and French institutionalism (Santi Romani, Hariou) for which it is the state, or more generally the institution, that makes the citizen and not the citizen the state. Finally, in part, it proceeds from the divisions of legal positivism, with which it shares the idea that there is no *effectivity* of a system of laws outside of the constraints imposed by state, even as it was engaged in an intestine quarrel with the contemporary representatives of legal positivism over the primacy of the juridical norm or political fact, and more profoundly over the foundation of "real" normativity: in the ideality of universal values for some or in the "concrete" political body's will to live for others.[18]

The object proper to an interpretation of the Schmittian œuvre is thus the way in which Nazism came to determine the point at which these different problematics overlapped: not so much as a regime (whose form never took on a univocal determination),[19] nor as a movement (or party), nor *a fortiori* as the charisma incarnate in the person of Hitler (a mediocre "*Führer*" in Schmitt's eyes), but as the *fact* of the *seizure of power* and thus as the manifestation of the *effectivity of power*. It seems that it was in this element that Schmitt saw, in accordance with his own theory, the "decision" that permitted, in a single instant, the overcoming of the tension between the logics of sovereignty, mass mobilization and the institution (or constitutional order). It is for this reason that the descriptions of his evolution in terms of opportunism, however accurate they may appear from a psychological perspective, are always inadequate.[20] It is more interesting to examine them on the basis of their intrinsic determinations.

The same is true in relation to the question of anti-Semitism, outrageous formulations of which may be found in Schmitt's *Leviathan*. Or rather, it is a question of a particular case, to which history compels us to assign an essential meaning, of the preceding considerations. Anti-Semitism can no more be considered external to the course of the European order than counter-revolutionary thought, on the one hand, and fascism and Nazism, on the other. It is certainly not the key to this order, but it is present in all its dimensions and in all its conflicts as a kind of "total ideological phenomenon." Schmitt's anti-Semitism is based on the persistent religious conviction that "the Jew" is the internal enemy of Christian civilization, the bearer of a contradiction lodged in the heart of the messianic promise ("Jesus is the Christ") as its rejection, its alternative, its simulacrum or its ruin. His anti-Semitism is above all an anti-Judaism. It is also a component of Christianity (and consequently one of the conditions of possibility of the very idea of "political theology"). Philosophically, it is the opposite of "biological" racism whose naturalistic and scientific references (the pseudo-Darwinism of the *Rassenkunde*) directly contradict his own philosophy of history.[21] This is why the term *Rasse* does not figure even in the texts totally aligned with the official discourse of the regime, where we find expressions as typical of Nazism as *Artgleicheit* (translated into French as "racial identity" (*identité raciale*) but that literally means "species identity") and *artgleich* (of the same species/kind/type) in opposition to *artfremd* (of a foreign species/kind/type).[22] The dominant theological notion of anti-Semitism in Schmitt and consequently its incorporation in schemes that evoke the link between the end of time and the fulfillment of the promise perhaps explains his uninterrupted dialogue with the Jewish philosophers and theologians who were fascinated by messianism and who were themselves tempted to provide a foundation for a "political theology" in opposition to Schmitt's (I refer here to Jacob Taubes rather than to Benjamin).[23]

Must we then conclude that Schmitt maintained a certain "reserve" or "distance" in relation to the ideology of the Third Reich that led to the extermination of Europe's Jews? On the contrary, his work testifies to the "speculative" diversity internal to this ideology, in which different varieties of European anti-Semitism joined together to create the conditions for an adherence to the program of the "purification" of the national community. We can even identify in Schmitt some of the lines of argumentation through which this conjunction was achieved.

Beginning with *The Crisis of Parlimentary Democracy* (1923) and *Constitutional Theory* (1928), he had advanced the idea that the constituent power in which the sovereignty of the people was expressed assumed a "homogeneity" (*Gleichartigkeit*) of the political body that parliamentary "pluralism" or the division of powers sanctified by liberalism precisely destroys. This homogeneity or "qualitative" unity of the general will is the stake of a decisive play on words that transforms republican (and notably Rousseauist) *equality* into similitude/identity (in German, the word *Gleichheit* signifies both equality and similitude), and democratic inclusion into the national-popular (*völkisch*) exclusion of "heterogeneous" elements, beginning with foreigners (*étrangers*) (or with those concealed foreigners who constitute internal enemies). Accordingly, anti-Semitism may appear as a privileged moment in the construction of the identity of the sovereign people, on the condition that Judaism itself is seen as the "last" (and most formidable) of the internal obstacles to the homogenization of the nation.[24] The construction or dissolution of the organic identity of the political body are the two terms of the founding alternative of politics.

Leviathan: Logos and mythos

We have thus arrived at the threshold of the themes that underlie Schmitt's book on the Leviathan. Although Habermas has called it "Schmitt's fundamental work," it is not in any formal sense one of his more successful works. It has neither the synthetic power of *Nomos of the Earth*, nor the beautiful linearity of *Dictatorship*; it has neither the capacity for the dialectization of juridical categories characteristic of the *Theory of the Constitution*, nor the genius for formulation seen in *Political Theology* and *The Concept of the Political*. On the contrary, it is a meandering work, whose scholarship is contestable (even if it proves, once again, his astonishing capacity to dramatize the given philological and philosophical stakes) and at least a part of whose intentions remain allusive (that allowed him to occupy a choice position from which to pursue his strategy of retrospective distantiation from his activity during the Nazi period and to continue to encourage opposing and incompatible interpretations).[25] But it is one of his most interesting works given the problems it raises concerning the relation between Schmitt's thought and the tradition of political philosophy, authorizing us to undertake a critical double reading: one, concerning the conflicts internal to "modern" natural law (according to Leo Strauss's terminology) that it reveals and the other concerning the aporias of Schmitt's own "concept of the political" of which the confrontation with Hobbes is particularly revealing. Written in the very middle of the Nazi period after Schmitt no longer held any official position[26] and then revisited and rectified (and on certain points his conclusions purely and simply reversed) after the war,[27] Schmitt's *Leviathan* is truly the site of a litmus test of the representation of the state as a *function of the unity* of the political body and in consequence of the categories of *totality, order, command* (or authority) and *subjection*.

It is not impossible that the composition of the book was precipitated by a "reception" of Hobbes in National Socialist philosophy (along with the reception of other, primarily German, authors: Fichte, Hölderlin, Hegel and Nietzsche, but also Machiavelli). This reception can be deduced from the constant references to Hobbes found in the work of Schmitt himself. At the same time, however, it tends to become dissociated from the typical Schmittian idea of "political theology," and even to problematize (*mettre en accusation*) this idea in the context of the regime's more general de-Christianization campaign, a kind of new Kulturkampf conceived by the ideologues of the Nazi party. Indications of these positions may be found in the discussion of the formulations of Helmut Schelsky, cited as representing a "German point of view" in opposition to the theses of "the learned Jew," Leo Strauss. Schmitt was compelled simultaneously to reclaim and defend his position.[28] More fundamentally, however, the confrontation with Strauss, which is not precisely presented as an ideological (not to say racial) rejection, but forms a link in a long exchange of arguments and ideas between the two authors, is, as we shall see, far more determinant.

Above all, the composition of the book on Hobbes appeared as the "indirect" means by which Schmitt attempted to re-establish his own problematic of the decision at the very moment that his engagement in the process of the foundation of the National Socialist regime and its evolution placed before him a series of intrinsic difficulties. We must keep this situation in mind in order to interpret the very strange rhetoric of a work that proclaims the grandeur of Hobbes in the form of his "failure." In his earlier works (in particular, *Political Theology* in 1922 and *The Concept of the Political* in 1932), Schmitt continued to designate Hobbes as the true founder of politico-juridical "decisionism" (by means of the formulation of the principle "*Auctoritas, non veritas, facit legem*" ("Authority, not truth, makes law"),[29] as well as one of the theoreticians of the *Jus Publicum Europaeum* (by means of the representation of the sovereign state as a "great individual" maintaining with other states relations of pure power (*puissance*), to the exclusion of any supra-national juridical order). Even as he expressed reservations about Hobbes's method or noted the contradictory presence of a naturalist metaphysics with a personalistic politics, he persisted in taking *Leviathan* as a model of a realistic notion of the state founded on the correct articulation of politics and law, and power and authority, which thus escaped the illusions of formal normativism and moral humanism. In the 1938 text on Hobbes, however, even if the same elements are present, the meaning of the argument seems to have been reversed: there, Schmitt privileges the critique of mechanism and the mechanization of political relations, as well as their relation to the *individualist* tradition that leads finally to the "technical" neutralization of politics, the autonomization of the sphere of private interests in relation to public power and the triumph of juridical positivism, constituted at its heart by the primacy of legality over legitimacy properly speaking – even if, finally, we have the sense that Hobbes's failure is less important than the magnitude of his attempt, which brings out through contrast the grandeur of the objective at which he aimed.[30]

Leviathan as Schmitt read it in 1938 exhibits a profound duality both of tendencies and effects. And Hobbes's *power* (*puissance*) exists side by side with his *impotence* (*impuissance*). This paradoxically made him the destroyer, by anticipation, of the very "machine" that he sought to constitute, the precursor of liberal theories (whose core was the individual's freedom of conscience, and more generally, the individual's *autonomization*, his "withdrawal" from the political community),[31] at the same moment he sought to absolutize the right of the state as the superior totality (by insisting in particular on the refutation of the "right of resistance"). Thus, Hobbes *simultaneously* prepared a defense and an illustration of the sovereignty of the state (whose insignia par excellence was the *jus circa sacra*, the authority of the magistrate in matters of religion and therefore the struggle against what Schmitt called "indirect powers"),[32] and an emancipation of civil society (that is, to put it another way, its "Jewish" side, which Schmitt attributes to such "Jewish" thinkers as Spinoza, Mendelssohn and Stahl, to explain and push it to its ultimate consequences).[33]

But this is only one, and perhaps not the most determinant or most original, aspect of the text. Its unique argument unfolds on two different planes: that of the "symbol" chosen by Hobbes to represent state absolutism (*l'absolutisme étatique*), the "Biblical monster" from the Book of Job, "to which no power on earth can compare" and that has been created "so that nothing can frighten it"[34] and that of the theory that assigns the function of assuring order and internal security to the "artificial" construction that is the state.[35] Schmitt had the genius to see and to say like no one before him that the allegory of the sea monster, as well as the *proper name* that it confers upon the state, possessed a function and history proper to it. He systematically employed this history to confront the doctrine of public power developed in the body of the work in order to extract from it a surplus of signification, that is, the manifest meaning it has acquired historically, irreducible to the simple idea of "representation" or "personification." The strange rhetoric of which we have spoken thus takes on another signification. Schmitt does not simply see Hobbes as the theoretician of certain antinomies inherent in sovereign power, but also as a witness to the profound inability of classical reason to master these antinomies totally. Discovering, little by little as he writes, the duality of the tendencies of Hobbesian thought, an idea certainly not peculiar to him, but that he insisted was the secret of the entire history of modern political rationality,[36] it is this inability that he wanted to show, without thereby really proposing another means of surmounting it (even if the concluding pages allusively evoke a political "combat" that would finally be oriented to the simple distinction between friend and enemy). But this inability only emerges by virtue of the heterogeneity of the two elements at work in the exposition or the art of writing *Leviathan*, the symbol or myth, and the reasoning or logos. Schmitt's originality (should we say his coup?) was to have held that these two elements must be taken as equally important, each to be interpreted through the other. In Hobbes, at least in *Leviathan*, the argumentation or the logos is only intelligible through the metaphorical detour of the symbol or the myth, which for its part had no other secret than a pure conceptual tension.[37]

The "mythic totality"

Schmitt felt that the importance of the symbol had been missed by traditional commentary except insofar as it projected the satanic "shadow" of *Leviathan* on Hobbes himself who was stigmatized as an enemy of religion and a theoretician of despotism. According to Schmitt, it was necessary to comprehend in its entirety the fact that the philosophy through which the theory of the nation-state and of sovereignty really entered modernity had attempted to create a political myth whose power over men today was as great as its power over those who lived during the time of archaic civilizations. This myth was destined to strike the imagination of subjects, to maintain the affects (respectful fear: *awe*, even *terror*)[38] necessary to the preservation of authority, but also to interpret the meaning of a human "creation" whose immeasurability defied reason, even as it found its most complete realization in reason alone.

In the 1938 text, these effects are summarized in a structure or "mythic totality" described at the beginning of chapter 2, immediately following the famous frontispiece (that for Schmitt illustrated the omnipresence of the founding *dualisms* of politics: friend/enemy and military powers/"indirect" spiritual powers), and before the definition of the "parity" between the two monsters (Leviathan and Behemoth), the one representing the forces of order and the other the forces of chaos: law and freedom, state and revolution. This structure brings to bear *four* terms, each of which refers to all the others and thus constitutes a different point of view on the enigma of sovereignty. Schmitt proposed to offer a complete explanation of the relation conferred by Hobbes on the power of names and images, rather than on the logic of discourse by emphasizing the symmetries on which it was based: first, that of the "great animal" of Biblical origin and of the "great human individual" (the colossus whose body is composed of a multitude of homunculi elevated above the inhabited land); then, that of the living (animal, human) and of the machine or automaton with which Hobbes identified the state insofar as it was an arrangement (*agencement*) of multiple "apparatuses" set into motion by the sovereignty that is like its "soul"; and, finally, that of the political body whose unity is evoked by these metaphors and the "representative" sovereign defined by Hobbes as a "mortal god."[39]

A later text takes up this analysis in a more concise way, in the form of a confrontation between Bodin and Hobbes, confirming that in Schmitt's eyes it reveals the symbolic nature of the Hobbesian structure:

> Bodin is certainly one of the inventors of the modern state. But he had not yet conceived of the modern Leviathan manifested in the four figures or the quadruple combination of God, animal, man and machine. He was not yet desperate enough for that. In contrast, the comprehension of this is much clearer in Hobbes. After another century of European theological struggles and civil wars, his despair was incomparably greater than that of Bodin. Hobbes was one of the great solitary figures, all of whom recognized each other, of the seventeenth century. He conceived not only the quadruple nature of the modern Leviathan, but also the way one must act in relation to it, the behavior an independently thinking individual must adopt in approaching such a perilous theme.[40]

Let us therefore begin by quickly explaining certain properties of this quadrangle or square, the most brilliant of Schmitt's intuitions (and that recalls the Heideggerian *Geviert,* (fourfold) even as it can be seen as a blasphemous version of the Trinity): they underlie both his argumentation and the possibility of confronting it with that of Hobbes. It is possible to make two elementary observations whose consequences we will examine.

In part, the very "geometry" of the square authorizes a privileging of each of its terms alternatively and gives us a sense of the meaning of the relation that each maintains in relation to the other three by isolating a conceptual tension inherent in Hobbes's metaphorics (*la métaphorique hobbesienne*). To conceive Leviathan as a "man" or a gigantic anthropomorphic collective individual is to bring out by contrast the element of inhumanity represented by God, the beast and the machine. It is thus to pose the question of the modality and effects of the invention of the state that is necessary in order to correct, control and convert the original inhumanity of man or, to put it another way, his bestial side, into its contrary. Paradoxically, man can only humanize himself by projecting himself into the inhuman, and can only accomplish his own work by placing himself outside of himself. At the same time, to conceive Leviathan as a machine or a mechanism, including as a thinking machine, is to bring out the element common to the group consisting of Animal, Man and God, that is, of *life* or the "natural" disposition of life. If we refer here to the great Aristotelian typology that situates the traits of human essence – the disposition to *logos* (reason/discourse) and the *bios politikos* (existence by and for the polis) – *between the bestial and the divine* in the continuity of life and the powers proper to it, it is to show the emergence of an *anti-natural* power in the heart of nature itself, where the dimensions of artifice and construction converge. It is this possibility above all that fascinates Schmitt, but also worries him in that it introduces a radical instability into the heart of the political institution.

In fact, the Hobbesian quadrilateral as Schmitt reconstructs it possesses another striking characteristic: each of the terms that compose it is a double or tends to divide into two and it is precisely in this way that it is linked to the others. This is obvious in the case of the beast since it bears two names: Leviathan and Behemoth. Although the latter is only mentioned in a later text, it is impossible that the reference to the Book of Job in the frontispiece of *Leviathan* would not evoke it, if only indirectly. In effect, this work had already explored the two aspects of politics that would later be made autonomous, as well as their internal opposition. In a profound sense, it was *Leviathan* itself that contained *Behemoth*, or was the unity of two contrary aspects (order and disorder, authority and subversion) and the monstrosity common to them. But this trait itself is linked to three other terms. Human nature exists according to two modalities or two "states": the one savage, violent and hostile (in which individuals repel and destroy one another), and the other, civilized, founded on peaceful commerce (in which they are so to speak collectivized, placed in a relation of interdependence). The one state is as typically human as the other and in fact both together form a single unity of contraries. The machine is also expressed according to two modalities: the one insofar as it is manufactured and moved by an external force and the other insofar as it is an automaton that regenerates itself. More precisely, as a political machine it is situated at the limit of these two determinations, the point at which the question of its permanence and its decomposition is posed.[41] Finally, and this is certainly the most essential and most enigmatic point, God or the divine is itself a double: mortal and immortal. This thesis is at once an ironic "repetition" of the central dogma of Christianity, that of the incarnation and of the redemptive sacrifice, summarized in the kerygmatic statement "Jesus is the Christ," and the key to the interminable historical conflict between church and state around which Hobbesian politics was organized.

If we consider the two types of variation characteristic of the terms of the quaternity isolated by Schmitt and of their relations, we arrive at the idea of a symbolic structure immediately characterized by the effects of ambivalence that it produces. It is not a matter of studying all of these effects, but of privileging three that illuminate both the hermeneutic possibilities opened by Schmitt's interpretation and the difficulties that it entails. The first concerns the ambivalence of human nature and the "monstrosity" proper to its political creation. The second concerns the unity of the political body, the models of which oscillate between the organism composed of material forces and gears (*rouages*) and the *corpus mysticum* inspired by theology. Finally, the third concerns the *mortality* of the God with which Hobbes identifies the political machine named Leviathan that may be associated not only with an eschatological perspective on the history of the modern state, but with the very development of its doctrine.

Violence and counter-violence

The ambivalence of human nature according to Hobbes is an omnipresent theme in Schmitt's work. From this background emerged both the idea that the state must "neutralize" political antagonisms and the idea that, returning in some sense against its human creator the inhumanity buried within him, it arouses a specific "terror" and represents a "danger" that we cannot hope to control absolutely. The ambivalence is therefore at the two extremities: at the anthropological point of departure and at the political endpoint, each of which in reality presupposes the other. If we consider that Hobbes's *exoteric* doctrine as it is developed in particular in *De cive* consists in postulating *the absolute exteriority of the two "states"* that succeed each other in the "conjectural history" of humanity (as Rousseau will put it), we may suggest that it is here a matter of the *exoteric* aspect of his thought: not that he concealed what was in question as if it were a mystery, but because it was a matter of a conclusion that could be arrived at only through a *reflection* on the terms of the doctrine whose key is its symbolic expressions.

To grasp everything that is at stake here, it is necessary to make a detour through the "dialogue" between Leo Strauss and Carl

Schmitt in which *Der Leviathan in der Staatslehre des Thomas Hobbes* may be considered a moment and through the evolution of Hobbes's doctrine between his two great treatises of political philosophy: *De cive* (1642) and *Leviathan* (1651).

After the publication of *The Concept of the Political* (first in a journal in 1927 and then, with certain modifications, as a book in 1932), the young Leo Strauss published a long review (that Schmitt would later agree to publish as part of the English language edition of his own work). This marked the point of departure of an indirect dialogue that was coextensive with the lives of the two authors. Strauss hailed Schmitt's essay for its authentic problematization of the essence of the political and its renewal of the interpretation of the relation of the political to modernity based on the postulation of the "failure of liberalism." But he articulated two criticisms of Schmitt's text. On the one hand, he observed that at the very moment Schmitt seems to take from Hobbes his conception of the "state of nature" as a state of war in order to make it "the specifically political condition of man," he completely transforms its meaning: instead of conceiving it as individual hostility, he makes it a war between groups (and notably between peoples), subsumed under the distinction between friend and enemy. For Hobbes, there are no friends, but only a civil peace imposed by the state in order *to leave* the state of nature. On the other hand, Strauss examined Schmitt's thesis according to which it is not possible genuinely to think in political terms the doctrine of the philosophers who believed in the "natural wickedness" of man, or in his "dangerosity" (*dangerosité*) and from that derived the necessity of government, in opposition to those (liberals, in the broadest sense) who held that man is naturally inclined to utility from which they deduce his spontaneous capacity to form a society. Of course, Strauss explains that this pessimism is as present in Hobbes as in Schmitt but for totally different ends: for Hobbes it is what must be denied in order to impose on the "antiliberal" nature of man the institution of freedom; for Schmitt, on the contrary, it is what must be *affirmed* in order to avoid the conclusion that civilization leads to a depoliticization of existence and to a materialist ideal of collective security and social protection. But the premises themselves are finally only apparently identical, for Hobbesian "wickedness" is fundamentally a pre-moral *innocence*, which is why it may be compared to an "animal" condition. Schmitt, in contrast, even if he doesn't admit it, makes "wickedness" a transgressive value directed against pacifist and liberal morality. This shows, according to Strauss's final note, that Schmitt does not go beyond the horizon of liberalism, succeeding only in opposing to it a critique or an *affirmation of what it denies* in order to make it the criterion of "politics" as such.

To this discussion, which had the particularity of making Hobbes the touchstone of Schmitt's theses on politics in general and that determined, from that point on, Schmitt's constant preoccupation with responding to him on the same terrain, we must add the new propositions from Strauss's own book, published in 1936, *The Political Philosophy of Hobbes*. Schmitt did not refer to it in 1938, but this does not mean that he was not familiar with it – on the contrary.[42] In any case, it is clear that Strauss retrospectively altered his reading of Hobbes's "anthropological pessimism," bringing it closer to the conception proposed by Schmitt.

The essential point lies in the fact that throughout his work Schmitt accentuates the role of *negativity* whose leitmotiv was the argument that the foundation of Hobbesian politics resides in the conjunction of two principles: 1) the nature of the human individual is what the Bible calls *vanity* or pride, that is, the desire for power or the tendency to seek "more power," rendering everyone in consequence the enemy of every other one; the animal "innocence" of the state of nature is designated here in its turn as an appearance behind which must be discerned a permanent transgression of social values; and 2) while there is no sovereign good in Hobbes, there is, in contrast, a sovereign or absolute evil, which is death, or that excess of death that is *violent* death. The "natural" foundation of law (*droit*) and of the state resides in the fear of violent death, whose founding value for politics Hobbes recognized and that prohibits any coincidence between obedience to the law and freedom.[43] But there is more: the fear of death that reigns over the *status naturalis* continues to govern the behavior and condition of men in the *status civilis*. It is their common foundation, which may be interpreted as the "primacy" of the state of nature, that persists into the heart of the civil state. The passage from the one to the other does not mean that men are liberated from the fear of violent death but that they displace or defer it by making political power the sole object of this fear, as if, to avoid the mortal threat that they represent to each other, they demand that the state terrorize them all. It is thus simultaneously necessary to postulate the distinction between the two states and *to relativize* this distinction since the fear of violent death reigns from one end to the other and the constitution of political authority is effected entirely within its unsurpassable element. From this generalized negativity, Strauss deduces the characteristics of Hobbesian political theory, namely, the surpassing of every antithesis between voluntary and involuntary subjection (violence is a legitimate means of the foundation of power), the idea that every *effective* political power (neutralizing the war of everyone against every other one) is *ipso facto legitimate* and finally the *absolute* character of sovereignty (in the sense that the subjects have obligations to the sovereign, while he has none to them).

We are now at a turning point in the long-distance "dialogue" between our two authors, but also in Hobbes's commentary in general. Strauss suggests that it is in this anthropology of negativity that we must seek the reason for Hobbes's choice of the allegorical title, Leviathan, illuminated by the citation from the Book of Job 41:26, where the biblical monster is said to be "king over all the children of pride," God having created him to inspire fear in humanity and dominate them. In the Latin version of the text, Hobbes says that his own Leviathan is sent to "refute" human pride. For only the state is capable of effectively exercising this domination over the earth. But at the same time, Hobbes was never capable of clearly drawing the conclusion (*from* the foundation of the state) that it imposes, that is, that "man is cruel by nature," even if it is possible to observe a progressive radicalization of anthropology from one study to the next (*Elements of Law, De Cive, Leviathan*) in proportion to the increasing importance of the critique of religion and the transformation of the meaning of the *credo* to which he continued to remain committed ("*Jesus is the Christ*"). It was this that seems to have posed a fundamental difficulty for him. Strauss observes that Hobbes was neither able to establish the anthropological foundations of his politics nor was he able to confer upon them a univocal significance. He will even maintain that the argument in *Leviathan* in which the system finds its most mature formulation, is also that that "dissimulates" most profoundly its true moral foundation. We have to specify this point before we return to Schmitt's elaboration of Hobbes's "contradictions." The conflict flares up between the two editions of the Latin *De Cive* (1642 and 1647). In the preface that he added to the second edition, Hobbes refrained from arguing that "men are cruel by nature." The way is short between the orthodox thesis of a *universal* wickedness and the blasphemous and heretical thesis of an *original* wickedness. A subtle distinction allowed him to separate an "animal nature" that cannot be bad in itself from "actions that are harmful and contrary to duty," that is, violent, which proceed from it, introducing on this occasion the famous metaphor of the "robust child."[44] But *Leviathan* will proceed to a striking reorganization of the symbolic, expressing the conflictual nature of the human that accompanies the development of the model of the political automaton.

In 1642, the opposition of the animal and the divine overlapped exactly with that of the two antithetical "states" separated by the institution of the statist *imperium*. Nature and civility were conceived in the same relation of opposition as animality and divinity: the lawless violence of the "war of every one against every other one" is understood in terms of the first, while the second refers to the institution of social relations that transform the "law of nature" or "divine law" into positive law. We are, even if it is in a heterodox way, in the classical dualism of a human nature torn between Good and Evil: "man is a wolf to man, man is a god to man."[45] Although *Leviathan* reproduced the same analyses of the state of nature as a state of war-violence-savagery, it was not based on the antithesis of "wolf" and "god." In contrast, it employs, in the same context and under the same mythical name, references to bestiality and divinity and associates them both with the model of artifice or the machine: it is the *same* "monstrous" collective being, at once bestial and divine, that contains within itself the powers of salvation and of death.

This complex allegory can have only one meaning, namely that the state of nature and the civil state are not really external to each other. Anthropology and politics are thus not separate domains: there is not on the one side a metaphysical foundation and on the other a technology of institutions, but, on the one side, a description of the mortifying effects of the lack of an institution, the pure reign of a fear that perpetuates itself and, on the other, a description of the institutional forms that *concentrate* the means of "terror" in the hands of one only, thus both maximizing fear and converting it into a power of reason – in principle, to the benefit of all. But in this conversion, fear continues to form the paradoxical basis of the social bond through which what makes men fundamentally foreign and hostile to one another is also the sole power capable of uniting them in a collectivity.[46]

The state is thus itself an anthropological structure whose existence and effects appear to be constitutive of "human nature." This is not to say that all theoretical ambiguity is thereby dissipated. In particular, the state of nature itself becomes in a certain way a concentrate of contradictions since it refers simultaneously to two opposing tendencies (violence and reason) each of which alternately represses the other and includes the entire series of the "historical" experiences of violence, from the incivility of individuals to organized civil war, notably those in which religious factions confront one another. It thus appears that the state of "nature" is just as retroactively determined by the civil state as the latter is through its opposition to the state of nature. The state of nature is essentially *anti-political and by this means is itself political*, or more precisely suggests that "political" in a general sense must refer *both* to the police, government and the rule of law *and* to the incivility that every moment haunts them and threatens to subvert them. This reciprocity of determinations explains the fact that government does not truly transcend the "maleficent" or even "demonic" powers inherent in human nature, but rather constitutes a conversion or a returning of their efficacy against their own domination. Government or the state is, as Weber would later say, a "monopoly of legitimate violence" or more precisely the *preventative counter-violence* that Hobbes calls "terror."

But the difficulty here can also be read in the opposite sense: if the essential function of the state is to "terrorize the terrorists" or to abolish fear by instilling an even greater fear, is it not necessary to conclude that at the heart of civility there resides an element of irreducible "natural" violence? The Leviathan is the power of the civilization of human savagery or, what amounts to the same thing, the repression of the tendencies to revolution and war that are perpetually born from the desire for power and from the force of individuals' imagination, but is it itself civilized? The form of the contractual scheme imagined by Hobbes as well as the connotations of the allegory he makes use of to symbolize its power, suggests exactly the opposite. The pact is concluded not between the subjects alone and the sovereign (the monarch) but between the subjects themselves who in this way agree to abandon their natural right (with the exception of the ultimate reserve, the right to defend their life against the sovereign's order that they be put to death) and institute a collective or individual public person who "represents" them and in their name decides their common utility. The pact only obligates them insofar as they have entered into a contract only with each other, while the third, precisely in order to benefit those who have entered into the contract, has assumed no obligation whatsoever. It may thus be maintained that the Leviathan, the sovereign, remains "in the state of nature" in relation to his subjects that, put plainly, means that he is as much their "enemy" as their "protector" (or even that he is their enemy *insofar as he protects them*).[47]

With this "dangerous" doctrine we find ourselves once again on the border between an exoteric and esoteric anthropology. For the constitution of civil society to represent a real exit from the state of nature, would it not also be necessary for the pact to commit the sovereign, involving tacit obligations responding to those of his subjects, or, what amounts to the same thing, to institute a *self-limited* power that submits itself to rules as a function of a superior end that would justify its constitution, namely, the peace, security and well-being of his subjects? But this doctrine, liberal by anticipation, is incompatible with the idea that individuals institute the state in order to repress or suppress *their own destructivity* and that it must be radically exterior to the civil society that it institutes and freed from any formal obligation to it (except that of a rational concern for its own preservation). This is why Hobbes continued to insist that the idea of "tyranny" is meaningless or is in reality the same thing as the absolutism of political power, whether of the monarchical or some other type. In Schmittian terms it is difficult to escape the conclusion that the form of politics in Hobbes is a sovereign dictatorship based on the indestructible "extremity" whose concept was formulated in the work of the same name.[48]

The basis of the difficulty is doubtless the fact that the Hobbesian sovereign as "representative" of the multitude is sometimes identified with the community (*commonwealth, res publica*) and sometimes with the government (*government, imperium*). What is required here is a *limit concept* that includes the two faces of the antinomy intrinsic to sovereignty and, when necessary, projects it in a visible figure.[49] Let us note that in the system of allegories whose grouping forms the structure studied by Schmitt, the term "machine" evokes a self-regulation in its insistence on the relation of complementarity or hierarchy that the different organs or "systems" that constitute the state maintain with one another, making it a community of communities. Conversely, the term "God" (even a "mortal" God) expresses the transcendence of the *imperium* in relation to the political body and its internal conflicts, or again the *incommensurability* of the sovereign's power and that of his subjects (therefore, the fact that compared to theirs, the sovereign's power is *immeasurable* or must be considered "omnipotence"). He tends to conceive the sovereign's relation to his subjects, whose fear he fights with fear, as a super-nature that overdetermines civility itself, at the same time that it insists on the fragility of the civility that represses rather than abolishes violence. For its part, the term "animal" or "beast" seems precisely to represent the incertitude or mixture of these two determinations: that which cannot be contained in the register of the natural or the artificial, neither in the relation of pure interiority not in that of pure exteriority and that, from this point on, can be employed in the attempt to think their "monstrous" coexistence...

It is clear that Schmitt never ceased to be fascinated by this presentation of the antinomies of sovereignty and was no doubt inspired by it himself, not only in the "decisionist" proposition that he attached to the Hobbesian formula "*Auctoritas, no veritas...*" but also in his "institutionalist" conception that makes the order of the state (*l'ordre étatique*) the constitutive mediation of the social order. And yet this presentation contains an element of *exteriority* that he is compelled to resist and that gradually implicates an entire line of juridical thought. Although it may seem strange at first, this element is central in the construction of the 1938 text that skips over Hobbes's exposition of the consequences of his own definition and passes directly to the evolution of the conceptions of modern political law. The turning point is situated in chapter 4, when Schmitt identifies in the *magnum artificium* both the origin of the "neutrality" characteristic of juridical positivism and the final form of an "absolute authority" that abolishes the right of resistance – an authority at once absolute and neutral: this is in Schmitt's view the difficulty and the origin of all subsequent contradictions, Hobbes's but also those of the state.

In the idea of a preventative counter-violence exercised by the state in order to protect human beings from their own destructivity, Schmitt could not have failed to recognize the essential form of what he would later call, in theological terms, the *Katechon*,[50] the power that "delays" or "holds back" the coming of the anti-Christ and in consequence the confrontation between good and evil that precedes the second coming of the messiah and the end of the world. Without the state institution (*l'institution étatique*), human history will end in an apocalypse of revolutionary violence. But through the state institution, history itself will also come to an end or, more precisely, becomes frozen in the interior of each political entity, confined to the margins in the clash between competing states in which the figure of the "enemy" is preserved and codified. Why then did Hobbes's manner of conceiving this regulation seem exaggeratedly "mechanistic" to Schmitt? Precisely because the relation of the subject to the law is defined in a purely external way: for Hobbes (who would be followed on this point by Kant and later by "juridical positivism," in particular Kelsen) the motive for obedience is grounded neither in a belonging to a traditional order nor in a conviction or adherence on the basis of conscience. This means that obligation is understood on the basis of a prohibition, behind which looms a "fear of the police." Once again we are confronted with an ambivalent characteristic that will be valorized in opposing ways, depending on whether one has a positive or negative conception of freedom: this means not only that criminal law (*le droit pénal*) constitutes the core of the juridical system and that *punishment* is the act par excellence of the sovereign in a "legal state," but also that the sovereign cannot claim totally to absorb the will or initiative of the subjects in a communitarian belonging or a "general will." At the very moment that the state suppresses the right of resistance, it creates the possibility of a *reserve of individual freedom*. It is true that, for Hobbes, on the terrain of the plurality of opinions and of religious affiliations, the terrain par excellence of conflict and the institution of power, this reserve of freedom is reduced to a bare minimum, or may be understood as vanishing: since it exists only in the secrecy of conscience and in every person's "right" to maintain their convictions without publicly expressing them or as a consequence "sharing them" (*les mettre en commun*) with others in order to make it the foundation of a social bond. The political unification that makes a people out of the multitude can never entirely reduce *multiplicity*, but it is decidedly exclusive of a pluralism. It is paradoxical that on this point Schmitt moves to restore to Hobbes what really belongs only to Spinoza. Such a thesis, one suspects, must have the significance of a *screen (écran)*.

Schmitt's struggle against "pluralism"

The basic problem with the reading proposed in his 1938 text was the way that Schmitt analyzed the "contradiction" in Hobbes's thought between the "decisionist" element from which Schmitt never strayed very far and the "liberal" element whose fatal consequences for the constitutional theory and practice of the state he sought to show. It was the conjunction of the mechanism, universalism (always proceeding from a pre-existing rule to its particular applications) and individualism (reducing totalities to their constituent elements) that was responsible for Hobbes's inability to inscribe the thesis that gave the sovereign the absolute right to determine the validity and content of the law within the framework of an organic conception of political community. It was in this way that the ferment of the dissolution of the authority of the state by the "indirect powers" of society was introduced. While nearly every commentator has noted its importance, there was perhaps another angle of approach that was even more decisive because it both formed a *constant* in Schmitt's critique of liberalism, in that it reappeared in all the anticipations and re-statements of the monograph on the Leviathan and finally because it immediately recalls what seemed in the 1930s and 1940s to constitute a new element in his juridico-political thought: the theory of the "concrete order" and the attempt to apply it to a "normalization" of the national-socialist revolution. That notion is *pluralism* and we must accordingly recall how the critique of pluralism articulated the different aspects of Schmittian anti-liberalism.[51]

Schmitt's critique of pluralism begins early on. It plays an important role in *Parlementarianism and Democracy* (1923), essentially providing the criterion of the distinction between the two concepts that liberalism confuses: 1) parliamentarianism, the institution of control of civil society and its powers within the state, founded on the principles of *representation, legality* and the *division of powers* and 2) democracy, the form of the people's sovereignty and therefore the principle of *legitimacy* that is inseparable from the "identities" that are subsumed by the General Will (the identity of the governors and the governed, the identity of the people and its representatives, of state and law (droit) and so forth). This analysis is further developed in *Constitutional Theory* (1928), where it presided over the articulation of the "constituted powers" and "constituent power" in modern parliamentary democracies (of the Weimar type), as well as the diagnostics of the "tension," even the "contradiction" inherent in their constitution.

Nor is this critique absent from *Political Theology* published in 1922, although it appears in another form, specifically tied to the question of sovereignty and its *personal* character. There, the discussion takes the form of an antithesis between *two ways* of reducing the multiplicity, pluralism and conflictuality of social forces and, in the last analysis, the power of the "chaos" it conceals through the *unity* of the state "form" (*forme étatique*) proposed by Kelsen and the juridical positivists that consists of submitting every practice to a single *system of norms*, itself attached to a "central point" whose formal normativity is "diffused down to the smallest element," excluding by definition any "personification" of the state and that that attaches the unitary form to a "concrete decision, arising from a determinate" and necessarily "subjective" instance. This discussion has the interest of showing that the notions of order and unity are themselves equivocal. It is to this second tendency, to which he himself adheres, that Schmitt links the Hobbesian model because he considers the unity of powers of decision as indissociable from the personified "representatives" or "actors" who exercise them, even if Hobbes is not absolutely consistent in this regard by virtue of his nominalism and naturalism. The articulation of these spheres of activity or relatively autonomous systems that constitute the political body thus is not the *automatic* result of their logical interdependence or, still less, of the imposition of an external juridical form as Kant or Kelsen would have it, but only of the personal dependencies (or relations of "subjection") that are established among their representatives and of the way in which the conflicts over power that set them in opposition to each other are decided.[52]

It is in *The Concept of the Political* from 1927 to 1932, however, that the critique of pluralism takes on its full significance in relation to the statement of the "criterion" of the political: the *friend–enemy distinction*. Chapter 4 is entirely devoted to this question, by means of a discussion of the contemporary doctrine of the autonomy of associations developed by G. H. D. Cole and Harold Laski that achieves a synthesis of classical liberalism and socialism accompanied by a devaluation of the idea of sovereignty.[53] Pushed to the limit, pluralist doctrine tends to regard the state as one "association" or juridical person among others, whose function is that of "governance," the establishment of consensus through the mediation of their conflicting claims, but without any power to suppress the entities with which it competes. The English theoreticians saw in pluralism the future of contemporary societies. But it was wrong in that it denied to the state the ability to confer on the *people* or the political *community* its own substance: for this ability derives from the right to determine *absolutely* the line of demarcation between "friend" and "enemy" and to decide conflicts or to suppress oppositions on this basis. Negatively at least there is a close interdependence between the absolute character of the sovereignty of states, the incarnation of the "political" as such and the repression of the "pluralist" pretentions that tend to neutralize the friend–enemy distinction, preventing the formation of an "existential community of interest and action," a *subject* capable of manifesting itself "in an extreme situation where there is acute conflict" (in particular, war, the national danger).[54]

Schmitt here plays a very subtle role. On the one hand, the categories of *totality* or *unity* no longer appear and have given way to that of *community*. Community not only does not exclude conflict, but presupposes it: community is born and preserves itself through confrontation with a mortal enemy. More generally, it calls for an *organizational decision* concerning the demarcation between friend and enemy.[55] It must thus be said that just as there is no substance proper to the political before a given domain is *invested* with and "politicized" by the friend–enemy distinction, so there can be no community that pre-exists war in its broadest sense. What makes community is neither the harmonization of antagonisms nor the regulation of conflict under the control and guarantee of the state, but the fact that it places itself in danger by directly confronting the antagonism it must overcome. In practice, this means that the political community has as its *negative* condition the reduction of "pluralisms" in favor of simple and "existential" antagonisms (that may be the struggle between classes, races, religions or rival nations) that in their turn are instituted by the state. Such a conception coincides with the book's central thesis, namely, that the state (*l'étatique*) *is not to be confused with the political* even as it represents historically the privileged *form* of its realization. But in this way the criterion of the political leads to an alternative that Schmitt does not hesitate to formulate. The reduction of pluralism is itself liable to be realized in two opposing ways: either in the modality of an anti-statist social revolution or in the counter-revolutionary modality of the repression of social movements that are "politicized" against the state or define other enemies than the state.[56]

It is therefore necessary, after having inscribed the primacy of community and the risk of death in the definition of the state and its historical function, to inscribe *a supplement of state sovereignty* in political antagonism. This is what *Political Theology* had already done by specifying that sovereignty did not reside solely in the "decision concerning the exception," the suspension of the established order, but in the exception insofar as it seeks the re-establishment of the juridical order and of a threatened *normality* that is possible only if the decision that liberates itself from the formal constraints of an order, always already itself proceeds from a prior order or from a *decision against "chaos."*[57] And it is this supplement that Schmitt attempts to think with Hobbes, borrowing from him the concepts forged in the "situation of exception" of the religious civil wars and in the struggle for a "strong" state capable of neutralizing its competitors, beginning with the Churches, against which in a certain way he turned their own theological power. It is thus very precisely here that the moment of truth in the Hobbes–Schmitt confrontation is situated: *how did Hobbes, for his part, think the relations between plurality and community, of sovereignty and enmity or antagonism?* Everything will depend on two questions: how is the category of *enemy* whether internal or external applied in his work? What does it mean for a social "association" and for the individuals who constitute it to recognize the *sovereignty* of the power of the state?

Hobbes: From "total alienation" to "subject systems" (*organizations sujettes*)

Not only is it possible to maintain that the question of pluralism is not foreign to Hobbes, but it may be regarded as central to *Leviathan* and that the enigma of the relations established there between absolutism and its apparent contrary, a certain liberalism *avant la lettre*, is illuminated only on the basis of this question. To see the matter clearly, it is not sufficient to speculate on the "individualist" foundation of Hobbesian politics, given that his conception of human individuality is irreducible to autonomy or self-sufficiency: either the individual radically lacks the conditions of the realization of his own ends (beginning with survival) or he finds them in the submission of his "forces" to a collective organism that no longer allows "property in oneself" any other than an unrealizable, purely residual function. And, although this theoretical *dispositif* introduced in *Leviathan* is crucial to an intellectual genealogy of liberal institutions, it nevertheless is not sufficient for an exploration of the possibilities of the development and the variation of the idea of representation as Hobbes conceived it: an operative juridical "fiction" through which the totality of citizens recognize themselves as authors of the decisions of the actor to whom they have abandoned their right to make and enforce laws in exchange for the peace of mind he guarantees them. This scheme (for which Rousseau would later invent the surprisingly Hobbesian expression "total alienation")[58] again only designates a principle of legitimacy that paradoxically associates the *constitution* of the people on the basis of the multitude with its *disappearance* into its own "actions." But it is necessary to conceptualize the unity of the representative principle and its power to organize the spheres of social activity, in other words, the reciprocal of the centralization of authority in the state, on the one hand, and the life of the "organs" of the political body and the relations between citizens, on the other.

And this is exactly what Hobbes will do in chapter 22 of *Leviathan*, "Of Systemes Subject, Politicall and Private," translated into French as "*des organizations sujettes*" (Tricot) or "*des organes assujetis*" (Mairet). "System" is a term that is simultaneously very general and directly linked to the theme of the artificial organism that can subsume every collectivity ("By Systems I understand any number of men joined in one Interest or one Business"), which leads in turn to the problem of differentiating these collectivities according to the relation they maintain with the sovereign "third."[59] Let us pause a moment at this crucial argument: Schmitt does not discuss it explicitly, but it is impossible that he did not know it. And in reality he continued to invoke it in his insistence that the practical criterion of sovereignty is the answer to the question, "who will judge?" (*quis judicabit?*).

What is striking in Hobbes's reasoning is that he combines two procedures. One is a descriptive procedure of *classification* that proceeds by means of dichotomies: it separates systems into two main categories, regular and irregular, and then subdivides them. The other is a normative procedure of *elimination* that establishes an opposition between the "lawful" and "unlawful" systems that may be found (at least in appearance) in the first two categories. But these procedures are not really independent, because some of the subdivisions in fact contain *only* lawful systems (such as *Politicall Systemes*, that is, systems of public law, still called "bodies politique" "persons in law," "or "corporations" that are "*ordained for government*"), while others in fact contain *only* unlawful systems – such as "private" systems other than families and associations of merchants engaged in a common trade or "traffique." These are, according to the astonishing list proposed by Hobbes, corporations of beggars, thieves and gypsies, or more generally of nomads, but also those who "by authority from any foreign person" engage in "making a party against the power of the Commonwealth" (aimed in fact at the Catholic Church that is subject to the authority of a foreign sovereign: the Pope). Finally, what is still more striking, is the "tumultuous assembly" or the "concourse of people" of a political, religious or moral character that by their number or conduct *cannot be suppressed* by the authorities.

The complete table obtained by cross tabulating the different criteria demonstrates quite clearly the two antithetical poles that delimit the totality of the social field (the pluralism of "systems"):

Regular Systems			Irregular Systems		
Sovereigns	Subjected		Licit?	Illicit	
	Public: «infinite variety» (provinces, colonies, cities, universities and colleges, churches, companies with monopoly privileges)			Factions, conspiracies	Tumults, Assemblies of an «unusual size»
	Licites: family, merchant corporations	Illicit: Corporations of beggars, thieves, gypsies, and the party of the foreigner (the Catholic church).		Political (parties)	Religious (sects)

On the one hand, we have the singular pole, by definition unique,[60] of *the sovereign system* characterized by the "unlimited" nature of its power, independent of any other system and that not only has the capacity to administer itself but represents *in the last instance* all the conflicts or disputes that emerge within other systems, although according to different modalities, depending on whether they are public or private. It is the sovereign system that "judges." This sovereign system, nothing other than the Commonwealth itself, *establishes the law* according to which every system or practice must be viewed as either lawful or unlawful. In opposition, there exists the diffuse and "multiple" pole of *unlawful actions* organized (that is, placed under the authority of a "representative" based on an internal power) or unorganized (arising from the "fermentation" of the movement of opinion or from "conspiracy"). They are virtually subversive because their very form implies a negation of authority (and there is obviously a circle here in that their seditious character arises from the fact *that the existing authority refuses to recognize them*). I would argue that it is important to recognize here a new version of the duality of "states," the finished juridical form under which it is transposed to civil space and formulated from the point of view of the law. The elimination of unlawful systems or organizations thus appears as the counterpart of the singularity of the state, the shadow cast by the power (puissance) over all systems or organizations, a power that can also be interpreted as the power *to organize organizations*.

A typology of this kind presents a number of characteristics that validate Schmitt's interpretation. It organizes the relation between the constitutive "systems" of social plurality, not as formal or functional relations, but as *relations of power* immediately invested with a juridical meaning through the intermediary of the notion of representation. Representatives order (articulate) organizations and not the inverse. Such a typology also confers an essential significance on the distinction between the public and the private, as Schmitt notes, in order to make it the point of departure for the "neutralization" characteristic of modern positivist systems: in one case, the representatives charged with "governing men" are vested with this responsibility by the sovereign who assigns them a specific mission and, in the other, representatives (such as the father of a family) proceed from the subject system, but can exercise their authority only within the limits and on the object defined by the law, that is, by the sovereign. But the difference between direct and indirect control that defines the two great modalities of social obedience, only reveals their common characteristic more clearly: the fact that in every case, the sovereign reserves the right to render judgment without the possibility of appeal, based on the sole condition that it was he who had originally *laid down the law*. No association, whether public or private (*not even the family*), can settle disputes between its own members or *punish* them in the case of criminal conduct. This *internal* recognition, direct or indirect, of the "unlimited" nature of sovereignty means that organizations that remain within the framework of legality are "lawful." This condition is especially important when we consider the case of religious organizations, in this case, the difference between Churches that are inscribed in legality (meaning that the Commonwealth defines the conditions of their activity: dogma, ritual, preaching and so forth) and the others: conspiracies based on religion (the Puritans) and the "party of the stranger" (Rome). The critical notion of "indirect powers" privileged by Schmitt appears constitutive of the very idea of public order.[61] The reign of collective opinion, in particular that of religious belief that directly affects the regime of obedience, cannot be dismissed as *private*: it can only oscillate between a public function and sedition where a "politicization" in terms of friend and enemy is clearly to be found. Finally, the conception of legality developed here (that has as its correlate the *negative* idea of civil liberty as the "silence of the law," as in chapter 21) implies the *criminalization of dissidence*: tendentially at least (but it is the state that determines that thresholds are significant, as in the case of "tumults") all opposition is criminal, and all disorder a political threat, if not treason.

Once these important convergences are noted, however, we will discover incompatibilities that are just as radical. They concern matters of principle and are already manifest in the figure of the "enemy." It is certainly notable that Hobbes's anthropological pessimism and his coercive, even punitive, conception of civil law leads to a conception of the organization of the political body that, to be able to "animate" the entire organism and reduce multiplicity to unity, must isolate an inassimilable remainder of social life and assemble it before the sovereign in the form of the public enemy. But this enemy, who necessitates the use of preventative "terror," and who is fundamentally heterogeneous (the Catholic Church, gypsies, the mob) does not have *substantial* or identitary traits. *It is the other of the people, not another people* identifiable internally or externally on the basis of permanent characteristics. Contrary to what Schmitt thinks, Hobbes's conception of the enemy in this sense is not an "indeterminate" whole but is destined to characterize the margin of indetermination and of the risk that the political institution works to reduce. Schmitt is certainly right to maintain that politics in Hobbes tends to be reduced to the police, as he repeats throughout his book on *Leviathan,* associating this analysis with his critique of the positivist conception of law that transforms the judge into a "recorder of infractions." But he doesn't see that it is simultaneously a question of thinking a "public hostility" without any preexisting unity, which is not in this sense concrete or whose concrete character would be aimed at *behaviors* and not at individuals who in themselves pose a threat. Unless, that is, it is acknowledged that *every individual* poses a threat.

What thus appears as a negative can also be conceived positively as a constructive characteristic of total alienation in the Hobbesian sense, that is, as the way representative procedure incorporates individuals into the sovereign by *extracting* them from their *attachments* (*appartenances*), the "corporative" organizations in which they act with and upon each other. If we suppose that the "originary" Hobbesian pact remains the object of a permanent renewal (if only because of insecurity and the fear it perpetually conjures up), it may be suggested that the relation of the sovereign to the "systems" in which the citizen-subjects experience the effects of the *authorization* that they have conferred upon him is a sort of virtual decomposition and recomposition of the plurality of collective relations (*appartenances*). At each instant, by submitting to a supreme jurisdiction, the subjects "return to the state of nature" in order to bring about its overcoming. In this way, they *dissolve* and then *re-form* the organizations of which they are members, insofar as these organizations are organs of security and civil peace. From the very interior of the diverse relations (*appartenances*) that civilize them, they see the personal/impersonal face of the sovereign (power and law) who makes a people out of the multitude, as if they themselves were looked upon, fixedly and discriminately, and "judged" by him.[62]

The characteristics of the *enemy* according to Hobbes, and of the juridical totality that for him institutes the "political bond," can be understood in relation to the symbolic and ideological stakes to which Schmitt accords great importance but which he does not at all treat in the same way. They suggest a movement of the "secularization" of the theological image – unless it is an ironic and blasphemous parody – that unites transcendence and immanence in the representation of the political body understood as a superhuman creation of man. Undoubtedly, it does not suffice here to speak of a political theology of the incarnation that would "bring down to earth" divine omnipotence in order to transfer its attributes to the state: we may even go so far as to speak of a mechanistic and anthropomorphic version of the *corpus mysticum*, the "glorious body of Christ" whose invisible unity the visible Church reflects and prefigures.[63] This would mean that the principle of unity at work in the political construction[64] truly acts from within each collective, in order from there to "interpellate" each individual or to demand his subjection, all the while involving *a radical alterity* in relation to the world of human actions. The human multitude can only be granted the unity proper to it by an Other who, for every particular individual, represents both what he most desires and what he most fears, and the need for which demands that it be *fabricated* – that leads Hobbes to call it, correctly, a "fiction."

The theologico-political dimension, however, is only the index of a more important question for Hobbes, as well as Schmitt, even if, again, their orientations diverge: the question of the political figure of the people and its relation to sovereignty or, to put it another way, the question of constituent power. The intrinsic universalism of the Hobbesian scheme of alienation in effect appears indissociable from the revolutionary proposition that concerns the relations between *equality* and *liberty*, with the meaning of the former reversed completely by Hobbes. In fact, he succeeds in constructing the strange theoretical configuration of a *counter-revolutionary egalitarianism* in which the state by means of the "pact" in which all alienate themselves, turns to its own purposes a subversive idea whose efficacy is directed against any possibility of a contestation of power. Schmitt, in contrast, deduced from his own critique of pluralism the principle of an essentially *hierarchical* "concrete" order.

Equality in Hobbes, as is well known, is first a "natural" equality arising from the fear of death and the ability to threaten the lives and possessions of others. Later, it is the civil equality that the state establishes by dissolving the multiple authorities proper to each organization or by disregarding them *completely* in the face of its own authority that places every subject before the law. It passes from the reign of liberty to that of obligation, or rather from a total, "savage," but self-destructive liberty to a restricted, "fettered" liberty, in which everyone's "hands are tied," that can only develop in the interstices of power even as it remains indissociable from its legitimacy.[65] Hobbes the counter-revolutionary has thus radically departed from the idea of the people's "constituent power" and from the insurrectional perspective from which it historically cannot be dissociated – except in considering the specificity of the vanishing moment of the pact by which the multitude vests its representative with authority in order to be unified by him. But he does so by remaining very close to formulations that will (in Rousseau, for example) produce a "reduction of the verticality" of power and lead it back to the immanence of the people and their collective being. In contrast, Schmitt, even if in his early texts he situates *the identity of the governors and the governed* among the characteristic theses of the democratic tradition with which he had allied himself against parlementarianism, systematically transposes equality into the *substantial identity*, even the *homogeneity*, of the people that he regards as the condition of the institution of the modern (national) state. By this alone, Schmitt repudiates the universalism that typically pertains to Hobbesian citizenship. In opposition, he maintains, implicitly or explicitly, the perspective of a *constituent power* that lies at the origin of constituted power or of the organization of powers within the state, beyond even the *Constitutional Theory* (1928) where this correlation acts as the guiding thread of the analysis, making it possible to think of the constitution as a unity of contraries. For the constitution is, according to Schmitt, indissociable from the opposition between legitimacy and legality and, using the very language of the law, designates the political conditions of this opposition. Constituent power is another name for sovereignty when it opts for order on the basis of its "exceptional" suspension. It is the "supra-statist" political unity that anticipates the unity of the state and confers upon it the force to destroy chaos. We thus observe an almost complete change of places between Hobbes's formulations and those of Schmitt that, from the beginning, closely link their decisionist conceptions of sovereignty.[66]

This situation is such that it illuminates Schmitt's reversals of position in relation to the contradictions he claimed to have uncovered in Hobbes's thought. But above all, and in conclusion, it opens the possibility of formulating a hypothesis concerning the nature of the link between the stubborn interrogation of the Hobbesian "symbolic" of power in 1938 and the political conjuncture contemporaneous with it, as well as the "turn" it determined in Schmitt's language and theoretical objectives.

Hobbes, Schmitt's "resistance"?

That hypothesis is the following and I offer it, not as if it had been established beyond dispute, but in a conjectural way, to open a discussion. It is well known that Schmitt, in a quite specious way, sought retrospectively to present his book on Hobbes's *Leviathan* as an example of the "Straussian" strategy for writing in a time of persecution that represented his personal form of resistance to "totalitarianism" (that was by definition secret, accessible to him alone or to a select group of initiates), going so far as to offer as proof of his irredentism the very position that – as will be seen – constituted his ultimate argument against Hobbesian individualism: the identification of liberty with the *silence* of thought in each individual's conscience. This in no way prevented Schmitt from being obliged to change the direction of this argument or even, purely and simply, to reverse its meaning retrospectively (that is the meaning stated in the "Postface" that breaks the connection between Hobbes and Enlightenment critique[67] and that, against all evidence, makes Hobbes the – non-ironic – theoretician of the opening to Christian transcendence in an age of the secularization of law). Would it not be more worthwhile to take the word *resistance* in a different sense? This is what I, for my part, will propose. *What has "resisted" is not Schmitt* by means of an interpretation of Hobbes that tends to "purify" his work by separating out the decisionist component or the conception of the sovereign from the liberal component, from the individualist mechanism or the juridical positivism *avant la lettre*. *It is instead Hobbes himself*, that is, the systematicity and paradoxical power of his theory, *in Schmitt*: in the uneasy relation that Schmitt maintains with elements of his own, personal problematic and with their contextual utilization.

But of course this was only possible insofar as the essential themes and terms of Hobbes's philosophy continued to play a mediating role in the relation of this "engaged jurist" (as Olivier Beaud put it) to himself. We may call this, if you like, Schmitt's "identification" with Hobbes. But more importantly, Schmitt himself, in particular through his exegesis of the new symbolic of Hobbes's thought and of the key that must be sought there in order to understand the "esoteric" side of *Leviathan*, gave himself (and continues to give us) the means to restore the conflictuality of the political that the reading of Hobbes as a simple "contractualist" or founder of modern individualism can only regard with suspicion.

If this hypothesis is tenable, other inquiries, other confrontations become necessary. For Schmitt's incessant return to the problems posed by Hobbes's book, and the incessant variation in his evaluation of the conflict between tendencies at play within it, do not mean that Schmitt evokes Hobbes either to safeguard a position in the struggles within the party, within ideology and for prestige, or to attribute to a political theory of authority whose meaning he thought he held in front of him, the historical depth and the *aura* capable of insuring his affinity with a great, "solitary" body of thought. It means instead that Schmitt sought "desperately" in Hobbes, through an experience of writing whose result could not be known in advance (that did not happen of course without the benefit of a certain aesthetic pleasure that was by no means "secondary") the possibility of responding to problems that *his own theory did not know how to, or could not, resolve*. And it is easy to see two terrains on which the investigation may be relaunched: the one more "political," the other more "theoretical" (or, if you prefer, epistemological).

The first concerns the question of the *constitution of the Third Reich*. Schmitt's activity from 1933 to 1936 consisted precisely in seeking that undiscoverable "constitution" – the alternative to the Weimar Constitution that he persisted in vilifying as a foreign imposition and a triumph of pluralism over the state. He pursued this end by synthesizing the notion of a "total state" that would control or politicize the totality of the spheres of social activity and that of a "concrete juridical order" in which the "constituent" power of a people endowed by history (and no doubt by divine decree as well) with an unshakeable spiritual identity and an imperial mission to reorganize the "old" European continent, in the face of new global (primarily, American) hegemonies was manifested.[68] But this synthesis was impossible both because the elements that it had to unite – the "Prussian" tradition and the "national-popular" revolution – were radically heterogeneous, and because the conjuncture of the institutionalization of the Third Reich, instead of providing political mediation, definitively distended these elements. This was the explosion of the "conservative revolution." Not only, as many historians have noted, were the conflicts between the different factions of national socialism, its internal "pluralism," or rather its institutional anarchy, not susceptible to constitutional formalization, but the dictator himself had no intention of occupying any of the places furnished by the juridical doctrine of legitimacy and legality. He neither wanted to be, nor could have been, the *Hüter der Verfassung* (guardian of the constitution) or Lord Protector of a new order. Schmitt's properly "Nazi" writings (that were, in any case, very poorly received), particularly *State, Movement, People: The triadic organization of political unity* that dramatically testifies to this impossibility, not only because of the servile character of the propositions concerning the *Führerprinzip* (leader or *Führer* principle) and the *Artgleichheit* (homogeneity) of the German people it contains, but also because of the mediocrity of the "dialectical" construction by which he proceeds to derive the spirit of the people at work in the hierarchization of "personal" competencies within the state from the "movement" that emanates from the *Führer*. It is not difficult to imagine that the author of *Political Theology* and the *Theory of the Constitution* sought to write something quite different on the relations between the mechanical and the organic, as well as between universal and historical singularity in the political field. In a sense, *Leviathan* is precisely his attempt to do so.

But there is another, no less important, terrain: that of the "typology" of meta-juridical discourses, the orientations of constitutional thought and the evolution of their political usage. The great debate here – as we know and commentaries in our own time return to it constantly – sets Schmitt in opposition to "legal positivism," notably the thought of Kelsen. Schmitt persisted in arguing that legal positivism, in order to avoid upholding the paradox of a right (or a legality) *without effectivity* (or to return to the idea, grounded in theories of natural right, of a "moral" effectivity, a kind of effectivity without force), had to *combine* two impulses that were in fact heterogeneous: "normativism" and "decisionism," under the domination of the first. Schmitt himself, beginning with *Political Theology* and above all in his late work, opposes this combination with a symmetrical combination of decisionism (the doctrine of sovereignty) and institutionalism (the doctrine of the objective sociopolitical order, not normativity, but normality). The only possibility that he finally does not explore is that of a combination of *institutionalism* and *normativism* that would be expressed in a rigorous postulation of the equivalence of "natural law" and "civil law" as is precisely found in certain passages in Hobbes's *Leviathan* (particularly in chapter 22 on "systems" and in chapter 26 on "civil laws," where we find the remarkable proposition according to which "The law of nature and the civil law contain each other and are of equal extent").[69] This would be the significance of the "artifice" or institutional construction whose motive is the foundation of law on the contract (and therefore on the freedom of individuals) and the exclusive expression of the contract in the form of law (and therefore the principle of obedience). Hobbes is the most profound *institutionalist*, capable of including in the doctrine of the institution both the notion of the norm (legality and its projected order: *nullum crimen sine legem* (no crime without law)) and the notion of the decision (the disproportion or non-reciprocity of power). But this paradoxical "institutionalism" is entirely conceived according to the modality of human art or creation, and thus does not require a natural, supernatural, traditional or customary foundation.[70] To examine such a hypothesis, however, would have compelled Schmitt to acknowledge that in a certain way legal positivism can claim to have descended from Hobbes as much – or as little – as he can himself.[71] And this is what Schmitt continues in some sense to say and to avow throughout his 1938 text, although in the form of a diagnosis of "failure." A great failure, it is true, for it acted as an obstacle to the perception of his own place in the "topography" of juridical discourses.

Finally, what undoubtedly appears from this perspective is the trans-temporal "encounter" between Hobbes and Schmitt (the actualization of Hobbes and the bringing into crisis of the Schmittian paradigms) as it is crystalized here constitutes a privileged way of approaching the antinomic nature of any approach that attempts to combine politics and law (*droit*) on equal terms or to find a stable conceptual "structure" in this combination. This is particularly true in the case of these two authors, and a few others. Such an attempt necessarily produces as its effect a resurgence not from the outside but from within the discourse of the "diabolical" element that Max Weber spoke of in *Politics as Vocation*.[72] Did Weber conceive this with reference to Hobbes, of whom his evocation of an "insoluble conflict" between the "genius or demon of politics" and "the God of the Christians" does not allow us to think? He cites only Machiavelli and Dostoyevsky. As for Schmitt himself, it is difficult to believe that he did not have Hobbes constantly in mind. For this element, whether in the conjuncture characterized by the confrontation between the "two gods" (mortal and immortal), that is, the State and the Church, or perhaps between material omnipotence and spiritual omnipotence, or in the conjuncture characterized by "total mobilization" for the identity of peoples and universal domination, leads to every kind of lucidity and every kind of blindness. But, conversely, can law be separated from politics and politics from law? "First we engage in battle and then we will see" (*on s'avance, et puis on voit*).

Notes

1. Doremus, André. "Introduction à la pensée de Carl Schmitt," *Archives de Philosophie*, 45.4 (1982), 637; also, Helmut Quaritsch, ed., *Carl Schmitt – Antworten in Nürnberg* (Berlin: Dunker und Humblot, 2000).
2. The most strking example of this servility is the 1934 text, "Der Führer schützt das Recht," in *Positionen und Begriffe im Kampf gegen Weimar-Genf-Versailles* (Berlin: Dunker und Humblot, 1994), 227–32. It was published in order to justify retroactively the "night of the long knives," while Schmitt, terrified by the summary execution of leading conservatives to whom he had been very close, including both former Chancellor Schleicher and the leadership of the SA, felt the need to give assurances to the faction of the regime that had carried it out. See Winkler, H. A., *Der Lange Weg nach Westen*, Zweiter Band, *Deutsche Geschichte vom "Dritten Reich" bis zur Wiedervereinigund* (Munich: Carl Hanser Verlag C.H. Beck, 2000), 36–7.
3. The apologetic text, *Ex captivitate salus* contains no reference to Judaism. This is not the case with the *Glossarium* (a journal covering the years 1947–51, but not published until 1991), where Judaism and Jewishness are simply designated by the letter "J."
4. The first was that of Raymond Aron who published pioneering translations of *The Concept of the Political* and *The Theory of the Partisan* in his series *L'esprit de la liberté* with the publisher Calmann-Lévy. He included a preface by Julian Freund that, through calculated silences and distortions, tended to deny Schmitt's adherence to Nazism and see him as the victim of an unfair trial. The second derives from Lenin's proclamation in *Materialism and Empirio-Critcism* that, paraphrasing Goethe, "*Ver der Feind will verstehen, muss in Feindes Lande gehen*" (whoever would understand the enemy must go to the country of the enemy). Phillipe Reynaud and others have argued that Schmitt's "radical critique

of liberalism undoubtedly gives us a number of reasons not to be 'Schmittian'," a fact that "should not prevent us from reading a corpus that demonstrates a penetrating knowledge of what it is fighting against" ("Le droit, la guerre et l'exception," *Le Monde des débats*, March 23, 2001). To confront the enemy at his strong points is to become stronger.

5. "*Ceci est-il un livre?*" asked Elisabeth de Fontenay of *Mein Kampf*, to which she devoted a lengthy analysis in her article "Hitler" in Chatelet et al. *Dictionnaire des œuvres politique* (Paris: Presses Universitaires de France, 1986).
6. Carl Schmitt, *Dictatorship* (New York: Polity Press, 2013) and *Political Theology: Four Chapters on the Concept of Sovereignty*, trans. George Schwab (Chicago: University of Chicago Press, 2006).
7. Carl Schmitt, *Theory of the Partisan* (New York: Telos, 2006).
8. Carl Schmitt, *The Crisis of Parliamentary Democracy* (Cambridge, MA: MIT Press, 1988).
9. The expression "extremismus der mitte" (the extremism of the middle) was fortuitously coined some years ago by the German philosopher and sociologist, Uli Bielfeld, to account for the rise of institutional racism and anti-immigrant attitudes in contemporary liberal European societies.
10. This is Arendt's phrase concerning Auschwitz, which extends through metonymy to Nazism as a whole. See *The Jew as Pariah: Jewish Identity and Politics in the Modern Age* (New York: Grove Press, 1978); also, Martine Leibovici, *Hannah Arendt, une Juive. Expérience politique et histoire* (Paris: Desclée de Brouwer, 1998).
11. Eric Hobsbawm, *The Age of Extremes: A History of the World, 1914–1991* (New York: Vintage, 1996).
12. See *Legality and Legitimacy* and its postwar reprise in 1945: *Verfassungsrechtliche Aufsätze aus den Jahren 1924–1954* (Berlin: Duncker und Humblot, 1985 (1958)). In his work *Les Derniers Jours de Weimar, Carl Schmitt face à l'avènement du nazisme* (Paris: Descartes & Cie, 1997), Olivier Beaud has perfectly demonstrated, it seems to me, the extent to which Schmitt attempted to "bar the way to Hitler" by obtaining the simultaneous prohibition of parties who were "enemies of the constitution" (the Communist Party and the Nazi Party) in 1932–3 from a succession of chancellors, Pappen, Schleicher and Hindenburg himself. Contrary to the legend propagated by a part of the Schmittian school in Germany and repeated in France by Julian Freund, this was not done to "save the Weimar Republic, but to destroy it as an expression of the order established

by the Treaty of Versailles and replace it with an authoritarian nationalist regime that expressed the real constitution of the German people" (Julien Freund, "Préface," in *Carl Schmitt, La notion du politique*, Paris: Calmann-Lévy, 1972, pp. 14–17).

13. See Carl Schmitt, *État, Mouvement, Peuple: L'organisation triadique de l'unité politique* (1933) (Paris: Kimé, 1997).
14. Carl Schmitt, *The Nomos of the Earth in the international Law of Jus Publicum Europaem*, trans. G. L. Ulmen (New York: Telos, 2006).
15. It is here that can be found the difference between Schmitt and Kantorowicz, a topic that deserves an analysis of its own that would explain the totally divergent evolutions of two authors whose points of departure seemed nearly identical. This difference was expressed in the reading of Hobbes on the basis of the "myth" of Leviathan rather than on the basis of the structure of the "fiction" of representation. Schmitt had no interest in the king's "two bodies"; on the contrary, he privileged the "real body" by granting it an immediately eschatological function.
16. The fundamental work on the conservative revolution has been for some time Stefan Breuer's *Anatomie de la revolution conservatrice* – substantial parts of which are devoted to Schmitt, in particular to the transfer of the Sorelian theory of "proletarian violence" to the "people" and to Schmitt's unfailing admiration for Mussolini and Italian fascism. Jean-Pierre Fayard's *Langages totalitaire* contains illuminating analyses, in particular of the discursive instability of the "extreme" positions during the crisis of the Weimar Republic.
17. On the question of the relations between the Hegelian idea of the mediation between the social and the political and the Schmittian problematic of the "concrete order," see the important work of Jean-François Kervégan, *Hegel, Carl Schmitt: le politique entre spéculation et positivité* (Paris: Presses Universitaires de France, 1992).
18. The project of tracing a genealogy of legal positivism and of assigning Hobbes a central place in this geneaology were the key objectives of Schmitt's book on Hobbes's *Leviathan*. It was therefore Schmitt himself who in this way established the conflictual proximity between his perspective and that of his adversaries, as has been noted by recent commentators. On the complexity of the Schmittian legal paradigm, see Olivier Beaud, "Carl Schmitt ou le juriste engage," who shows in particular how the anti-positivist demand for a "material" or "substantial" constitution crossed political dividing lines in Weimar Germany (Schmitt, Rudolf Smend, Hermann Heller).

Kervégan, for his part, has insisted on the heterogeneity of Schmitt's arguments againt Kelsen's normativism according to whether they are based in decisionism or institutionalism – a question that as we shall see lies at the heart of his commentary on Hobbes.

19. See Franz Neumann's *Behemoth: The Structure and Practice of National Socialism 1933–1944* (New York: Octagon Books, 1963), where the encounter with Schmitt in the context of a discussion of Hobbes cannot be a matter of chance. Neumann argues that Schmittian institutionalism (his theory of the "concrete order") is what most approximated a theory of the National Socialist state ... if National Socialism was in fact a state (that is, a Leviathan and not a Behemoth).

20. I agree with the position laid out in Séglard, *Trois Types*, on this point.

21. On the general opposition of the "revolutionary conservative" movement to "Darwinist" racism, see Beuer, *Anatomie*, 102ff. In his memoires, Nicolaus Sombart evokes Schmitt's representation of the history of the nineteenth century as a cosmic struggle between *Deutschtum* and *Judentum*, that is, Christian "Germanity" and universalist "Judeity" allied with the Anglo-Saxon empire in the figure of Disraeli who is designated, by means of projection, as the inventor of the philosophy of history as a struggle between races, which must prevail. Nicolaus Sombart, *Jugend in Berlin; 1933–1943; ein Bericht* (Berlin: Fischer Taschenbuch Carl Hanser Verlag, 1991), 259–64.

22. Schmitt, *État, Mouvement, Peuple*, 59ff. The term "Gleichheit" is translated, depending on context, as "similitude" or "equality" (or, with more difficulty, as "identity"). In his investigation of the "racist moment" in Schmitt's work, Hasso Hoffmann shows very clearly how the paradigm derived from the term "Art" functions: *Gleichartigkeit* (homogeneity), Artgleicheit (similitude of genus or species), Eigenart (the type of the German people). Hoffmann, Hasso. *Legitimität gegen Legalität: Der Weg der Politischen Philosophie Carl Schmitts* (Berlin: Duncker und Humblot, 1995), 177–97.

23. See Jacob Taubes, *The Political Theology of Paul*. Trans. Dana Hollander (Stanford: Stanford University Press, 2003).

24. Olivier Beaud, *Jurist engagé* reminds us of the importance of the theological scheme of popular acclamation demanding the exclusion of heretics, borrowed from a certain patristics (Peterson) and converging with the practice of fascist and more generally populist regimes.

25. Cited in Carlo Galli, *Genealogia della politica. Carl Schmitt e la crisi del pensiero poltico moderno* (Bologna: Il Mulino, 1996), 785.
26. After the war Schmitt attempted to distort his involvement in the conflicts internal to National Socialism (with the very real risks that they entailed) as a form of secret opposition to the regime, the allegorical figure of which was Melville's Benito Cereno. It was not impossible that Schmitt himself was convinced of this version of his history that corresponded to his conception of his "intellectual adventure" in the field of politics. Attacked by the leadership and official organs of the SS (Himmler, Der Schwarze Korps) and the ideologues of the Nazi Party (Rosenberg) in 1934 and deprived of his official functions in 1936, he was under the protection of Göring who provided the security that allowed him to develop his theory of the Grossraumordnung (the German domination of continental European space) and to outline his conception of the relation between state sovereignty and the international order. See Séglard, *Trois Types*, 32–8. It is all the more striking to see that one of the most important themes of Schmitt's book on Hobbes's *Leviathan* concerns the distinction that Hobbes makes between public opinion controlled by the state and the internal freedom of private conscience.
27. With the exception of the honorific title of counselor of the Prussian State. Teresa Orozco, however, points to the fact that in 1939 Schmitt joined the scientific council of the Gesellschaft für Europäische Wirtschaftsplanung und Grossraumwirtschaft organized from the perspective of a war of European conquest. See Teresa Orozco, *Platonische Gewalt, Gadamers politische Hermeneutik der NS-Zeit* (Hamburg: Argument Carl Hanser Verlag, 1995), 185. The author devotes a significant section of the book to Schmitt's work on Hobbes in the context of the "philosophical strategies" for reform within the Nazi State.
28. Helmut Schelsky's "Die Totalität des Staates bei Hobbes," *Archiv für Rechts- und Sozialphilosophie*, 31.2 (1937/8): 176–93, represented in part a critique of an essay that Schmitt had published in 1937, Carl Schmitt, 'The State as Mechanism in Hobbes and Descartes', in *The Leviathan in the State Theory of Thomas Hobbes: Meaning and Failure of a Political Symbol*, trans George Straub and Erna Hilfstein (Chicago: University of Chicago Press, 1996), 91–103. This young philosopher later described himself as close to the Nazi party and after the war would become with Arnold Gehlen one of those responsible for the rebirth of sociology in the German Federal Republic. He proposed attaching the conception of the "total state"

in Hobbes (using a terminology he shared with Schmitt) to a critique of any political theology as well as any individualist or pessimistic anthropology in order to found a philosophy of "power" and "action." See Helmut Rumpf, *Carl Schmitt und Thomas Hobbes: Idelle Beziehungen und aktuelle Bedeutung* (Hamburg: Duncker und Humblot, 1972), 93–4.

29. This gnomic figure only appears in the Latin version of *Leviathan* (chapter 26, "Of Civil Laws"). Schmitt always insisted that Hobbes marked a turning point in the history of sovereignty and the birth of the modern conception of the state by "fusing" the concepts of temporal *potestas* and spiritual *auctoritas*.

30. We see from Schmitt's own indications ("my brother Thomas Hobbes" *Glossarium*) an identification with Hobbes. But, if it exists, it is in the form of a chiasmus: Hobbes immediately constructed a grandiose justification of the modern state, thereby contributing to its "foundation" but a foundation riven by an internal fault by means of which its dissolution is being prepared. Schmitt, for his part, failed immediately to lead Nazism to a new legal order but his conception will be able to triumph in the future.

31. This is what distinguishes Schmitt from the conceptions expressed in C. B. Macpherson, *The Political Theory of Possessive Individualism* (Oxford: Oxford University Press, 1962), to which Schmitt refers in his postscript of 1965: Schmitt sees Hobbes's authoritarianism undermined by the "germ" of individualism founded on the freedom of conscience, while Macpherson sees the possessive individualism that Hobbes develops as based on the authoritarian structure that regulates the conflicts of interest inherent in the market.

32. The expression *Potestas indirecta* was invented by Robert Bellarmine (*De potestate summi pontificus in roebus temporalibus*, 1610), in support of the Roman Catholic Church's claim that it had the power to exercise spiritual authority within states, each of which demands for itself alone the entirety of political *imperium* and thus the right to determine its orientation to its own goals. Schmitt, who returned repeatedly to Hobbes's fundamental merit, which was to have fought this claim without making any concessions and to have defended the sovereign's right to determine the validity of opinions and norms in the public sphere, extended the concept of *Potestas indirecta* to any of the ideological forces whether national or international that claimed to represent *universality* and from this fact to provide individuals or groups with criteria of judgment independent of those of the sovereign political power, to free them from its definition of

friend and enemy and even place these individuals or groups in a position to judge the sovereign's actions in the name of a superior ethics. For Schmitt, this was particularly the case with the mystique of socialism and the cosmopolitical humanism of the League of Nations, in the name of which certain states were declared "aggressors" and placed outside the civilized world.

33. The absence of any reference to Hegel in the context (while *The Crisis of Parliamentary Democracy* made him the theoretician par excellence of "public opinion" and its constitutional function within the state, and contrasted him on this point to Marx, the restorer of a "concrete" conception of revolutionary dictatorship and the dialectic) is at first sight strange. It may be explained by the fact the book on Hobbes was written at the moment Schmitt stressed the "institutionalist" side of his thought and undertook to recuperate for his own purposes certain aspects of the Hegelian conception of the state as an "organic" totality unified by a single "popular spirit." It is nevertheless very surprising to find this place occupied from this point on by the theoretician of the Restoration, F. J. Stahl (who in *Political Theology* is ranked as one of the "reactionaries," along with Donoso Cortès) reduced for the sake of the cause to his Jewish origins (under the name Stahl-Jolson). On the Hegel–Schmitt relation as a whole, see Kervégan, *Hegel, Carl Schmitt*.

34. The citation ends "He looks down on all high things. He is king over all the children of pride" (Job 41:26). In chapter 15 of *Leviathan*, Hobbes specifies that pride arises from a rejection of natural human equality. By breaking this pride, the Leviathan restores the principle of equality.

35. A constant in Schmitt's interpretation of Hobbes is the privilege he accords the conclusion of *Leviathan*: "And thus I have brought to an end my discourse of civil and ecclesiastical government, occasioned by the disorders of the present time, without partiality, without application, and without other design than to set before men's eyes the mutual relation between protection and obedience." This is a reprise of chapter 21: "The end of obedience is protection." Shortly after Hobbes's return from exile and the publication of *Leviathan*, Cromwell was proclaimed Lord Protector of the Commonwealth of England.

36. Schmitt was undoubtedly inspired by Leo Strauss's critique. Leo Strauss, "Notes on Carl Schmitt, the Concept of the Political," in *The Concept of the Political* (Chicago: Chicago University Press, 1996), 83–107.

37. This is why finally Schmitt's erudite arguments concerning the respective roles of a "Jewish tradition" and a "Christian tradition" (primarily Lutheran) in the transformation of the Biblical Leviathan into a satanic figure or a theologico-political monster endowed with an eschatological function and the mythopoeic project that it represents. Nevertheless, they created the conditions for the metamorphosis of the myth that Schmitt hoped to bring about by remaking the Leviathan into a "sea monster" and associating those he was sent to terrify with the perspective of the "end of the state," or at least the state as understood according to the European principle of sovereignty. This philology has been called into question by contemporary critics who contest Schmitt's distortion of the Talmudic tradition, which was in any case based on dubious sources, in order to support the supposition of an interpretive tradition according to which the Leviathan represents the powerful enemies of the Jewish people who will take their revenge at the end of time. See Ruth Groh, *Arbeit an der Heillosigkeit der Welt. Zur politisch-theologischen Mythologie und Anthropologie Carl Schmitt* (Frankfurt: Suhrkamp Taschenbuch, 1998), 87ff. Hobbes, *Leviathan*, chapter 17.
38. Hobbes, *Leviathan*, chapter 17.
39. The quasi-structural idea of "mythic totality" is progressively constructed in Schmitt's commentaries on Hobbes. In *Political Theology*, Schmitt writes that "despite his nominalism and his natural-scientific approach, and his reduction of the individual to the atom, Hobbes remained personalistic and postulated an ultimate concrete deciding instance. This is why he heightened his state, the Leviathan, into an immense person and thus straight into mythology. For him this was no anthropomorphism – from which he was truly free – but a methodical and systematic postulate of his juridical thinking" (47), that is, an indirect, metaphorical attempt to express the unity of contraries to which his thought was opposed. When in 1945 Schmitt sought to "save Hobbes's soul" by revealing the presence of an indestructible element of religious transcendence (and not only the limit-point of sovereign decision) in Hobbes's work, he would create another structural figure: that of the "Hobbesian crystal," arranging the five formulations that defined the reciprocal relations between truth, authority, law, power and the security of individuals, evoked very allusively here in a note to the afterward to *The Concept of the Political* (Carl Schmitt, *La notion de politique. Notes et références de 1963*, pp. 188–9 and 192).

40. Carl Schmitt, *Ex Capitivitate Salus. Erfahrungen der Zeit 1945–1947* (Cologne: Greven Carl Hanser Verlag, 1950), 60.
41. See Hobbes, *Leviathan*, chapter 29.
42. It is possible that Schmitt was being cautious here. The book that Strauss wrote in France and in England was supported by a grant from the Rockefeller Foundation awarded on the basis of Schmitt's recommendation and it allowed him to move beyond the reach of Nazi antisemitism. Leo Strauss, *The Political Philosophy of Hobbes* (Chicago: University of Chicago Press, 1996).
43. Hobbes, *Leviathan*, chapter 14. Strauss, using the Schmittian term word "secularization" (in quotation marks) in a clearly deliberate way poses the question of whether there is here a transposition of the Christian antithesis between spiritual pride and the fear of God (who would become in politics the "mortal God," that is, the state). He concludes that it is instead a matter of a new anti-naturalist political morality.
44. Thomas Hobbes, *De Cive: Philosophical Rudiments Concerning Government and Society*, 6, <http://www.unilibrary.com/ebooks/Hobbes,%20Thomas%20-%20De%20Cive.pdf> (accessed May 29, 2016). The ambiguity of the distinction is confirmed by the frontispiece in the two editions of *De Cive*, engraved as *Leviathan* would later be, according to Hobbes's specifications in which the antithesis of the two states, civil authority (imperium) and natural liberty (libertas), illustrated by a sovereign figure facing a savage cannibal from the Americas, is made to correspond to the theological of paradise and hell as they are sent to one or the other by Christ at the Last Judgment. See Horst Bredekamp, *Thomas Hobbes: Visuelle Strategien. Der Leviathan:Urbild des modernen Staates. Werkillustrationen und Portraits* (Berlin: Akademie Carl Hanser Verlag, 1999).
45. On the origin and uses of this formula repeated by Hobbes in the Epistle Dedicatory of *De Cive*, see Jacqueline Lagrée, "L'homme, un loup ou un dieu pour l'homme?" in *L'amitié* (Paris: Autrement, 1995), 116–32.
46. On fear as a universal horizon of Hobbes's thought, see Roberto Esposito, *Communitas: The Origin and Destiny of Community* (Stanford: Stanford University Press, 2009).
47. This interpretation is argued in Frieder Otto Wolf, *Die neue Wissenschaft des Thomas Hobbes* (Stuttgart-Bad Cannstatt: Friedrich Fromann Carl Hanser Verlag, 1996). Wolf begins with the Schmittian notion of the political to rethink the antithesis of the

natural and the artificial in Hobbes's œuvre. In *Naissance de la politique moderne – Machiavel, Hobbes, Rousseau* (Paris: Payot, 1977), Pierre Manent defends a variant that finally leads to the opposite conclusion. The basis of the Hobbesian contract, which absorbs all the forces of the subjects into that of the sovereign and reduces them to a definitive silence, is a "rational panic" (57) but one that suppresses itself dialectically: as soon as the subjects are stripped of their forces, they no longer represent a threat to the sovereign, and there is no reason for the sovereign to conduct himself in a way that harms his subjects; better still there are natural reasons for him to show his benevolence towards them. According to an incontestably theological scheme (even if it is "secularized"), it is the perfection of the omnipotence incarnate in the sovereign, who will use this power only partially and reasonably. Finally, Franck Lessay in *Souveraineté et legitimité chez Hobbes* (Paris: Presses Universitaires de France, 1988) goes to the other extreme: after having recognized that in Hobbes the two "states" are not separate, he seeks to demonstrate (on the basis of the historical context of the controversies over absolute monarchy) that contrary to appearances, Hobbes's sovereign is a party to the contract and therefore subject to obligations analogous – if not equivalent to those of his subjects.

48. Carl Schmitt, *Dictatorship*, 45–7. Schmitt explains this idea in *Political Theology* and returned to it in 1934 at the moment he apparently took his distance from "pure decisionism": for Hobbes, the most important representative, of the decisionist type, sovereign decision is the *statist* dictatorship, creating law and order on the basis, and in the heart, of the anarchic insecurity of a pre- and -sub-statist state of nature. Carl Schmitt, *The Three Types of Juristic Thought*, trans. Joseph Benderesky (New York: Praeger, 2004).
49. This notion of sovereignty as a limit concept referring contradictorily to the inside and the outside has been developed by Giorgio Agamben, particularly in *Homo Sacer* where he explicitly invokes the beginning of Schmitt's *Political Theology*: "Sovereign is he who decides the state of exception. Only this definition can do justice to a borderline concept . . . a borderline concept is not a vague concept" (5).
50. Borrowed from Paul, II Thessalonians 2.
51. The question of pluralism and its relation to the principles of the "neutral state" and the "strong state" is at the center of Beaud's *Les Derniers Jours de Weimar*. Its primary objective is the analysis of the meaning and conditions of Schmitt's proposition prohibit-

ing "extremist" political parties before Hitler took power. See also Kervégan, *Hegel, Carl Schmitt*, chapter 2.
52. This thesis that leads to the postulation not only of inferior and superior "orders," but of "superior and inferior rights" is taken up, as always with reference to Hobbes, in *The Concept of the Political*, chapter 7. In truth, Schmitt's argumentation is conditioned by the fact that the "power" to which he refers as the paradigm of the demand for autonomy in relation to the state is once again the spiritual power (the *potestas indirecta*) of the Church and its leaders.
53. Cole and Laski were "Guild socialists" who represented a continuation of the Fabian society that sought a socialist-liberal synthesis (in opposition to "social democracy"). They saw themselves as continuing the pragmatism of William James and his pluralism of "experience." On this occasion, Schmitt provides an interesting genealogy of the idea of social and political pluralism. It includes, of course, Proudhonian federalism and its anarcho-syndicalist offshoots (out of which came Berth's exclamation "the state is dead"). Above all, it contains numerous references to the work of Otto von Gierke on "associative" (or corporate) right in the German tradition (Otto von Gierke, *Das Deutsche Genossenschaftsrecht* (Berlin: Beidmann Buchhandlung, 1868)) that was very influential in the Anglophone world. von Gierke holds that there exists a continuity between the "corporations" and the status of autonomy of medieval collectivities and contemporary associative right as expressed in trade unions and municipal socialism. On the tradition leading from Gierke to Cole and Laski, which leads to a return to Hobbes, see David Runciman, *Pluralism and the Personality of the State* (Cambridge: Cambridge University Press, 1997).
54. Schmitt, *Concept*.
55. Schmitt, *Concept*.
56. The reference to Marxism and Bolshevism here is explicit. Schmitt cites the "Hegelian" interpretation of Lenin expressed in Lukács's *History and Class Consciousness* (1923), but it is difficult not to see that his formulations lead to the alternatives articulated by the young Marx in *Class Struggles in France* (1850): when the class struggle "rises to extremes," there are only two possibilities, the "dictatorship of the bourgeoisie" (or the "party of order"), or "the dictatorship of the proletariat" (the party of the movement, of permanent revolution).
57. Schmitt, *Political Theology*.
58. Rousseau, *The Social Contract*, I.6. Hobbes doesn't speak of alienation but of "total submission" (*Leviathan*, p. 439). I have borrowed a

number of analyses from Lucien Jaume, *Hobbes et l'état représentitif, moderne*, without necessarily sharing all the conclusions he draws from them. The principle point of passage between Hobbes and Rousseau is obviously, as Jaume insists, the fact that for both authors private property in the juridical sense of the term has as its condition the decision of the sovereign to "render" to the possessors, within determinate limits, the goods over which he alone has eminent disposition. For his part, Yves-Charles Zarka distinguishes between "unlimited authorization" and "total alienation" and sees in the construction of *Leviathan* a critique of Rousseau *avant la lettre*. Yves-Charles Zarka, *La Décision métaphysique de Hobbes* (Paris: Vrin, 1999), 330–8.

59. Hobbes, *Leviathan*, chapter 22. Runciman provides a detailed commentary on this chapter, but one that differs from what I have proposed.
60. Except by taking into consideration, as Hobbes rarely does, the plurality of Leviathans, that is, sovereign states in international space.
61. The distinction in status between different churches will be discussed by Hobbes at length in the fourth part of *Leviathan*, "Of the Kingdom of Darkness," especially chapter 47.
62. In his remarkable work on Hobbes's "visual strategies," Horst Bredekamp, in *Visuelle Stategien*, 68–78, conducts an exhaustive study of the frontispiece of *Leviathan*, composed by Hobbes in collaboration with his engraver (Abraham Bosse). One of his most interesting comments concerns the attitude of the homunculi with whom Hobbes fills the torso and limbs of the Royal Giant: they are seen from behind (as coats and hats) so that they appear to be contemplating the face of the monarch whose body they simultaneously form. In their eyes, we can see the respectful fear they feel, just as we, by projection, can picture ourselves inserted among them. In this way, in a veritable staging of the political optic, the operation of representation or the phenomenon of total alienation that institutes the subjection, at once collective and singular, of the multitude to power is illustrated.
63. Strangely, the only iconographic analogy that appears not to have occurred to Bredekamp, *Visuelle Stategien*, 144ff, as a means of illuminating the composition of the image of the Leviathan is that of Christ in his glory rising above the inhabited earth and drawing all men to him, even as he carefully retraces the evolution of the allegories of power, beginning with the frontispiece of *De Cive*, whose figuration of the Last Judgment constitutes its most important part.
64. Hobbes, *Leviathan*: "This is more than consent, or concord; it is a real unity of them all in one and the same person" (chapter 17, 106).

65. These formulas are from chapters 18 and 21 of *Leviathan*. It seems to me that the secret of the opposition between Hobbes's doctrine and the traditional discourses of legitimation of the monarchy (and therefore also the reason for his less than enthusiastic reception among the monarchists) is to be found on the side of Hobbes's absolutism of equality rather than the residual function of liberty in the civil state. Hobbes was able to turn the egalitarianism of his revolutionary (politically as well as religiously) adversaries to the profit of a refoundation of the state. Among modern commentators, I would particularly call attention to Raymond Polin, whose perspective I share ("By restoring a soul to the political body, by making it a person [Hobbes] takes up the theory of sovereignty and the rights of the people, but by inverting it"). Raymond Polin, *Politique et Philosophie chez Thomas Hobbes* (Paris: Vrin, 1977), 228. This could be interpreted in a purely theoretical, as well as historical and conjunctural, way. The textual and iconographic indications would then take on a particular importance. From Hobbes's earliest manuscripts, the formula "equal liberty and free election" became a hallmark of the discourse of the Levellers in the English revolution of the 1640s (see Wolf, *Die neue Wissenschaft*, 150). In this connection, Bredekamp's study includes an extraordinary document: a caricature from the period of the English civil war representing the "monster of the royalty" as a composite figure in which the One of the monarch (l'Un du monarch) covers with his coat and incorporates into himself the multiplicity of little people who represent the institutions of the kingdom (church, parliament, town . . .) that seems to have directly inspired the image of the Leviathan (Bredekamp, *Visuelle Stategien*, 82–3).

66. In his *Constitutional Theory*, Schmitt cites as a criterion of the exercise of the constituent power of the people "some recognizable expression of their direct comprehensive will, which is targeted at a decision on the type and form of the existence of the political unity." Carl Schmitt, *Constitutional Theory*, trans. Geoffrey Seitzer (Durham, NC: Duke University Press, 2008), 130, a combination of his own definition of sovereignty and Rousseauist formulations concerning the General Will. As in the earlier work on dictatorship, it recalls some of the original formulations advanced by Sieyès in order to read in them an echo of the Spinozist distinction between "Natura naturans" and "Natura naturata." But this reference only suggests a vague notion of a "vital source" and in no way constitutes an overturning of the unity of the people in favor of the autonomy of

the multitude, as is the case today with Antonio Negri, *Insurgencies: Constituent Power and the Modern State*, trans. Maurizia Boscagli (Minneapolis: University of Minnesota Press, 1999).
67. who saw himself as Schmitt's heir in his earliest text, *Kritik und Crise: Eine Studie zur Pathogenese der bürgerlichen Welt* (Freiburg, München: Carl Hanser Verlag Karl Alber, 1959).
68. Both Kervégan and Beaud discuss the question of the "total state" and the "concrete order" (or *ethical order* of the state).
69. Hobbes, *Leviathan*, chapter 26.
70. Bredekamp, *Visuelle Stategien*, proposes the hypothesis that the Corpus hermeticum and the idea of a "human fabrication of the superhuman" influenced the image of the "mortal God." This hypothesis deserves its own discussion.
71. This hypothesis is of course classic: on the "Kelsenian" reading of Hobbes, for which the fundamental norm would be represented by the contract (and therefore the contract understood as a Constitution), see Lessay, *Souveraineté*, 178ff.
72. Max Weber. *Le savant et le politique* (Paris: Union Générale d'Éditions, 1963).

Bibliography

Agamben, Giorgio. *Homo Sacer: Soveriegn Power and Bare Life*. Stanford: Stanford University Press, 1998.

Arendt, Hannah. *The Jew as Pariah: Jewish Identity and Politics in the Modern Age*. Ed. Ron H. Feldman. New York: Grove Press, 1978.

Beaud, Olivier. "Carl Schmitt ou le *juriste engage*." In Carl Schmitt, *Theorie de la Constitution*. Paris: Presses Universitaires de France, 1993. Pp. 5–113.

Beaud, Olivier. *Les Derniers Jours de Weimar, Carl Schmitt face à l'avènement du nazisme*. Paris: Descartes & Cie, 1997.

Bredekamp, Horst. *Thomas Hobbes: Visuelle Strategien. Der Leviathan: Urbild des modernen Staates. Werkillustrationen und Portraits*. Berlin: Akademie Carl Hanser Verlag, 1999.

Breuer, Stefan. *Anatomie de la revolution conservatrice*. Paris: Les Editions de la MSH, 1996.

de Fontenay, Elisabeth. "Hitler." In François Chatelet, Olivier Duhamel and Évelyne Pisier. *Dictionnaire des œuvres politique*. Paris: Presses Universitaires de France, 1986. Pp. 410–16.

Doremus, André. "Introduction à la pensée de Carl Schmitt." *Archives de Philosophie*, 45.4 (1982): 585–665.

Esposito, Roberto. *Communitas: The Origin and Destiny of Community*. Stanford: Stanford University Press, 2009.
Fayard, Jean-Pierre. *Langages totalitaires*. Paris: Hermann, 1972; réédition augmentée, Paris: Hermann, 2004.
Foisneau, Luc. *Hobbes et la toute-puissance de Dieu*. Paris: Presses Universitaires de France, 2000.
Galli, Carlo. *Genealogia della politica. Carl Schmitt e la crisi del pensiero poltico moderno*. Bologna: Il Mulino, 1996.
Groh, Ruth. *Arbeit an der Heilosigkeit der Welt. Zur politisch-theologischen Mythologie und Anthropologie Carl Schmitt*. Frankfurt: Suhrkamp Taschenbuch, 1998.
Hobbes, Thomas. *De Cive: Philosophical Rudiments Concerning Government and Society*. University of Adelaide, n.d.
Hobbes, Thomas. *Leviathan*. University of Adelaide. April 23, 2016. <https://ebooks.adelaide.edu.au/h/hobbes/thomas/h68l/>
Hobsbawm, Eric. *The Age of Extremes: A History of the World, 1914–1991*. New York: Vintage, 1996.
Hoffmann, Hasso. *Legitimität gegen Legalität: Der Weg der Politischen Philosophie Carl Schmitts*. Berlin: Duncker und Humblot, 1995.
Kervégan, Jean-François, *Hegel, Carl Schmitt: le politique entre spéculation et positivité*. Paris: Presses Universitaires de France, 1992.
Koselleck, Reinhart. *Kritik und Crise: Eine Studie zur Pathogenese der bürgerlichen Welt*. Freiburg, München: Carl Hanser Verlag Karl Alber, 1959.
Lagrée, Jacqueline. "L'homme, un loup ou un dieu pour l'homme?" In *L'amitié*. Paris: Autrement, 1995. Pp. 116–32.
Leibovici, Martine. *Hannah Arendt, une Juive. Expérience politique et histoire*. Paris: Desclée de Brouwer, 1998.
Lessay, Franck. *Souveraineté et légitimité chez Hobbes*. Paris: Presses Universitaires de France, 1988.
Lucien, Jaume. *Hobbes et l'état représentatif moderne*. Paris: Presses Universitaires de France, 1986.
Lukács, Georg. *History and Class Consciousness*. Cambridge, MA: MIT Press, 1972.
Macpherson, C. B. *The Political Theory of Possessive Individualism*. Oxford: Oxford University Press, 1962.
Manent, Pierre. *Naissance de la politique moderne – Machiavel, Hobbes, Rousseau*. Paris: Payot, 1977.
Marx, Karl. *Class Struggles in France*. Marxists.org, 2009. <https://www.marxists.org/archive/marx/works/download/pdf/Class_Struggles_in_France.pdf> (accessed September 2016).

Mastnak, Tomaz, ed. *Hobbes's Béhémoth. Religion and Democracy*. Exeter: Imprint Academic, 2009.
Negri, Antionio. *Insurgencies: Constituent Power and the Modern State*. Trans. Maurizia Boscagli. Minneapolis: University of Minnesota Press, 1999.
Neumann, Franz. *Behemoth: The Structure and Practice of National Socialism 1933–1944*. New York: Octagon Books, 1963.
Orozco, Teresa. *Platonische Gewalt, Gadamers politische Hermeneutik der NS-Zeit*. Hamburg: Argument Carl Hanser Verlag, 1995.
Polin, Raymond. *Politique et Philosophie chez Thomas Hobbes*. Paris: Vrin, 1977.
Quaritsch, Helmut, ed. *Carl Schmitt – Antworten in Nürnberg*. Berlin: Dunker und Humblot, 2000.
Reynaud, Phillipe. "Le droit, la guerre et l'exception." *Le Monde des débats*. March 23, 2001.
Rousseau, Jean-Jacques. *The Social Contract*. University of Adelaide, 2014.<https://ebooks.adelaide.edu.au/r/rousseau/jean_jacques/r864s/> (accessed September 2016).
Rumpf, Helmut. *Carl Schmitt und Thomas Hobbes: Idelle Beziehungen und aktuelle Bedeutung*. Hamburg: Duncker und Humblot, 1972.
Runciman, David. *Pluralism and the Personality of the State*. Cambridge: Cambridge University Press, 1997.
Schelsky, Helmut. "Die Totalität des Staates bei Hobbes." *Archiv für Rechts- und Sozialphilosophie*, 31.2 (1937/8): 176–93.
Schmitt, Carl. *Ex Capitivitate Salus. Erfahrungen der Zeit 1945–1947*. Cologne: Greven Carl Hanser Verlag, 1950.
Schmitt, Carl. *Verfassungsrechtliche Aufsätze aus den Jahren 1924–1954*. Berlin: Duncker und Humblot, 1985 (1958).
Schmitt, Carl. *The Crisis of Parliamentary Democracy*. Cambridge, MA: MIT Press, 1988 (1923).
Schmitt, Carl. *Parlementarisme et démocratie*. Paris: Editions du Seuil, 1988 (1923).
Schmitt, Carl. *Der Leviathan in der Staatslehre des Thomas Hobbes*. Stuttgart: J.G. Cotta Buchhandlung, 1993. English trans. *The Leviathan in the State Theory of Thomas Hobbes*. Trans. George Schwab and Erna Hilfstein. Chicago: University of Chicago Press, 2008.
Schmitt, Carl. "Der Führer schützt das Recht." In *Positionen und Begriffe im Kampf gegen Weimar-Genf-Versailles*. Berlin: Dunker und Humblot, 1994. Pp. 227–32.
Schmitt, Carl. *The Concept of the Political*. Chicago: University of Chicago Press, 1996 (1932).

Schmitt, Carl. *The Leviathan in the State Theory of Thomas Hobbes: Meaning and Failure of a Political Symbol*. Trans. George Straub and Erna Hilfstein. Chicago: University of Chicago Press, 1996.

Schmitt, Carl. 'The State as Mechanism in Hobbes and Descartes'. In *The Leviathan in the State Theory of Thomas Hobbes: Meaning and Failure of a Political Symbol*. Trans. George Straub and Erna Hilfstein. Chicago: University of Chicago Press, 1996. Pp. 91–103.

Schmitt, Carl. *Legality and Legitimacy*. Raleigh: Duke University Press, 2004.

Schmitt, Carl. *The Nomos of the Earth in the international Law of Jus Publicum Europaem*. Trans. G. L. Ulmen. New York: Telos, 2006.

Schmitt, Carl. *État, Mouvement, Peuple: L'organisation triadique de l'unité politique*. Paris: Kimé, 1997 (1933).

Schmitt, Carl. *The Three Types of Juristic Thought*. Trans. Joseph Benderesky. New York: Praeger, 2004.

Schmitt, Carl. *Political Theology: Four Chapters on the Concept of Sovereignty*. Trans. George Schwab. Chicago: University of Chicago Press, 2006 (1922).

Schmitt, Carl. *Theory of the Partisan*. New York: Telos, 2006.

Schmitt, Carl. *Constitutional Theory*. Trans. Geoffrey Seitzer. Durham, NC: Duke University Press, 2008.

Schmitt, Carl. *Dictatorship*. New York: Polity Press, 2013.

Séglard, Dominique. "Présentation." In Carl Schmitt, *Trois Types de pensée juridique*. Paris: Presses Universitaires de France, 2015.

Sombart, Nicolas. *Jugend in Berlin; 1933–1943; ein Bericht*. Berlin: Fischer Taschenbuch Carl Hanser Verlag, 1991.

Strauss, Leo. "Notes on Carl Schmitt, the Concept of the Political." In *The Concept of the Political*. Chicago: Chicago University Press, 1996. Pp. 83–107.

Weber, Max. *Le savant et le politique*. Paris: Union Générale d'Éditions, 1963.

Winkler, H. A. *Der Lange Weg nach Westen*, Zweiter Band, *Deutsche Geschichte vom "Dritten Reich" bis zur Wiedervereinigund*. Munich: Carl Hanser Verlag C. H. Beck, 2000.

Wolf, Frieder Otto. *Die neue Wissenschaft des Thomas Hobbes*. Stuttgart-Bad Cannstatt: Friedrich Fromann Carl Hanser Verlag, 1996.

Zarka, Yves-Charles. *La Décision métaphysique de Hobbes*. Paris: Vrin, 1999.

2

The Mortal God and his Faithful Subjects: Hobbes, Schmitt and the Antinomies of Secularism

Etienne Balibar

Translated by Warren Montag

The preface I wrote in 2002 for the French translation of Schmitt's book, *The Leviathan in the State Theory of Thomas Hobbes*, published by Éditions du Seuil,[1] had already become so long that I was unable to include as I had originally intended a section entitled "God's Impotence" (*"L'impuissance de Dieu"*), concerning the doctrine of the Katechon.[2] For this reason, I had to set it aside. I wanted to take advantage of the opportunity offered to me here to return to this theme. The conjuncture is no longer entirely the same. It is overdetermined in particular by the resumption of the debates over the meaning of "secularism" and the modalities of its application in the French context (*à la française*). The legal projects in preparation at that time concerning the prohibition against the wearing of the burka or the niqab in what were called "public spaces," a category that seemed to designate any place from which a third-party was not excluded, showed quite clearly the extremities to which this category could lead when it was considered not only a constitutive element of the sovereignty of the state, but as the principle source of the legitimacy of its republican form. But it is always in the urgency of the conjuncture that we identify the point of the question that must be posed to the classical texts to determine what, even today, gives their theoretical statements their vitality.

Inversely, there is little doubt, on the one hand, that the Hobbesian conception of the separation of Church and State with the fluctuations that may include its institutional realization, but also the intransigence of the principled position of which it is the incarnation, constitutes the typical "source" of the French doctrine of a secularism of the state or, if you prefer, of secularism as an attribute of public power, that lies at the heart of the classical doctrine of *ius circa sacra*, developed in different ways by Locke and Spinoza.[3] On the other hand, it is on this point even more than on others that the double influence of Hobbes's thought on the Schmittian concept of the political and of Schmitt on the interpretation of the tensions that animate Hobbes's thought, proves illuminating, even indispensable: it allows an examination of its very center, that is, the relation between the absolute nature of political sovereignty and constitution of the subject of the state, the double movement of de-theologization and re-theologization (probably without end) that characterizes the Hobbesian Leviathan, but also, to one degree or another, its practical applications in modern European history. In what follows and in what is nothing more than a sketch (*programme*), I am going to outline three points: first, how may we relate Hobbes's anti-clericalism as expressed in particular in Parts III and IV of *Leviathan* to his doctrine of the artificial personality of the state? Second, in what way does Schmitt's reading and its "forcing" of Hobbes (that I made the axis of my 2002 commentary) allow us to identify the central difficulty at the heart of the Hobbesian conception of the subjection (*assujettissement*) of citizens, and of the associations they form under the authority of the law, which leads to the sacralization of this authority? Third, how finally do we evaluate as precisely as possible the tendency of sovereignty to theologize the function of the internal enemy of the state, and the way it has evolved from the Hobbesian prototype to its Schmittian reprise, the relevance of which can be seen in certain contemporary transformations of the political functions of "secularism"?

Hobbes: The necessity of an anti-clericalism of the state

Hobbes's anti-clericalism, whose explicit target was the Catholic Church, but that could be extended to other formal and informal organizations (or, as Hobbes puts it in chapter 22 of *Leviathan*, "systems") that unite their adherents in a common pursuit of the same objective of salvation and a common recognition of the same spiritual authority within civil society, is forcefully developed in the third and fourth parts of the book, which are often overlooked in modern commentaries, although they hold the key to the work's objectives. This anti-clericalism includes a very complex set of critical, hermeneutic and juridical operations, from the analysis of the anthropological foundations of religious belief (that resides in a metaphorical faculty proper to human language that permanently diverts it from its natural cognitive function), to the denunciation of the use by the Church as a separate hierarchy of power and by its ministers, of superstition and of the need for the obedience of individuals to order to subject them to a power, in competition with the state, that promises them a salvation beyond this world.

His anti-clericalism obviously forms the counterpart – in anticipation of a certain current of the Enlightenment and later of positivism – of a conception of rational education and of the pragmatic essence of obedience to the law that are essential to the Hobbesian notion of politics insofar as it is a purely human construction. It coexists, however, in a surprising fashion, surprising to the interpreters who tend to minimize or, on the contrary, make it the hidden truth of this doctrine, with a valorization of the mythic, if not mystical, dimensions of the legal state (or of the state as juridico-political "machine") summarized in the expression "Mortal God" that Hobbes employed to characterize the *excess of power* that resides in the attribution to the state alone of the right to punish criminals or simple delinquents, when he introduced the Biblical metaphor of the "Leviathan" borrowed from the Book of Job. Would there thus be a good and bad practice of metaphor, depending on the political ends it served? I think that it is possible to address the question from two opposing points.

It can be addressed on the basis of the essential positivity of the artificial person of the state – that is the positivity of its function of protecting the life and property of its subjects and the positivity of the judicial system constituted by laws that can require obedience and impose sanctions in the case that they are violated, only if they have been published previously in the forms of and as a counterpart to this positivity. In effect, this positivity means that the state, combining the legislative function with its prerogatives, but essentially organized as the juridical power to adjudicate conflicts between citizens in the last instance and to impose a legal order, has a monopoly of authority. In order for it to be sovereign, all other sources of authority must be nullified. We know that this is obtained ideally through the mechanism of *representation* that makes it so that the subjects themselves abandon their authority to recognize it, after the fact, in the essentially fictive person that they have all simultaneously invested with the power to represent them. *Total alienation*, as Rousseau will call it. This alienation in no way implies that the subjects (or citizens) do not form particular associations and do not have the freedom of initiative. It is not totalitarianism. But it does signify that there cannot exist opposite the state any organization whose power would be in competition with the power of the state to require obedience and, even more, individuals' acceptance of the authority of a judgment that concerns their own lives. And this would be – or is – precisely the case of any Church (and more generally of any "spiritual power") that promises salvation to the faithful and for this reason disrupts, even partially or on another plane, their exclusive relation to the law. Hobbes's materialism, here absolutely rigorous, postulates that such an association (beginning with the common acceptance of a *doctrine* or *teaching*) is nothing other than a composite *body*, as artificial as that of the state and standing in opposition to it, whose very existence destroys the state's power (for there is no absolute or sovereign power where there is no monopoly, but rather a sharing or division of jurisdictions and thus permanent negotiation). Such a body thus must be either subjected, that is, dissolved as a separate body, or completely eliminated.

But the question may also be addressed in an opposing sense, on the basis of the *negativity* that runs like a guiding thread from the description of the anthropological bases of the state in the "war of every one against every other one," to the account of the causes of its dissolution, described in terms of social pathology according to an old organicist tradition, particularly in chapter 29 of *Leviathan*. Their common characteristic is that they *divide the soul of the political body* by means of "seditious doctrines" that propel it into war against itself, a notion that, thirty years later, Hobbes's *Behemoth* would apply to the history of the English Civil War, caused by religious controversies.[4] We may say then that what essentially characterizes the construction of *Leviathan* insofar as it involves not only a statics, but a dynamics, even an economics, of the passions, as well as the fact that it is deployed not only in the field of political theory, but also, to take up Roberto Esposito's term, in the field of the *impolitical,* is that it must be designed to resist the dissolution to which the forces of death, which will inevitably prevail, are driving it. It is precisely the idea of delaying or restraining (*retardement*) that Schmitt will find in the notion of the *katékhon*, but it is also and more precisely the idea of the *immunitary* function that protects the political "body" against the germs of death that it contains. Its essential instrument is, as is well known, the capacity of the state to inspire terror in its subjects (we may even say to inspire in its subjects the terror that they demand from it to protect themselves against their own violence) according to the two registers of religious, reverential fear and physical fear (awe and terror). It will be seen that this doctrine of the state (and of the law that is its essential instrument) as a function of immunity, translates in practice into an identification of *public enemies* situated either outside the state's territory or internally and who must be eliminated or neutralized.

The key question posed by the political construction of *Leviathan* in its entirety and that will, without any doubt, clarify the historical argumentation of its long delayed "double," *Behemoth*, is the relation between the designation of the main enemy, the *kingdom of darkness* of ecclesiastical power, and the multiplicity of identities behind which the power of subversion or of individual or collective resistance to the law may be hidden. But we see that it is here that the most profound justification of the state machine as a *monstrous human creation* expressed by Hobbes's recourse to the Biblical myth of the Leviathan, on which Schmitt focused, and perhaps even more the metaphorical power of the work's frontispiece, the object of Horst Bredekamp's unsurpassed commentary in his book on "Hobbes's visual strategies," must be sought.[5] Immunity and the monster have in common an excess of the monopolistic function. And this latter, as is clear, concerns not only what Weber would later call legitimate violence, but also the "metaphorical power," mythological and mythopoetic, that is at the heart of theological language. Hobbes only denies legitimacy to metaphor as it is employed by the spiritual power of the Church so that the state may appropriate metaphor for itself and concentrate it in a single point of origin that is also, in the strict sense, fictional. From this fact itself, Hobbes believes that it is possible to affirm that the state will cease to proliferate throughout society, and will on the contrary, like violence, withdraw and yield its place to the rational operations of science, pedagogy or rhetoric, and law that are the "civil sciences" par excellence, to use Quentin Skinner's expression.[6] We thus arrive at the profoundly paradoxical figure, much more "French" than English, of a secularism whose conditions of possibility and whose destination is its own doubling as a theology in competition with the historical religions.

Pluralism and individualism

From here we may pass on to the second point noted above. I must be brief here, even though we have arrived at the heart of the institutional construction of sovereignty and its effect of subjectivation in the etymological sense of the construction of the figure of the "subject" (*subjectus, subditus*) who recognizes a certain authority or forms the correlate of a political obligation that is all the more incontestable in that it emanates from the subject itself. At the risk of outrageous simplification, I can isolate certain themes based on the argument I sketched out in my preface to Schmitt's book. What appears to me most important for my question, once we have recognized Hobbes's pertinence or rather his contribution to the construction of the foundations of modern "liberalism,"[7] is to attempt to situate Hobbes's position between two very different modalities according to which we can grasp the emergence of *the individual as subject* in political philosophy. It is possible to regard the individuality of the subject that forms the basis of its autonomy as a *natural* fact (or a fact of "natural law") presupposed by the very constitution of civil society and that gives its coercive force to obligation – that is precisely where the allegory of the "pact" or the originary contract figures. Or, in contrast, we may regard the isolation of the individual (at least "in law" and as a legal subject endowed with a will that belongs only to him) is never originary, but emerges from the more or less complete, more or less violent, *dissolution* of *collectivities* or pre-existing ties of attachment (whatever the modalities of this dissolution: as the effect of commerce, education, action by the state, "individualistic" religion and so forth).

The common conception – and it obviously cannot purely and simply be refuted – is that Hobbes is situated on the side of the first position and even that he provided its most radical exposition, that is, its prototype. Things, however, are more complicated if we agree that Hobbes's problem is not simply a matter of a statics or a metaphysics, but a matter of dynamics and political science. In this way, we encounter the problem we posed earlier, but from a different perspective: the problem of the conservation or immunity of the political body when it encounters the germs of dissolution or death that it contains, but this time in the form of what Hobbes calls the "systems" constituted by the association of a plurality of citizens (chapter 22, "Of Systemes Subject, Politicall and Private"). The goal of civil association is certainly not to prevent citizens from forming corporations or systems, whether commercial companies or mutual aid societies or cultural or even family associations. But civil association is perpetuated only if these systems remain subjected (*assujettis*) "subjects," that is, fundamentally, only if they renounce any claim to being able to judge their own members and to render justice themselves in a closed circuit, and recognize, on the contrary, the permanent right of the state to intervene within their own system – *quis judicabit* (*who judges*)? This is the great criterion stated by Hobbes, to which Schmitt, as well as legal positivism of the Kelsenian type, accorded a decisive function in the constitution of sovereignty or of the unitary legal norm insofar as it coincides with a statist norm.[8] We may then conclude that, at the limit tendencially and politically, a single task underlies the conditions of the production of an individualized subjectivity capable of authorizing the sovereign and thus founding the state by dissolving, at least virtually, in the realm of law, pre-existing communities. But it also underlies the conditions that make possible and permanently animate a politics designed to prevent the automatization, not of individuals but of collectivities, the transformation of attachments (appartenances) into claims that must be satisfied before those of the state, in short, the appearance of what are called today "communalisms" (*communautarismes*).

And it is here that we see the need to develop a more complex conception of Hobbesian individualism, one in which the history of the state in a certain sense retrospectively explains the conditions of its constitution. Schmitt helps us do this, although in a paradoxical form, by decreeing that this dialectical process is the site of "Hobbes's failure," even if it is a "grandiose" failure, to liberate himself from mechanism and adopt an organicist conception of the state and of the link that – to speak this time as Rousseau does – "that makes a people the people" within the state, and no longer an atomized "multitude." By making the radical fear of the death of which the other man is potentially the bearer, the ultimate motive for the constitution of the state, Hobbes identifies the most powerful motive for this organic unity, but by maintaining in it an essential *pluralism* of associations, although under the jurisdiction of the sovereign, he has "missed" the logical conclusion of his pessimistic anthropology. The paradoxes that Schmitt constructs on the basis of this point have the immense interest of allowing us to understand that Hobbesian theory, especially in *Leviathan*, is inhabited by a tension that can neither be resolved nor even stabilized, but only "forced" or decided by the "force" of sovereignty and its theological aura. Hobbesian "pluralism" is so clearly a reality that some (David Runciman, for example) have argued convincingly that it is the origin of a lineage in political philosophy and the sociology of law that does not lead to theories of national sovereignty, but to the "corporatisms" and "solidarisms" of the nineteenth and twentieth centuries, in particular, in the liberal socialist tradition.[9] This makes it possible to avoid any contamination of the idea of equality or even equal liberty, of which Hobbes is one of the classical proponents, by the idea of the *homogeneity* or common identity of the citizens that, in contrast, triumphs in Schmitt, including through references to Rousseau, to the benefit of the term *Gleichheit* ("equality" but also "sameness") in the broadest sense and its proximity to *Gleichartigkeit* (homogeneity) in the texts from the Nazi period. But this supposes an interpretation of Hobbesian sovereignty, and the subjection (*assujettissement*) that it entails, as a "pure" form of the authority of the law, universal and undivided, duplicated in the constraint exercised by the state to enforce it. Is this really the case? We may well doubt it, if we examine the function in Schmitt's work of the distinction between *public* and *private* that provides the foundation of the universality of the law that largely corresponds to the distinction between corporative "systems" and civil society (that is, the state) itself. This functioning is completely asymmetrical: it is not a matter of a reciprocal demarcation or limitation of entities of the same nature. On the one side, there is a limitation or a self-limitation (private associations must *always* recognize the right of the sovereign to intervene within them as judge or arbiter), and, on the other, there is an illimitation (the state must "totally" penetrate these systems, not to destroy them, but to decompose and recompose them virtually and to make them subordinated organs of civil society). There is, of course, a "last instance" and there must therefore be an *excess of the power* of the state over the collectivities, without which there would not be an absolute individualization of the subjects. Or worse, a subversive simulacrum of individualization through which individuals resist the law (and therefore the state) *in the name of the collectives* of which they are a part and whose material or spiritual interests they embody. In this way we rediscover the thesis of the "mortal God," the political analogue of an all-powerful sovereignty, or rather we discover the paradox captured by the following expression: that of an absolute that would nevertheless be historical, politically constructed and reconstructed (and thus, as may be the case, destroyed), and that is based on a denial of its own limits by means of a myth of the origin.[10]

Secularization, secularism (*laïcité*), hostility

Let us return, in order to conclude or rather to open a discussion, to the question with which we began: that of the model of a secularism ("*laïcité*") of the state and of politics inherited from Hobbes. It is necessarily a very paradoxical model in that it combines the most virulent anti-clericalism with an appropriation of the attributes of divine power – that is even transposed to the juridical register – to the profit of political sovereignty, itself reestablished on an anthropological level by a theory of fictions and an overturning of the metaphorical function.

Have we not thus arrived at precisely the case defined and generalized, even absolutized, by Schmitt and transformed according to a philosophy of the history of modernity that began with his celebrated 1922 book *Political Theology*? This would explain without difficulty Schmitt's fascination with Hobbes, his infinite contestation of the latter's statements. "All political concepts [and therefore also juridical concepts insofar as they are eminently political] are secularized theological concepts," Hobbes being the proof par excellance of this thesis. *Yes and no*, that is, here again, we must recognize, it seems to me, the complexity of a double movement: what characterizes the problem permanently posed by the reading of Hobbes, is the difficulty of invoking in a univocal way, either the application of the "Schmittian" thesis (that is why Hobbes "resists" Schmitt, as I suggested in 2002), or the application of the *inverse* thesis, that of Spinoza in the *Tractatus Theologico-Politicus* and the *Ethics* as it has been reactivated in our time by a theorist like Jan Assman, in order to "reverse" the meaning of Schmitt's argumentation by recognizing its relevance on the basis of the idea that the models of "decision" and "divine omnipotence" (Egyptian, Hebraic) were themselves always already *theologizations of pre-existing political forms,* monarchical and imperial.[11] Why is this discussion of significance to us?

Not only because we are interested, speculatively or even aesthetically, in an interpretation of Hobbes and Schmitt, but because the question of knowing if the religious communities internal to the modern "secular" state constitute a particular, but perhaps very important, case of the general problem of "communitarianism" with which a unitary conception of national affiliation and citizenship, oscillating between universalism and organicism, collides or whether it is the case that religious affiliations and, conjuncturally, certain among them (Catholicism in England in the seventeenth century and Islam in France and perhaps Europe in the twenty-first century) become that upon which are projected all the historical, sociological and cultural differences and represent in the eyes of the discourse of sovereignty the primary obstacle that must be removed, because these attachments refuse to be "dissolved" by purely juridical means into individualities subjected to the law, or, what amounts to the same thing, because their "public" or even "political" character does not spontaneously disappear to the benefit of a radically asymmetrical "privatization"? I do not pretend to resolve this dilemma, but I want to relate it to a question that recurs throughout a reading of Hobbes and that I mentioned earlier: the question of the implicit relation between the designation of public enemies or "systemic" forces of resistance to the legal order, and the constitution of ecclesiastical power as an antagonistic spiritual force of political sovereignty in the construction of *Leviathan* itself. It would be easy to show the affinity between this question and the *state of exception* that Agamben has privileged in his attempt to apply certain of Schmitt's postulates to the interpretation of the extreme forms of political violence in contemporary societies and, in doing so, to incorporate a reference to Hobbes in the discussion around this point. It should be remembered here that the critique of the ecclesiastical machine developed by Hobbes (in chapter 42 of *Leviathan*) was not based on an arbitrary invention, but on the return of the doctrine of the Pope's *potestas indirecta* in relation to temporal sovereigns developed by Cardinal Bellarmine (who will be, a century and a half later, the source of the theorization of "spiritual power" by Auguste Comte). The classification of "subject systems" by Hobbes, divided into regular and irregular organizations and, within each category, into the lawful and the unlawful, brings out a list of "residues" or uncontrollable associations that must therefore by combatted by the state as, at least potential, enemies of the juridical order and that seem at first sight deprived of any unity. What is nevertheless striking is that at each step we find a conjunction of two poles, which, taken together, may be said without exaggeration to form the "subversive" obsession that haunts Hobbesian politics. This conjunction outlines in advance the dissolution of the political body and the return to the state of nature through sedition: on the one side, there are groups of sub-proletarians or popular gatherings of "unusual size," and, on the other, religious sects, above all that "foreigner's party" in the field of the belief that the Catholic Church represents. It may be suggested that Hobbes's argument outlines negatively *the formation of the public enemy*, whose ideal (that is, diabolical) figure would be constituted by the capacity of a religious sect and above all a centralized, transnational Church, like the "universal" Catholic Church, to organize or inspire popular movements, notably those virtually present in the pauperized masses . . . This would be, in anticipated form, the figure of a revolutionary party that would be at once a class party and an obscurantist movement, that is, a movement based on superstition and faith. This exists in negation in Hobbes, that is, it is a hypothesis in some sense *held back* by Hobbes, in the same way that this hypothesis became for Schmitt the very object of a "politics" that, because it had given itself the fundamental task of *holding back the revolutionary catastrophe* and therefore of constructing a sovereignty engaged in permanent, preventative counter-revolution, must begin by *creating its adversary* as an internal enemy. It is only in a theological form that the "friend–enemy distinction," the original ground of politics according to Schmitt, but also the organizing principle of the difference between the interior and the exterior of the state, can come to be re-inscribed *in the interior* and from there create the catastrophic figure of a foreign body whose very presence or whose actions are deadly to the political community.

In sum, what I want to suggest is that the theologization of the enemy of the established political order coincides with the passage from a virtual threat to a real threat or rather a threat *projected on the real* to derive the effects of sovereignty from it. The theological moment of the passage from the legal state (*État de droit*) to the state of social and ideological defense is what is at stake in the continuity and discontinuity between Hobbes and Schmitt. It is clearly one of the meanings that must be associated with the political theologies of secularism or secularization in the current conjuncture that become more virulent as the sovereignty they claim becomes, in practice, more uncertain.

Notes

1. Carl Schmitt, *Le Léviathan dans la doctrine de l'état de Thomas Hobbes: Sens et échec d'un symbole politique (1938)*, trans. D. Trierweiler, préface E. Balibar, postface W. Palaver (Paris: Seuil, 2002); Carl Schmitt, *The Leviathan in the State Theory of Thomas Hobbes: Meaning and Failure of a Political Symbol*, trans. George Straub and Erna Hilfstein (Chicago: University of Chicago Press, 1996).
2. "Le Hobbes de Schmitt, le Schmitt de Hobbes," preface to Carl Schmitt, *Le Léviathan dans la doctrine de l'état de Thomas Hobbes: Sens et échec d'un symbole politique (1938)*, trans. D. Trierweiler, préface E. Balibar, postface W. Palaver (Paris: Seuil, 2002); see Chapter 2 of this volume.
3. This must be specified: in one of its interpretations, opposed by a conception that may be called "liberal," according to which secularism is not an attribute of public power (rendering it, as in Hobbes, a substitute for the Church in matters of education and the legitimation of authority), but the rule of law that permits the freedom of religious institutions and the compatibility of beliefs in society. See my essay, "Secularism and Universality: The Liberal Paradox," *Hommes et libertés. Revue de la ligue des droits de l'homme*, n° 143, 2008 (included in *Equaliberty*, Durham: Duke University Press, 2014).
4. On *Behemoth*, its place in Hobbes's thought and its relation to *Leviathan*, see Tomaz Mastnak, ed. *Hobbes's Béhémoth. Religion and Democracy* (Exeter: Imprint Academic, 2009).
5. Horst Bredekamp, *Thomas Hobbes: Visuelle Strategien. Der Leviathan: Urbild des modernen Staates. Werkillustrationen und Portraits* (Berlin: Carl Hanser Verlag, 1999).
6. Q. Skinner, *Visions of Politics*, Vol. III, *Hobbes and Civil Science* (Cambridge: Cambridge University Press, 2002).
7. Not, however, or not essentially, in the sense of Macpherson's *possessive individualism*, and even less in the sense of a liberalism of the autonomy of civil society in relation to the state, but in the sense of an organic or institutional liberalism in which the state, through the intermediary of the law, the public regulation of individual rights, permanently assures and reproduces the conditions of the autonomy of the individual. See, in particular, the work

of Lucien Jaume: *Hobbes et L'État représentatif moderne* (Paris: Presses Universitaires de France, 1986) and *La liberté et la loi. Les origines philosophiques du libéralisme* (Paris: Fayard, 2000). On Macpherson and later explorations of his thesis, see my essay "Le renversement de l'individualisme possessif," in *La Proposition de l'égaliberté*, cit., 91–126.

8. For a discusssion of the points of convergence and divergence between Hobbes and Kelsen on the relations between law and state, see Franck Lessay, *Souveraineté et légitimité chez Hobbes* (Paris: Presses Universitaires de France, 1988), 178.
9. David Runciman, *Pluralism and the Personality of the State* (Cambridge: Cambridge University Press, 1997).
10. On the articulation of the conceptions of the "omnipotence of God" and the "absolute power of the sovereign" in Hobbes (in particular concerning the dissymetry of obligations) see Luc Foisneau, *Hobbes et la toute-puissance de Dieu* (Paris: Presses Universitaires de France, 2000).
11. Jan Assmann, *Herrschaft und Heil. Politische Theologie in Altägypten, Israel und Europa* (Munich: Carl Hanser Verlag, 2000).

Bibliography

Assmann, Jan. *Herrschaft und Heil. Politische Theologie in Altägypten, Israel und Europa*. Munich: Carl Hanser Verlag, 2000.
Balibar, Etienne. "Le renversement de l'individualisme possessif." In *La proposition de l'égaliberté. Essais politiques 1989–2009*. Paris: Presses Universitaires de France, 2012. Pp. 91–126.
Balibar, Etienne. "Secularism and Universality: The Liberal Paradox." In *Equaliberty: Political Essays*. Trans. James Ingram. Durham, NC: Duke University Press, 2014. Pp. 223–30.
Bredekamp, Horst. *Thomas Hobbes: Visuelle Strategien. Der Leviathan:Urbild des modernen Staates. Werkillustrationen und Portraits*. Berlin: Akademie Carl Hanser Verlag, 1999.
Foisneau, Luc. *Hobbes et la toute-puissance de Dieu*. Paris: Presses Universitaires de France, 2000.
Lessay, Franck. *Souveraineté et légitimité chez Hobbes*. Paris: Presses Universitaires de France, 1988.
Lucien, Jaume. *Hobbes et L'État représentatif modern*. Paris: Presses Universitaires de France, 1986.
Lucien, Jaume. *La liberté et la loi. Les origines philosophiques du libéralisme*. Paris: Fayard, 2000.

Mastnak, Tomaz, ed. *Hobbes's Béhémoth. Religion and Democracy.* Exeter: Imprint Academic, 2009.
Runciman, David. *Pluralism and the Personality of the State.* Cambridge: Cambridge University Press, 1997.
Schmitt, Carl. *The Leviathan in the State Theory of Thomas Hobbes: Meaning and Failure of a Political Symbol.* Trans. George Straub and Erna Hilfstein. Chicago: University of Chicago Press, 1996.
Schmitt, Carl. *Le Léviathan dans la doctrine de l'état de Thomas Hobbes: Sens et échec d'un symbole politique (1938)*, trans. D. Trierweiler, préface E. Balibar, postface W. Palaver. Paris: Seuil, 2002.
Skinner, Q. *Visions of Politics.* Vol. III. *Hobbes and Civil Science.* Cambridge: Cambridge University Press, 2002.

II Transindividual/Universal

3

The "Other Scene" of Political Anthropology: Between Transindividuality and Equaliberty

Jason Read

The political thought of Etienne Balibar is framed between transindividuality and equaliberty. These terms frame much of Balibar's writing on politics, citizenship, race and philosophy in recent decades yet they do not have the same status. One is borrowed, a citation from Gilbert Simondon, while the other is Balibar's neologism, a word that combines equality and liberty. The first is situated with respect to Balibar's investigations in the history of philosophy, constituting a tradition of Spinoza, Hegel and Marx, while the second is deployed in Balibar's investigations of the intersection of race, nation and class in contemporary politics. One term refers to a question of political anthropology, or even ontology, an articulation of the fundamental problems of individual and collective, while the other is framed between the relation between equality and liberty, rights and freedoms, in the history of political practice. The points of overlap are just as salient as their differences. Transindividuality and equaliberty challenge conventional, which is to say both philosophical and ideological, notions of the individual and society, collectivity and individuality. The point, however, is not that these terms are the same, referring to identical terms and questions, nor that they are rigorously distinct, referring to different fields of inquiry – specifically social ontology and politics – but that the differences and relations may itself be a way of articulating what are some of the most pressing questions in contemporary philosophy, not just the relation between the individual and collective, but also the relation between politics and economics, and ultimately the relation between ontology and politics. The relation between transindividuality and equaliberty defines not just a field of political questions on citizenship, civility, the nation and race, but defines a particular philosophical practice, a particular way of engaging in political problems.

Transindividuality *chez* Balibar

The term "transindividuality" is drawn from the work of Gilbert Simondon, most specifically the posthumously published *L'individuation psychique et collective*. As much as Balibar acknowledges this as the source of the term, his own development of the concept is drawn more from the work of Spinoza, or more specifically Spinoza as initially read by Alexandre Matheron in *Individu et commauté chez Spinoza*. For Balibar the overlap between Matheron and Simondon's work constitutes a particular kind of coevolution in the history of philosophy; Matheron could not have been aware of Simondon's thesis, and, for his part, Simondon tends to see Spinoza as not so much a transindividual thinker but as thinker who dissolves the individual into the larger totality of God or nature, losing any individuation whatsoever.[1] In contrast to this, Matheron insists that what Spinoza presents is both an ontology and politics in which the standard oppositions between the individual and the totality no longer hold. Each individual thing is defined by its particular striving, its particular conatus, but its particular conatus only exists and is oriented in and through its affects, encounters and relations.[2] Everything is at once rigorously individual and collective. This irreducibility at the level of ontology is doubled at the level of ethics and politics. As Matheron demonstrates, the task of Spinoza's *Ethics* is to demonstrate that "nothing is more useful to man than man," that the opposition between egoism and altruism, between the pursuit of self-interest and the good of the community, is an illusion generated by inadequate ideas and distorted ambitions.[3] The individual and the collective are not opposed, or reducible to one another, but most be thought in their mutual irreducibility.

It is from this point, from the mutual irreducibility of the individual to the collective or the collective to the individual, that Balibar constructs his lineage of transindividual thinkers, a list that encompasses Spinoza, Hegel, Marx and (sometimes even) Freud.[4] The thinkers on this list have an uneven status in Balibar's thought; Spinoza and Marx have been the subject of both (short) monographs and essays and interventions, while Hegel has recently

Between Transindividuality and Equaliberty 113

appeared in several essays, and Freud often only appears conjoined with other thinkers. Taking this publication history as something of a guide it is possible to argue that the two principal thinkers of Balibar's conception of transindividuality are Spinoza and Marx. Or, more to the point, transindividuality is a concept that Balibar develops according to a transversal logic that passes through the different systems and conjunctures of Spinoza and Marx. This itinerary is not one of influence or lineage between the philosophers under consideration, but constitutes different problems and questions within Balibar's examination of transindividuality. (As I will argue below, Hegel represents a different problem for Balibar, one associated with equaliberty, or more specifically, the relation between equaliberty and transindividuality.)

Spinoza's definite statement of transindividuality is "desire is man's very essence." As Balibar argues, such a formulation redefines the very nature of not only humanity, defining a philosophical anthropology, but the very problem of essence. "The metaphysical notion of essence has thus undergone a profound change instead of referring to a class or a genus, it now refers to the singularity of individuals."[5] Everything that exists, exists in terms of its singular striving, but this singular striving, is, as Matheron asserted, nothing outside of the relations that affect it. Transindividuality is ultimately not just a way of bypassing the oppositions of individual and collective, but of thinking a new figure of causality – causality in the sense that the old opposition between external and internal causes, between being affected and having effects, must be dispensed with in order to understand everything, every striving, as simultaneously a cause and an effect, as a conatus and the affects that orient it.[6] Transindividuality means that any opposition between social causes and individual desires necessarily collapses, the individual exists in and through its relations and these relations only exist insofar as they are individuated in specific strivings. Thus, the very formulation repeats the idea of structural causality, of a cause that exists in and through its effect, and as with structural causality it is less a matter of a transcendent ontological assertion, a claim that would remain the same for all times and places, than a general structure that can only be actualized in specific situations and problems. The combination of external and internal causes, of singular desires and shared affects, can only be thought in and through their specific articulation, their specific character, what Balibar calls, following Spinoza, *ingenium*.

Ingenium, which is translated as nature or character, is the word that Spinoza uses to refer to both the specific character, or comportment, of an individual, and the specific nature of a city or polis. It is through this specific *ingenium* that it is possible to think of both the stability and transformation of a given individual's desires and a given collectivity.[7]

That Balibar finds a turn towards relational and historical specificity at the heart of Spinoza's ontology, at the core of a philosophy often summarized as *sub specie aeternitatis*, is perhaps surprising, but it also explains why Balibar turns to Marx to develop and expand the concept of transindividuality. At the level of propositions, the definitive statement of Marx's transindividual thought is the sixth of the *Theses on Feuerbach,* or, more specifically Marx's statement that "the human essences is no abstraction inherent in each single individual. In its reality it is the ensemble of social relations."[8] Once again it is a question of essence, essence now framed less in terms of the singularity of its manifestation, the desire that underlies every individual, but the relational nature of its articulation.[9] Balibar emphasizes that Marx uses the French word *ensemble* stressing the non-totalizable nature of the relations that constitute and affect this essence. Spinoza and Marx represent twin assaults on the most commonplace nature of a philosophical anthropology, of a human essence that is both universal, a shared essence, and transcendent, existing prior to and outside of its relations. In its place there is the necessity to think of both the singularity and relational dimension of this supposed essence, to think it as transindividual. The human essence is singular, but this singularity is nothing other than the way in which it intersects with determinate relations.

Marx's thought of transindividuality is not limited to the uncharacteristically speculative moment of the *Theses on Feuerbach* but continues through his critique of political economy in *Capital*. Transindividuality is the under-theorized and unnamed concept underlying Marx's more prosaic examinations of the relations of capitalist exploitation. As Marx writes in the chapter on cooperation:

> [T]he special productive power of the combined working day, is under all circumstances, the social productive power of labour, or the productive power of social labour. This power arises from cooperation itself. When the worker co-operates in a planned way with others, he

strips off the fetters of his individuality, and develops the capabilities of this species [*Gattungsvermögen*].[10]

In this passage the capacity of the species, or species being, appears less as that that is alienated by selling one's labour than as that that is put to work by capital. Capital does just not exploit individual labour power understood as the physical or mental expenditure of this or that individual; it exploits the collective labour of not only those gathered in the factory or workshop, but also the collective inheritance of language, skill and knowledge embodied in any individual's productive labour. As Balibar writes,

> We must give this thesis its maximum force to understand the conclusions that Marx wants to reach. Not only is labor socialized historically, so that it becomes transindividual. Essentially it always was, insofar as there is no labor without cooperation, even in its most primitive forms, and the isolation of the productive labourer in relation to nature was only ever an appearance.[11]

Marx then represents one of the most important reversals of possessive individualism, contesting the equation between individuality, labor and possession. Labour is irreducibly collective and individual: in a word, it is transindividual.

Spinoza and Marx would each seem to represent two different theses of transindividuality. With Spinoza there is the assertion of an irreducible minimum of individuation at the heart of any collective process. Desire remains a singular striving. As Spinoza argues in the *Tractatus Theologico-Politicus*, individuals cannot alienate or give away their rights to the sovereign; right, which is to say power, remains an irreducible aspect of individual striving. Individuals cannot suppress their striving, histories and encounters.[12] If Spinoza asserts the irreducible minimum of the individual in the collective, then Marx can be understood to assert the irreducible minimum of the collective in the individual. Labor, but also language and thought, are irreducibly collective. The skills that we use and the language that we speak are collective products. The opposition, or contradiction, on this point is solely heuristic or relative. Spinoza's assertion of the irreducible minimum of the individual has as its corollary the irreducible relational, or collective nature, of this individual striving. Desire is always oriented, determined by the affects and encounters that shape it. In a similar manner, Marx's materialism demands that the collective nature of the labor has as its necessary corollary the singular, embodied performance of this labor. It is always a singular body and mind that is put to work, and it is the kernel of living labor that constitutes the limit of capitalist exploitation.[13] The minimum of the individual cannot be separated from its communication and relation, just as the minimum of the collective cannot be separated from its singular embodiment in the laboring body or thinking mind.[14] We may put to work the combined "general intellect" of humankind, but we always do so with our head and hands and in our particular finite time. The two theses of transindividuality, the irreducibility of the collective in the individual and the individual in the collective, are not only each present in each transindividual thinker, but are the necessarily corollary of each other.

The salient difference between Marx and Spinoza is not that the first is more collectivist and the second is more individualistic. That would negate the very premise of transindividuality. Nor is it a difference of philosophical speculation and concrete analysis: Spinoza's conjunctural analysis of religion and politics is as important as the *Ethics* for grasping his account of transindividuality and Marx's philosophical anthropology found in such early fragments as the "Theses on Feuerbach" is as important as the critique of political economy. If they differ and complement each other it has to do with the way that the relation between politics and economics is framed in each. As Balibar writes,

> It would be easy to conclude that Marx is basically unaware of the "other scene" of politics, the scene of communitarian affiliation, and therefore unaware of symbolic violence as well (although he names it or has bequeathed us with the word ideology, on of the aptest names for it); and to conclude that Spinoza, for his part, basically ignores the irreducible level of economic antagonism (doubtless because, at the economic level, where conatus can perhaps be conceived of as a "productive force," Spinoza is basically an optimist and a utilitarian).[15]

Marx is then the thinker of economic exploitation, with little to say about the conflict over symbolic identities, while Spinoza is the thinker of the ambiguity of political identities, with little to say about exploitation. As much as this is perhaps true, it does not entirely address the way in which their thought can be articulated with respect to these problems (as Balibar's parenthetical statement reveals). It is a matter of tendencies rather than divisions.

It is at this point that we confront the ambiguity of transindividuality as a politics. As much as Spinoza recognized the irreducible singular striving of the individual as a limit that tyrannical powers would have to confront, he also understood that the strength of superstition, which is to say ideology, is to incorporate, or interpellate the individual. Superstition, by which Spinoza means religion, begins from the fact that men are "conscious of their appetites, and ignorant of the causes of things." As Balibar demonstrates, politics, political authority, continues this interpellation. This is the ultimate significance of the contract for the history of politics; it is an ideology that constructs the state as something individually chosen or willed. Hence the continued importance of Spinoza's critique of theocracy: theocracy is not just a state founded on religious authority, but a state founded upon imaginary participation of the individual in the collective through the act of consent.[16] In a similar manner Marx's analysis of commodity fetishism demonstrates the manner in which the irreducible collective, or social nature, of production appears first as the value of commodities, and ultimately as the productive power of capital.[17] The terms could be reversed here as well: an ideological or imaginary dimension of collectivity can be found in Spinoza, in the community founded upon imagined identifications, just as an imaginary of ideological dimension of individuality can be found in Marx, in the market relations of isolated individuals. We can find in Spinoza an analysis of the way in which the irreducible collective nature of striving constitutes both the basis of not only rational agreement, "nothing is more useful to man than man," but also imaginary identification, the entire affective economy of ambition and envy. For Marx there is also an analysis of the way in which capital, specifically the market, appears as a regime of "freedom, equality, and Bentham," as the very realization of individual aspiration and desire. What Balibar writes of Spinoza, that "[s]ociability is . . . the unity of a real agreement and an imaginary ambivalence, both of which have real effects," can be understood to apply to not only to both Spinoza and Marx, but transindividuality in general.[18] "One divides into two" with respect to transindividuality, in that both the irreducible individual nature of the collective and the irreducible collective nature of the individual have their imaginary (or symbolic) and real dimensions.

Individual identity and collective belonging are each both symbolic and real, affective and rational.

The incomplete history of equaliberty

There is an unmistakable overlap between transindividuality and equaliberty. What the former does with the anthropological, or ontological, postulates of the individual and the collective, the latter does with the political articulations of individual and collective through such concepts as rights, citizenship and nation. Their conceptual overlap can thus be seen in their objects of criticism; each of the terms is critically positioned against a persistent binary or opposition that posits the relation between the collective and the individual as necessarily a zero sum game, as a choice between the individual or the collective. Equality has often been understood, especially since the cold war, as the demand of the collective, while liberty has been understood as the rights of the individuality. Equaliberty, like transindividuality, must ultimately posit the irreducibility of the individual to the collective and the collective to the individual. This conceptual overlap is doubled by the fact that many transindividual thinkers, including Spinoza and Marx, have as their political ideal a realization of the individual in the collective and the collective in the individual (to borrow a Hegelian phrasing).[19] The transindividual ontology is completed and realized in a political ideal that seeks the realization of the individual in the collective, in other words, equaliberty.

Despite this overlap of problems and terms Balibar does not develop equaliberty on the same philosophical terrain as transindividuality, nor does he refer to the same figures. As we have seen above, transindividuality is grounded on the ontology and political thought of Spinoza and Marx (to name two transindividual thinkers), or, more precisely, the point where politics and ontology intersect. The points of reference for equaliberty, however, are primarily political and historical. Equaliberty is not developed through an ontological examination, but through political transformations and historical experience. As Balibar writes:

> [I]f it is absolutely true that equality is practically identical to liberty, this means that it is materially impossible for it to be otherwise – in other words, it means that they are necessarily always contradicted

together. This thesis is itself to be interpreted in extension: equality and freedom are contradicted in exactly the same conditions, in the same situation, because there is no example of conditions that supress or repress freedom that do not suppress or limit – that is, do not abolish – equality, and vice versa. I am not afraid of being contradicted here by the history of capitalist exploitation, which by negating the equality proclaimed in the labor contract ends up in the practical negation of freedom of speech and expression, or by the history of socialist regimes that, by suppressing public freedoms, end up constituting a society of privileges and reinforced inequalities.[20]

Balibar turns the cannons of cold war ideology against that ideology by arguing that it is history itself that demonstrates the impossibility of liberty without equality, the Western Ideal, or equality without liberty, its Soviet counterpart. The American ideal of liberty without equality is contradicted by the various liberties, from speech to participation in the political process that are effectively annulled by massive inequality of material resources. Freedom of speech without access to the very material conditions of being heard effectively annuls itself, just as the equality of state socialism is annulled by the differences that set party members apart from non-party members. As Balibar writes,

> There are no examples of restrictions or suppressions of freedoms without social inequalities, nor of inequalities without restrictions or suppressions of freedoms, be it only to put down resistance, even if there are degrees, secondary tensions, phases of unstable equilibrium, and compromise situations in which exploitation and domination are not homogeneously distributed across all individuals.[21]

Cold war ideology was framed in terms of a choice between liberty or equality, understood as competing as political ideals; the history of the same period posits the impossibility of separating equality and liberty. The separation between equality and liberty is also the separation between economics and politics, between economic equality (coupled with political repression) or political liberty (coupled with economic inequality). Thus, the proposition of equaliberty is aimed as much against the divide between economics and politics, the idea that economic transformations do not affect political relations and vice versa, as it is between freedom and equality, the individual and collective.

Balibar's turn toward history, towards the historical evidence of the Cold War, does not entirely dispense with the philosophical articulation of the concept. Equaliberty is not a fact of nature, some law of the universe that dictates that equality must always accompany liberty and vice versa. This is not a positivism in which the facts of history trump conceptual analysis, but an examination of the institution and transformation of political ideas in and through political practices. The efficacy of equaliberty stems from a particular institutionalization of politics and humanity, a particular political anthropology. The initial point of reference for this institution is the Declaration of the Rights of Man and of the Citizen – the historical institution of the identity of man and citizen, humanity and the right to politics. Balibar's assertion contests Marx's famous reading of this Declaration in "On the Jewish Question" that argued that "man" was ultimately bourgeois man, the private citizen of market existence, and the conjunction "and" ultimately reduced all rights of the citizen to man, to an isolated, self-interested and private existence.[22] As Balibar argues, "Reread the *Declaration* and you will see that there is in reality no gap between the rights of man and the rights of the citizen, no difference in content: they are exactly the same."[23] This proclamation constitutes something of an event, a transformation of the terms of politics. As such it is shaped by both what precedes it, and as Balibar argues the French Revolution was simultaneously a revolution against tyranny and inequality, against the absolute powers of the king and the entrenched inequalities of feudal society. Like Marx, Balibar argues that the revolution is shaped by his conditions, but these conditions do not restrict it, leave it at the status of merely political emancipation, but shape its particular political transformation understood as a universal right to politics. At the level of political anthropology, it is a break with the ancient conception of politics, in which citizenship, political belonging, had to be qualified with respect to the different aspects of humanity. The result was that women, children, slaves and even manual labourers were disqualified from citizenship. In the ancient period "the concept of the citizen is subordinated to anthropological differences."[24] It thus institutes a new era of political thought and practice, one that is less the decisive transformation of politics, than an era riddled with its own contradictions and tensions. The history of equaliberty, the struggles against the separation of equality and liberty, is the history of the way the various tensions of this relation is worked out and displaced through multiple identities and institutions. It is a history in which the identity of citizen and man are driven beyond any anthropological limitation, any qualification by nation, race or gender.

The citation of the historical evidence of equaliberty is thus understood as the intersection between institutions and insurrection. For Balibar, the citizen instituted by this revolution is split between its constitutive dimension and its insurrectionary dimension. It is at the basis of state authority, but it is so only through its capacity to constantly contest this authority, to revolt once again. Equaliberty is thus a thoroughly historical or historicized concept, which is to say that not only does it unfold over history, and constitute the basis for making sense of a particular history, but it can only unfold historically. "This is why citizenship is historically engaged in an uninterrupted process of the extension, deepening, and adaptation of norms."[25] This history has two defining moments. The first is the attempt to reconcile the tension of maintaining equality and liberty in something other than moments of insurrection, between social and political existence, through a third term, through a concept of fraternity or, understood as either social citizenship or through property, or self-possession, understood as the only viable equality and the basis of liberty.[26] These two ideals and institutions represent the two dominant ways, ways that could be distinguished as left and right, of stabilizing equality and liberty, either through the institution of fraternity through social citizenship that encompasses some ideal of equality under its basic liberties, or the protection and guarantee of property as means to reconcile liberty and the equal right to prosperity.

It is the same intersection of social and politics, economic and political transformations that threatens the very identity of man and citizen, of humanity and political participation. This is the second moment, the unravelling of fraternity or property as the mediation of the tensions between equality and liberty. On the side of fraternity, there is the division of man, of humanity, into the sexes, plural, not just men and women but the myriad identities and relations that do not neatly fit into such a division. On the side of property, there is the fundamental transformation of property to encompass "intellectual property," a transformation that affects not only the social conditions of labour but also the political conditions of participation. These transformations challenge equaliberty not just in that they disrupt the identity of man and citizen, suggesting new inequalities irreducible to ancient exclusions, but any solution to these transformations exceeds what is conventionally understood as equality or liberty. The inequalities and exclusions of sexual difference cannot be resolved by a simple appeal to equality, nor can the intellectual property be resolved by the free access to information.

The history of equaliberty, or equaliberty as an understanding of the history of modern politics, then returns us to the concept of transindividuality. Its limits, sexual difference and intellectual difference, are nothing other than radical challenges to the very conditions and possibility of the citizen as a form of political transindividuation. As such, these limits remind us that political individuation is itself situated among other individuations, the individuations of social reproduction and the labour process. Sexual difference reminds us that identity, even the most intimate and naturalized, is always framed in relation with others, is always transindividual.[27] The politicization of sexual difference can be considered an extension of the initial identification of man and citizen, extending it beyond its gendered exclusion to eventually problematize the very concept of human nature, or human individuality underlying politics, revealing the gendered and thus non-neutral nature of any politics in the name of man. It pushes beyond the identity of man and citizen to question, in the name of political universality and participation, any attempt to ground politics in a naturalized figure of man. Intellectual difference relates less to the internal transformations of citizenship than to the division between politics and economics. What Balibar refers to as intellectual difference returns us to Marx's understanding of the transindividual nature of labour, reminding us, as Marx did in *Capital*, that this anthropological fact is not without its divisions, most notably the division between mental and manual labour, divisions that are extenuated by the radical transformation brought about by the capitalist subsumption of labour. Capital increasingly transforms man from the wielder of tools into nothing other than a conscious organ of the machine, making skill and knowledge part of the machine rather than the worker. This has profound effects for the constitution of individuation. As Balibar writes,

> This process of autonomization-intellectualization-materialization of "knowledge" determines more and more the exercise of the "property rights" and thereby individuality. But at the same time it renders

more and more uncertain the identity of proprietors, the identity of the "subject" of property. Then we are no longer dealing merely with a mechanism of division of human nature that practically contradicts the requirement of freedom and equality. Instead we are dealing with a dissolution of political individuality.[28]

Sexual difference and intellectual difference challenge the very identity of man and citizen, of citizenship as a transindividual individuation. This is not a return to the ancient inequalities of exclusion, although the incomplete and uneven development of transindividuation means that it is never free of such inequalities. As Balibar argues, the "current conjuncture" carries with it elements of ancient, modern and postmodern transindividuation.[29] Sexual difference and intellectual difference challenge equaliberty, the constitution of the citizen, in a different manner than such ancient exclusions in that their very resolution demands a redefinition of both equality and liberty. Sexual difference cannot be resolved by a simple appeal to equality, nor can the transformations of intellectual difference, the materialization and transformation of knowledge, be resolved by a simple appeal to liberty, to the freedom of information (or information "wanting to be free"). Sexual difference and intellectual difference challenge equaliberty, not simply by introducing hitherto unimagined inequalities and dominations, but because their emancipatory transformation will necessarily involve new concepts and practices of equality and freedom, challenging both terms in the conjunction.

Conclusion: Dialectics of the other scene

The relation between the concepts of transindividuality and equaliberty is conflictual and uneven. Transindividuality would seem to be the necessary ontological postulate underlying equaliberty. As such it is a necessary, but not sufficient condition, as equaliberty is the institutionalization and "becoming explicit" of transindividuality. At the same time, the broad meaning of transindividuality, the ensemble of relations it encompasses, political, economic and technical, would constantly threaten equaliberty as a particular political institutionalization of transindividuality. One the one hand, equaliberty completes transindividuality, while, on the other, transindividuality threatens equaliberty.

One way to resolve this tension would be to posit politics as a necessarily becoming equaliberty of transindividuality – in which the task of politics would be a matter of proceeding from an inadequate to adequate idea of transindividuality, to use Spinoza's terminology. We are always already transindividual, constituted even in our isolated, egocentric and ambitious relations through our encounters and relations, but there is a fundamental difference between the transindividual identity that sees itself as isolated, separate or even hostile to society, and one that recognizes its constitutive relations with others, and recognizes itself in those relations. One could argue that such a transformation underlies Spinoza's politics in the shift from the inadequate ideas of ambition to the adequate ideas of people's common usefulness to each other. Spinoza's politics are thus in some sense a politics of communication, of a transformation of how people understand and think about their constitutive relations.[30] It is also possible to argue that Marx's, or at least Marxist politics, are shaped by a fundamental epistemological transformation, a different understanding of social relations in the passage from ideology to class consciousness (or science). "The true society of individuals can only exist in their effective socialization."[31] Politics in Marx and Spinoza is both a transformation of social relations and a transformation of the understanding of those relations, a transformation of base and superstructure, the order and connection of things and ideas.

Politics as a recognition of the transindividual takes on a much more explicit form in Hegel. This is perhaps why Balibar turns his attention to Hegel, specifically the *Phenomenology of Spirit* in *Citoyen Sujet*. Balibar examines two of Hegel's statements, each of which could be understood as formulations of the transindividual, "Ich das Wir, und Wir, das Ich ist" or "I that is We and We that is I," and "das Tun aller und Jeder" or "The work of all and each."[32] As such, these formulations constitute a particular moment in the becoming subject of substance, of the becoming universal of the common, the point at which spirit, the constitutive historical and relation aspects of subjectivity, is explicitly recognized. There are two limitations to this absolute identity of the individual in the collective, of the we that is an I and the work of all and each. First, as Balibar argues, there is a fundamental problem as to whether any specific community, any given social relation can ultimately realize transindividuality as such. There is a fundamental and eternal difference between the common, transindividuality as the very condition of individual and collective life, and the universal, the recognition and institutionalization of that common life.[33] This difference cannot be transcended or sublimated. There is no community of the community, no social relation that corresponds to absolute knowledge; the closer that specific social formations come to realizing the very idea of such a community, the more they universalize their own particular articulation of the common, the more that they expose their particular and contingent basis.[34] The conditions of this limit are given in the two formulations of spirit, one that posits it as a social relation of recognition, as a universality, in the I that is We, and the other as a task, an activity, a common project, in the task for all and each. One splits into two, in that any community, any social relation, is always at once common and universal, an activity, a practice and its representation and recognition. Or, put in the terms we are examining here, transindividuality is the condition of equaliberty but is neither reducible to it, nor completely resolved into it.

If we turn our attention to Hegel's *Philosophy of Right* it becomes clear that it is not just a matter of the individual recognizing itself in its transindividual conditions, the I that is We, or acting in relation to the common, the work of all and each, but of both at once, of an individual constituted in and through different political and social individuations, including the division between collective work, the economy and collective identity, the state or nation. As Balibar writes,

> The Hegelian political subject is thus citizen and burgher [bourgeois] at the same time, a "man without qualities," and a "man with qualities," these qualities being at once subjective and objective, that is, dispositions (*habitus*) and properties (*proprietas*). The state thus conceived, however, has two faces; we should perhaps go so far as to say that it divides into two, that it contains *two communities in one*.[35]

This division is in turn split, as private life is torn between civil society and the family, between individual self-interest and substantial belonging. The politics that Hegel proposes in *The Philosophy of Right* is one of the destruction and constitution of different overlapping transindividual individuations, family, civil society and state.[36]

Returning now to the problem of the relation between transindividuality and equaliberty from this perspective it is now possible to see equaliberty, the ideal of the citizen, as one transindividual individuation. It is perpetually threatened by not only its own limits, the limits ascribed to citizenship demarcated by national borders and other forms of belonging, but by its external conditions, by economic and political transformations, as well as familial relations.[37] These economic and familial transindividual individuations differ from Hegel's in two substantial ways. First, following the latter works of Marx, "civil society," or the economy is not one transindividual individuation, that of ego-centric self interest, that can simply be opposed to the universal individuation of the citizen or state, but is itself split between market-based isolated subjectivity and work that is necessarily transindividual if not collective. The economic does not have a univocal individuation, but is itself split between its symbolization in competition or cooperation, the market or the labour process. As Balibar remarks of the contemporary neoliberal symbolization, demonstrating the flexibility of this symbolization, "The capitalist is defined as a worker, as an 'entrepreneur'; the worker, as the bearer of a capacity, of a 'human capital.'"[38] To which we must add a third individuation, the loss of individuation and transindividuation through the technological and social fragmentation of the labouring body and subjectivity.[39] This last transformation can be understood to be a product of the contemporary reorganization of the labour process. Balibar argues that Marx's concept of class politics was always divided between the proletariat understood as a class and the process of precariatization and fragmentation of workers.[40] The proletariat was always both a political identity and the capitalist undermining of the collective unity and individual security necessary to constitute any identity, a collective subject and a process. The gap between the process and identity is instructive. There is no institution or practice – economic, political or social – that univocally constitutes a determinate individuation; each must pass through the other scene. Symbolic identifications of the citizen must pass through economic relations, and economic relations must pass through their symbolic articulation. Second, whereas Hegel could posit a linear progression through the various institutions, family, civil society and the state, culminating in the recognition of universality, such a progression seems difficult to maintain today. This is both a theoretical and historical point. As Balibar argues, Marx's writing from the early critiques of Hegel to *Capital* interrupted Hegel's linear progression from particularity to universality.[41]

Commodity fetishism is one name of this interruption, of the way in which the individual is interrupted in its progress from isolation to transindividuality, the recognition of the constitutive and necessary nature of collective relations. Rather than recognizing oneself in the constitutive relations of transindividuality these relations are fetishized, made into qualities of the commodity. Such a progression is also called into question by the historical experience of the twentieth century, which far from being one of the dissolution of violent particularity into universality has been marked by the return of various forms of violent exclusion, of pre-modern limitations of the universality of the citizen.[42] Hegel's historical optimism in which particularity is elevated to universality, violence to a new legal order, is one of the causalities of the long twentieth century.

Equaliberty, the universalization of man and citizen, is thus a fragile, and precarious constitution of the political. It is only one transindividual individuation among others, situated among different practices and relations that both extend and threaten it. Politics are rare. The corollary of this is provocation that perhaps goes beyond Balibar's formulation. There is no reason to necessarily limit equaliberty to the citizen, to the instituted sphere of the state; there are practices of equaliberty that can be extended in and through the sites of production and social reproduction, transforming work and the family. As much as the citizen is threatened by other transindividual individuations, or by the destruction of individuation through the labor process, the fact that all identities, all subjects, are constituted transindividuality means that there is not one relation, one identity, that cannot be extended, or transformed by equaliberty. The intersection of equality and liberty can be articulated with labor process, the family and social relations, transforming them and being transformed in the process. As Yves Citton writes:

> Equaliberty is a matter of pressures, multiple, complex and often contradictory dynamics in which we must try to intervene to increase the share of real freedom enjoyed by all, limiting the tensions and distortions introduced by entrenched inequalities in which one only benefits at the expense of others.[43]

It is not a matter of returning to the citizen, or mourning its loss, but of constituting equaliberty in multiple relations, making it a part of the transindividual individuations that traverse political, economic and social life.

Notes

1. Etienne Balibar, "Individualité et transindividualité chez Spinoza," in *Architectures de la raison. Mélanges offerts à Alexandre Matheron*, ed. P. F. Moreau (Fontenay-aux-Roses: ENS Editions, 1996), 37.
2. Alexandre Matheron, *Individu et Communauté chez Spinoza* (Paris: Éditions de Minuit, 1969), 19.
3. Ibid. 274.
4. Etienne Balibar, *The Philosophy of Marx*, trans. Chris Turner (London: Verso, 1995), 120.
5. Etienne Balibar, "Spinoza: From Individuality to Transindividuality," in *Mededelingen vanwege het Spinozahuis*, Vol. 71 (Delft: Eburon, 1997), 5.
6. Ibid. 13.
7. Etienne Balibar, "Jus, Pactum, Lex: On the Constitution of the Subject in the *Theologico-Political Treatise*," trans. Ted Stolze, in *The New Spinoza*, ed. Warren Montag and Ted Stolz (Minneapolis: Minnesota University Press, 1997), 185.
8. Karl Marx, "Theses on Feuerbach", in *Marx/Engels Reader*, ed. Robert Tucker (New York: Norton, 1978b (1845)), 144.
9. Etienne Balibar, "From Philosophical Anthropology to Social Ontology and Back: What to Do with Marx's Sixth Thesis on Feuerbach?" *Postmodern Culture*, 22.3 (2012): 5.
10. Karl Marx, *Capital: A Critique of Political Economy*, Vol. 1, trans. Ben Fowkes (New York: Penguin, 1977 (1867)), 441.
11. Etienne Balibar, *Equaliberty: Political Essays*, trans. James Ingram (Durham, NC: Duke University Press, 2014), 85.
12. Etienne Balibar, *Violence and Civility: On the Limits of Political Philosophy*, trans. G. M. Goshgarian (New York: Columbia University Press, 2015), 11.
13. Balibar, *The Philosophy of Marx*, 101
14. Etienne Balibar, *The Philosophy of Marx*, trans. Chris Turner (London: Verso, 1995), 11.
15. Ibid. 12.
16. Balibar, "Jus, Pactum, Lex," 193.
17. Etienne Balibar, *Citoyen sujet et autres essais d'anthropologie philosophique* (Paris: Presses Universitaires de France, 2011), 325.

18. Etienne Balibar, *Spinoza and Politics*, trans. Peter Snowdon (London: Verso, 1998), 88.
19. Balibar, *Violence and Civility*, 138.
20. Balibar, *Equaliberty*, 49.
21. Ibid. 49.
22. Karl Marx, "On the Jewish Question," in *Marx/Engels Reader*, ed. Robert Tucker (New York: Norton, 1978a (1843)), 45.
23. Balibar, *Equaliberty*, 44.
24. Etienne Balibar, *Masses, Classes, Idea: Studies on Politics and Philosophy before and after Marx*, trans. James Swenson (New York: Routledge, 1994), 59.
25. Balibar, *Equaliberty*, 123.
26. Ibid. 53.
27. Etienne Balibar, *Politics and the Other Scene*, trans. Christine Jones, James Swenson and Chris Turner (London: Verso, 2002), 27.
28. Balibar, *Masses, Classes, Ideas*, 58.
29. Ibid. 59.
30. Balibar, *Spinoza and Politics*, 98.
31. Balibar, *Equaliberty*, 85.
32. Balibar, *Citoyen Sujet*, 270.
33. Ibid. 283.
34. Ibid. 280. Balibar's position here is in many senses similar to Jameson who also stresses the social and non-totalizable nature of spirit. As Jameson writes, "Yes, Spirit is the collective, but we must not call it that, owing to the reification of language, owing to the positivities of the philosophical terms or names themselves, which restore precisely that empirical common-sense ideology it was the very vocation of the dialectic to destroy in the first place. To name the social is to make it over into a thing or an empirical entity, just as to celebrate its objectivity in the face of idealistic subjectivism is to reestablish the old subject–object opposition which was to have been done away with." Frederic Jameson, *The Hegel Variations: On the Phenomenology of Spirit* (London: Verso, 2010), 13.
35. Balibar, *Violence and Civility*, 112; emphasis in the original.
36. Ibid. 113.
37. Louis Carré, "Violence, institutions, 'politique de la civilité': Étienne Balibar et les enjeux d'une anthropologie politique,'" in *Pourquoi Balibar. Raison Publique* 19 (Fall 2014): 30.
38. Balibar, *Masses, Classes, Ideas*, p. 52.
39. The destruction of individuation brought about by the transformations of the labor process has become the central focus of the work

of Bernard Stiegler (Bernard Stiegler, *La Société automatique: 1. L'avenir du travail* (Paris: Fayard, 2015), 353). For how this conception of the short-circuit of transindividuation relates to the work of Balibar see Jason Read, *The Politics of Transindividuality* (Leiden: Brill, 2015).
40. Balibar, *Masses, Classes, Ideas*, 127.
41. Etienne Balibar, "The Infinite Contradiction," trans. Jean-Marc Poisson with Jacques Lezra, in *Depositions: Althusser, Balibar, Macherey, and the Labor of Reading. Yale French Studies*, 88 (1995): 146.
42. Balibar, *Violence and Civility*, 49.
43. Yves Citton, *Renverser L'insoutenable* (Paris: Seuil, 2012), 107 (my translation).

Bibliography

Balibar, Etienne. *Masses, Classes, Idea: Studies on Politics and Philosophy before and after Marx.* Trans. James Swenson. New York: Routledge, 1994.

Balibar, Etienne. "The Infinite Contradiction." Trans. Jean-Marc Poisson with Jacques Lezra. In *Depositions: Althusser, Balibar, Macherey, and the Labor of Reading. Yale French Studies* 88, 1995. Pp. 142–64.

Balibar, Etienne. *The Philosophy of Marx.* Trans. Chris Turner. London: Verso, 1995.

Balibar, Etienne. "Individualité et transindividualité chez Spinoza." In *Architectures de la raison. Mélanges offerts à Alexandre Matheron.* Ed. P. F. Moreau. Fontenay-aux-Roses: ENS Editions, 1996. Pp. 35–46.

Balibar, Etienne. "Jus, Pactum, Lex: On the Constitution of the Subject in the *Theologico-Political Treatise.*" Trans. Ted Stolze. In *The New Spinoza.* Ed. Warren Montag and Ted Stolz. Minneapolis: Minnesota University Press, 1997. Pp. 174–94.

Balibar, Etienne. "Spinoza: From Individuality to Transindividuality." In *Mededelingen vanwege het Spinozahuis.* Vol. 71. Delft: Eburon, 1997.

Balibar, Etienne. *Spinoza and Politics.* Trans. Peter Snowdon. London: Verso, 1998.

Balibar, Etienne. *Politics and the Other Scene.* Trans. Christine Jones, James Swenson and Chris Turner. London: Verso, 2002.

Balibar, Etienne. *Citoyen sujet et autres essais d'anthropologie philosophique.* Paris: Presses Universitaires de France, 2011.

Balibar, Etienne. "From Philosophical Anthropology to Social Ontology and Back: What to Do with Marx's Sixth Thesis on Feuerbach?" *Postmodern Culture*, 22.3 (2012). <http://muse.jhu.edu/journal/160>.

Balibar, Etienne. *Equaliberty: Political Essays*. Trans. James Ingram. Durham, NC: Duke University Press, 2014.

Balibar, Etienne. *Violence and Civility: On the Limits of Political Philosophy*. Trans. G. M. Goshgarian. New York: Columbia University Press, 2015.

Carré, Louis. "Violence, institutions, 'politique de la civilité': Étienne Balibar et les enjeux d'une 'anthropologie politique.'" *Pourquoi Balibar. Raison Publique*, 19 (Fall 2014): 21–33.

Citton, Yves. *Renverser L'insoutenable*. Paris: Seuil, 2012.

Hegel, G. W. F. *The Phenomenology of Spirit*. Trans. A. V. Miller. Oxford: Oxford University Press, 1977.

Hegel, G. W. F. *Elements of the Philosophy of Right*. Trans. Allen W. Wood. Cambridge: Cambridge University Press, 1991.

Jameson, Frederic. *The Hegel Variations: On the Phenomenology of Spirit*. London: Verso, 2010.

Marx, Karl. "On the Jewish Question." In *Marx/Engels Reader*. Ed. Robert Tucker. New York: Norton, 1978a (1843). Pp. 26–52.

Marx, Karl. "Theses on Feuerbach." In *Marx/Engels Reader*. Ed. Robert Tucker. New York: Norton, 1978b (1845). Pp. 143–5.

Marx, Karl. *Capital: A Critique of Political Economy*. Vol. 1. Trans. Ben Fowkes. New York: Penguin, 1977 (1867).

Matheron, Alexandre. *Individu et Communauté chez Spinoza*. Paris: Éditions de Minuit, 1969.

Read, Jason. *The Politics of Transindividuality*. Leiden: Brill, 2015.

Spinoza, Baruch. "The Ethics." In *The Collected Works of Spinoza*. Trans. and ed. Edwin Curley. Princeton: Princeton University Press, 1994. Pp. 408–620.

Spinoza, Baruch. *Theological Political Treatise*. Trans. Samuel Shirley. Indianapolis: Hackett, 2001.

Stiegler, Bernard. *La Société automatique: 1. L'avenir du travail*. Paris: Fayard, 2015.

4

Intersubjectivity or Transindividuality? The Leibniz–Spinoza Alternative

Vittorio Morfino

Translated by Dave Mesing[1]

Monadology and Spinozism

Among the most curious and insistent features in the history of misunderstandings of Leibniz's philosophy is the attempt to see within it a form of Spinozism. This is a misunderstanding in a double sense, because in order to affirm it, the complexity of Spinoza must be reduced to the same extent as the complexity of Leibniz. Already in the final years of his life, Leibniz had unequivocally expressed the problem with such a reduction in response to a letter from Louis Bourguet:

> I do not see how you can deduce any Spinozism from this; to do so is to jump to conclusions. On the contrary, it is through these very monads that Spinozism is destroyed, for there are just as many true substances, as many living mirrors of the universe which subsist always, or as many concentrated universes, as there are monads; according to Spinoza, on the contrary, there is only one substance. He would be right if there were no monads; then everything except God would be of a passing nature and would vanish into simple accidents or modifications, since there would be no substantial foundation in things, such as consist in the existence of monads.[2]

Leibniz's response grasps the fundamental point of divergence between the two philosophies, which Balibar, using a fine expression of Foucault's, has defined as their "point of heresy."[3]

On a strictly metaphysical level, it is Jacobi who took up the opposition between the two systems: the presence of the concept of substantial form in Leibniz, a *principium individuationis*, renders the two systems not only different but opposed.[4] This opposition was at once canonized and dialecticized by Hegel in the Remark to the third section of chapter one in the Doctrine of Essence[5]: here the Leibniz–Spinoza opposition loses the contingent characteristics of its historical horizon in order to become a categorical game that the mind of God conducts in the eternity of the logical element. This opposition, in its historical existence, expresses the dialectic of two one-sidednesses that must be overcome by the self-unfolding of the process: while in Spinozist philosophy, the subject drowns under the totality of substance, in Leibnizian philosophy the subject can be posed only if it takes on the law of its relations with other monads, that is, if its activity is an activity understood only in a relative sense. Upon closer analysis, Hegel repeats Leibniz's judgment by putting the dialectic of the two one-sidednesses in the service of his own philosophy: substance without subject on the one hand and subjects without totality on the other prepare the way for the substance becoming subject that is the core of his own thought.

Despite the contours of Hegel's sketch, the Leibniz–Spinoza opposition has not been a mere repetition. When posed on a purely metaphysical level, it seems to be sterile: the eternal repetition of the dialectic between the One and the Many, central to the Western tradition since Plato's *Parmenides* is refracted in the Leibniz–Spinoza dyad through the lens of substance. One or many substances – this is the dilemma. If we renounce a panoramic view of the history of thought and draw closer to the two authors' terminology, however, it becomes immediately clear that every simplistic oppositional schema proves to be inadequate and reductive, as demonstrated by the extraordinary reading protocol that is Leibniz's *Ad Ethicam*, whose salient aspect is precisely the impossibility of Leibniz's retranslation of the terminology of Spinozist metaphysics into his own philosophy. Renouncing a panoramic approach to Leibniz and Spinoza, then, displaces the question by means of a double move: on the one hand, it situates the opposition not on a metaphysical level (the unity of substance against the plurality of monads) but rather on the level of the finite and its internal relations (monads against modes) and, on the other, it disengages the opposition from a strictly historiographical level in order to evaluate its power in terms of the history of its effects, projecting it on to a theoretical terrain.

Transcendental intersubjectivity

If there is an author in nineteenth-century philosophy who restored vigor to the Leibnizian project of a monadology, it is without doubt Edmund Husserl. As the *Cartesian Meditations* progresses, the figure of Leibniz seems to undermine the figure of Descartes from the center of the theoretical backdrop, up until the fifth meditation dedicated to intersubjectivity, in which Husserl offers his own theory as a new monadology.

We can briefly recall the essential steps of this journey. Husserl's first well-known move consists in the repetition of Cartesian universal doubt that leads to a pure *ego* (or a "reduced *ego*"), a pure interiority equipped with the character of apodictic obviousness. In this way, the *ego cogito* becomes "the ultimate and apodictically certain basis for judgments, the basis on which any radical philosophy must be grounded."[6] Towards the world and all others, I do not have a claim to being, a *Seinsanspruch*; in other words, I lose "all the formations pertaining to sociality and culture [*die ganzen Gebilde der Sozialität und der Kultur*]"[7] in their existential belief, *Seinsglauben*. The *epoché*, this "transcendental-phenomenological reduction" is indeed the repetition of a Cartesian move, and yet at the same time it is an attempt to tap into a deeper radicality: the bracketing of the world as a method through which I take myself as a pure I is also a distancing from the Cartesian identification of *cogito* and *substantia*, in which Husserl sees a sort of reification of the pure *ego*.

This first move, however, thanks to which I access the obviousness of the *cogito*, is not an end in itself. It allows me to have access to the multiplicity of experiences of the self in transcendental life:

> The bare identity of the "I am" is not the only thing given as indubitable in transcendental self-experience. Rather there extends through all the particular data of actual and possible self-experience – even though they are not absolutely indubitable in respect of single details – a universal apodictically experienceable structure of the Ego.[8]

Transcendental phenomenology is therefore an absolutely subjective science, inasmuch as its object in its being is independent from the decision about the existence or non-existence of the world. However, according to Husserl we are only apparently facing a transcendental solipsism, because "the consequential elaboration of this science, in accordance with its own sense, leads over to a phenomenology of transcendental intersubjectivity"[9]: solipsism is essentially a subordinate stage, a necessary methodological consideration in order to put into play the methodological problematic of transcendental intersubjectivity. We will see how.

The scope of the reduced *ego* includes the entire world and objective science, an *ego* that remains identical in its multiple *cogitationes*, "the flowing conscious life in which the identical Ego lives [*das strömende Bewusstseinleben*]": the more accurate expression of apodictic obviousness is therefore according to Husserl *ego cogito* + *cogitatum* in the double direction of the noetic and noematic.[10] This flux of *Erlebnisse* in consciousness is not given without connection, but rather as a synthesis:

> I see in pure reflection that "this" die is given continuously as an objective unity in a multi-form and changeable multiplicity of manners of appearing, which belong determinately to it [*in einer vielgestaltigen wandelbaren Mannigfaltigkeit bestimmt zugehöriger Erscheinungsweise*].[11]

It is the synthesis of consciousness that stabilizes the unity of the object in the plurality of its manifestations: "the whole of conscious life is unified synthetically."[12] The task of the phenomenologist is not to naively describe the object but also the ways in which consciousness constitutes it as such:

> Thus alone can the phenomenologist make understandable to himself how, within the immanency of conscious life and in thus and so determined modes of consciousness belonging to this incessant flux, anything like fixed and abiding objective unities can become intended and, in particular, how this marvelous work of "constituting" identical objects is done in the case of each category of objects.[13]

In the *Herakclitean flux* of consciousness every object designates a structure of rules of the transcendental *ego*.

Now, if the first three meditations move in the direction of a transcendentalization of the Cartesian cogito, it is with the fourth meditation that the Leibnizian path opens. Here Husserl poses the fundamental question for his project: how to exit from the "field of consciousness [*Bewusstseinsbereich*]," from the "island of consciousness [*Bewusstseinsinsel*]"?[14] Or how is it possible that the obviousness has more than a conscious character? It is precisely here that the problem of intersubjectivity opens: it does not make sense to pose, as Descartes did, the universe of being as external to the universe of consciousness by establishing a fixed law of correspondence between the two (correspondence as the necessity of a divine guarantee); it is sufficient that other egos and an objective world are constituted in me. It is here that we can exit from the transcendental solipsism, from the immanence of consciousness, by moving towards the transcendence of the other.

Husserl approaches the question by analyzing how the sense of the *alter ego* is formed for the *ego*. This works first by a methodological reduction to the "sphere of ownness," that is, excluding "from the thematic field everything now in question," or "*abstracting from all constitutional effects of intentionality relating immediately or mediately to other subjectivity [fremde Subjektivität]*."[15] However, Husserl maintains that

> such abstraction is not radical; such aloneness in no respect alters the natural world-sense, "experienceable by everyone" [*Für-Jedermann-Erfahrbahr*], which attaches to the naturally understood Ego and would not be lost, even if a universal plague had left only me.[16]

Therefore, within that which is in me as a monad, existing "purely in myself and for myself with an exclusive ownness [*in abgeschlossener Eigenheit*],"[17] there is the intentionality of the other:

> there becomes constituted for me the new sense of being that goes beyond my monadic very-ownness; there becomes constituted an ego, not as "I myself," but as mirrored in my own Ego, in my monad [*sondern als sich in meinem eigenen Ich, meiner Monade spiegelndes*].[18]

This second *ego* is not "present" or given "authentically," but is constituted as *alter ego*. However, the question of the possibility of the other's intentionality remains difficult to solve. "There must be," Husserl writes, "a certain *indirect intentionality* here," going out from the substratum, "primordial world [*primordinale Welt*]."[19] This mediation must render the *Mit-da* representable without it ever being able to present itself as a *Selbst-da*. It is an act of rendering-as-present, a kind of appresentation, but one of a different species than that present in external experience, according to which the visible side of an object appresents the hidden posterior side. The appresentation of the other is of a different type: "Ego and *alter ego* are always and necessarily given in an *original 'pairing'* [*ursprüngliche Paarung*],"[20] a pairing that is a self-presentation configured as a couple, group, multitude or passive synthesis of association according to which, by the fact that I have a living body, if a body similar to mine appears in my primordial field of perception, "a body with determinations such that it must enter into a phenomenal pairing [*phänomenale Paarung*] with mine,"[21] then that body assumes sense as a living body by means of a transfer of sense.

The question now concerns how this sense can have the value of a being. According to Husserl,

> The appresentation [*Appräsentation*] which gives that component of the Other which is not accessible *originaliter* is combined with an original presentation (of "his" body as part of the Nature given as included in my ownness). In this combination, moreover, the Other's animate body and his governing Ego are given in the manner that characterises *a unitary transcending experience.*[22]

This experience of the other can be verified "*by means of new appresentations that proceed in a synthetically harmonious fashion.*"[23] Therefore, through appresentation, another monad is constituted in my monad, but I can never grasp this monad *originaliter* (originally) because it has the character of transcendence.

This experience of the other founds the objectivity of the world and the community of monads, that is, their common temporality:

> With its complicated structure, it effects a similar connection mediated by presentiation: namely a connection between, on the one hand, the uninterruptedly living self-experience (as purely passive original self-appearance) of the concrete ego – accordingly, his primordial sphere – and, on the other hand, the alien sphere presentiated therein. It effects this, first, by its identifying synthesis of the primordially given animate body of someone else and the same animate body, but appresented in other modes of appearance, and secondly, spreading out from there, by its identifying synthesis of the same Nature, given and verified primordially (with pure sensuous originality) and at the same time appresentationally. In that way the coexistence of my <polar> Ego and

the other Ego, of my whole concrete ego and his, my intentional life and his, my *"realities"* and his – in short, a common time-form [*eine gemeinsame Zeitform*] – is primally instituted; and thus every primordial temporality [*primordinale Zeitlichkeit*] automatically acquires the significance of being merely an original mode of appearance of Objective temporality to a particular subject. In this connexion we see that the temporal community [*zeitliche Gemeinschaft*] of the constitutively interrelated monads is indissoluble, because it is tied up essentially with the constitution of a world and a world time [*Weltzeit*].[24]

The contemporaneity of the monads, their *being in the same time*,[25] founds the uniqueness of the monadic community, the uniqueness and objectivity of the world, the uniqueness of space and the uniqueness of real temporality.

This community has two levels of formation: at a lower level the other monad is constituted in me as other and the other monads are *realiter* (really) separate from me or there is no real link between their moments of consciousness and mine; at a higher level, if I direct my understanding (*comprensione*) towards the other man, I discover that as his living body is found in my field of perception, my own body is found in his field of perception. This reciprocity founds the monadic community, the transcendental intersubjectivity that "bears within itself, as its necessary constitution, the same Objective world."[26] Very briefly, we could say that the first level is Cartesian, while the second is Leibnizian. As Husserl himself writes:

> The constitution of the world essentially involves a "harmony" of the monads: precisely this *harmony among particular constitutions* in the particular monads; and accordingly it involves also a *harmonious* generation that goes on in each particular monad.[27]

The constitution of transcendental intersubjectivity therefore requires the concept of the monad as a synthetic mirror of an environment-world, and the concept of the monadic community as a reciprocity of reflections, a synchronicity of worlds. However, such harmony would not have a metaphysical structure, nor would the monads be metaphysical inventions or hypotheses: the escape from solipsism would not at all be rendered possible, as Husserl himself emphasizes, by "an unacknowledged metaphysics, a concealed adoption of Leibnizian traditions."[28]

Metaphysical intersubjectivity

The primary question of transcendental intersubjectivity concerns this non-metaphysical conception of monad and harmony that Husserl places at the foundation of his theory. What exactly does Husserl understand by a non-metaphysical conception of monad and harmony? It seems to me that the theory of transcendental intersubjectivity does not require certain of Leibniz's metaphysical assumptions, which can be synthetically listed as running through the paragraphs of the *Monadology* as follows:

1) the substantiality of the monad;
2) that the monads "can only begin by creation and end by annihilation";[29]
3) that "every present state of a simple substance is a natural consequence of its preceding state, [so that] the present is pregnant with the future";[30]
4) that "the ultimate reason of things must be in a necessary substance in which the diversity of changes is only eminent, as in its source. This is what we call God";[31]
5) that God's intellect is the ontological foundation of possibility;[32]
6) that "in simple substances the influence of one monad over another can only be ideal, and can only produce its effect through God's intervention";[33]
7) that God has chosen the best possible universe from among an infinity of possible universes;[34]
8) that "the soul follows its own laws and the body also follows its own, and they agree in virtue of a pre-established harmony between all substances";[35]
9) that there is a harmony "between the physical kingdom of nature and the moral kingdom of grace."[36]

What Husserl rejects is the concept of harmony dominated by the mirroring conceptual pair of onto-theology: finite substance/infinite substance, monad/God. What becomes valorized from the standpoint of transcendental intersubjectivity is the question of the immediate relationality of the monad, paradigmatically expressed in this passage:

> This interconnection or accommodation of all created things to each other, and each to all the others, brings it about that each simple

substance has relations that express all the others, and consequently, that each simple substance is a perpetual, living mirror of the universe. Just as the same city viewed from different directions appears entirely different and, as it were, multiplied *perspectively*, in just the same way it happens that, because of the infinite multitude of simple substances, there are, as it were, just as many different universes, which are, nevertheless, only perspectives on a single one, corresponding to the different points of view of each monad.[37]

The world, or the unity of the world in its spatial-temporal dimension, is nothing but a phenomenon grounded in the inter-relationality of the monads. Intersubjectivity precedes and founds the objectivity of the world.

However, Husserl maintains that the harmony between monads is not metaphysical. In this claim, apparently deprived of problems, there lurks the veritable linchpin (*scacco*) of Husserlian intersubjectivity. What does non-metaphysical harmony mean? Let's re-read Husserl's key passage:

> The constitution of the world essentially involves a "harmony" of the monads: precisely this *harmony among particular constitutions* in the particular monads; and accordingly it involves also a *harmonious* generation that goes on in each particular monad.

What does this harmony of the monads that founds the objective world consist of? In Leibniz the response is well-known – God discloses and settles the relational games in the calculus that originates the world – while in Husserl the relational games would remain open. However, this response is unsatisfactory on a theoretical level: Husserl rejects the Leibnizian solution that synchronizes the time of each monad by making their internal time the mirror situated differently from the history of the world, proposing instead the idea of the monadic community as essential contemporaneity.

> It is essentially necessary that the togetherness of monads, their mere co-existence [*ihr bloßes Zugleichsein*], be an essential contemporaneity [*wesesnotwendig zeitlich Zugleichsein*] and therefore also an existence temporalized in the form: "real" temporality [*Verzeitlicht-sein in der Form realer Zeitlichkeit*].[38]

However, this togetherness of the monads can never really be perceived, because one monad can never *originaliter* tap into the vital flux of another monad. The temporality of the *alter ego* is always only appresented, and never directly presented. In the togetherness of the monads, the harmony without metaphysics, we find hiding nothing less than a god, whether the transcendent god of Berkeley or the immanent god of Hegelian objective spirit: *essential contemporaneity is the Husserlian name for god*. Intersubjectivity can only be metaphysical: as soon as the Augustinian move of seeking the truth *in interiore homine* is repeated, which Husserl does in the conclusion to his *Meditations*,[39] only a god can allow us to escape from interiority and find the way back to the world.

Simondon and the transindividual

If transcendental intersubjectivity therefore reveals itself to be at root a metaphysical intersubjectivity, it will be necessary to try to traverse another path in the attempt to found the existence of a community and an objective world without resorting to a god (even if his role is reduced to a mere guarantee of the synchronicity of worlds beyond good and evil). To this end, I propose a detour that will allow me to establish, in extremely synthetic terms, the historical coordinates of the emergence of the concept of the "transindividual," which I will then use to underline the Leibniz–Spinoza alternative in all of its force.

The term was introduced in Gilbert Simondon's posthumously published book, *L'individuation psychique et collective* (1989), which made up the final part of a doctoral thesis written in the 1950s, the first two parts of which were published in 1964 under the title *L'individuation et sa genèse psyco-biologique*. The central concept, as is apparent even from a superficial glance at the two titles, is individuation, and Simondon proposes to focus on processes of individuation against a tradition that has conceded ontological privilege to an already-constituted individual. In fact, both the substantialist and hylomorphic traditions have hypothesized the existence of a principle of individuation that is anterior to individuation itself, and capable of explaining, causing and directing it. Both begin from a ready-made individual, trying to retrace the conditions of its existence.[40]

According to Simondon, we can attempt to know the individual through individuation rather than grasping individuation by starting from the individual. In other words, we can know the individual by first radically overturning the perspective from which the individual has been observed, strongly affirming the primacy of individuation:

> The individual would then figure as a relative reality, as a phase of being that presupposes a preindividual reality. Even after individuation, the individual does not exist in total isolation, because individuation does not exhaust the potentialities of preindividual reality and, moreover, because individuation does not produce only the individual, but rather the pair individual/environment. The individual is therefore relative in a double sense: because it is not all of being, and because it derives from a state of being in which it does not exist as an individual or as a principle of individuation.[41]

Such an overturning of perspective was made possible by the concept of metastable equilibrium, which allows being to be thought not in terms of substance or material, but as a stretched, oversaturated system. Simondon presents physical individuation and living individuation as cases of resolution of a metastable system, with the difference that while physical individuation happens "in an instantaneous, quantitative, abrupt, and definitive way, leaving behind itself an individual/environment dualism," living individuation "preserves a permanent activity of individuation in itself."[42]

It is precisely this characteristic of individuation in the context of living that allows Simondon to think the psychic and collective levels in terms of successive individuations with respect to vital individuation. However, psychic individuation and collective individuation should not be thought as successive to one another, according to a diachronic model of development, but rather in synchronic terms, as one and the same process that gives rise to an inside and an outside. It is at this level that the concept of individuation interweaves with the theme of the transindividual:

> The two individuations, the psychic and the collective, stand in a reciprocal relationship and allow us to define the category of the transindividual: it should be understood as an attempt to give an account of the systematic unity of (psychic) individuation and (collective) external individuation. The psycho-social world of the transindividual is neither bare sociality, nor inter-individual; it presupposes a

pre-individual reality, connected to individuals and capable of determining a new problematic endowed with its own metastability.[43]

The transindividual is therefore the name of the complex weave of relations that constitutes psychic and collective individuation at one time. Here the third key concept in Simondon's theory emerges, that of relation, which is never a relation between two pre-existing terms, but rather the constitution of the terms at stake in the relation. In this sense, for Simondon, we can delineate a new method at the level of the concepts of individuation and the transindividual:

> The method does not consist in attempting to outline the essence of one reality by means of a conceptual relation between two pre-existing external terms, but in attributing to every authentic relation the rank [*rango*] of being. Relation is a modality of being; it is simultaneous to the terms of which it guarantees existence. A relation should be understood as a relation in being, a relation of being, and a mode of being; not indeed as the mere relation between two terms that, arranging a preliminarily separate existence, are adequately knowable by means of concepts.[44]

To summarize, the concept of the transindividual is defined by two philosophical theses:

1) the primacy of the process of individuation over the individual
2) the primacy of the relation over the terms of the relation.

The transindividual is the name of the metastable system that gives rise to psychic and collective individuations, the weave of relations that traverses and constitutes individuals and society, methodologically prohibiting the substantialization of one or the other: "society," Simondon writes, "is not the product of the reciprocal presence of many individuals, but neither is it a substantial reality superimposed on individual beings, as if it were independent of them."[45]

Spinoza and the transindividual

We can now ask ourselves in what way the concept of the transindividual can belong to the path we have proposed so far. It should constitute the twentieth-century extension of Spinozist theory in the same way that Husserlian intersubjectivity provided the twentieth century extension of Leibnizian monadology for us. However, the connection between Spinoza and Simondon is not at all immediate. Spinozism is not only absent as an influential source for Simondon, but is even explicitly eradicated as a pantheistic position in which individual reality is negated. It is therefore once again to the history of effects and a theoretical coup de force that we must appeal in order to think the conception of the transindividual as the extension of Spinoza's philosophy, or better and more likely, in order to produce a chemical reaction between Spinoza's text and the concept of the transindividual. Such a theoretical coup de force was proposed by Étienne Balibar in the wake of the Althusserian project of rethinking Marxist philosophy through the thought of Spinoza. In *Spinoza: From Individuality to Transindividuality*, he proposes not so much the adaptation of Spinoza to Simondon's formulations, but rather

> to discuss the extent to which *Spinoza himself* can be considered a consistent theoretician of "transindividuality," thus helping us to transform this notion from its initially negative definition (a doctrine which is neither individualistic nor holistic, just as it is neither mechanistic nor finalistic) into a positive, or constructive notion.[46]

In order to follow-up on this sketch, Balibar retraces three levels through which "the idea of individuality as transindividuality or as a transindividual process of individuation"[47] can be probed in the *Ethics*:

1) transindividuality as a specific schema of causality;
2) transindividuality as a determinate element in the construction of successive levels of individuality;
3) transindividuality as a latent concept that articulates both imagination and reason. First, Balibar maintains that in the Spinozist schema of causality, complexity does not constitute a derived moment, but is already present from the beginning: The infinite connection does not take the form of independent linear series, or genealogies of causes and effects . . .: it typically takes the form of an infinite network of singular modes, or existences, a dynamic unity of modulating/modulated activities.[48]

Intersubjectivity or Transindividuality 145

This means that every individual is passive and active at the same time. Or better, the essence of causality would be "the unity of activity and passivity" or, as Balibar again suggests, "in quasi-mathematical terms . . . the 'differential of activity and passivity,' a unity that 'defines the individual's singular *conatus* and relates it to an infinite multiplicity of other individuals.'"[49] Here transindividuality would consist in the *infinitus nexus causarum*, the order through connection of which *Ethics* 2P7 speaks.

Second, this level of complexity, defined by Balibar as "first order," which stabilizes an equivalence between the concept of the actual existence of an individual and the plurality of different individuals, finds a deepening in Spinoza through the introduction of a "second order" of complexity:

> This is the concept of the individual as a determinate level of integration, incorporating other individuals ("lower" levels of integration) and itself incorporated in "higher" levels or forms of integration.[50]

A representation of this kind of second order complexity carries with it a risk, according to Balibar, which consists in thinking of nature as a hierarchy of forms, or an order of the inclusion of one individual in another, according to a model that would be static in the last instance (the point of view, in Spinozist terms, of *natura naturata*). Such complexity should instead be understood in a dynamic sense (that is, according to the point of view of *natura naturans*), by thinking of individuals as forms given with a stability and identity that are actually the effect "of a continuous regeneration of [an individual's] constituent parts, i.e., what in modern terms we would call a regulated inward and outward flow":[51]

> Spinoza's idea is simple, but daring: what is exchanged are parts of the individuals under consideration, that is, "regeneration" means that a given individual (let's call it "I") continuously abandons incorporating some *part(s) of itself*, while at the same time continuously incorporating some *part(s) of others* (let's call them "they"), provided this substitution leaves a certain "proportion" (or essence) invariant . . . The more complex an individual is, the more relationships it will have with the external world; i.e. the more intensively it will exchange its own "parts" with other (similar or dissimilar) individuals, the more it will *need* these exchanges to preserve its own existence.[52]

This means that every individual exists between an inferior level and a superior level. For this reason, Balibar writes,

> I spoke of a "second order of complexity" in the understanding of natural causality, because the transindividual pattern which we are dealing with is not only understood as horizontal interaction or reciprocity at the same level, but also as a process of interaction which, for any type of individual . . ., regresses to the inferior level *and* simultaneously progresses to the superior level.[53]

It is here that the meaning of transindividuality Balibar finds in Spinoza approaches Simondon's concept of transindividuality. As we outlined, the latter maintains that the individual is a relative reality, the effect of a process of individuation that on the one hand does not exhaust pre-individual potential and on the other does not give rise to an isolated individual, but rather to the individual-environment pair.

Third, this second order complexity opens on to a treatment of the human world, and specifically on to the concept of the transindividual as the mediation between imagination and reason. Balibar shows first of all how the structure of both the imagination and reason are essentially transindividual. Concerning the imagination, Balibar writes,

> it can be suggested (1) that Spinoza's theory of imagination is not a theory of some human *faculty* . . ., but a theory of the *structure* in which individual "selves" are primarily constituted . . .; and (2) that this structure is originally relational or transindividual: not only does it confront us with a picture of consciousness in which every relationship that "I" can have with "Myself" is mediated by the Other (more precisely: an image of the Other), but it also shows that the life of imagination is a circular process of successive "identifications", where I recognize the Other from Myself, and Myself from the Other.[54]

Moving on to analyze the Spinozist concept of reason, Balibar notes,

> It is presented, not as a faculty . . ., but as a structure or system of mutual implications in which, for each individual, the *conatus* to preserve his existence is connected with the knowledge of his proper good . . . and the necessary establishment of a *commercium* with other men.[55]

Given the relational constitution of the imagination and reason, Balibar proposes to consider transindividuality not as a rigid model (or as two opposed models), but as a process in which the relations between individuals "are considered *in the transition from Imagination to Reason*, i.e. from a lesser to a greater power to act."⁵⁶ This third level of reading Spinozist thought through the concept of the transindividual therefore shows how "a new kind of knowledge is also, by its very nature, a new kind of community."⁵⁷

Monad and mode

Having shown the context of the concept of the transindividual and the occasion of its encounter, through Balibar, with Spinozist thought, it is now possible to try to confront the question of the Leibniz–Spinoza alternative as read through the two theoretical models of intersubjectivity and transindividuality in order to indicate, in all of its force, the difference between them. Certainly, we could instead proceed, as in fact has been done repeatedly in the history of interpretations, with an individualistic – monadological, so to speak – reading of this difference. In other words, we could think in terms of an individual who pre-exists and founds the relations: the essence of the human would be defined by the mind–body dyad, of which the fundamental properties would be desire, joy and sadness. The mode, just like the monad, would therefore have an essence that precedes existence, the basis of the relational play. Undoubtedly in Spinoza as in Husserl there would not be a pre-established harmony – the relational play would remain open, but still would be between individuals who logically precede the relation. In this theoretical horizon the passions would only be possible variations of an essence. An argument only apparently contrary, but actually favorable to an interpretation of this kind, is the emphasis some interpreters place on Spinoza's theory of affective imitation. Warren Montag has in fact rightly noted that

> this theory in no way excludes the notion of originally dissociated individuals who remain dissociated even in their imitation of the affects of others. In fact, Spinoza's text contains the basis of a reading according to which affective imitation would become nothing more than an act of projection, which requires only that I imagine that the other feels pleasure or pain in order to imitate what I imagine the other to feel.⁵⁸

In other words, affective imitation would constitute at an ontological level the analogic appresentation of the *alter ego* at the methodological level in Husserl: the bridge between individuals is drawn by departing from a projected interiority in an analogous way (it is not an accident that in this context Husserl uses, albeit with extreme caution, the term "empathy" (*Einfühlung*)).

However, reading the mode in light of the concept of the monad, even temporarily, is extremely problematic. To show this, we can first take the scholium that closes the small treatise on physics in part two of the *Ethics*, a treatise that unchains (*svincola*) the concept of a corporeal individual from every form of substantiality by setting the *principium individuationis* in a determinate proportion (*certa ratio*) of movement and rest of the parts that enter into the process of its composition and regeneration with the environment:

> A composite Individual can be affected in many ways, and still preserve its nature. So far we have conceived an Individual which is composed only of bodies which are distinguished from one another only by motion and rest, speed and slowness, i.e., which is composed of the simplest bodies. But if we should now conceive of another, composed of a number of Individuals of a different nature, we shall find that it can be affected in a great many other ways, and still preserve its nature. For since each part of it is composed of a number of bodies, each part will therefore ... be able, without any change of its nature, to move now more slowly, now more quickly, and consequently communicate its motion more quickly or more slowly to the others.
>
> But if we should further conceive a third kind of Individual, composed [of many individuals] of this second kind, we shall find that it can be affected in many other ways, without any change of its form. And if we proceed in this way to infinity, we shall easily conceive that the whole of nature is one Individual, whose parts, i.e., all bodies, vary in infinite ways, without any change of the whole Individual.[59]

The scholium has drawn critical attention because of Spinoza's reference to *corpora simplicissima* and nature understood as a whole individual. In my view, this attention is a *Holzwege*: in other words, these are limit-terms that do not correspond to any ontological reality. It seems clear that Spinoza is not saying that there exist infinite levels of existence between simple bodies and that nature should be understood as an aggregate individual, but rather that there exists an infinite level of the increasing existence of individuality and complexity *tout court*, and that this is what nature consists in.

Now, at first sight the scholium could make us think of a set of paragraphs in the *Monadology*:

> Each organised body of a living being is a kind of divine machine or natural automaton, which infinitely surpasses all artificial automata. For a machine constructed by man's art is not a machine in each of its parts... But natural machines, that is, living bodies, are still machines in their least parts, to infinity. That is the difference between nature and art, that is, between divine art and our art.
>
> And the author of nature has been able to practice this divine and infinitely marvelous art, because each portion of matter is not only divisible to infinity, as the ancients have recognised, but is also actually subdivided without end, each part divided into parts having some motion of their own; otherwise, it would be impossible for each portion of matter to express the whole universe.
>
> From this we see that there is a world of creatures, of living beings, of animals, of entelechies, of souls in the least part of matter.
>
> Each portion of matter can be conceived as a garden full of plants, and as a pond full of fish. But each branch of a plant, each limb of an animal, each drop of its humors, is still another such garden or pond.[60]

However, if the two passages are analyzed carefully, one notices that in Leibniz there is a structural analogy between the different levels of individuality (the metaphors of the pond and the garden express this precisely), while in Spinoza the complexity of the superior level does not have any structural analogy with the inferior level. Rather, the inferior level constitutes the emergence of a grade of individuality that was not contained in advance in the grades of individuality that entered into its composition.

The difference will appear in all its clarity by reading this paragraph of the *Monadology*:

> Each living body has one dominant entelechy, which in an animal is the soul; but the limbs of this living body are full of other living beings, plants, animals, each of which also has its entelechy, or its dominant soul.[61]

In Leibniz, the body, life, is ordered (*comandata*) by a hierarchy of forms whose level is given once and for all even though the perpetual flux of bodies renders it unthinkable that a soul has a genuine possession of living things inferior to it.[62] In Spinoza, the mind is not in fact the form of the body, but instead the same body expressed through a different attribute. This means that minds must be thought according to the same model of infinite levels of complexity that Spinoza describes for the structure of bodies, as required by *Ethics* 2P7. Therefore, the mind-body individual is not thinkable as a closed monad, but rather as a composition of individuals that in turn enter into the composition of individuals at a superior level: considered at any level, we always find the individual as a doubly provisional moment between two levels of individuality. In other words, we find, to use Simondon's terminology, that the individual is actually second with respect to the process of individualization that constitutes it as such.

To return to the confrontation with Leibniz on the theme of relations, we can observe that the theory of pre-established harmony requires that every extrinsic determination actually be founded within an intrinsic determination, or that every exterior relation be founded both in a property of the monad, and in an internal state of the monad (and each state is infinitely complex because it must express the whole inter-individual at the intra-individual level). In Spinoza, however, every intrinsic determination is actually founded on a complex play of extrinsic determinations (without the extrinsic determinations thereby containing the intrinsic determination in advance), or every property of an individual is produced by the complex relational play of relations that has constituted its individuality. It seems to me that it is in this sense that the monad–mode opposition, read through the contemporary opposition between intersubjectivity and transindividuality, takes on its full meaning.

Passions: Not properties but relations

We can now try to show how the application of the model of transindividuality makes possible a new reading of Spinoza's theory of the passions, understood not as the properties of a transhistorical human nature, but rather as a transindividual weave that constitutes forms of individuality that are historical in the last instance.

It is true that in deference to the *mos geometricus* (geometrical style) of the *Ethics*, and to several of Spinoza's formulations, one would be tempted to read Spinoza's theory of the passions as properties, or intrinsic classifications, that is, as characteristics of the *essentia intima* of human nature taken separately from all the rest. But can we really take, in Spinozist ontology, one reality separately from all the rest? Can we truly understand passion in a technical way as *proprietas*, or as the *proprium* to an *essentia* that precedes relations and existential circumstances? In his translation of the *Political Treatise*, Paolo Cristofolini has proposed translating the expression *passionibus obnoxius* as "attraversati dalle passioni, traversed by, shot through with, crossed through by the passions."[63] By taking Cristofolini's translation as a starting point, we can try to think the passions not as the *proprietates* of a generic human nature given once and for all, but as the relations that cross through the individual and constitute her in her social and historical dimension.

For Spinoza, the individual is neither substance nor subject, but a relation between an exterior and an interior that is constituted in the relation. This relation constitutes the essence of the individual that is nothing other than its power (*potenza*) of existing; its essence is not, however, a power given once and for all, but rather something that is variable, precisely because the relation that constitutes it is unstable and not given. Now, the passions are not the properties of a given human nature, properties that exist prior to the encounter and are in some way activated by it, but rather the constitutive relations of the social individual: the original place over which they act is not interiority, but the space *between* the individuals for whom interiority itself is a historical effect. Certainly, Spinoza defines the three primary affects as desire, joy and sadness:[64] these primary affects could therefore be understood as fundamental properties of human nature, properties that anticipate the encounters that are produced by the individual–environment relation and receive different gradations on the basis of them. In reality, if these affects are primary for the individual, they are not primary if considered from the point of view of immanent causality, that gives rise to the individual as a *connexio singularis*, a unique weave. From this perspective, such primary affects are only abstract elements prior to entering into relations; not only this, they cannot even exist in a pure state, as originary elements whose combination gives birth to all the others.

These primary affects only exist within the infinite metamorphoses that relations with the outside impose on them: hate, love, hope (security/gladness), fear (despair/remorse) and so forth. Moreover, we cannot even speak of a singular affect as a transitive relation to an object,[65] because through the effect of immanent causality, which appears in the finite sphere as *nexus causaurum*, a causal weave, every affect is always overdetermined by other affects.

The passions, therefore, cannot be thought through the category of property, the inherence of a predicate to a subject, but rather should be thought as a complex weave of relations. As Montag perfectly summarizes,

> the imagination (which to a certain extent mediates between my body considered as a singular thing and other equally singular bodies) gives way to an unmediated imitation that is less a reduplication of one person's affect in another than . . . a perpetuation or persistence of affect without the mediation of the person. The affect is thus not contained in me or the other but lies between us.[66]

The weave of affective life therefore exists between individuals and constitutes them as such. This means that no interior mirroring of the other is given, from the monad of the other in my monad, precisely because the other is that of which we are woven.

Conclusions

Through this long historical and theoretical path, we have tried to follow the Leibniz–Spinoza opposition from a perspective that is not limited to repeating the tired Hegelian song of the dialectic of the One and the Many, but rather examines it in all of its force and actuality. Immersed within the terms of the philosophical results of this path is the fact that Husserl's transcendental reprise of monadology finds itself confronted with a definitive checkmate (*scacco*) of the unobtainability of the Other for consciousness: intersubjectivity is either metaphysical or it is nothing. Transcendental intersubjectivity in fact surreptitiously introduces a concept of metaphysical harmony without which the *ego* and the *alter ego* cannot appear at the same time, in the same way. How does the model of transindividuality allow us to avoid this checkmate? It avoids it precisely because the other is not beyond the closed circle of the *ego*, but always-already in the *ego* (and certainly in such a perspective the very opposition between *ego* and *alter ego* is nothing more than the substantialization of a grammatical function), traversing it, constituting it as a complex weave of bodies, passions, ideas, words – a complex weave of temporality irreducible to the essential contemporaneity of a community.[67] As Lucretius writes in a splendid verse that I would like to think inspired Spinoza:

Inter se mortals mutua vivunt.[68]

Notes

1. TN: I would like to thank Christopher Noble for his assistance in various matters pertaining to Leibniz.
2. G. W. Leibniz, *Philosophical Papers and Letters*, trans. and ed. Leroy E. Loemker (Dordrecht: Kluwer Academic Publishers, 1989), 663.
3. Étienne Balibar, "Prefazione," in *Spinoza contra Leibniz*, ed. Vittorio Morfino (Milano: Unicopli, 1994), 8.
4. F. H. Jacobi, *Beylagen zu den Briefen über die Lehre des Spinoza*, in Werke, Bd. 4 (Leipzig: Fleischer, 1819), 114.
5. G. W. F. Hegel, *Science of Logic*, trans. A. V. Miller (New York: Humanities Press, 1969), 536–40.
6. Edmund Husserl, *Cartesian Meditations: An Introduction to Phenomenology*, trans. Dorion Cairns (The Hague: Martinus Nijoff, 1960), 18.
7. Ibid. 19.
8. Ibid. 28.
9. Ibid. 30.
10. Ibid. 31.
11. Ibid. 39.
12. Ibid. 42.
13. Ibid. 48.
14. Ibid. 83.
15. Ibid. 93 (translation slightly modified); emphasis in the original.
16. Ibid. 93.
17. Ibid. 94.
18. Ibid. 94 (translation slightly modified).
19. Ibid. 109 (translation slightly modified); emphasis in the original.
20. Ibid. 112; emphasis in the original.
21. Ibid. 113.

22. Ibid. 114; emphasis in the original.
23. Ibid. 114; emphasis in the original.
24. Ibid. 127–8; emphasis in the original.
25. Ibid. 139.
26. Ibid. 130 (translation slightly modified).
27. Ibid. 108 (my emphasis).
28. Ibid. 148.
29. Leibniz, *Monadology*, §6. TN: All references to the *Monadology* are by paragraph number and use the Ariew and Garber translation.
30. Ibid. §22.
31. Ibid. §38.
32. Ibid. §43.
33. Ibid. §51.
34. Ibid. §53–5.
35. Ibid. §78.
36. Ibid. §87.
37. Ibid. §56–7 (my emphasis).
38. Husserl, *Cartesian Mediations*, 139 (translation slightly modified); emphasis in the original.
39. Ibid. 157.
40. Gilbert Simondon, *L'individuazione psichica e collettiva*, trans. Paolo Virno. Rome: Derive Approdi, 2006), 25. TN: I have translated from the Italian edition, translated and edited by Paolo Virno.
41. Ibid. 27.
42. Ibid. 30.
43. Ibid. 32.
44. Ibid. 35.
45. Ibid. 144.
46. Étienne Balibar, *Spinoza: From Individuality to Transindividuality* (Delft: Eburon, 1997), 11; emphasis in the original.
47. Ibid. 12.
48. Ibid. 14.
49. Ibid. 15.
50. Ibid. 16.
51. Ibid. 18.
52. Ibid. 18–21; emphasis in the original.
53. Ibid. 22; emphasis in the original.
54. Ibid. 25–6; emphasis in the original.
55. Ibid. 28.
56. Ibid. 31; emphasis in the original.

57. Ibid. 31. It should be noted that Balibar adds: "I find this likely, but I am not sure that it can be completely demonstrated from the text of the *Ethics*."
58. Montag, "Who's Afraid of the Multitude," 667–8.
59. Spinoza, *Ethics*, 2 P14L7S.
60. Leibniz, *Monadology*, §64–7.
61. Ibid, §70.
62. Ibid. §71.
63. TN: Morfino here draws on a discussion explored to different lengths in his essay, "Spinoza: An Ontology of Relation?" Vittorio Morfino, "Spinoza: An Ontology of Relation?" in *Plural Temporality: Transindividuality and the Aleatory between Spinoza and Althusser* (Leiden: Brill, 2014), 46–71. The entire essay is a helpful backdrop for the present essay, but cf. especially 61–6. As Morfino notes, there are fourteen occurances of *passionibus* or *affectibus obnoxius* in the *Ethics*. I happily reproduce Jason E. Smith's excellent translation of Cristofolini's "attraversati delle passioni" here.
64. "[A]part from these three I do not acknowledge any other primary affect. For I shall show in what follows that the rest arise from these three" (Spinoza, *Ethics*, 3 P11S).
65. The same relation that binds subject and object has no universality, as Spinoza emphasizes: "Different men can be affected differently by one and the same object; and one and the same man can be affected differently at different times by one and the same object" (Spinoza, *Ethics*, 3 P51).
66. Montag, "Who's Afraid of the Multitude," 668.
67. On the *multitudo* as a complex weave of temporality, c.f. Vittorio Morfino, "Temporalità plurale e contingenza: l'interpretazione spinoziana di Machiavelli," *Etica e politica*, 6.1 (2004): 1–37.
68. "Mortal creatures live dependent on one another." Lucretius, *De Rerum Natura* II, trans. W. H. D. Rouse and Revised by Martin Ferguson Smith (Cambridge, MA: Harvard University Press, 1975), 76.

Bibliography

Balibar, Étienne. "Prefazione." In *Spinoza contra Leibniz*. Ed. Vittorio Morfino. Milano: Unicopli, 1994. Pp. 1–17.
Balibar, Étienne. *Spinoza: From Individuality to Transindividuality*. Delft: Eburon, 1997.

Hegel, G. W. F. *Science of Logic.* Trans. A. V. Miller. New York: Humanities Press, 1969.
Husserl, Edmund. *Cartesian Meditations: An Introduction to Phenomenology.* Trans. Dorion Cairns. The Hague: Martinus Nijoff, 1960.
Jacobi, F. H. *Beylagen zu den Briefen über die Lehre des Spinoza.* In Werke, Bd. 4. Leibzig: Fleischer, 1819. Pp. 183–271.
Leibniz, G. W. *Philosophical Papers and Letters.* Trans. and ed. Leroy E. Loemker. Dordrecht: Kluwer Academic Publishers, 1989.
Leibniz, G. W. "The Principles of Philosophy, or, the Monadology." In *Philosophical Essays.* Trans. and ed. Roger Ariew and Daniel Garber. Indianapolis: Hackett Publishing Company, 1989. Pp. 213–25.
Leibniz, G. W. *Discourse on Metaphysics and other Essays.* Trans. Daniel Garber and Roger Ariew. Indianapolis: Hackett, 1991.
Lucretius, *De Rerum Natura.* Trans. W. H. D. Rouse and Revised by Martin Ferguson Smith. Cambridge: Harvard University Press, 1975.
Montag, Warren. "Who's Afraid of the Multitude? Between the Individual and the State." *South Atlantic Quarterly,* 104.4 (2005): 655–73.
Morfino, Vittorio. "Temporalità plurale e contingenza: l'interpretazione spinoziana di Machiavelli." *Etica e politica,* 6.1 (2004): 1–37.
Morfino, Vittorio. *Plural Temporality: Transindividuality and the Aleatory between Spinoza and Althusser.* Leiden: Brill, 2014.
Morfino, Vittorio. "Spinoza: An Ontology of Relation?" In *Plural Temporality: Transindividuality and the Aleatory between Spinoza and Althusser.* Leiden: Brill, 2014. Pp. 46–71.
Simondon, Gilbert. *L'individuation psychique et collective.* Paris: Aubier, 1989.
Simondon, Gilbert. *L'individuation et sa genèse psyco-biologique.* Paris: Presses Universitaires de France, 1964.
Simondon, Gilbert. *L'individuazione psichica e collettiva.* Trans. Paolo Virno. Rome: Derive Approdi, 2006.
Spinoza, Benedictus de. "Ethics." In *The Collected Works of Spinoza Volume 1.* Trans. and ed. Edwin Curley. Princeton: Princeton University Press, 1985. Pp. 408–617.

5

A Parallelism of Consciousness and Property: Balibar's Reading of Locke
Warren Montag

No word more accurately captures the originality of Etienne Balibar's reading of Locke than "parallelism," a word commonly applied to (but not used by) Spinoza rather than Locke. Balibar's argument that there exists in Locke "a parallelism of responsibility and property, of self-consciousness and 'property in oneself'"[1] allows us in turn to speak of a kind of parallelism of the two works in which Locke established these concepts, namely *An Essay Concerning Human Understanding* and the *Two Treatises of Government*. This is not to say that they form a logical sequence, as if one followed necessarily from the other, but rather that they develop simultaneously in relation to a common object and set of objectives. It is important to keep in mind that "parallelism" as Balibar uses it belongs to a very specific historical and semantic field. First used in its philosophical sense by Leibniz to describe Spinoza's argument in the *Ethics* that "the order and connection of ideas is the same as the order and connection of things" (*Ethics* II, P7), the notion of parallelism allowed Hegel to criticize "Spinozism" as a dualism of thought and extension, mind and matter or even form and content rather than the philosophy of immanence that Spinoza thought he had constructed.[2] And while there are many reasons to reject the application of the notion of parallelism to Spinoza, in the case of Locke, it makes visible what we may call the materialist element in his philosophy: the indissociability of his theory of consciousness from his political theory (or perhaps politico-ontology) of property and the disciplinary and punitive strategies that have historically followed from their conjunction. To assert such a parallelism, which is another way of saying that no philosophy is innocent of its practical effects will, Balibar fears, strike many readers as either "paradoxical or intolerable."[3]

If indeed Balibar's reading is intolerably paradoxical it is certainly because of his insistence that there exists a disavowed solidarity between Locke's speculation on personal identity (at the center of which is consciousness), on the one hand, and on the political (at the center of which is property), on the other, as if the production of Locke's essential concepts takes place in two registers simultaneously: political and philosophical, practical and theoretical. The effect of this simultaneity is to prevent the attribution of logical or historical priority either to 1) the political theses concerning the vital necessity of property (including ownership of one's self) and its place as the primary object of government as argued in chapter 5 of the *Second Treatise*, or 2) the theory of personal identity that requires as its condition of possibility a conception of consciousness that reduces it to individual or self-consciousness and thus eliminates the horizontal ties between individuals based on a transmission or shared existence of ideas and affects, even by means of language. In the void left behind by the exclusion of a transindividual dimension, there emerges a vertical or topographical model according to which the individual's perception of his own perceptions (to which no other person is privy) must in turn be perceived from the position of a transcendent last instance of absolute knowledge, which for Locke is the Christian God at the moment of the Last Judgment. I specify God in this way to emphasize that the reference to an omniscient and transcendental God is neither an expression of the depth and sincerity of Locke's belief nor a way of disguising a profoundly secular project. The God that Locke composes in his text is the last instance without which, "what passes in a man's own mind," the mind that is proper to him or that is his property, would be absolutely inaccessible not only to others, but even to the individual himself who cannot possibly recollect the lifetime of perceptions that have passed through his mind, even at the moment his salvation is at stake.

From Locke's position, neither a "materialist" reduction of the ideality of consciousness to the material existence of bodies and things, nor an idealist regime in which the body is subjected to the mind as an instrument of its will is possible. Instead, Balibar allows us to understand the parallelism of Locke's two major works as of unity of opposites, according to which the solitary individual, united to himself by the fact of consciousness, and the individual understood as proprietor of himself presuppose each other. But if we can in this way speak of the unity of Locke's philosophico-political project, it is in the sense that it is as a whole organized around the same set of unresolved contradictions that Locke's theoretical practice necessarily produces.

Balibar changed our sense of the history of philosophy, above all, the history of the subject as *subjectum* (agent, actor or author) rather than *subjectus* (under the authority of another) when he demonstrated in *Citizen Subject* that the dominant modern conception of the subject did not emerge from Descartes, but was instead a Kantian invention retrospectively attributed to Descartes by means of a nominalization of "ego cogito" as "*das: Ich Denke,*" or "the I think."[4] In this way, Balibar allowed us not simply to reassign a point of emergence or mutation in an otherwise linear history (the history of the process by which subjection produced, as a kind of byproduct or side effect, subjectivity), but to see the way that the subject is historically linked to a series of related, if not exactly synonymous, terms: "individual," "person" and, above all, "consciousness." Although, like "subject," the term "consciousness" derives from a Latin translation of a Greek word, it is a relatively recent invention in English, dating back to the late seventeenth century, where it was given its full significance only in chapter 27 of Locke's *An Essay Concerning Human Understanding*. This was the focus of Balibar's recent book *Identity and Difference, John Locke and the Invention of Consciousness* but his discussion there, I want to argue, has a significance beyond the interpretation of Locke he offers, namely, a further specification of the genesis of the concept of the subject in a double sense: Balibar both demonstrates the function of the concept of consciousness in the emergence of the subject in Kant's sense (the "I think" must think that it thinks or must think itself thinking), and describes the role of consciousness, in all the complexity that Locke attributes to it, in the reproduction of the subjected subject, the subject who is the result of his own subjection (as he who subjects and is subjected) the simultaneous *subjectum/subjectus*, master/servant of himself.

What I want briefly to explore here is perfectly summarized in a two-sentence passage from *An Essay Concerning Human Understanding* (ECHU II.27.23):

> Could we suppose two distinct incommunicable consciousnesses acting the same body [NB: "act" is a transitive verb here], the one

constantly by day, the other by night; and, on the other side, the same consciousness acting by intervals two distinct bodies: I ask in the first case whether the day and the night-man would not be two as *distinct* persons as Socrates and Plato? And whether in the second case, there would not be one person in two distinct bodies as much as one man is the same in two distinct clothings? (ECHU II.27; emphasis in the original)

Let us consider these two alternatives: (1) the possibility of a person whose consciousness is so divided that it can no longer be regarded as a single consciousness, and (2) the possibility of a single person "acting" (to use as Locke does the now obsolete transitive form of the verb "act," which meant to put into motion) two or more distinct bodies, uniting what Locke will show must remain divided. Far from being merely a meditation on "split" or multiple personalities, on the one hand, and the transmigration of souls and (demonic) possession on the other, these are the unasked questions the response to which constitutes what Althusser called "a primary 'obviousness' (obviousnesses are always primary)," like, "that 'obviousness' that you and I are subjects."[5]

Locke's texts, even more than those of Hobbes, may be understood as a form of *ursprüngliche akkumulation*, a primitive or original accumulation in theory that "frees up" individuals from the "bonds" (in both the positive and negative senses of the term), as well as the entanglements, of social existence, the confusion of affects, desires and identities that stood in the way of the partitioning of human action (that in turn provides the foundation of the private property necessary to the life of the individual).[6] The operation of consciousness as a concept is here: consciousness both guarantees the unity of the individual with "his own thought," so that there can be no other within, and with the organization of the body that he calls his own, so that by means of the notion of its vital unity with the body, Locke insures that the individual cannot feel or think what the other outside feels or thinks. Consciousness, Balibar constantly reminds us, is the perception of what passes not simply in a man's mind, but in a man's *own* mind, as if Locke, by means of the adjective "own," both acknowledges and rules out the possibility that there may pass through a man's mind something, a feeling or an idea, that is not his or his own, but that has infiltrated his consciousness, an affect he may perceive as his but that properly belongs to the mind of another. The political function of consciousness is thus to distinguish the person (and what is his, his own, what is proper to him) clearly or, as Locke will say, "forensically," from all other individuals in order that he may be a "person" possessed of his own legal personality and thus liable for what he and he alone has done (ECHU II.27.26).

As Balibar has shown, the term "consciousness," as employed by Locke, that is, not simply "self-awareness" (a usage already well-established in Locke's time), but a faculty essentially united to thought itself and necessary to the individuation understood to be a property of the human species, was an invention. To understand its semantic specificity, however, requires a knowledge of a long and complicated history of translation, transmission and transformation involving a number of languages. Perhaps most significantly, the term "consciousness" is marked by a forgetting, precisely the objective forgetting that does not take place in consciousness – through a fault, lack or failure – but a forgetting internal to the discourse that precedes it, as if consciousness emerges as a concept only on the basis of a refusal or exclusion of another meaning or meanings. Both "consciousness" and "conscience" in English are derived from the Latin term "*conscientia*," which is in turn derived from the Greek "*syneidēsis (συνείδησις)*."[7] The statistically predominant sense of both the Greek and Latin terms is that of shared knowledge: the Latin prefix "con" or "com," like the Greek "syn" or "sym," denotes a shared or common experience. The Greek *syneidon* (συνεῖδον) means to see together, that is, to see the same thing as others, and by extension to know what others know. Thus, in opposition to Locke's argument that the individual could be conscious only of what passed in his own mind, the Greek and Latin terms suggest that consciousness, in the full sense of the term, cannot be restricted to one's own self but is finally a transindividual experience.

It was only with the beginnings of Christianity that the noun συνείδησις took on the meaning of an individualization or interiorization of a shared knowledge, something like the application of a shared knowledge by an individual to himself, and thus self-judgment.[8] The works attributed to Paul, above all, Romans and I-II Corinthians, clearly represent a redirection or, more precisely, a contraction of the range of the term, such that the implication of "knowing with" is limited to the relation between the individual and God, and concerns the individual's knowledge of his (and no one else's) inclinations and desires and thus of the conflict within him between the flesh and the spirit, rather than knowledge in a general sense. Commentators have often associated this semantic shift with Paul's rejection of the law and outward, bodily obedience in favor of an internal obedience to God no longer visible to others, whose judgments, whether positive or negative, would carry no weight on that day when God alone, from whom nothing can be hidden and who cannot be deceived, will judge.

Similarly, in the Latin world, the term "*conscientia*" shifted from a designation of a "knowing-with" others to a sense internal to the individual, the capacity for a self-scrutiny that enabled him to submit his thought to a *foro interno* or internal tribunal. The English term "conscience" by the seventeenth century had been emptied of any reference to the horizontality of a "knowing with" or a seeing something at the same time as others. Perhaps the polemics associated with the reformation, particularly with Luther, had contributed to a re-fashioning of the concept of conscience that rendered the collective prefix of the German "*Gewissen*" (the equivalent of the English "conscience") purely vestigial. Henceforth, conscience would be understood as the individual's relation to himself mediated by God or through the law that God has inscribed in every heart. It designates that essential part of every human being that others precisely cannot know or judge, as if the solitary individual were abandoned by his fellows before God.

As Balibar has argued, Locke might have simply retained the term "conscience," by his time well established in the lexicon of the English language as in French and Spanish, exploiting and perhaps recovering some of the meanings of *conscientia* as it was used by Cicero and others, particularly the meaning of self-scrutiny, reading the prefix "con" as if it were a reflexive form: something like self-knowledge. Why would Locke choose instead to employ a term, and to do so systematically, that had been used in his sense no more than half a dozen times before him? Balibar has analyzed in detail the enormous difficulty that Locke's decision caused his French translator, Pierre Coste, as he sought to supply a French equivalent.[9]

Apart from the fact that by the seventeenth century "conscience" had a far more limited semantic range in English than *conscience* in French, there existed difficulties that the notion of "conscience" not only did *not* address, but in fact aggravated. Accordingly, we may understand Locke's introduction of the term "consciousness" as a means of solving two related but unequally developed problems: (1) the very notion of "conscience" suggested that there were at least two divergent and often opposed wills in every individual, the will to sin and the will to obey God. Which of these wills could justifiably be said to pertain to the individual in question? Is it the same man, or more precisely the same person, who wills himself to sin and to obey God? Locke formulates the problem by calling up a forensic scene, not that of the Last Judgment, but a perfectly banal courtroom drama: if a man when drunk (that is, so drunk he cannot later remember what he said or did – or at least claims that he cannot remember) or "asleep," that is, sleepwalking (a phenomenon of great interest to seventeenth-century philosophers, including Descartes, Spinoza and, above all, Gassendi who produced a study of what he called "les noctambules"),[10] violates the law, can the act be said to have been performed by the "same" man who the individual is when sober or awake? In part, this is a question of what Locke calls identity: "the identity of the same man consists; viz. in nothing but a participation of the same continued life, by constantly fleeting particles of matter, in succession vitally united to the same organized body" (ECHU II.27.7). But this only tells us that the identity of his bodily substance lies not in the continuity of its parts but of its organization or composition: even if we can rule out a transmigration of souls that would allow Socrates to live on in a succession of different bodies, is what answers to a proper name and is vitally united to an organized body necessarily one and the same person? Indeed, is a man who answers to one name (one of the marks of his identity) the same person when sane and when mad? Are the actions he performs when mad really his own and can he be said to be responsible both causally and legally for them simply because these actions were carried out by the same body? Here, the problem is that of a multiplicity and a diversity internal to the individual (or at least to the individual body present to the senses of others), which would make it impossible to answer a simple question like "who is responsible for this?"

Locke's solution lies in the concept of consciousness: "the perception of what passes in a man's own mind" (ECHU II.i.19). For Locke, this perception "is inseparable from thinking and, as it seems to me, essential to it": when we perceive something, we, in one and the same act, perceive that we perceive; when we think, we know that we think or think that we think. This doubling or duplication is necessary given that "to suppose the soul to think and the man not to perceive it is to make two persons in one man" (ECHU II.1.19). The fact that we always and necessarily perceive that we perceive and know that we know, Locke argues, means that "every one is to himself that which he calls self" (ECHU II.27.11). It is consciousness that unifies past and present thoughts and imposes a sufficient degree of unity and continuity to refer all the passes in a man's own mind to a single person who corresponds to the pronoun I. And Locke leaves little doubt concerning the urgency of establishing with certainty the unity of the person. Without reducing him to the single individual he is and separating him from others, there can be no judgment of his actions: "punishment is annexed to personality and personality to consciousness" even in the case of the drunkard who upon awakening has no consciousness of having committed a crime (it is just to punish such a man "because the fact is proved against him but the want of consciousness cannot be proved for him" (ECHU II.27.22)). The judgment of innocence or guilt rests on two contrary hypotheses: the observable unity of an individual's body and the opacity of the consciousness encased in it. Thus, while each person knows that he himself knows, he cannot thereby know that anyone other than himself knows or knows that he knows. If the body is an essential part of the man for Locke, it is because the body as perceived by others is that to which consciousness and thus legal and moral personality may be imputed or ascribed. Even if the man who while drunk or sleepwalking commits a crime without any thought or consciousness of that thought, the very inaccessibility of consciousness to others necessitates the supposition, which Locke freely admits may be mistaken, of responsibility: because no one other than himself participates in the consciousness of what passes in his mind, it is impossible to know whether or not, when he says he has no conscious recollection of the action in question, he is telling the truth. But if a man can deceive others about what has passed in his mind, can he deceive himself? And who in such a case would seek to deceive and be deceived? In a sense, everything Locke says in chapter 27 is designed to exclude such a possibility, even as the work of exclusion seems to produce increasingly difficult questions.

It is here that what Balibar has called a topography of the subject arises as a kind of solution to this problem: personal identity emerges not simply from the fact that an individual thinks, but from the fact that he observes that he thinks in what Locke calls not simply consciousness but self-consciousness. But the very fact that he "appropriates" his thought to himself precisely by affirming that it is his own and no one else's renders it inaccessible to the knowledge and judgment of others. The presumption of guilt in the case of the drunken man or the sleepwalker who commits a crime, a presumption made necessary by the fact that he alone can know whether the act was a conscious decision or not and, in his capacity as the sole witness to his intentions, cannot be expected to testify against himself, calls the very notion of justice into question by punishing the innocent along with the guilty. As a "solution" to the problems that arise from the impermeability of individuals' minds and the difficulty of determining "intent," as it is said in the legal system today, Locke is compelled to postulate the existence both of a transcendental position from which the contents of every consciousness are visible and someone to occupy that position as supreme judge: God. For there will come, he tells us, a "Great Day, wherein the secrets of all hearts shall be laid open," to be seen and then judged by God who will recognize and reward those among the innocent who nevertheless, within the limits of human knowledge, were rightly judged guilty and punished accordingly.

It is thus consciousness that transmutes the thing that thinks into a person ("Nothing but consciousness can unite remote existences into the same person") (ECHU II.27.23), who, because he knows what he thinks and has thought, is accountable for the actions that he imputes to himself. It is crucial here that the person thus defined must not only know, but know that he knows what he has done, and further must also know that even if he cannot now be known to anyone but himself, there will come a time when he is "laid open," when the inner becomes outer, and that which he has concealed is revealed. And because he knows that he knows and thinks that he thinks, he knows that when he is known at the Last Judgment there can be no excuse or alibi for his evil deeds. We live under the uninterrupted self-surveillance that Locke calls consciousness, knowing that we are, or will be, in turn observed, visible not by other persons we may hope to deceive, but by an observer who cannot be deceived and from whom nothing can be concealed. As Balibar has noted,

> for Locke, the truth of consciousness (or self-consciousness) and that of absolute judgment, freed from the veils that language and communication impose, constitute one and the same problem: that of *the last*

instance of judgment. It is possible to take this as a kind of myth, but it would be more accurate to see in it an ideality, precisely the ideality that Locke, through the concatenation of the terms consciousness, memory, identity, "self," responsibility and judgment, seeks to place at the limit of his theory of mind.[11]

In this topography, the person, whose thought is visible to himself but concealed from the other persons around him, must know his thought is, or rather will be, visible and judged on the basis of all that he has ever thought or done, including that that, having been forgotten, remains a secret from himself. All will be revealed to him at the moment he is judged (and Locke uses the passive voice here and elsewhere as if to emphasize the judgment rather than the judge, rendering it strangely impersonal), as if consciousness comprehends all that it has known in that last instance (understood both logically and chronologically), the instance of judgment in which all is revealed to the individual in question. Jeremy Bentham's panopticon, whose significance Foucault articulated with such lucidity, was perhaps nothing more than the allegorical figure of Locke's topographical scheme of the subject who knows himself knowing and knows that he will be known when he is summoned to judgment. We are in this way reminded that Locke's person is indeed a subjected being, even if his subjection is finally a self-subjection, as if he were endowed with consciousness in order to be liable to judgment both here and now and on the Great Day to come: it is not enough that he sees and knows himself – he must be seen seeing himself, known knowing himself, for only through this last instance can he both know all that his consciousness has perceived and know that he knows. It is this self-knowledge that is revealed on the day of judgment and for which the person will be called to account.

But just as we cannot "suppose two distinct incommunicable consciousnesses acting the same body, the one constantly by day, the other by night," so we cannot suppose "the same consciousness acting by intervals two distinct bodies" (ECHU (II.27.23)). This highlights the importance of the body for Locke: consciousness acts the body that, "vitally united to it," is its own. The body retains its identity not because it is made up of the same particles of matter, but because consciousness of the body's actions vitally unites the body to the rational spirit, which allows us to speak of the same man. In this way, Locke is able to tie the self to a single body, thus rendering the body the means of separation and individuation:

> The body, as well as the soul, goes to the making of a man. And thus may we be able, without any difficulty, to conceive the same person at the resurrection, though in a body not exactly in make or parts the same which he had here, the same consciousness going along with the soul that inhabits it. But yet the soul alone, in the change of bodies, would scarce to any one but to him that makes the soul the man, be enough to make the same man. (ECHU II.27.15)

The reference here to the resurrection is crucial: the individual knows and knows that he knows only the actions of his own body, the body that in Locke's words is acted by "its" consciousness and held accountable on Judgment Day:

> the sentence shall be justified by the consciousness all persons shall have, that they themselves, in what bodies soever they appear, or what substances soever that consciousness adheres to, are the same that committed those actions, and deserve that punishment for them. ECHU (II. 27.26)

The separation of bodies here is the condition of the separation of conciousnesses, which in turn guarantees the separation of persons for "forensic" purposes. I am aware of what happens in my own body and no one else's, just as no one else can be conscious of what happens in my body: no one can feel my pain or pleasure, my ease or uneasiness of body. There can be no mingling or sharing of bodily sensations between consciousnesses. The separation is absolute; if one were "to find himself conscious of any of the actions of Nestor, he then finds himself the same person with Nestor" (ECHU II.27.14).

Here, Locke stands in opposition to his contemporaries Spinoza and Malebranche for whom one of the most powerful forces in social and political life was the imitation or contagion, that is, reproduction or transmission, of affects between individuals. For them, passions and images passed so freely between persons that the question of whether what passes in my mind is mine or somebody else's became an insoluble problem, calling into question the very notion of "a man's own mind" and thus the proprietary relation between me and what I call mine or my own. It is in this context that Balibar notes that "the thematic of the 'own,' 'owning' and 'ownership' entails a parallelism of responsibility and property, of self-consciousness and 'property in oneself.'"[12] At this point we may begin to see that the importance of the body extends beyond the guarantee it provides of the separation of consciousnesses and therefore of persons. The body is not simply an object in space, even an object that retains its identity through the changes it undergoes. The body is an "animate" and therefore living thing, a fact that opens the way to what we may call the biopolitical dimension of Locke's philosophy that indissolubly unites the doctrine of property developed in the first five chapters of the *Second Treatise of Government* to the concept of personal identity Locke elucidates in chapter 27 of the *Essay*. For if my ownership of the body I act, in both senses of own (I acknowledge it mine and I am its proprietor), is the foundation of all subsequent appropriation (and Locke will make frequent use of the term "annexation" to describe the act of appropriation), the condition of such ownership is the continued life of the body, without which (at least until the Resurrection) there can be no consciousness, no self, no person. It is this fact that gives primacy to what we may call the act of living, not simply the involuntary movements of respiration or the circulation of blood, but those voluntary actions by which an individual procures the nourishment and shelter without which the body cannot remain animate.

What I have here, following Locke, termed "procuring," that is, not simply ingesting nourishment, but first obtaining what is to be ingested, is both a physical act and a political act, an appropriation that, beyond the simple fact that what I procure for my survival is something I happen to have in my possession, confers a right upon me, the right of proprietorship. To support our being, our life, we must "appropriate" the fruits that nature provides by "joining" and "annexing" them to our body.[13] But while, for Locke, "he that that is nourished by the acorns he picked up under an oak ... has certainly appropriated them to himself,"[14] the process of appropriation that occurs through and in the body, which being separate from all other bodies, as the consciousness is separate from all other consciousnesses and therefore the person from all other persons, simultaneously involves the exclusion of all other bodies, consciousnesses and persons. To follow Balibar's argument about "the parallelism of responsibility and property" we can say that consciousness in its vital unity with the body both "owns and imputes to itself past actions" for which the person alone is accountable and over which the person alone has right of proprietorship. In this way, the very act of living produces a double exclusion: just as another person by virtue of the incommunicability of consciousnesses and bodies cannot share in the guilt or innocence attached to my actions, my own actions, so that person cannot share in what I have, through the actions of my body, appropriated and annexed to myself.

The commons, the idea that the fruits of nature belong to everyone and no one, is thus literally an impossibility given the fact that appropriation and annexation are necessary to the support of life, the life of the individual person: there can be no property without life and no life without property. This is of course an early version of the so-called tragedy of the commons, but if anything a more violent and threatening version. The commons is not a remnant of an original, natural condition; it is rather an imposition on nature, the exclusion of the exclusion necessary to life and therefore a pre-emptive expropriation of all that is proper to the person. Henceforth, life itself will be a struggle by a self that thinks and feels as it will be judged, alone, to annex what is common and to exclude both the rights and the consciousness of others.

To appreciate Locke's conception of the relation of property to life we may recall the famous Roman adage captured and translated in a brief passage from a work written 300 years before the publication of *Two Treatises of Government*. It will help make visible the heretofore illegible stakes of Locke's text to reveal not the underlying coherence and unity of his argument, but the specific conflict that makes the text what it is.

In Passus 20 of William Langland's *Piers Ploughman*, we read the following lines:

And nede he hath no lawe,
Ne nevere shal falle in dette:
For thre thynges he taketh,
His lif for to save.

I cite this passage not only because it represents a popularization of the debates that occupied the Church throughout the twelfth and thirteen centuries concerning the rights of the poor to subsistence and whether that right granted them dispensation to engage in taking for themselves what outside of the condition of life-threatening need (for food, water, clothing or shelter) lawfully belonged to another, but even more because it represents a particular interpretation of "*Necessitas non habet Legem*" (often translated as "necessity has no law"). The phrase has been understood in different and even opposing ways by a series of twentieth and twenty-first century commentators, including Schmitt and Agamben, as an expression of the fact that the sovereign must operate in the realm of necessity, employing whatever force is necessary (and perhaps an excess designed to inspire terror) to preserve or restore the legal order that nevertheless cannot be allowed to restrain it. Clearly, Locke's political philosophy in its entirety opposes such a position by installing certain primary laws in nature prior to any human legislation, a law coextensive with the use of reason itself and thus immediately knowable. And the law of nature is formulated as a right of ownership: killing an individual is above all a violation of his rights as proprietor of his own person, just as the expropriation of what he has mixed his labor with and thus annexed to himself, above all, according to Locke's own examples, the food necessary to his existence (Locke's examples: apples, acorns and deer) is not simply an attempt on what is his property, but on what is proper to him, that originary and essential prosthesis without which his existence is inconceivable.[15] The sovereign who disregards the law of nature is less a Leviathan sent by God to chasten and terrify the children of pride, than the figure of the inhuman, a man who has "become degenerate," as a "*lion* or a *tyger,* one of those wild savage beasts, with whom men can have no society nor security: and upon this is grounded that great law of nature."[16] The necessity that requires a suspension of law is nothing more than the machine-like operation of a predatory animal incapable of obeying any law other than that of the promptings of the body. Indeed, as Roberto Esposito has shown, the sovereign power has no other function than the protection of the property that is a man's own life and the life that through labor ceaselessly converts the things around him into himself, not so much interiorizing them as transmuting them indistinguishably into his very being. Thus, when Locke declares "no one ought to harm another in his Life, Health, Liberty or Possessions,"[17] he resorts to the highly unusual construction "to harm a man in his X" not simply to render life and possessions equivalent, but to suggest that to take another man's possessions (and let us note that possession, mere possession, and ownership are not and cannot be the same for Locke) represents an attack on or a subtraction from a man's physical, corporeal existence. And while Locke initially holds that in the state of nature the punishment meted out to the violator of natural law must be "proportionate to his transgression," and carried out in order to "make him repent the doing of it and thereby deter him, and by his example others, from doing the like mischief,"[18] he soon exempts the victim of even petty theft from such restrictions. Thus, "I may kill" a "thief" when he

> sets on me to rob me but of my horse or coat because the law, which was made for my preservation, where it cannot interpose to secure my life from present force, which, if lost, is capable of no reparation, permits me my own defense, and the right of war, a liberty to kill the aggressor, because the aggressor allows not time to appeal to our common judge, nor the decision of the law, for remedy in a case where the mischief may be irreparable.[19]

Locke's argument here, that when I am directly exposed without the physical protection of an agent of the law to those actions on the part of the thief necessary to the accomplishment of the theft, I am in his absolute power and could be killed by him, has the effect of rendering every act of theft from his person (pickpocketing, for example, which may indeed involve "setting on" the victim, by jostling, grabbing or pushing him) a potential attempt on his life (here again the forensic function of Locke's privative definition of consciousness comes into play: we cannot know what is in the pickpocket's mind and must assume guilt where we cannot be certain of innocence) that can and indeed should punished by death. Even the use of the term "thief" is significant here: it allows Locke to avoid specifying whether the thief is a man, woman or child, old or young, strong or weak, and therefore the extent to which the "thief" is actually capable of posing a threat to my existence. Moreover, the proximity of "my Horse or coat" to my body, the fact that they are mine in the sense that, to use the language introduced in chapter 5, I have "annexed" them to me, means that they are now a kind of prosthetic extension of my body in the absence of which I am not the person I was when I "possessed" them. The *Second Treatise* thus moves, not only in the sequence of its arguments, but in the illustrations designed to help us picture the arguments, to problematize and interfere with every attempt to separate the notions of my self, my life and my property in its drive to render them both equivalent and indiscernible.

It is this fact that allows us to understand Locke's apparently restrictive definition of *"Political power"* as the *"right* of making laws with penalties of death, and consequently all less penalties, for the regulating and preserving of property"[20] as something other than an abandonment of the responsibilities traditionally associated with governing. The verb "preserve" and the noun "preservation" together occur twenty-one times in the *Second Treatise*. In nineteen of the twenty-one ocases, they refer to life, that is, to self-preservation or the preservation of the species. Locke allows or rather compels us to read the preservation of property as part of self-preservation, not only because the definition of every man as the proprietor of himself eliminates any distinction between the propertied and the propertyless, given that every individual owns at least his own person and thus gives every human being a stake in the defense of property, but also because appropriation, the transmutation of what is not mine, what is common and not (yet) appropriated into my property and thus myself, is not simply a change in ownership but a material transformation necessary to life itself, of which ingestion and digestion are the privileged examples.

But this expanded sense of the preservation of property that is the sole end of government, itself rests precariously on the fault lines that Locke's own argument opens. If government exists to defend individuals understood as the rightful proprietors of their own lives, as well as their own goods, from those who would take one or the other in violation both of that "original law of nature" and of the "positive laws to determine property" made and multiplied by humankind, it must also defend their freedom "to order their actions, and dispose of their possessions and persons, as they think fit, within the bounds of the law of nature, without asking leave, or depending upon the will of any other man."[21] Indeed, the limitations on private accumulation that Locke proposes in chapter 5 do not refer to the desires or, more to the point, the needs of any other man, but to the extent to which what is appropriated by an individual can be consumed and made part of his being. That original law of nature, the preservation of which is coextensive with the self-preservation of the individual, cannot provide a justification for requiring an individual to give up what may now or in the future be used for the support and maintenance of his being to another man. But this does not mean that the individual in question, at least "when his own preservation comes not in competition," does not do his part, "as much as he can, *to preserve the rest of mankind.*"²² He leaves *or* abandons what he himself cannot use now or in the future (what will, if it remains in his possession, spoil – which raises the question of whether basic provisions could not be "preserved" and stored for future use) for others to appropriate as they can – allowing them the chance through their labor to annex, ingest and digest the food necessary to their preservation. Thus, the law of nature does no more than forbid the individual to waste what others may possibly consume, just as he is forbidden to take their lives or property. But he is under no enforceable obligation to feed them and is immunized against their claims to whatever food he possesses that will not spoil (or can be sold on the assumption that what is purchased will be distributed for consumption and not wasted), in the same way that the needs of the coatless man in an English winter cannot justify "harming another in his possessions" even if he takes only what is necessary to his self-preservation from someone whose life will not be threatened by the loss. Need, for Locke and against Langland, is thus always subject to law, if only the "original law of nature," a law that because it precedes and founds positive law as its condition, a law that is not made but discovered by the industrious and the rational, cannot be suspended and suffers no exceptions, whether from above, in the case of absolute sovereignty, or below, in the case of those, the majority in Locke's world, without any property other than their own person.

At this point, I am tempted to quote a line from the *First Treatise* in which Locke cautions the reader after a sustained examination of Filmer's text that "[w]e have been so long detained, not by the force of arguments and opposition, but by the intricacy of the words, and the doubtfulness of the meaning."²³ Thus, if it is clear that the sovereign cannot suspend the law of nature, property, established in the very act of self-preservation in which the necessity of establishing property is inseparable from the necessity that governs life itself, the case of the man in need, dire need, who lives, not in the wild woods and forests of the state of nature, but among the civilized where everything has been divided up among legitimate owners is less clear. Locke would openly defy absolute monarchs who presume to violate the natural and inalienable rights of their subjects by taxing them against their will, no matter how small the tax and how substantial the holdings of those who must pay it: theft is theft. But the problem of the destitute, above all those not maintained by the voluntary charity of the prosperous, a population whose numbers increased substantially during Locke's life time and led him to devote significant thought to the problem of the poor in his last years, appears only fleetingly, half-represented, and at the margins of the *Second Treatise*: the coatless man, the savages shivering in the wilderness of the new world whose image merges with that of the improvident villagers who depend on the commons for food, fuel and lumber. They are the quarrelsome and contentious who resist the appropriation of what they mistakenly regard as their land by "the industrious and the rational,"[24] to whom Locke insists God gave it.

If, according to one of the positions in the Medieval debates about the relation of property to life, the law of property cannot apply to the man who is starving who, in taking what he must "his lyf for to save," is thus neither a thief nor a criminal in any sense, we can say with reasonable certainty that Locke's arguments in the *Second Treatise* exclude any such possibility. There can be no life without nourishment and no nourishment without individual appropriation of the source of nourishment that transforms it both legally and physically: in appropriating an apple from what God has given to humankind in common, Locke's individual both joins something of his own, of himself, to the apple, and annexes it to his own self of which it becomes a part. The fact that the appropriation "without which the common is of no use"[25] precisely excludes the claims of others, is underscored in Locke's text by his exclusive use of solitary individuals to illustrate the natural right of property ("He that is nourished by the acorns he picked up under an oak," "The fruit, or venison, which nourishes the *wild Indian*").[26] The absence of others allows Locke to avoid the problem of what, if anything, is due to them from all that I have appropriated and made my own, and under what conditions (and the spoliation clause that appears later in chapter 5 addresses this problem so obliquely that it merely perpetuates it). What happens when my property in food, unspoiled and unlikely to spoil before I will have occasion to consume it, encounters need, the others' need for food that, if unmet, brings the risk of death? It is possible to compose a response from Locke's texts: the state of nature as it appears in chapter 5 is bountiful, no one willing to exert himself in labor will go hungry. In his later "Essay on the Poor Law" (1697), he uses the same words to describe the England of his time. "The multiplying of the poor," he tells us, the all too apparent increase in the number of vagrants and beggars, has "proceeded neither from scarcity of provisions, nor want of employment for the poor, since the goodness of God has blessed these times with plenty."[27] Instead, their numbers have increased by virtue of an unfortunate "relaxation of discipline and corruption of manners."[28] Those who are hungry where both provisions and employment are plentiful are thus hungry by consent; it is they alone who bear the responsibility for their need. But if I am thus exempted from any responsibility to them, what would be the nature of my responsibility to the starving prior to the exemption their consent allows me to claim?

Locke does not entirely avoid this question, although by responding to it in the *First Treatise*, specifically in chapter 4, "Of Adam's Title to Sovereignty by Donation," he isolates it from the discussions of the state of nature and the state of war, as well as the theory of property which, as we have seen, provides the foundation of his conception of "political society." The effects of this isolation are clear: the passage has been overlooked by some of the most penetrating readers of chapter 5, "Of Property," from Macpherson to Balibar and Esposito, while a new "religious turn" in the reading of Locke cites the passage from the *First Treatise* in an attempt to connect him to medieval and Reformation discussions of charity and property by minimizing or explaining away what is most historically significant and perhaps most disturbing about Locke's texts.[29] I will neither attempt to reconcile the discussions of property in the First and Second Treatises nor will I treat them as the two poles of a contradiction; I will assume that just as the chapter "Of Property" is marked by the play of its inconsistencies and discrepancies, by what it avoids saying as much as what it has to say, so Locke's discussion of property and need in the *First Treatise* takes shape around the contradiction proper to it.

As part of his refutation of Robert Filmer's argument that the earth was given by God to Adam who, as sole sovereign and proprietor, passed it on to those he designated his heirs, and they to theirs, until the present, and that this donation was the origin and foundation of all legitimate sovereignty, Locke admits that God gave the world to Adam to hold as his property. But, as he asks, if

> by this donation of God Adam was made sole proprietor of the whole earth, what will this be to his sovereignty? And how will it appear, that

propriety in land gives a man power over the life of another? or how will the possession even of the whole earth give any one a sovereign arbitrary authority over the persons of men?[30]

Of course, there are any number of possible arguments for a derivation of sovereignty from dominion or possession, as the experiments in colonialism with which Locke was very familiar showed, and we may expect him to acknowledge these positions, if only to refute them. Instead, his argument takes what should be a surprising turn. The hypothetical proprietor of the earth may, according to Locke, exercise his natural right to use his property as he alone sees fit, as a means of coercion, that is, to starve, or threaten to starve, those without property in land to extort from them submission to his absolute authority:

> he that is proprietor of the whole world, may deny all the rest of mankind food, and so at his pleasure starve them, if they will not acknowledge his sovereignty, and obey his will. If this were true, it would be a good argument to prove, that there never was any such property, that God never gave any such private dominion; since it is more reasonable to think, that God, who bid mankind increase and multiply, should rather himself give them all a right to make use of the food and raiment, and other conveniencies of life, the materials whereof he had so plentifully provided for them; than to make them depend upon the will of a man for their subsistence, who should have power to destroy them all when he pleased.[31]

While Locke's argument here points to the conceptual necessity of an original commons the supersession of which through individual appropriation constitutes the possibility both of life and of political society, an origin that Filmer's argument for Adam's proprietorship of the earth displaces and calls into question, Locke quickly moves to qualify and limit the right of property on very different grounds than those of the spoliation clause proposed in chapter 5 of the *Second Treatise*. Assuming an origin of property other than that of the individual laboring to satisfy his vital needs, Locke, following Filmer's argument, asserts that if property is given to man by God, the gift cannot be given to him, or for his benefit, alone. "The property in his peculiar portion of the things of this world," given by God to one man not only does not exclude the rights of others, but is simultaneously "a right to the surplusage of his goods ... given his needy brother."[32] Locke further stipulates that this right "cannot justly be denied him, when his pressing wants call for it."[33] It is true that Locke in some sense compromises his position by arguing against Filmer that the needy man may indeed be subjected to the authority of the proprietor who feeds him from his surplus, but is careful to note that such subjection is purely voluntary, originating neither in a natural hierarchy nor in a violent appropriation of the needy man's natural liberty, but rather in his consent alone:

> the authority of the rich proprietor, and the subjections of the needy beggar, began not from the possession of the lord, but the consent of the poor man, who preferred being his subject to starving. And the man he thus submits to, can pretend to no more power over him than he has consented to, upon compact.[34]

In this way the "Man of Estate" fulfills his obligation to relieve the needy man through a contractual arrangement by which the latter is fed on the condition that he freely consents to submit to the authority of the former who nevertheless has "no more power over him than he has consented to, upon compact." The unequal relation that arises from this agreement is perfectly legitimate, as is the use of need to obtain by means of a contract the "voluntary" obedience and subjection of others. Thus, as Locke rejects dominion as the foundation for absolute sovereignty in response to Filmer, he simultaneously shifts the onus on to the needy man who can no longer expect to be fed without conditions; if he wants to eat, he must consent to serve the man who feeds him. If he does not so consent, he, in anticipation of the language of the "Essay on the Poor Law," starves by free choice.

It is here that this already elliptical passage begins to break apart under the pressure of the questions to which it leads the reader, even as it cannot pose them: if the gift given to the proprietor simultaneously confers upon the needy man a right to the proprietor's surplus (however defined), is the needy man who takes food from the former's supply after being refused a thief? Does the widespread refusal to feed the starving even through a mutually beneficial compact imply a revocation of the immunity of property owners? Is immunity granted to those who, faced with starvation, must take what the men of estate have not consented to give? Finally, and most intolerable of all for Locke: what happens when the exclusive right of property, instead of forming the basis for existence, threatens to exclude the needy from life itself?[35]

This then is the parallelism that marks the complicity between Locke's concepts. Having confined the human individual to his own self, Locke abolishes the horizontal dimension in which thoughts or feelings may be shared and lived with others to replace it with the verticality of a topography in which individuals, knowing only themselves and unknown by all but him whose knowledge is absolute, come to resemble the solitaries who inhabit the *Second Treatise*. Wandering the forests of America or English highways, they are modern subjects, declared after the fact to be the subjects of their own subjection, composed by movements of annexation and exclusion, appropriation and punishment, each immured in a tower into which only a God who watches over all can see.

Notes

1. Etienne Balibar, *Identity and Difference, John Locke and the Invention of Consciousness*, trans. Warren Montag (London; New York: Verso, 2013), 101.
2. Pierre Macherey, *Introduction à l'Éthique de Spinoza. La seconde partie: la réalitié mentale* (Paris: Presses Universitaires de France, 1997), 72–3.
3. Balibar, *Identity*, 101.
4. Immanuel Kant: Kritik der reinen Vernunft – 2. Auflage – Kapitel 37, § 16, Der Spiegel, <http://gutenberg.spiegel.de/buch/kritik-der-reinen-vernunft-2-auflage-3502/37> (accessed September 2016).
5. Louis Althusser, "Ideology and the Ideological State Apparatuses," in *The Reproduction of Capitalism*, trans. G. M. Goshgarian (London: Verso, 2014). Pp. 232–72.
6. Karl Marx, *Capital, Volume I* (London: Penguin, 1994), XX. Martin Heidegger offers his own interpretation of the moment that individuals were freed, or freed themselves, from the ties characteristic of feudalism. "The Age of the World Picture," in *Off the Beaten Track*, trans. Julian Young and Kenneth Haynes (Cambridge: Cambridge University Press, 2002), 66–7.
7. Balibar, *Identity*, 39.
8. Balibar, *Identity*, 39.
9. Balibar, *Identity*, 2–17.
10. Baruch Spinoza, *Ethics III*, P2, *scholium*, René Descartes, *The Passions of the Soul* and Pierre Gassendi, "De la phantasie," in

Abrégé de la philosophie de Gassendi, Vol. 3, 7 vols (Lyon: Anisson, 1684). Pp. 182–93.
11. Balibar, *Identity*, 109–10; emphasis in the original.
12. Balibar, *Identity*, 100–1.
13. John Locke, *Two Treatises of Government*, ed. Peter Laslett (Cambridge: Cambridge University Press, 1963), II.5.27.
14. Locke, *Two Treatises*, II.5.28; emphasis in the original.
15. Roberto Esposito, "The Paradigm of Immunization," in *Bios: Biopolitics and Humanity*, trans. Timothy Campbell (Minneapolis: University of Minnesota Press, 2008), 45–77.
16. Locke, *Two Treatises*, II.2.11; emphasis in the original.
17. Locke, *Two Treatises*, II.5.28.
18. Locke, *Two Treatises*, II.2.8.
19. Locke, *Two Treatises*, II.3.18–19.
20. Locke, *Two Treatises*, II.1.3; emphasis in the original.
21. Locke, *Two Treatises*, II.2.4.
22. Locke, *Two Treatises*, II.2.6; emphasis in the original.
23. Locke, *Two Treatises*, I.4.21.
24. Locke, *Two Treatises*, II.5.33.
25. Locke, *Two Treatises*, II.5.27.
26. Locke, *Two Treatises*, II.5.24., II.5.27.
27. John Locke, "An Essay on the Poor Law," in *Locke: Political Essays*, ed. Mark Goldie (Cambridge: Cambridge University Press, 1997), 184.
28. Locke, "Essay on the Poor Law," 184.
29. For an overview of the "religious turn," see Paul E. Sigmund, "Jeremy Waldron and the Religious Turn in Locke Scholarship," *The Review of Politics*, 67.3 (2005): 407–8.
30. Locke, *Two Treatises*, I.4.41.
31. Locke, *Two Treatises*, I.4.41.
32. Locke, *Two Treatises*, I.4.42.
33. Locke, *Two Treatises*, I.4.42.
34. Locke, *Two Treatises*, I.4.43.
35. On the importance of the debates over the right of the starving to steal food in Canon law, see Gilles Couvreur, *Les Pauvres ont-ils des droits? Recherches sur le vol en cas d'extrême nécessité depuis la Concordia de Gratien (1140) jusqu'à Guillaume d'Auxerre (1231)* (Rome: Libreria Ecitrice dell'Università Gregoriana, 1961).

Bibliography

Althusser, Louis. "Ideology and the Ideological State Apparatuses." In *The Reproduction of Capitalism*. Trans. G. M. Goshgarian. London: Verso, 2014. Pp. 232–72.

Balibar, Etienne. *Identity and Difference, John Locke and the Invention of Consciousness*. Trans. Warren Montag. London; New York: Verso, 2013.

Couvreur, Gilles. *Les Pauvres ont-ils des droits? Recherches sur le vol en cas d'extrême nécessité depuis la Concordia de Gratien (1140) jusqu'à Guillaume d'Auxerre (1231)*. Rome: Libreria Editrice dell'Università Gregoriana, 1961.

Descartes, René. *The Passions of the Soul*. Trans. Stephen H. Voss. Indianapolis: Hackett Publishing Company, 1989.

Descartes, René. *Les Passions de l'âme*, La philosophie dans l'Académie de Créteil. <http://philosophie.ac-creteil.fr/IMG/pdf/Les_passions_de_l_ame.pdf> (accessed May 27, 2016).

Esposito, Roberto. "The Paradigm of Immunization." In *Bios: Biopolitics and Humanity*. Trans. Timothy Campbell. Minneapolis: University of Minnesota Press, 2008. Pp. 45–77.

Gassendi, Pierre. "De la phantasie." In *Abrégé de la philosophie de Gassendi*. Vol. 3, 7 vols. Lyon: Anisson, 1684. Pp. 182–93.

Heidegger, Martin. "The Age of the World Picture." In *Martin Heidegger: Off the Beaten Track*. Trans. and Ed. Julian Young and Kenneth Haynes. Cambridge: Cambridge University Press, 2002. Pp. 57–85.

Heidegger, Martin. "Die Zeit des Weltbildes." In *Holzwege*. Frankfurt: Vittorio Klostermann, 1952.

Kant, Immanuel. *Critique of Pure Reason*. Trans. Norman Kemp Smith. New York: St. Martin's Press, 1965. Pp. 75–113.

Locke, John. *Two Treatises of Government*. Ed. Peter Laslett. Cambridge: Cambridge University Press, 1963.

Locke, John. *An Essay Concerning Human Understanding*. Ed. Peter H. Niddich. Oxford: Clarendon Press, 1975.

Locke, John. "An Essay on the Poor Law." In *Locke: Political Essays*. Ed. Mark Goldie. Cambridge: Cambridge University Press, 1997 (1697). Pp. 182–200.

Macherey, Pierre. *Introduction à l'Éthique de Spinoza. La seconde partie: la réalitié mentale*. Paris: Presses Universitaires de France, 1997.

Marx, Karl. *Capital, Volume I*. London: Penguin, 1994.

Sigmund, Paul E. "Jeremy Waldron and the Religious Turn in Locke Scholarship." *The Review of Politics*, 67.3 (2005): 407–18.

Spinoza, Baruch. *Ethics,* Spinoza House Association, 2000. <http://users.telenet.be/rwmeijer/spinoza/works.htm> (accessed May 20, 2016).

6

Figures of Universalism: Notes on Philosophy and Politics in Etienne Balibar

Mohamed Moulfi

Translated by Vanessa Brutsche

My intention here is to trace the ways in which the confrontation between the problematic of universalism in its internal diversity and the reality of anthropological difference has determined the part of Etienne Balibar's œuvre that remains a work in progress. The course he has taken in his works and the continuous movement of his ideas together reveal the essential articulations of his philosophical meditations. The impressive range of his texts is equaled by his desire to confront both the blind spots of classical political theories and the inescapable problems posed by the contemporary situation. The perpetual motion proper to his approach undermines any attempt to identify a given demarcation in the development of his work over the long term as a decisive or irreversible turning point. It brings out, among other things, the problematizations that correspond to "what might be understood as a 'contemporary confrontation' with the heritage of Marx and Marxism."[1] It is undoubtedly necessary to point out that he has never ceased to rework or rectify (without any renunciation of this activity) the "marxological," Marxist and Althusserian[2] foundation of his thought. Is it then a question of self-criticism? Not really, since it is less a repudiation than a matter of re-investigating and extending this foundation based on his desire to found or refound the theory of the political in the light of new "historical figures of *emancipation*."[3] His project is thus reaffirmed: to face the "essentially 'contested' character of political philosophy" for the explicit purpose of renewing the "dynamics of the political" through this contestation itself.[4] The result has been an impressive and essential œuvre. And, if it were not unseemly and presumptuous to describe his theoretical development, we would have to acknowledge that if Balibar were not speaking of Hannah Arendt in the following passage, we might have seen it as a case of *de te fabula narrator*:

> Every great work has its history, both interior and exterior. It reflects a development characterized by powerful continuities, by the recurrence of obsessive questions on which the very expansion of the philosophical horizon and the movements of his analysis depend.[5]

Further, rather than reproduce the terms and themes of the debates surrounding Balibar, it would seem more appropriate to examine one of the "compact theoretical scenes," to cite Remo Bodéi,[6] that is simultaneously a deployment sequence and an "essential section."[7] Recognizing both the extent of this theoretical deployment and the precision of the analytical instrument, I will outline the theoretical scene in which the unceasing movement, by which Balibar returns to the achievements of his own mode of thought to restate in a new and better form that he has already repeatedly interrogated, formulated and reworked, is crystallized.

Our choice – but is it a choice? – is to focus on the articulation of the concept of anthropological difference that first appeared in 2010,[8] and on the notion of equaliberty, the "perfect equivalence of liberty and equality,"[9] in their comprehensive reconceptualization. Balibar's project is indissociable from the tendency he discovers at the heart of the "process of civilization" of the contemporary world or "*Humanitas*." His object here is to bring about the conjunction, not previously seen, of these two notions and to establish a political philosophy potentially capable of thinking the real and evolving relation of the political and the impolitical beyond the old dualist antinomies, in the sense that it is impossible to construct a community or a citizenry without deconstructing it, of the universal and the cultural.[10] On this terrain, Balibar's enterprise, as badly understood as it has been in the more or less recent period, that is, as a voice dissenting from Marxism, or at least less Marxist, nevertheless has continued to develop Marxism and to confer upon it its historical and theoretical reach. At the same time, the openness that he continues to exhibit allows him to borrow conceptual and methodological elements from other established movements of thought and philosophical schools (Althusser, Canguilhem, Arendt, Deleuze, Foucault, Derrida, Negri, Habermas and so forth) as well as from a number of other sources and domains (sociology, psychoanalysis, linguistics and so on).

It is in this way that Balibar, following the thesis of C. Colliot-Thélène, acknowledges that modern political philosophy cannot do without a philosophy of history in which the relation between rationality and Western modernity is produced as an effect.[11] From here, he draws a line of demarcation between tendencies in political philosophy whose multiple stakes are recognizable in the classical categories of community and conflict, right and power, legislation, sovereignty and justice, authority, representation, responsibility and so forth.[12] This is why, as Balibar notes, the merit of the controversies of the second half of the twentieth century is to have reinvented the association between political philosophy and philosophy as such, torn from every metaphysical form of politics by means of such categories as action, judgment, rationality and constitution. This association henceforth projects itself as the reciprocal determination of the meaning of political practice and of human existence or of being in the world. So be it.

But according to what unstated emphasis does the relation between the universal and the anthropological, initially characterized as one of the fundamental questions of political philosophy, come to raise the question of the very basis or essence of philosophy itself? This is what is to be seen in Balibar's philosophico-political inquiry. We cannot be content, however, with a problematization according to which political philosophy presupposes a philosophy of history, which would lead to the risk of seeing it simply as a theory insufficient to itself, and thus in turn contradict the meaning of Balibar's project, even in relation to the analysis of anthropological difference introduced in his work. This is why, in the face of this avowed homogeneity, it remains to be determined in what way anthropology, in spite of its intrinsically philosophical side, contains, if not a philosophical problematic of history and process (*devenir*), at least a logical excess around these questions. The intention here is not to provide a philosophy of history for anthropology, or to construct a meaning for history and for politics, but to attempt to construct on the basis of anthropology a meaning for politics and consequently for history, in the absence of which we would be forced to conclude that from the moment of its emergence anthropology provoked a confrontation with the very universal that would guarantee the future of civilization and that would always and forever complete its mission. We may see in

Philosophy and Politics in Etienne Balibar 185

what way Balibar will attempt to restore – without reducing – the significance of its methodological requirements. This significance in turn makes audible the meaning once expressed by Althusser when he evoked the knot that produced a certain homology between *philosophy* and *politics*, such that, as he said, "all philosophy is therefore *political or* practical: 'ethical.'"[13] However, the articulation of philosophy and politics, that is, the effective transfiguration of philosophy into politics, their relation or rather the "metonymic relay"[14] between them, to use Patrick Tort's expression, is such a problematic point that a number of tropisms have developed, particularly within Marxism, in response. In any case, with the emergence of the concept of anthropological difference, we find ourselves confronting an epistemological and theoretical event within which political philosophy is not only put in perspective, but is placed in a situation of coherent integration with its own conceptual universe.

Thus, Balibar's philosophy has set itself the task of thematically illuminating the anthropological difference of the human from a new point of view insofar as this difference corresponds to the cultural disposition of a being produced by political and social evolution. It is thus around this category that the interpretation of the universal or of universalities will be effectuated. A reading that confuses these two orders in their historical and cultural complexity has little chance of grasping the profound meaning of his work. The theoretical order that Balibar has constructed is intelligible on the condition that the reader succeeds in reconstructing at least the heuristic or problematizing chains that appear in the texts constituting the corpus under consideration in this essay: *Citizen Subject, and other essays in philosophical anthropology*, the *Proposition of Equaliberty*, *Saeculum. Culture, Religion, Ideology*, among other works. This is the wager behind the present reading.

The concept of anthropological difference is the key to Balibar's interpretation of the *continuum*/reversal of modernities. Before approaching its content, let us indicate what is established within it. The formation of a concept that succeeds in radically overturning the interpretations that had up to that point dominated philosophy, assumes in one and the same movement a triple gesture:

- the introduction of a new protocol of reading that is based on the points of heresy, aporia, textual variants and mechanisms of interpellation (originating from afar)[15] that engage

political thought while putting in perspective the entirety of its development;
- the affirmation of the ruptures and rebounds that have occurred in the history of philosophy;
- and finally, as I have noted, the desire for a refoundation of political philosophy.

The concept in question traverses a considerable part of Balibar's corpus, as its recursively critical operation shows. By adopting this approach, he opposes the malicious orientation of a "fractioned rewriting" of the very texts of political philosophy, whose most important consequence was the illegitimate fiction of the doublet universal and particular, or that of cosmopolitanism and secularism.[16] This is why with respect to his project he proposes three directions to take, and, implicitly, as many he wishes to avoid.

1. For him, it is not a matter of simply problematizing the relation between cosmopolitanism and secularism,[17] but also "of discussing its presuppositions and in consequence of *complicating* the way this relation is represented."[18] Is it rather a matter of advancing towards an analytic of the concepts of political philosophy, the very analytic that by defining a new, specific domain as well as by a determination of the instruments that allow it to be analyzed? Everything would seem to indicate that this is the case. From the outset, Balibar has demarcated himself from those who articulate it to an "unfinished" modernity (Habermas) and those who subsume it in a hegemonic Eurocentric discourse.[19]

2. Further, he postulates the principle of a modification of the universal as a reality bearing within itself the effects of different representations as fiction and as ideal.

3. Beyond these markers, he adds as a warning the idea of the relation between the translation and the tradition as a possible means of access to the universal. The language or "idiom" of the philosopher contains within it that with which it compensates the lack of universality.[20] On this subject, he explains that, in part, philosophy "began to go through the systematic examination of the effects of translation in philosophy, and hence also of the 'untranslatable,' and the process of the 'translation of the untranslatable' as a moment of conceptual invention."[21]

Let us continue by following the "philosophical" reasoning and argumentation produced at each of his steps by integrating the problematizing homogeneity of Balibar's reworkings of texts in each case, in order to arrive at *effectively conclusive* statements. He rejects the so-called "abstract universalism" denounced by Joan Scott,[22] which he rejects as "dreadfully abstract and ahistorical."[23] He also points out the contradictions, in particular regarding the respective influences of market equivalence and equality before the law, both of which have the formal characteristic of "impartiality," but that are obviously not addressed to the same type of "subject."[24] He evaluates what he calls the current modalities of the theologico-political complex, in which the religious is reserved for the sphere of the *particular* or particularisms, and the secular, referring to public reason, would take the place of the *universal*.[25] Here the existence of "*conflicts between competing universalisms*" comes to light because of "a generalized relativization."[26] Would this not mean that this conflict recognizes itself as a conflict of particulars, in which case the universal under certain conditions would itself be a particular? Is this not what Hegel called the concrete universal. "a universal . . . that is within itself the particular and the determined"?[27]

Balibar thus approaches the universal/particular opposition as integrated *hic et nunc* into the evolution of the idea of citizenship, from which this opposition takes its contents and their effects in the particular historical context of modernity. According to him, modernity develops as a first and second modernity – the latter by another name, postmodernity – but does so not according to a merely diachronic process, but as a complex entanglement of events and advents that have the potential to introduce decisive reversals. It is precisely the *equality/liberty relation that allows the unfolding of* the order of the two modernities and in this way makes manifest the figures of the universal.

The first modernity[28] can be recognized by two essential traits. First, the *Bestimmung* of history presents itself as a *continuum* in which the so-called symbolic or formal rights are realized, "of which the combination of equality and freedom forms the essence."[29] Then, via the theories of Kant, Fichte and Marx, the representation of "a process that aims to transform the world"[30] takes shape. However, there occurs in Marx, precisely through both the representation and the slogan understood in relation to political practice, a flow in the direction of the meaning of the proposition of equaliberty, which "already moves in the direction of the second, post-revolutionary modernity,[31] and implies a tendential reversal of the relation between the formal and the material, or the symbolic and the real."³² Between the first and second modernities there is a kind of reversion effect that involves a new configuration of the open dynamics between the formal and the material. These developments are decisive for the determination of citizenship, which is gradually wrested from the "universalist tradition dominant in the first modernity and the Enlightenment."³³ In this spirit, the man of the first modernity³⁴ is a "man/citizen" whose status is subsumed under what is called the intensive emancipatory principle based on the idea of a universal right to politics. This means that citizenship, returned to an anthropological level, thus depends on historical conditions that are transformable, even if not directly.

Before going any further, we should note that Balibar makes a distinction that proves decisive in the determination of citizenship: universalism appears in two forms, *extensive* and *intensive*. The first form is the empire of the law, exercised by definition in a space without limits or borders and in which the same principle reigns or the same positive law is exercised. That is to say, this form relies on a state or a state institution. In contrast, the second form is defined "negatively as the *refutation* or *negation* of differences"³⁵ as well as of constraints and the forms of discrimination. It is clear that intensive universalism is on the side of equaliberty. It will act as the antidote to the arbitrariness of political power (tyranny or despotism). It turns every community and every nation into mere groups without any privilege of rank. This is the image of the human community, the ultimate or absolute community, as Balibar describes it.

But this principle of intensive universality, that is, this universal right to politics, this active politics, opens the "right to rights," as prescribed by Arendt. Indeed, it is this level of universality that, in his eyes,

> tends at least virtually to identify man with the citizen, to (re)think man within a horizon of citizenship and political participation that makes him 'autonomous,' master of his own destiny. It makes everyone a 'citizen in power' (*citoyen en puissance*) disqualifying in advance the anthropological difference that, in the ancient city in particular, restricted access to citizenship.³⁶

From this point forward, philosophy enjoys the right to rethink the human in its political dimension. And both philosophy and political philosophy find themselves on the same horizon of intelligibility of modern citizenship.

From this follows certain consequences related to the status of the human. In effect, Balibar notes that the very idea of man produces a movement toward the idea of the citizen contained in the modern dialectic of equality and freedom that is at the core of the revolutionary vocation, as the hope of political movements; equaliberty, this "portmanteau word" demanded by modernity, "has totally transformed our idea of 'man'"[37] The relationship of the man of the first modernity – as potential citizen (*citoyen en puissance*) – to the social norm appears under two modalities: as "a subjective possibility based on interiority and the interiority of the law to self-consciousness, and as an objective possibility based on utilitarianism and the observance of rules and conventions"; these relationships, he adds, determine in turn

> two ways of articulating the individual and society, which have been perceived as antithetical from the Enlightenment up to our own day. But we must immediately note that they are equally universalist, and even more that both carry within them the possibility of an exclusion inscribed at the very core of the principle of inclusion.[38]

In response to the demands of an archaeology of modernity, Balibar evokes concepts that are correlated to the history of political philosophy. What is at stake here is a rethinking – through Locke, Smith, Rousseau, Kant and Tocqueville – of the dualism of "institutional mediations" and the principle of the "constitutionalization" of the rights of man via the state and the market, the political body and civil market society, and their formalization as rights of the citizen. This is also a rethinking of "the anthropological dualism that derives from the tendential opposition between a discourse of *subjectivity* (in the sense of interiority) and a discourse of *individuality* (implying the primacy of a philosophy of exteriority)."[39] This double dualism leads to a reconsideration of the ideas of equaliberty and universal citizenship, and thus, of the status of political universalism. Yet these demands imply "the idea of a 'foundation' for political philosophy, at least to the extent that it has to do with historical figures of emancipation"; the concept of the political is defined here as *emancipation* and not as *transformation*.[40] Its narrative is articulated in two dimensions, simultaneously superimposed and parallel: one is historical and the other is logical. With respect to the first dimension, Balibar establishes the existence of a

> dilemma ... in the modern institution of citizenship, opposing a universalist notion of the citizen (such as is founded on the unconditional declarations of the rights of man) and a materialist notion of social rights (or "social justice"), from which follows the distinction (and generally also the point-by-point opposition) of formal and substantive concepts of freedom and equality.[41]

As for the *logical* dimension, Balibar attributes it "to the anthropological determination of the articulation between subjectivity and community as they are revealed by displacements of the object and objectives of emancipation movements that demand freedom and equality before and after the turning point of modernity."[42] Is the logical dimension the prelude to a second-generation historical dimension? Balibar's demonstration leaves open a horizon of comprehension where the differential anthropological dimension will emerge.

The interrogation of normality seems to lead us there. Normality is, in effect, "the ethical counterpart of any 'majoritarian' conception of politics – especially a democratic politics, made 'by and for the people.'"[43] But in reality, there is an opposition between a *formal* conception and a *material* conception of liberty and equality. Hence the dilemma, or *elenchus* of the simultaneous refutation of two possible "negations" that places us before an impossible choice of "one against the other."[44] Balibar's remarks never lack attention to methodology; his critique of classical philosophy is marked by its precision. Thus, to understand the articulation between society and the state is to "reflect on the 'foundation' of universality."[45] Classical philosophies, as we know, can be distinguished according to "two ways of hierarchically organizing the constitutive relation between society and the state (but also ... their contestation): one that foregrounds the question of *community* and another that foregrounds the question of *property*."[46] The status of the philosophical categories of the subject and the individual is at play here – categories that will condition the passage to new paradigms, announcing the second modernity.

The second (so-called postmodern) modernity constitutes a decisive historical turning point in favor of a social-democratic revolution that can be identified by the emergence of the welfare state or the social state. These historical moments disrupt the political relationships between rights, citizenship and the state, to such an extent that the political side becomes more important than the anthropological side, which "comes after the fact, as a necessary consequence more than in the form of declarations of principles."[47] Hence the persistent tension between the two concepts of politics,[48] the politics of emancipation and the politics of social and institutional transformation. In other words,

- there can be no movement of progress, that is, revolution, due to the classic stability of the alternative of the subject and the individual, as well of that of the concept of activity and the heightened association of the ideas of citizenship and normality.[49] This is why, to put it briefly, Balibar privileges the concept of praxis, as formulated by A. Sen, as capacity for action.[50]
- the principle of "anthropological" exclusion persists. Balibar goes so far as to doubt its effectiveness: "Perhaps in reality the idea of a form of political universality that would be or become absolutely nonexclusive is an anthropological absurdity."[51]

This is why, he believes, that in order to grasp the new meaning of the dialectic of equality and liberty, and the aspects of the transindividual relation that it causes to emerge,[52] we must consider the state, and therefore the necessity of its transformation into a welfare state, preferably democratic, characterized by the practical acknowledgment of social rights, and by a purely political, as well as a social, definition of citizenship. From this point forward, there is a strong relationship between social rights and social citizenship, which calls for them to be analyzed together, from both the historical and theoretical perspectives.[53]

Balibar admits that the concepts of social rights, social citizenship and the welfare state are interdependent and linked to the problematic of justice. The most complex concept among all of these is social citizenship. It is the mediation between the idea, the demand and the definition of social rights, understood as *unconditional*, acting "to be admitted into what we can call, with Claude Lefort, the democratic invention – which is nothing other than a history of the universal – and the constitution of a new type of state."[54] This new state would be different from the one that tends "to conform to the human, as if it were a second nature, by imposing the whole series of anthropological norms,"[55] with the understanding that the limit of humanity is inhumanity, the "only possible way of restricting a universal (or universally human) political capacity from the inside."[56]

Thus, in political modernity, equaliberty is "before and after the rise of the social question at the center of the political space of modern states that aspire to be democratic."[57] From this emerges the *historicity* of the proposition of equaliberty, as well as the refusal of a teleological schema within which Marx is assigned a particular place. This points back to "intensive" universality.[58]

Indeed, in the context of political modernity, where the social question arises, the state is transformed and its services overwhelmed. The relations between individuals, the community and the state are reconstructed to the point that Balibar does not exclude the impossibility of constructing community and citizenship without their deconstruction. And if such a deconstruction were to prove impossible, this would indicate that we are in the impolitical. We can thus see that Balibar is in search of other, radically new openings and access points, that is, politics from a new point of view. And this is where he situates the precise place from which to articulate the "question concerning politics with a question concerning anthropology."[59] In what way? He sees it in the comparison of the status of anthropological difference

> before and after the invention of universal citizenship as social citizenship, and thus before and after the formulation of the norms of natural humanity and social norms that draw a line of demarcation between the human and the inhuman, social being and asocial or desocialized being, in order to deduce from it the conditions of active citizenship or effective participation in politics.[60]

To this effect, he appeals to the concept of *paideia* in order to explain that it is a process of civilization and emancipation that demands the complementarity of public space (*polis*) and private space (*oikos*), while, in postmodernity, anthropological differences are "heterotopical" (to use Foucault's term), "never really localizable or territorialized, confinable within boundaries, within simply dichotomous spaces."[61] Their ontological reality has "the disturbing (but fundamental) trait that *one cannot elude them (or deny their reality), nor fix them in a stable, univocal, or incontestable fashion.*"[62] Once again, insists Balibar, we must be aware that postmodern anthropological differences are characterized by a "permanent *double bind*" in their relation to citizenship, by virtue of their ambiguity and deterritorialization.

Through the clarity of his demonstration, Balibar develops a manner of thinking that is capable of producing essential elements of the theorization of the evolution of politics. He does so through a reflection on citizenship as the reign of politics, by definition opposed to the hegemony of state institutions,[63] in which it (citizenship) is defined by obedience to the law. In this privileged theoretical scene, anthropological differences play a decisive role. Nevertheless, let us return to the procedure that led to their breakthrough and significance. Referring to general or philosophical anthropology, he sets out both to elucidate and to move beyond a certain tautology in order to say "that it is a matter of the human and its own variability."[64] To indicate this, he takes the counter-position of difference through recourse to the concept of *anthropological difference* and the way in which it has been constructed and has varied historically: "throughout history, 'man' is never the same – except, perhaps, as a biological *species*."[65] The concept of difference refers back to the continual tension between a recognition in fact that takes the form of exclusion and a de jure recognition that is always to come in the form of rights. However, it can become, through a "'performative reversal,' the slogan of a demand for rights, dignity, or recognition, whose political modality remains, by definition, problematic."[66] In an allusion to the work of Foucault, Balibar lists

> not only sexual difference as differences between gender and sexuality, the "bio-social" difference between the "normal" and the "pathological," or health, and physical as well as mental, illness, the difference between the upstanding person and the criminal and, further, the differences of these differences (like that of the madman and the criminal), but also "cultural" differences that have to do with the opposition between mind and body, manual (or physical) and intellectual competences, oral and written cognitive competences, etc., the division between ethnic or ethno-religious cultures, communitarian models of identification in Georges Devereux's sense, and so on.[67]

Political thought finds itself weighed down by the various minorities, "defined by culture, sexuality, administrative status, but also by biological or biopolitical difference."[68] The emergence of anthropological differences outlines and regulates political space differently. There, a "majority" politics, inherent in the democratic tradition, and a "minority" politics are articulated at the point of emergence of new forms of transindividuality, even if they do not transgress *norms* in the construction of community and even if what he calls a "renunciation of the universal" does not take place. He sees in it "on the contrary, ... (even if the expression is paradoxical) a supplement of universality that corresponds to the incorporation of differences and singularities in the very construction of the universal."[69] That, in other words, articulates the *norm* and the *exception,* the *universal* and *singularities,* although this combination "is precisely 'impossible,' that is, affected by its contrary in its very realization."[70] As a result, the antagonism that must insure them an unprecedented and politically active ontological status is organized. In a projection towards a future that is in part by definition unknown and unpredictable, their task is to demand "'negative' rights or liberties, that is, the abolition of certain incapacities or repressive constraints" and to demand "the possibility of contributing to a recasting of the political."[71]

To conclude, let us remember that the history of citizenship is as open as the history of equaliberty. He will recall this later by indicating the correlation between historical mutation and the effect in its change of content:

> *The whole* of its institution inevitably ends up being put back into play, and that presents itself to us in a paradoxical form, because we struggle to imagine the new (and therefore, to invent it) in the very language of the old.[72]

This is the entire paradox of the emergence of the new in the old that Balibar brings to light. Is this not the paradox of creation? And yet, is it in the form of conflict that creation must occur? It would seem that he has offered the elements of a theorization capable of incorporating at the very least the modalities put to work by philosophy – a philosophy that "is never independent of determinate conjunctures," determined in the

> qualitative and not quantitative sense, as it connotes the event – whether very brief or prolonged – of a crisis, a transition, a suspension, a bifurcation, and that is expressed by its irreversibility, that is to say, by the impossibility of acting and thinking like before.[73]

Conjuncture and texts unite and from the effects of their complex intersection comes the particular form of thought that elucidates some contemporary questions, such as citizenship or universality, the concept of which bears the weight of both the conceptual heritage and the conjuncture.

Pursuing his reflections, Balibar notes the cosmo-political nature of a conflict that originated in a religious or theological difference, leading him to conclude that the *cosmopolitanism* of the ancient or classical philosophical tradition, and *cosmopolitics*, overdetermined by globalization, although similar, cannot exist simply as an idea and its application or practical translation.[74] The relation of cosmopolitics to cosmopolitanism cannot be a relation of negation. On the contrary, it must become a relation of reference:

> Contemporary *cosmopolitics is a particularly equivocal form of politics;* it is made up of nothing but conflicts between universalities without a pre-given solution ... It would be more accurate to say that it opens the entire field of competition between *incompatible cosmopolitanisms*.[75]

He adds that these conflicts "do not exist in opposition to *particularisms* (in which case the solution would consist of either separating them under the aegis of a superior, transcendent universality, or progressively integrating them into some syncretic civilization), but instead sets *incompatible universalisms*" against each other.[76] Thus, he puts himself in a difficult position when he returns to the central "turning point" of *Phenomenology*, that

> long investigation of the possibility of *universalizing being in common* and, correlatively, of *instituting the universal* in the framework and modality of a community, of which the "historical" (or, as we would say today, "cultural") figures that it then reconstructs represent so many attempts at realization.[77]

In order for the (moral, juridical, religious, political, pedagogical, scientific) universal to become concrete, this double movement abandons "utopia or pure ideality," on the condition that "the community possesses in itself a *power of unification* capable of transcending the differences and conflicts that it subsumes, not by rejecting them outside of itself, but by 'reflecting' them as *its* differences."[78] Does the meaning of this projection derive from a stochastic effect? Indeed, the orientation can be exposed to what Balibar calls the "singularity effect" due to "a sort of tragic destiny of communities":

> [T[he moment at which they come closest to instituting universality, that is, to inventing a historical language or original culture for the universal (for example the "law" for the city, or the intelligence of the Enlightenment and critical reason, or the moral, "Protestant," vision of the world) – is also the moment at which they demonstrate once again their particularity or their finitude as the reverse side of their pretention to universality, the mark of its internal contradictions, which can lead to collapse.[79]

Does this mean that particularity – the promise and the reverse side of universality in certain conditions, if it is prevented from becoming universal – can be reduced to a specificity whose essence resists its future, or resists what its future will have been? This is the question that Balibar poses and asks us to consider. The future of revolution must be rethought in this light.

Notes

1. Etienne Balibar, *La proposition de l'égaliberté. Essais politiques 1989–2009* (Paris: Presses Universitaires de France, 2012), 9.
2. It is not possible to characterize his relations with Louis Althusser in a few words. Beyond his Althusserian theoretical "unconscious" now largely on the surface, Balibar has come to be inspired by Althusser's thought in the same way as he has been inspired by other teachers.
3. Balibar, *La proposition de l'égaliberté*, 128; emphasis in the original.
4. Ibid. 8, 12.
5. Ibid. 201.
6. Cited in Etienne Balibar, *La philosophie au XXe* (Paris: Flammarion, 1999), 7.
7. Althusser defined the essential section as "an intellectual operation ... a vertical cut in the present such that all the elements of the whole revealed by this cut are in an immediate relation which immediately express their internal essence." Louis Althusser, *Lire le Capital*, Vol. I (Paris: Maspéro, 1968), 116.
8. *L'introuvable humanité du sujet moderne: L'universalité "civique-bourgeoise" et la question des différences anthropologiques,*

in *L'Homme*, Juillet/Décembre 2012, n° 203-2040; to situate the elaboration of this concept, see *Citoyen Sujet et autres essais d'anthropologie philosophique* (Paris: Presses Universitaires de France, 2011), 465, note 2, and Etienne Balibar, *Saeculum. Culture, religion, idéologie* (Paris: Galilée, 2012), 81, note 1.

9. *La proposition de l'égaliberté*, 151.
10. *Mutatis mutandis*, this confrontation is in many ways comparable to that alluded to by Merleau-Ponty when he invoked the exchange between Husserl et Lévy-Bruhl in 1935: "He (Husserl) seems to admit here that the philosopher cannot immediately arrive at universality based on simple reflection and that he is neither in a position to move beyond anthropological experience, nor to construct through a merely imaginary variation on his own experiences, that which constitutes the meaning of other civilizations." Maurice Merleau-Ponty, *Éloge de la philosophie* (Paris: Gallimard, 1960), 132.
11. *La proposition de l'égaliberté*, 168. In relation to this conception of political philosophy, Balibar will underscore the necessity of the critique of historicism and evolutionism.
12. Ibid. 169.
13. Cité par F. Matheron, *Des problèmes qu'il faudra bien appeler d'un autre nom*, in L. Althusser, *Machiavel et nous* (Paris: Tallandier, 2009), 198; emphasis in the original.
14. Patrick Tort, *La raison classificatoire. Quinze Etudes* (Paris: Aubier Montaigne, 1989), 11. It is necessary to specify that the notion of metaphor refers to similarity and resemblance, while metonymy refers to connectivity, that is, contiguity, association and geneaology.
15. *Citoyen Sujet et autres essais d'anthropologie philosophique*, 21.
16. Cosmopolitanism and secularism, he notes, "are two aspects of a project of the *democraticization of democraticization*" (*Saeculum. Culture, religion, idéologie*, 19; emphasis in the original); Etienne Balibar, "The Antinomy of Citizenship," in *Equaliberty: Political Essays*, trans. James Ingram (Durham, NC: Duke University Press, 2014), 1–32.
17. Balibar, *Saeculum. Culture, religion, idéologie*, 14.
18. Ibid. 14.
19. Ibid. 14.
20. He also writes of an "excess of universality," 60.
21. Ibid. 21; on this subject, see his contributions in Barbara Cassin, ed., *Vocabulaire européen des philosophies. Dictionnaire des intraduisibles* (Paris: Le Seuil-Le Robert, 2004); B. Cassin, ed., *Philosopher en langues. Les intraduisibles en traduction* (Paris: Les Editions

Rue d'Ulm, 2014); Barbara Cassin and Daniele Wozny, eds, *Les intraduisibles. Du patrimoine en Afrique subsaharienne* (Paris: Demopolis, 2014).
22. Joan Wallach Scott, *The Politics of the Veil* (Princeton: Princeton University Press, 2007).
23. *Saeculum. Culture, religion, idéologie*, 30; Balibar recalls that it is the "very notion of abstraction that is, without a doubt, equivocal, and this cannot help but reverberate in what is understood, in return, by 'difference' (in particular by implying that differences are always or somewhat 'concrete')" (31).
24. Ibid. 30; *Citoyen Sujet et autres essais d'anthropologie philosophique*, 286, 287, 327. For Marx, he notes, universality is an exclusion (328).
25. *Saeculum. Culture, religion, idéologie*, 42. Balibar borrows the expression from Judith Butler (her contribution in E. Laclau and S. Žižek, *Contingency, Hegemony, Universality. Contemporary Dialogues on the Left* (London: Verso, 2000), 11–43).
26. *Saeculum. Culture, religion, idéologie*, 42; emphasis in the original.
27. Georg Wilheim Friedrich Hegel, *Lectures on the History of Philosophy*, trans. E. S. Haldane (Lincoln: University of Nebraska Press, 1995), 24.
28. *Equaliberty*, 105; he calls "first modernity (before and during the bourgeois revolutions, which are themselves designated as insurrections of the rights of man, made by *insurgés* – in English 'insurgents,' in Spanish, *insurgentes*) the moment when the idea of citizenship stopped referring to a closed, privileged status and for the first time in history was related to the principle of a universal right to political participation" (105–6).
29. Ibid. 104.
30. Ibid. 104.
31. The second modernity is "where the problem of citizenship appears inseparable from claims for social justice, and consequently from an infinite dialectic of universality and practice, or of social transformation, in which equality tends to appear as a historical construction rather than a given, and freedom as a material conquest rather than a principle" (110.); as for the postmodern problematic of citizenship, it is "a problematic that designates the contingent or aleatory future of modernity" due to the renewed existence of "anthropological differences" (127); it is "to-come (*à venir*)" after modernity, "which in a certain way is always already there" (ibid.).

32. Ibid. 104.
33. Ibid. 104.
34. Ibid. 109.
35. Ibid. 106 (translation modified); emphasis in the original.
36. Ibid. 106 (translation modified).
37. Ibid. 99.
38. Ibid. 109.
39. Ibid. 107 (translation modified); emphasis in the original.
40. Ibid. 100.
41. Ibid. 100.
42. Ibid. 101.
43. Ibid. 101.
44. Ibid. 101.
45. Ibid. 107.
46. Ibid. 108; emphasis in the original.
47. Ibid. 122.
48. Ibid. 118.
49. Ibid. 118.
50. Ibid. 122.
51. Ibid. 124.
52. Ibid. 111.
53. Ibid. 111, 121.
54. Ibid. 113; furthermore, he specifies, "The decisive fact in this regard seems ... to be that the state we are dealing with here is always already a *national* state" (113; emphasis in the original).
55. Ibid. 117 (translation modified).
56. Ibid. 121.
57. Ibid. 120.
58. Ibid. 123.
59. Ibid. 126.
60. Ibid. 126.
61. L. Robin has already pointed out the difficulty of fully rendering the meaning of *paideia* in French: neither civilization, nor culture, nor education, nor tradition; however, he warns: "The Ancients believed that education and culture were as one with the objective, historical structure of the spiritual life of a people – a spiritual life of which literature is the highest form of expression" (*Critique* 15–16, 1947, Paris, 199, cited by V. De Magalhaes-Vilhena, *Socrate et la légende platonicienne* (Paris: Presses Universitaires de France, 1952) 9, note 1).
62. *Saeculum. Culture, religion, idéologie,* 79; emphasis in the original.

63. On this subject, it is useful to point out the conclusion of his *Spinoza and Politics*, where he notes that "the theory of the 'body politic' is neither a straightforward 'physics' of power, nor a method for formalising a juridical order, but the search for a strategy of collective liberation, whose guiding motto would be *as many as possible, thinking as much as possible* (*Ethics*, VP5–10)" (trans. Peter Snowdon, 98; emphasis added).
64. *Saeculum. Culture, religion, idéologie*, 79.
65. Ibid. 79; emphasis in the original.
66. *Citoyen Sujet et autres essais d'anthropologie philosophique*, 467.
67. *Equaliberty*, 128.
68. Ibid. 126.
69. Ibid. 131.
70. Ibid. 126.
71. Ibid. 127.
72. *Saeculum. Culture, religion, idéologie*, 18; emphasis in the original.
73. *Citoyen Sujet et autres essais d'anthropologie philosophique*, 19.
74. *Saeculum. Culture, religion, idéologie*, 98; the works of R. Bastide and M. Leiris on an anthropology of "contacts of/between civilizations" (see translation "thus a disidentification that is at least virtual, able to go as far as 'double conscience'" (46)).
75. *Saeculum. Culture, religion, idéologie*, 43; emphasis in the original.
76. *Saeculum. Culture, religion, idéologie*, 48, 95; emphasis in the original.
77. Etienne Balibar, "*Zur 'Sache selbst'. Du commun et de l'universel* dans la *Phénoménologie* de Hegel," Savoirs, Textes, Langage, Université de Lille, <http://stl.recherche.univ-lille3.fr/textesenligne/auteursdivers/2007balibarHegel.html> (accessed November 2, 2015).
78. *Citoyen Sujet et autres essais d'anthropologie philosophique*, 278; emphasis in the original.
79. Ibid. 280.

Bibliography

Althusser, Louis. *Lire le Capital*. Vol. I. Paris: Maspéro, 1968.
Althusser, Louis and Etienne Balibar. *Reading Capital*. Trans. Ben Brewster. London: Verso, 1997.
Balibar, Etienne. *Spinoza and Politics*. Trans. Peter Snowdon. London: Verso, 1998.
Balibar, Etienne. *Citoyen Sujet et autres essais d'anthropologie philosophique*. Paris: Presses Universitaires de France, 2011.

Bailbar, Etienne. "L'introuvable humanité du sujet moderne: L'universalité 'civique-bourgeoise' et la question des différences anthropologiques." *L'Homme* 203-4 (2012): 19-50.

Balibar, Etienne. *La proposition de l'égaliberté. Essais politiques 1989-2009*, Paris: Presses Universitaires de France, 2012.

Balibar, Etienne. *Saeculum. Culture, religion, idéologie*. Paris: Galilée, 2012.

Balibar, Etienne. "The Modern Subject's Humanity Cannot Be Found: Universality of 'Civic Bourgeois' and the Question of Anthropological Differences." *L'Homme*, 3 (2012): 19-50.

Balibar, Etienne. *Equaliberty: Political Essays*. Trans. James Ingram. Durham, NC: Duke University Press, 2014.

Balibar, Etienne. "The Antinomy of Citizenship." In *Equaliberty: Political Essays*. Trans. James Ingram. Durham, NC: Duke University Press, 2014. Pp. 1-32.

Balibar, Etienne. *Violence and Civility: On The Limits of Political Philosophy*. Trans. G. M. Goshgarian. New York: Columbia University Press, 2015.

Balibar, Etienne. "Zur 'Sache selbst'. Du commun et de l'universel dans la *Phénoménologie* de Hegel." <http://stl.recherche.univ-lille3.fr/textesenligne/auteursdivers/2007balibarHegel.html> (accessed November 2, 2015).

Balibar, Etienne. *Citizen Subject: Foundations for Philosophical Anthropology*. Trans. Steven Miller. Oxford: Oxford University Press, 2016.

Bodei, Remo. *La philosophie au XXe*. Paris: Flammarion, 1999.

Cassin, Barbara and Daniele Wozny. *Les intraduisibles. Du patrimoine en Afrique subsaharienne*. Paris: Demopolis, 2014.

Barbara Cassin, ed. *Vocabulaire européen des philosophies. Dictionnaire des intraduisibles*. Paris: Le Seuil-Le Robert, 2004.

Cassin, Barbara, ed. *Dictionary of Untranslatables: A Philosophical Lexicon*. Trans. and ed. Emily Apter, Jacques Lezra and Michael Wood. Princeton: Princeton University Press, 2014.

Cassin, Barbara, ed. *Philosopher en langues. Les intraduisibles en traduction*. Paris: Les Editions Rue d'Ulm, 2014.

De Magalhaes-Vilhena, V. *Socrate et la légende platonicienne*. Paris: Presses Universitaires de France, 1952.

Hegel, Georg Wilheim Friedrich. *Lectures on the History of Philosophy*. Trans. E. S. Haldane. Lincoln: University of Nebraska Press, 1995.

Laclau, E. and Žižek, S. *Contingency, Hegemony, Universality. Contemporary Dialogues on the Left*. London: Verso, 2000.

Legendre, Pierre. *Tour du monde des concepts*. Paris: Fayard, 2013.
Matheron Francois. "Des problèmes qu'il faudra bien appeler d'un autre nom." In L. Althusser, *Machiavel et nous*. Paris: Tallandier, 2009.
Matheron Francois. "Des problèmes qu'il faudra bien appeler d'un autre nom." *Multitudes*, 22 (2009): 21–35.
Merleau-Ponty, Maurice. *Éloge de la philosophie*. Paris: Gallimard, 1960.
Merleau-Ponty, Maurice. *In Praise of Philosophy and Other Essays*. Trans. John O'Neill. Evanston: Northwestern University Press, 1988.
Robbins, Bruce and Pheng Cheh, ed. *Cosmopolitics: Thinking and Feeling beyond the Nation*. Minneapolis: University of Minnesota Press, 1998.
Scott, Joan Wallach. *The Politics of the Veil*. Princeton: Princeton University Press, 2007.
Tassin, Etienne. *Un monde commun. Pour une cosmo-politique des conflits*. Paris: Seuil, 2003.
Tort, Patrick. *La raison classificatoire. Quinze Etudes*. Paris: Aubier Montaigne, 1989.

7

Balibar and the Philosophy of Science: The Question of the "Epistemological Break"

Giorgos Fourtounis

In what follows I will discuss Etienne Balibar's return, in a series of seemingly untimely articles,[1] to a project of which he once was a protagonist and that at the time appeared outdated. I refer to Althusserianism's epistemological project, that is, the project of developing an epistemological discourse on science,[2] adequate to what I will call *the epistemological claim of Marxism*, namely the rather provocative contention that Marxism is or, better, should become what it is: the science of the theoretical object that it alone had elaborated and defined, the social and the historical, responsible for and capable of producing all the relevant objective knowledge. The circumstances could not be more unfavorable: the project in question was by then generally perceived as a "degenerating program"[3] and was either tacitly dismissed or openly denounced. This occurred not only as an effect of the crisis of Marxism, but was also due to the spreading skepticism, connected to the rise of post-Kuhnian Science Studies, concerning the sustainability of epistemological difference in general, that is, of science's positive distinction in terms of objectivity and rationality, or of science's *asymmetry* regarding other kinds of "belief systems." At that time, at the height of the Science Wars, when the only possible defense of science's objectivity against the assault of Science Studies was coming from mainstream philosophy of science (whose tenets Balibar decisively rejected), those articles risked appearing outmoded or even reactionary. Taken together, though, they constitute one of the longest, most systematic and thoroughly developed accounts of the singular epistemology involved in the work of the group around Althusser. But Balibar does not simply furnish a summary of this project; more importantly, he reflects upon it anew by returning to what is unthought in it in order to determine the extent to which it may continue to help us think about the inescapable problems that surround the notion of science.

I

But in what way would the epistemology in question be adequate to this bizarre claim that Marxism is the science of the social and the historical? What is the nature of this peculiar "premise," which is stated as a *thesis*, aspiring to announce a *fact*? It is obviously a very provocative and even paradoxical thesis. Most critics would immediately reject it as outrageous, while the most charitable ones would accept it not as a thesis but as *a hypo-thesis* to be philosophically or epistemologically judged, a conjecture to be theoretically proved or refuted. In other words, it could be accepted not in the affirmative but in the interrogative, as a question to be answered by the sole legitimate "authority," one that would have previously and independently established what science is, a concept or *essence of science*.

But for the Althusserians' epistemological project, and here is its most provocative and counter-intuitive point, this precisely is *not* the case: for them, Marxism's epistemological claim can function epistemologically *only as a thesis*. If it is to contribute to the development of a distinct epistemology, it must itself be posited as a non-negotiable, that is, necessary, thesis. In other words, this thesis does not take the form of a *question*, whether explicit or implicit, to be answered by an unprejudiced epistemology. A major premise of the whole project is that Marxism's objectivity is not to be established through a license granted by the philosophy of science, and thus it is not submitted to a *judgment* that would operate by subsuming Marxism under a general concept of science produced in turn by a philosophy external to it. Hence, the rather scandalous reversal of the "obviously" legitimate relation to an epistemology: here *the epistemology is subordinated to the thesis*, and not the (hypo)thesis to the epistemology. As scandalous as that may be, it draws upon the epistemology of Gaston Bachelard, for whom the validity and scientific character of *every* science does not depend on such an epistemological judgment; as Balibar argues,

> Bachelard's epistemology breaks with the idealism of all "theory of knowledge" in that for it the objectivity of scientific knowledge *is not*

a problem. Objectivity is not the name of a "critical" questioning followed by the reassurance of a fictitious "guarantee". Rather it is *posed* initially, as a fact, not a simple fact but one which is not to be doubted of.[4]

At the same time, Balibar adds, this encounter with Bachelard's position "reinforces the [latter's] materialist element" by extending it to "a domain of objectivity which Bachelard in no way envisaged,"[5] liberating it from "the idealist tendency linked with the privilege of mathematics and mathematical physics" and thus recognizing the irreducible plurality of the scientific. This represents a peculiar generalization of the epistemological claim, this time in relation to the existence of the sciences: there is (objective) scientific knowledge, there are sciences or, more precisely, the existing sciences are sciences. The tautological aspect of this affirmation signals the fact that nothing here, neither the existence nor the scientificity of the sciences, depends on a theoretical guarantee furnished by an epistemology. The existence of the sciences as sciences is not subordinated to an essence of science. The existing sciences are not posited as merely instantiations of science, in the singular. Instead, what is essential is the irreducible plurality of the sciences, which in turn implies as its corollary (as we shall see in more detail) the similarly essential singularity of each science. The result is that there can be no hierarchy among the sciences: none is closer to some archetype of science, none is more scientific than the others; there can be no meaningful distinction between "hard," rigorous or demonstrative sciences and "sciences" that are less so.[6] Specifically, Marxism, as "social science" (or, according to its own epistemological claim, the social science), is neither less scientific nor scientific in another, different, sense than they: all are equally sciences even in their singularity; let us say that they are all sciences in the same sense and in the same way.

Therefore, if this many-sided thesis necessitates an epistemology, it must be a *materialist, non-essentialist* one, in which all existing sciences are equally and univocally sciences. This does not entail a kind of epistemological egalitarianism of "discourse formations"; on the contrary, this epistemology is constitutively obliged to assert the *epistemological difference* between science and non-science. The question then is how this difference does not re-introduce essentialism; how to speak of "the same way" or "the same sense," in which all existing sciences are sciences, does not make them instantiations of a unitary concept. Anticipating what follows, we may advance a seeming paradox: the common way in which the existing sciences are equally and univocally sciences consists in the fact that every science is a science in its own way. The peculiar generality of this position, which disturbs the logic of the subordination of the particular to the general, is (as we shall see) in keeping with the similarly paradoxical concept of the "epistemological break," itself necessary to any philosophical discourse capable of articulating Marxism's epistemological claim.

2

What we have called a materialist epistemology must, in opposition to any essentialism, confront the topic of the *history* of science; as Balibar notes, opposition to idealist philosophies of science forces us to confront

> the whole tradition which flounders interminably in the obvious incompatibility between the idea of an objectivity of sciences (hence the idea of a truth in their results) and the idea of their *historicity* (hence the idea of the "relativity" of their results, theories, concepts and givens of fact).[7]

We may add that this supposed incompatibility emerges when the idea of incommensurability is introduced into the history of science in contrast to the representation of commensurable progress, according to which historically limited scientific results can be considered as precursors of subsequent results – a notion of "history" that essentialist philosophy of science can accommodate, as in the case of the "unified discipline" of the History and Philosophy of Science (HPS).

Of particular importance is the controversy between HPS and post-Kuhnian Science Studies, which in turn led to the so-called Science Wars. To summarize the terms and stakes of this conflict succinctly, we may say that mainstream philosophy of science can only think of a concept of "normal science" in the singular, as the normative exemplar of universal scientific rationality, the transcendent norm of science along with the epistemological criteria of the distinction between science and non-science. Here, history of science can only mean the continuous and cumulative succession of the commensurable accomplishments of scientific rationality and, at the same time, the uninterrupted, evolutionary genealogy of scientific truths. Kuhn's intervention undermined this idea and posited "normal science" in the plural, as distinct normal sciences, each one guided by its own "paradigm": this produced a plurality of scientific "normalities," partial or local structures of rationality, not themselves rationally related, non-totalizable and irreducible – in a word, incommensurable. Thus, a non-normative, non-epistemological notion emerges: the normality of science is reducible to contingent facts (sociological, psychological, anthropological and so forth), susceptible to an exhaustively descriptive account. The notion of incommensurability implies in turn the idea of discontinuity in the development of science: there is no normal way to pass from a normal science to another. Despite the title of Kuhn's book, scientific revolution is a non-structured instance between structures, a revolutionary incident between essentially conservative regimes.

Thus, in its Kuhnian conceptualization, incommensurability is understood as an essentially symmetrical relation (or non-relation): a "two-way" incommensurability, a relation that is in principle reversible. Different formations, then, are symmetrically incommensurable, that is, mutually incommensurable. This symmetrical understanding has been subsequently generalized and radicalized by Science Studies, which seems to complete Kuhn's anti-essentialist move towards a nominalist stance: the term "science," instead of an essence, or a concept with definable meaning, is reduced to a simple name or title, which can sustain only the epistemological fallacy of renaming incommensurable differences in terms of the now untenable opposition of scientific and non-scientific. This development has been condensed into the principle of symmetry, the very symbol of faith of Science Studies, based on Kuhnian symmetrical incommensurability, the radical absence of any rational and normative context for what are now conceived as "belief systems," "discourse formations" and so forth, which makes them all epistemologically equivalent.

This descriptive stance towards the scientific phenomenon was from the start interwoven with the critique of continuist "philosophical" historiography as reconstruction of what is, in principle, a timeless rational development, a *retrospective* teleology of truth, an anachronistic projection of today's science to a fictitious past, the past that in an imaginary way explains and justifies the scientific present. As Pierre Macherey has put it, "this history is obviously false; but what is more, *it is not even a history.*"⁸ In contrast, Kuhnian and post-Kuhnian approaches tend to a non-normative, non-epistemological historiography of the phenomenon of science; the concept of incommensurability, along with the principle of symmetry, writes the history of science in a non-anachronistic way, that is, not from the perspective of today's science that looks back in order to select the past that does justice to itself. This seems to comply with the methodological standards of any adequate historiography, claiming the past "for itself," and thus to be genuinely historical. Nevertheless, the rational void between incommensurable formations and the epistemological abstinence that this incommensurability entails, makes this historiography incapable of providing the criterion to determine which of these formations belong to the history of the same "science" or even of science in general. Despite its historiographical credentials, the past and the history it constructs are neither the history of any actually existing and particular science, nor of science *tout court.*

In other words, post-Kuhnian Science Studies, with their symmetrical notion of incommensurability, share with their opponent, History and Philosophy of Science, the essentialist notion of the incompatibility of science and history. Neither side of the Science Wars can think the history of science, properly speaking: in the case of commensurable continuity, there is only a "history of science" that is not history; in the case of incommensurable discontinuity, there is a "history of science" that it is not a history of science. Both fail to answer the two crucial questions that Canguilhem posed regarding science's historicity: first, what is the history of science a history of?⁹ And, second: is past science a past for today's science?¹⁰ As is often the case, this systematic opposition is organized around a shared tacit assumption, which allows continuous, commensurable historiography to be epistemological but forbids it to be historical, and discontinuous, incommensurable historiography to be historical but forbids it to be epistemological: the assumption that incommensurability can only be symmetrical incommensurability, or that epistemological asymmetry and difference can only be possible at the cost of abandoning incommensurability altogether.

It is precisely around these points that Balibar's epistemological writings, produced as the Althusserian project was in steep decline and the Science Wars were at their height, represent a rethinking of the materialist, anti-essentialist epistemology required by

Marxism's epistemological claim. Balibar shows that such an epistemology not only escapes the dilemma described above, but (registering itself in Bachelard's and Canguilhem's tradition of historical epistemology, correlated with an epistemological history) it constructs its central category, the epistemological break, in terms of a non-Kuhnian, non-symmetrical incommensurability. Thus, it is in a position to think epistemologically the history of science, including the emergence and the always precarious development of an individual science.

3

Referring to an unpublished text by François Regnault, Balibar writes that the break represents "a mutation in the order of knowledge (savoir)," an event with "a before and an after," so that we can "fix a date which interrupts continuity."[11] Thus, Balibar associates the break with the category of discontinuity, though often he warns that it is not a "simple" discontinuity. The question of incommensurability remains unsettled in the writing of this period: sometimes he refuses to attribute it to the break, while other times he describes the break in terms of *Kuhnian* incommensurability, as "the development of a fissure within language between two linguistic universes without communication nor translation."[12] By analyzing these ambiguities, I will show that Balibar's epistemology involves both incommensurability and discontinuity, but in a non-Kuhnian sense.

For Balibar, the epistemological break is primarily the *event* of the emergence of "a new scientific problematic," interweaving "concepts without precedents,"[13] a new conceptual structure[14] and norm of rationality. The break thus brings together *novelty* and *scientificity*: within a theoretical or discursive field, scientificity is the condition of novelty, and *vice versa*. The new problematic is irreducible to each one of the pre-existing theoretical traditions or discursive formations, but also to the field that *all* of them constituted, even in their rivalry; the break cannot be reduced to the type of ruptures characteristic of science's pre-history: "the break is a rupture with those ruptures: it makes us see what they always presupposed without ever questioning it."[15]

This leads to what is perhaps the more recognizable and controversial theme of Althusserian epistemology: science's "other," both its inescapable ground and its obstacle, is associated with the Marxist concept of *ideology*. Pre-scientific ruptures are "intra-ideological" ruptures.[16] What they presupposed and what structured the relevant discursive field is an ideological problematic. I cannot dwell on this here; let me just say that the pre-scientific field is determined as ideological by a structure of *obviousness* (Balibar uses the plural: *évidences*[17]), which remains unthematized, while governing what these theoretical discourses thematize, the invisible condition of what is "spontaneously" and unproblematically offered in vision. The break with the pre-scientific ideological field, then, is a "rupture with obviousness."[18]

What determines the philosophical meaning of all of the above, the most distinctive characteristic of the break as an event, which complicates its temporality of a "before" and an "after," is the crucial category of Balibar's epistemology: the "epistemological recurrence, which distinguishes after the fact (*après coup*) truth and error, science and non-science."[19] The break is a "recurrent process," meaning that it "repeats itself and returns to its own past."[20]

Let us start with the latter point. How are we to understand this "return to the past," this "after the fact" *epistemological* distinction of true and false? To start with, it does *not* refer to an epistemological fallacy, to the *simple* passage from one theoretical landscape to another and the biased, merely *retrospective* distribution of the values of false (to the past) and true (to the present). On the other hand, neither is it the *retrospective* recognition, enabled by present truth, of something that was already there as such, namely the falsity of the past. The common presupposition of those two schemes of retrospection is that past and present are assumed to be in principle identifiable and in possession of their epistemological value independently of their retrospective distinction: they are true or false, or neither (just incommensurable), *in themselves*.

In opposition, for Balibar *there is* true and false, scientific and non-scientific, but *not* before or independently of the break that separates them. The identity and the epistemological value of past and present depend on the "instance" that separates them. Present true and past false are not such *in themselves*; their distinction, the break itself, is *active*: the epistemological distinction produces the terms it opposes. The scientific and the non-scientific are effects of the break. The recurrence that characterizes it is not just retrospective (despite Balibar's sporadic use of the word), but retroactive.

Hence, while the break can be represented also in terms of spatial metaphors, such as the crossing of a border or the shifting of terrains,[21] nevertheless, none of the "*loci*" involved can be thought of as in principle pre-existent to the passage between them. "The break is not the simple fact of discontinuity or incommensurability between problematics, between discursive formations, which would then be definable in themselves, each on its own."[22] On the contrary, the break is a peculiar transition that determines the "places" involved, a crossing that produces both the border and the realms that it separates.

Thus, it is the break that determines what it "breaks" with, which of the traditions and norms of the past form the field in which it takes place. Paraphrasing Canguilhem, the break selects and structures, out of the past of science, the *science's past*, its "pre-history." But, what is more, this retroactive delimitation of the science's past is *epistemological* in character: the relevance of the past "elements" as pre-scientific amounts to their disqualification as non-scientific; determining the science's past, the break determines – and devaluates as false – *science*'s ideology, the ideology proper and relevant to it. There is no question here of a disclosure or unearthing of ideology *as such*, which would be false *in itself*; ideology cannot be indentified with error or false, which would substantialize both. Thus, the pre-scientific is "ideology from the view point of science";[23] nothing is in itself *distinctively* ideological; being ideological is not an essential quality, capable of demarcating what is in itself ideological. Or, from another angle, everything is ideological; ideology is everywhere (including within science, as we shall see shortly). By the same token, nothing is false as such, but only in its constitutive relation with the true that is also its true, that is, it is false by and through a break: according to Balibar, each one of the pre-scientific "errors" that are "assigned in a recurrent manner . . . is an error in relation to a well determined scientific truth; none represents the error in itself."[24] This, at the same time, is the counterpart of the emergence and confirmation of the scientific as true; the true is produced by that peculiar transition to it: "[a science's] problematic is constructed in and by the break."[25] The scientific problematic is not in principle independent of the break; the break is not incidental to the emergent science. The scientific terrain was not "there," awaiting its discovery.

So, the individuation and epistemological distinction between the scientific and the non-scientific are *relational*: it is their relation, the break itself, which determines them. As Balibar points out, "the recurrent definition of ideology has nothing to do with the announcement of a criterion of demarcation. Far from being susceptible to a disassociation in advance, the concepts of science and those of ideology begin to be that only by the fact of the break."[26] The break falsifies its ideological past and, by the same token, verifies the science whose emergence it marks in the most literal sense of the terms: it constitutes the specific distribution of the false and true, respectively. The simultaneity of the verification of the scientific and the falsification of its ideology amounts to the fact that "science is identified with the scientific process of destroying obviousness or initial [ideological] abstractions."[27] This dual event has a name with a specific weight within Marxism: critique[28] – and this critique can only originate in the emergent scientific problematic. This is crucial for the recurrent, epistemological character of the break: on the one hand, the break has to be an event of rational critique if the "relativistic," retrospective distribution of the values of false and true is to be avoided; on the other, if it is to avoid also the "rationalist," essentialist ascertaining of what is absolutely true and false, this critique cannot be guided by a mythical, universal rationality. This necessary critique can only be guided by the new structure of rationality. In other words, if the constitution of true and false is relational, it is not relative; the break is objective, but its objectivity is not a function of an Archimedean-point rationalism. The objectivity of the event is correlated with the "viewpoint of science," a constitutive perspective, which does not simply distinguish the scientific and the ideological, the true and the false, but produces them as such.

This then is the significance of the break's epistemological recurrence and its retroactive character: the break is brought forth by the very scientific problematic that it brings forth. Science extricates itself, detaches itself from what it determines as its ideological past; it (actively) distinguishes itself from its non-science. Science *produces* itself out of its past by its own means, confirms and validates itself as science; in a peculiar way, then, it presupposes itself. Science commences by an "absolute beginning," as Althusser says in his *Machiavelli and Us*[29] or, as Balibar himself puts it, as "absolute method," in a surprisingly Hegelian "concept of science preceding itself in the production of its own means of production."[30]

The break then "belongs" to the emergent scientific problematic, which "will" be the outcome of the whole process. On the one hand, to the precise extent that it is a break, it essentially involves incommensurability that is correlative with science's radicality and novelty. The new science was *essentially unpredictable*; it was literally *impossible* to reach the scientific problematic on the basis of the pre-scientific norms from which it broke; the transition *was* inconceivable. On the other, from the inverse perspective, there *is not* and there *was not* incommensurability, to the extent that the break was a constitutive, epistemological *act*, that of *critique*. The impossible transition *did happen*, but not in a vacuum of any rationality; the transition was rational, and the rationality in question was the one that this very transition would arrive at. In opposition to the prevailing, symmetrical understanding of incommensurability, where a structure of rationality begins irrationally, here the beginning of the new, scientific rationality is already its first and constitutive act. The break is, thus, an instance of "one-way" incommensurability, a non-symmetrical incommensurability. In fact, Balibar never stops insisting that the break is irreversible. The specific forms of the scientific and the ideological, the true and the false, insofar as they are produced in and by the break, are not interchangeable. He also persistently characterizes the break, citing Regnault's phrase, as a "point of no return." The transition could not, even in principle, be reversed. The break thus is an *irrevocable* event; because of its truth-effects a structure of obviousness has been definitely *destroyed*: what has been falsified can no longer be taken as (obviously) true.

However, the thesis of the irreversibility of the break is necessarily complemented by a thesis that seems to contravene it, and that concerns the second aspect of Balibar's "epistemological recurrence," its *repetitive* character. Balibar in fact insists that the break, being an irreversible event, does not happen once and for all; correlatively, once the new science has been inaugurated by the break, it does not develop in a linear, continuous and accumulative manner. Thus, "the break must be thought, however strange it seems, not simply as an event but as a process," which is ultimately identical with the science itself; "contrary to what certain critics of Althusser have thought ... the epistemological break is a 'continuing break' and not a result definitively completed in the instant."[31] In other words, the break between a science and *its* ideology is never complete. The break "is characterized by its irreversibility and by its incompleteness, the one being as important as the other."³² The break does not represent a definitive separation between the scientific and the ideological (that would contradict their relational determination). There is no pure science, pure scientific rationality (as the *rationalist* notion of rationality would have it), purged of all ideology. Hence, "the presence, and the pregnancy, of the 'pre-scientific' within the history of knowledge which, nevertheless, is grounded on the exclusion of it as *non-scientific*."³³ Science's self-distinction and self-extrication from ideology is forever unfinished precisely for the science to continue to be, and to be a science. Since the scientific can only be the effect of the break, it is dependent on it: science is perpetually subjected to and reliant on consecutive, recurrent epistemological acts of self-demarcation from the ideology proper to it:

> [E]very break is at the same time irreversible and precarious, threatened with an impossible return to its ideological prehistory, without which it would not last, it would not progress. It is thus a continuous break (in the sense of continuation, not of continuity).³⁴

Balibar will term this differential repetition of the break within science, this "intra-scientific rupture," the recasting (*refonte*) of science by science itself, a privileged example of which is the relativist remaking of classical mechanics. Once again, while Balibar attributes Bachelardian discontinuity to the recasting, he refuses to characterize it using a Kuhnian notion of incommensurability: "it is impossible to consider that classical and relativist theories are 'incommensurable', as two linguistic universes or two exclusive conceptions of the world."³⁵ But, as Balibar makes clear, such a recasting represents a "new development of the idea of recurrence,"³⁶ that is, both the foundational break and the recastings that follow are differential instantiations of the central category of epistemological recurrence, conceived according to a non-Kuhnian, non-symmetrical incommensurability.

The epistemological acts of recasting amount to a constituted science's return to what Balibar calls, following Regnault, science's own *"unthought"* (both writers use always the term in the plural: *les impensés*): "for a given science, we will name epistemological recasting the point of return to the unthought of the science in question, which is at the same time a new point of no-return for that science."³⁷ Science's unthought is the site of the persistence of science's ideology within this very science, in the form of implicit, metaphysical "absolutes."[38] It is here that the Bachelardian concept of epistemological obstacles becomes most relevant. Contrary to what the metaphor of an obstacle may suggest, epistemological obstacles are not exterior to science and neither do they act merely negatively, as simple impediments to science. Epistemological obstacles pertain to science and have a crucial, positive role in the constitution and the development of its problematic: they are enabling obstacles, as it were. Recalling the metaphor of the river-bed, in Wittgenstein's *On Certainty*,[39] the epistemological obstacles are both constraints and conditions of possibility for the ongoing, rational and critical tradition that each science is, the unthought that enables science to think what it thinks, the grounds for its rationality, which can support it on condition that they remain inaccessible to it. Each time, then, science's vision is conditioned by a structure of blindness that is necessary for a specific science to be able to "see" what it "sees"; those conditions, which remain unproblematized as such, determine the existence of what appears to be an unconditioned visual field: they represent another instance of the ideological structure of obviousness.

Overcoming epistemological obstacles is for a science to return to its unthought, to *think* its unthought in its plurality, and to neutralize it: it *destroys* the relevant obviousnesses such that they can no longer act as obstructions. This is a critical act of thematizing, problematizing and questioning that was impossible from the perspective of the initial rational structure. Such critical questioning presupposes a new conceptual ground that did not exist before. The act of thinking this unthought, impossible in the previous framework, ipso facto brings forth the new framework in which it is both possible and actual. This act coincides with the *recasting* of the science, that is, its conceptual restructuring on a new basis, itself "unthought" in its turn, that is, as a new scientific problematic that has emerged from the initial one. An epistemological rupture thus takes place here, one that exhibits all the retroactive characteristics of the initial break. On the one hand, it is an act of critique in which the new scientific rationality is already active; on the other, this new rationality does not exist before or independently of that act of critique, but is established by it. The rupture that "will" launch the new rationality is already performed by that new rationality: the emergent conceptual structure is present and guides the process through which it emerges. Once again, the retroactivity at issue here must be distinguished from simple retrospection, which would concern only the way we regard and evaluate the past.

Thus, a "one-way" incommensurability is involved here, too, a non-symmetrical, irreversible incommensurability, which undermines in advance any "epistemological" equivalence between the structures in question. The absence of logical relations and the impossibility of transition exist only from the "before" to the "after"; the new rationality, on the contrary, critically assesses both the possibilities and the limits of the previous rationality in a self-inaugurating act. The new problematic has access to the visual field of the former, but also to the invisible conditions that both made it possible and constrained it at the same time. Thus, according to Regnault, "it is from the point of view of the [relativist] recasting that we can master Galilean physics in its entirety. It is now that we have overstepped its limits and reformulated its presuppositions."[40]

Once again, the asymmetry involved eludes the dilemma presented by the opposition between rationalist commensurability and irrational incommensurability: there is no transcendent, privileged perspective, capable of encompassing both the "before" and the "after" without pertaining to one or the other of these perspectives; however, in another sense *there is* a privileged perspective, that that is immanent in the event: the perspective of the scientific structure that emerges by and through it, which can and actually does theorize and assess the former perspective as guided by grounds that support it while remaining inaccessible to it. It thus opens up an objectively greater logical space, wherein more things than before are thinkable: both what could previously be thought and the relevant "unthought" principles. In short, the objectivity of the whole process lies in this asymmetrical relation.

And this gives the measure of the difference between this materialist epistemology and Kuhn's position. For Kuhn, the threshold between two successive scientific norms is the blind spot of both; "scientific revolution" is the instance when scientific rationality in general is silenced and yields the stage to other forces (psychological, social and so forth). As a consequence of this symmetrically non-rational relation and transition, the succession could in principle have been the inverse of what it was; none of the paradigms involved is "essentially" posterior to the other. Furthermore, other than the sociology of the scientific community and its reproduction, there is no epistemological criterion assigning two paradigms to the same history, that is, the history of the same *science*, since, as we may recall, after the revolution, scientists are transplanted to another world.[41] At the limit, successive paradigms are not even episodes of the same history based on a common object.

Instead, science's self-recasting by virtue of its asymmetrical, retroactive character is historical because it is epistemological (and vice versa). On the one hand, far from being a moment of irrationality between irreducible structures of partial rationality, the recasting is the rational act of a science *par excellence*, not only at an epistemic level, at a "first degree" of rationality as it were, but also at a "second degree," in an *epistemological* sense, where the epistemic perspective is rationally criticized. And this, in its turn, is what allows this whole conception of epistemological recurrence to think a science historically: the past perspective does not simply precede the perspective that follows in an epistemologically indifferent way; the epistemological, retroactive incommensurability of which we have spoken has transformed past science into science's past. In this way, both become co-articulated in the history of the same individual science; they both pertain to a history, the history of the same science. This relation of past and present, through precisely the epistemological nature of the break, acquires a surplus of meaning, connoting *historicity*: the past becomes precisely *past*; it is over, bygone, obsolete – it is history. It is impossible to return to it. In other words, the recasting, too, represents an irreversible and irrevocable, critical and cognitive event, a point of no return.

To sum up, the asymmetrical incommensurability proper to any act of epistemological recurrence becomes the privileged topos of the distinction between the scientific and the non-scientific – and not the exact opposite, the point where this distinction becomes meaningless. But as it is not a distinction that could be performed from a transcendent philosophical point, it is not philosophy's business to judge the legitimate claims to scientificity. Instead, it is each science itself, in each critical moment of its history (including the moment of its inauguration), that produces, distinguishes, confirms and legitimates itself as science. That asymmetrical incommensurability is placed now in the heart of the scientific process, canceling the Kuhnian distinction between normal science, extraordinary science and scientific revolution; in that sense, incommensurability and discontinuity – in a word, historicity – are the privileged point of science's rationality and objectivity – and not the opposite, that is, their unsurpassable limit.

The meaning of the "epistemology of the break" for science in general, then, the equivalent of its "concept of science," is that *each* science *is* its self-confirmation as science, in contradistinction to what it rejects as its "other," its ideology. The distinction between a singular science and the relevant non-science falls within the "jurisdiction" of this science itself. It is of course a very peculiar "concept" (as we shall see in more detail), a strange form of generality, in that it hands over the right to subsume the particular into the general to the authority of the particular itself, in an epistemological act that does not leave the general intact. It is as if a "minimum of generality" is posited in order to be canceled. And it is precisely here that the anti-essentialism and materialism of this epistemology lies: the emancipation of existence from essence, of the actual from the possible. Thus, the "common" way in which each particular and individual science is science is its own singular way: each science brings forth its own scientificity, irreducibly differentiating the "concept" of science.

4

We began with the quest for an epistemological discourse adequate for the *thesis* of Marxism's scientific status and ended up with an "epistemology of the break," with no apparent specific relation to Marxist theory and its epistemological claim. Balibar shows that this relation cannot be one of application, not even in the atypical sense that this epistemology allows; Marxism cannot be understood as if it simply fell within this epistemology's specific generality, as one more science that initiates itself through an epistemological break. Such a notion would amount to resuscitating the logic of the "speculative guarantee" of an epistemology.[42] To have been inaugurated by a break would entail the risk of playing the role of a criterion for Marxism's scientificity, which would undermine the logic of the break, implicitly transforming the initial thesis into a question (while furnishing its response). Balibar, instead, indicates another, inverse, way in which the historical epistemology of the break may be the epistemology of Marxism's break: instead of subsuming the theory to the epistemology, it is the epistemology that has to be inserted within theory as one of its truth-effects, so as to affirm factually theory's break:

[starting] from the *existence* of a scientific Marxist theory ... the objective [would be] *materially to implant the history of sciences in the field of plain history*, something which can be done only by means of a scientific theory of that history.[43]

The link between the two has already been identified: it is the Marxist concept of ideology; it is thus a question of *"transporting the whole problem of the constitution of sciences into the field of the materialist (historical) theory of ideologies."*[44] Thus, a truly exceptional situation emerges, where an epistemological discourse becomes continuous with a science's epistemic discourse, a situation that produces serious complications for both discourses. In some of his most subtle, at times elliptical, writing, Balibar takes up some of the above difficult questions, discussing specifically the work of Althusser's self-critical period as well as his late writings publically available at the time.

According to one tendency in Althusser's work, Marxism is finally a *theory of practice*, according to which "all the levels of social existence are the sites of distinct practices,"[45] arranged in relations of *overdetermination* or *structural causality* within a *topography*, which represents the condition of *historicity* itself. The concept of practice is explicitly conceived according to the "model of production,"[46] that is, as a structured transformation of a distinct object through the use of the appropriate "means of production." Immanent in each practice is its "practical ideology," which misrecognizes the practice through an imaginary presentation of it in terms of the category of praxis between self-subsistent subjects and objects. Practical ideology, thus, has a material existence, is inseparably interwoven with the practice's materiality, the structured relations between its object, means of production and human agency.

In one of his most radical theoretical moves, Althusser places the theoretical inside the topography of the social practices, as a distinct practice, theoretical practice, the distinctive materiality of which is discursive. Thus, a theory of theoretical practice is inscribed, as a "regional theory," within the "global" theory of practice, whose object would be the historicity of theoretical knowledge.

Theoretical practice is connected with ideology in a double way: first, as a practice among others, it is interwoven with its proper practical ideology, an imaginary presentation of the theoretical as cognitive praxis between pre-determined subjects and objects of knowledge, where the subject has access to and abstracts the object's essence. This presentation depicts what Althusser terms "empiricism,"[47] an empiricist and essentialist epistemology in a "practical state": it has a material existence, immanent in the discursive materiality of theoretical practice and embedded in the "theory-form" of its discourse. And, by the same token, it is relevant to what Althusser again will term theoreticism,[48] the absolute, unconditioned viewing (*theorein*) of an object's being what it is in itself, in its essence.

Second, as *theoretical* practice, it is correlated with ideology in a *specific* way: by virtue of its distinctive "product," the *theoretical ideologies,* which claim (precisely by means of the "theory-form" of their discourse) the capacity to grasp the essence of the theoretical-ideological objects that ultimately originate in the various "practical ideologies." There is thus a correlation between theory-form and essence-category, the effect of the empiricist and essentialist "form" of theoretical discourse on its "contents." Theoretical practice necessarily tends to absolutize both the subject and the object of theory.

Theoretical practice also theorizes *its own* practical ideology: it produces theoretical ideologies of the theoretical, competitive renditions of the empiricist-essentialist and theoreticist matrix of its practical ideology. Those theoretical ideologies, which claim access to the essence or concept of knowledge, constitute the philosophical field of idealist epistemologies, in the sense of empiricist and essentialist theories of knowledge, and philosophies of science in particular. Those theoretical constructions, which represent the ideology of the theoretical in both a practical and a theoretical state, inherently presuppose the concept-essence of science as the prerequisite for the epistemological judgment by which a science can be confirmed as such.

In this context, the theory of theoretical practice has to consider science (scientific practice) as a "species" of the theoretical (practice) in general. However counter-intuitive and perplexing this may be, in that it includes science among the theoretical ideologies, it evades the already familiar dilemma between: (a) a rationalist notion of science as transcending the ideological horizon of the theoretical, so that only non-scientific, ideological theories could be included in the social topography and historicized (in the manner of the old "sociology of knowledge"), and (b) a notion of the immanence of science, albeit an immanence that comes at the cost of the trivialization of science as an epistemological category, which is then reduced to a mere "practice" or "belief system" (in the manner of the current "science studies"). Moving beyond this dilemma, science is characterized by its specific *and* epistemological difference from its ideological "genus." It is at this precise point that the theory of practice merges with the epistemology proper to it, its epistemic discourse becoming continuous with the epistemological discourse by which the scientific status of the former is established. The epistemology of the break is thus inextricably bound up with the theory of theoretical practice, as if the theory of theoretical practice has become both an instance of the theory of practice and an epistemology.

But then science becomes a very peculiar species, which denies essential features of the genus – even more, a "species" that opposes, in a peculiar way, its own genus. Science is an open process of *questioning* its presuppositions, either in its inaugurating moment of the break, or in its subsequent history, when it returns to its "unthought," while theoretical ideologies are subjected to their unthought presuppositions, which they reproduce unquestioned. Sciences are conditioned by recurrent, continuous and retroactive break, while theoretical ideologies, despite their "intra-ideological ruptures," always respect the principles of their ideological problematic. Thus, science is a continuous de-essentializing process that, by virtue of its own genus, is continuously obstructed by an essentializing "practical" ideology, through the essence-effect of the theory-form. According to Balibar's rendering of the epistemology of the break, this tension is "essential" for science: it constitutes the base of its most "essential" trait, the thematization and problematization of the unthought "absolutes," which are always regenerated within the product of every epistemological act.

Science then is a non-normal species: there is no typical "specific difference" here, no proper definition or concept of science. In place of specific difference there is the factual and historical epistemological break. According to its own explicit and positive conceptual content, the "epistemological break" and, consequently, "science" cannot be finished concepts, only incomplete concepts characterized by a peculiar lack of generality: they cannot discern which objects fall within their extension, they cannot recognize and confirm by themselves particular sciences *as sciences*. The relevant theory cannot by itself subsume particulars by means of its concept of science. This conceptual incompleteness is, paradoxically, the point of its completion, its accomplishment, what is most novel and radical in what it has to say about science, its "concept" of science, by virtue of which this very epistemology delegates the epistemological task of distinguishing the sciences from the non-sciences to the sciences themselves.

Here, the tension between theoretical "form" and "content" is of another order. Theory explicitly acknowledges that it cannot have what is most central to it – that is, a concept of science understood in terms of the epistemological break – nor can it be a systematically "complete" self-enclosed – and, a fortiori, a scientific – theory. At the same time, however, through precisely this "concept" (that constrains this epistemology to deny itself the ability to discern its objects and demarcate its extension), the theory of theoretical practice "breaks" with the relevant theoretical-ideological field: the "epistemological break" represents the epistemological break of this theory, which then has to be what, through its "scientific" knowledge, it forbids itself to be: a science, precisely, a scientific theory.

The conditions of possibility of the theory of theoretical practice, then, are the conditions of its impossibility: the object of the practical "theoreticist" ideology that it bears as theory is identical with its own *theoretical* object; the essentializing effect of its form on its content is not indirect, as in all other sciences (whose object is not the "theoretical"). The tension between form and content here has the specific effect of nullifying the theory at the very moment of its accomplishment: in so far as it is the theory it is, it cannot be a theory at all. Given its self-canceling antinomy, the theory of practice does and does not include a theory of theoretical practice. The theory of theoretical practice has its determinate place within the theory of practice, corresponding to both the critique of the de-historicizing ideology of the theoretical and the ability to explain the historicity of theoretical knowledge (that necessarily includes the scientific). That place, however, is at the same time full and empty; it is empty because it is full.

According to my reading, Balibar sees this antinomy as the focus of Althusser's self-criticism regarding the epistemology of the break *as* the Theory of theoretical practice. It is the moment of what Balibar calls "the break 'corrected.'"[49] The break in its new formulation appears not as a concept, but as a "metaphor": the "break" cannot represent an epistemological break itself because there can be no epistemological breaks in philosophy. Of course, this means that idealist philosophies and epistemologies cannot be deemed theoretical ideologies anymore; philosophy is not just one more theoretical field among others, but a distinctive practice, mediating theory and politics, representing class struggle within theory. This self-critical "correction" (and the selection of the word here is significant), concerning precisely the specific antinomy of this theory, is not a refutation of its earlier content, nor even a recasting of its principles; on the contrary, the content remains as it is – and indeed, Althusser, in his self-critical writings (and Balibar doesn't miss this) re-asserts the break and its epistemology uncompromisingly. The *theoreticism* that Althusser denounces regarding his own epistemological work primarily concerns the fact that it has been cast in the theory-form, which tends to essentialize and absolutize whatever it theorizes: in this case, *science* itself, in its difference from ideology. The theoreticist *deviation* of the *Theory* of theoretical practice is finally symptomatically expressed in the capital T.

Althusser's self-criticism, the "correction" of the break, raises the question of a form adequate to this content, in order for it to be the content that it is. But this exceeds the theory of theoretical practice and concerns the theory of practice as a whole, Marxism itself. The full/empty place of the theory of theoretical practice within it is a not just a regional place that could remain provisionally vacant. The present/absent historicization of the theoretical is a crucial and urgent content for Marxist theory. According to Althusser, indeed, the epistemological break introduced by Marxism against the theoretical ideologies of history (including those most devoted to sublimation, the various philosophies of history) passes through history's emancipation from any theory of history, the rejection of any isomorphism between history and theory, any subordination of history to theoretical knowledge. The historicization of the theoretical would imply as its correlate the critique of the "theorization" of history, in the sense of a continuous and essential identity between history and theory. This is or had to be a break from the essentialism of both theoretical knowledge, in particular its transcendence from the horizon of social determinations, and the social, along with the theoretically governed "history" that necessarily characterizes it. This is why, for Althusserianism, Hegelian philosophy became the privileged locus of the break. According to Balibar, "the 'content' of the break described by Althusser is precisely the historical mutation of the dialectic,"[50] and this regards both the complexity of the social practices and the theoretical practice in particular: "there are in fact two 'dialectics' that we have to choose between ... a dialectic of consciousness and a dialectic of production."[51]

Thus, the historicization of the social, the critique of essentialism, amounts precisely to a theoretical construction of the topography of practices.

> In its theoretical form [this scheme] already constitutes a reformulation of the dialectic or, if you wish, of the "motor of history," absolutely incompatible with Hegelianism. Althusser stated it strongly: *in Hegel there is no topography*, or rather, the only "topography" that Hegel knows ... is in reality a *non-topography*.[52]

The non-topography of Hegelian dialectic, on the other hand, is correlative with its non-history, the only "history" that Hegel knows: the dialectic, teleological transformations of this non-topography. Instead, the topography becomes now the condition of historicity itself; it is the materialist, anti-essentialist and historical conception of the social: "Althusser thus inscribes the *materialist topography* of social relations and of their 'differential efficacy' in the very heart of his definition of Marxist theory as scientific theory."[53]

If this is a *first*, absolutely necessary instance of Marxism's materialist endeavor, it nevertheless puts Marxist theory to a very strained relation to itself: at the very moment that it conveys history's incongruousness with theory, it raises itself "in practice" to the position implied by the ideology of the theoretical, from where it supposedly supervises and "governs" history. The topography necessarily becomes the "content" of the break; theory constructs the topography: as Balibar implies, it is the "moment" of the subordination of the topography to the break and, consequently, to the theory of practice, which contains and determines it. Balibar elaborates this point by focusing on Althusser's last published text, which he cites *in extenso* in an endnote: there, writes Althusser, when Marx's "presentation takes the form of a topography," he "presents his own ideas ... twice and in two different forms." In the first, "he presents them as principles of analysis of the whole ... Here his ideas are present everywhere, because it is a matter of using them to explain a global reality. And they are here present in their theoretical form."⁵⁴ But, to be able to encompass a "global reality," Marxist theory must itself originate in an Archimedean point external to that reality: to "explain" the whole topography, its point of view must be outside the topography. Thus, Marx presents his theory as *transcendent*: if its gaze is everywhere, it is because it is a "view from nowhere,"⁵⁵ capable of grasping social reality "as it really is," as "essentially" historical.

But how does Marx *present* his "ideas" like that? It is not a matter of their explicit content, but a function of their form: they are omnipresent "in their *theoretical form*." This theoreticist presentation of Marxist's theory stands for the moment when Marxism inevitably, carrying through its anti-essentialist break, succumbs in practice to the ideology of the theoretical; it adopts for itself this essentialist epistemology, in its "practically" effective state, by investing itself in the inescapable *theory-form*. Thus, the non-essentialist and historical content par excellence (the topography) subordinates itself to the essentializing and un-historicizing theory-form. And, ipso facto, Marxist theory takes on a very specific version of "performative contradiction": it becomes singularly blind to what it specifically and exclusively produces, and thus to its most proper and exclusive contents that exist and become visible only within it. Its own discovery, the heart of its field of visibility, that is, precisely history's "essential" disobedience of any theory, *historicity itself*, becomes its blind spot. It is a blindness to its own proper visual field, a blindness therefore that it alone is in a position to ascertain. Thus, not only the theoretical, but all the crucial and critical "contents" or "concepts" of Marxist theory that, in their structural interrelation, constitute the problematic of historicity, are inherently unstable concepts, always precarious, present/absent from Marxist theory, its concepts/non-concepts.⁵⁶ These concepts are all characterized by this elliptical/defective and undecidable status, which signals both the attempt to grasp and the perpetual flight of the corresponding "objects." Its "concepts" escape theory's hold at the moment precisely that it grasps them. Hence the paradox to which Althusser alludes: "even though it refers to the capitalist society and to the worker's movement, Marxist theory says almost nothing about the state, ideology, politics, or the class struggle organizations." It is a "blind spot that signals undoubtedly the theoretical limits that Marx encountered."⁵⁷ This presence/absence of concepts culminates, according to another of Althusser's late texts, in Marx's "absolute limit," that is, "this theoretical lacuna concerning the nature of the relation between the base, on the one hand, and the superstructure, on the other":[58] in short, the theory of topography "misses," precisely, the topography.

At the crossroads of these concepts, there appears yet another one, once again at the threshold of presence and absence: the famous "fusion of Marxist theory and the worker's movement," the very event of historical communism, which would amount to the historicity of Marxist theory itself. The theoreticist "presentation" of Marxist theory conditions one well-known interpretation of that fusion, an interpretation that has an important place in the Marxist tradition: Marxist theory emerged and developed *independently* of the workers' movement, and only secondarily was it "fused" with it. The fusion is incidental and epistemologically indifferent to the theory itself, which is determined by its access to the totality of its object, the topography. Once more, the implicit assumption of theory's transcendence entails its omnipresence. The "fusion" is thus trivialized; it does not raise any questions regarding the scientific status of Marxist theory and it involves no epistemological aporia, just as historical communism does not pose specific conceptual demands to insure its comprehension. The "fusion" represents thus another instance of Marxist theory losing its sense of historicity: this in turn entails a theoretical loss of the meaning of the fusion and, consequently, the loss of any possibility of understanding the communist movement itself: thus, the "tendency to communism" is characterized by a deficit of self-knowledge, that is, a deficit of a Marxist knowledge of Marxism.[59]

And this is where a second "moment" intervenes, Marx's second presentation of his theory that is inscribed in it as its constitutive theoretical consequence: after presenting his "ideas" as transcendently omnipresent in the global reality of the topography, Althusser goes on to argue that

> Marx has his ideas appear a second time, situating them this time in a determined and limited place in the same reality of the whole, ... among the "ideological forms where men become conscious of (class) conflict and fight it to the end."[60]

That is, the historicity of Marxism itself amounts to the positioning of the theory of the topography within that very topography, in its proper time and place, in a historical site both of structural determinations but also of structure's overdeterminations. It is the reversal, even the subversion, of the subordination of the topography and history to the break and, consequently, to theory characteristic of the first moment. It is here that history is really emancipated from theory: as Balibar points out, the break is subordinated to the topography;[61] the topography contains and determines the break and its outcome, Marxist theory:

> there is no longer any question of making the materialist topography ... into a simple content of the revolutionary problematic put in place by an epistemological break. Rather ... the question of topography ... commands all reflection on "theoretical practice."[62]

It is important to note that this second "moment," although in a sense subverting the first, does not invalidate it, since, without the latter, it would be meaningless: the insertion of Marx's theory within the topography presupposes what this theory conveys, the topography itself. Both these "presentations" must be taken together, in opposition once again to the dilemma of transcendent science and a "science as (just) practice." Together, those two instances constitute what Althusser terms the "double inscription," or Balibar the "double position" of a theory that posits itself within the object that it posits. Thus, as Althusser notes and Balibar confirms, Marx's materialism does not consist merely of the contents of a theory of history; rather, according to Balibar, "Marx's materialism consists in the *fact* that Marx inscribed in theory itself the *limits*, and thus the *conditions*, imposed on its historical efficacy by the fact that theory consists of 'ideas.'"[63]

But this second "presentation," insofar as it combines itself with the first, that is, Marx's materialism, also finds its "practical" correlate; this "double inscription" of the theory entails ipso facto a change in its "form": "As a result of this fact, [Marx's ideas] also change shape: they move from the theory-form to the 'ideology-form'."[64] A virtual "content," then, is impelled to seek the "form" in which it can be formulated. There thus emerges the problem of an alternative form for Marxist "theory," adequate to its most indispensable contents (including a Marxist knowledge of Marxism), the form in which alone these contents can appear.

But what does "ideology-form" mean here? Does it mean that the circle is now closing, and the product of the break is reabsorbed into that from which it has already extricated itself? Does the epistemological break revoke itself? Balibar seems to imply something like that when he discerns, in Althusser's late writings, a "disappearance of the break."[65] But, as his argument develops, it is clear that ideology-form designates the form in which Marxism is or can be historically effective, not *only* breaking with but also *acting* upon ideology, in order that the "ideas" it formulates become active. Ideology-form is then the consequence of Marxist *science* as a social and historical force, and this, in its turn, amounts to the historicity of Marxism, its existence within the topography, within the play of determination and overdetermination, a determined but also a determinant instance of the structure, characterized by its own efficacy by virtue of which it can have historical effects. And the place and time of what we earlier called insertion is the "fusion," except that now Marxist "theory" is not even in principle thinkable as prior to or independent of its fusion with the workers' movement; Marxist "theory" is constituted as always-already "fused" with the workers' movement. The fusion is a relation that has priority over its *relata*, and thus it is *constitutive* of Marxism. But, in accordance with its "double inscription," the latter cannot be just ideological; in order for the "fusion" not be trivialized in an inverse sense, which would reduce Marxism to nothing more than another ideology, and where the specificity of the communist movement would be lost again, the "fusion" is of necessity epistemologically constitutive for Marxism. The "fusion" with the workers' movement is determinant of Marxism's scientificity. As Althusser claims, Marxist science is an inherently conflictual science, a partisan science, taking sides within the conflicts – the objective knowledge of which it makes possible.[66] The question of the form of Marxism is now inseparable from the problem of the revolutionary science.

Althusser and Balibar designate this question, in its immense difficulty and complexity, as a "conceptual," epistemic problem and an epistemological problem (both "theoretical" and "practical") for Marxism. More than that, as Balibar notes, it is a philosophical problem, concerning "the reality of thought about the real ... and above all true thought," conditioned by some of the most profound elements of the "unthought" of Western metaphysics, and at the same time by the political problem of the "revolutionary thinking of the masses"[67] that is necessarily both ideological and scientific (both immanent in and radically breaking with the ideological horizon). What Althusser once wrote about Marx, could be paraphrased and applied to his own late writings regarding the question of the revolutionary science: some insightful formulations, a few lines and "then silence."[68] The conditions of Althusser's silence are both known and unimaginable. And at the time Balibar was writing the texts discussed here, it was simultaneously too late and too early to pose anew this multifaceted question.

Notes

1. Etienne Balibar, "From Bachelard to Althusser: The Concept of 'Epistemological Break,'" *Economy and Society*, 7.3 (1978): 207–37; Etienne Balibar, *Lieux et noms de la vérité* (Paris: Éditions de l'aube, 1994); Etienne Balibar, "Althusser's Object," *Social Text*, 39 (1994): 157–88.
2. I qualify as "epistemological" any approach to science that, even if it accounts for its social and historical dimensions, involves the (inescapably evaluative) distinction between the scientific and the non-scientific.
3. I refer loosely to the term coined by Imre Lakatos (1978), to account (among many others) for Marxism itself.
4. Balibar, "From Bachelard to Althusser," 212; emphasis in the original.
5. Ibid. 215.
6. "Every science is, as such, demonstrative, but *in its own way*" (Balibar, *Lieux et noms de la vérité*, 110; emphasis in the original).
7. Balibar, "From Bachelard to Althusser," 212–13; emphasis in the original.
8. Pierre Macherey, "George Canguilhem's Philosophy of Science: Epistemology and History of Science," in *In a Materialist Way: Selected Essays by Pierre Macherey*, ed. Warren Montag (London: Verso, 1998), 168; emphasis in the original.
9. Georges Canguilhem, "Introduction: L'objet de l'histoire des sciences." in *Études d'histoire et de philosophie des sciences* (Paris: Vrin, 2002), 14.
10. Georges Canguilhem, "Introduction: Rôle de l'épistémologie dans l'historiographie scientifique contemporaine," in *Idéologie et rationalité dans l'histoire des sciences de la vie* (Paris: Vrin, 2000), 13.
11. Balibar, *Lieux et noms de la vérité*, 102–3.
12. Ibid. 128.

13. Balibar, "From Bachelard to Althusser," 218.
14. Even though Balibar, in accordance with the Bachelardian epistemological tradition, prioritizes the *concept* as "the unit *par excellence* of scientific knowledge" ("From Bachelard to Althusser," 232, n.2), to the detriment of an emphasis on theories, nevertheless, he does not posit concepts "in an arbitrary isolation . . . but in their interrelation, their 'interdetermination'" ("From Bachelard to Althusser," 233, n.2).
15. Balibar, *Lieux et noms de la vérité*, 104.
16. Regnault, quoted in *Lieux et noms de la vérité*, 104.
17. Balibar, *Lieux et noms de la vérité*, 119–23.
18. Ibid. 121.
19. Ibid. 102 (last emphasis added).
20. Ibid. 124.
21. Balibar, "Althusser's Object," 162–3.
22. Ibid. 163.
23. Balibar, *Lieux et noms de la vérité*, 128.
24. Ibid. 127.
25. Balibar, "Althusser's Object," 157–88, 163.
26. Balibar, *Lieux et noms de la vérité*, 129.
27. Balibar, "Althusser's Object," 163.
28. Thus, the full title of Marxism's major scientific work emphasizes the inseparability of the "positive," epistemic content with the "negative," epistemological opposition with its other: *Capital: A Critique of Political Economy*.
29. Louis Althusser, *Machiavelli and Us*, trans. Gregory Elliott (London: Verso, 1999).
30. Balibar, "Althusser's Object," 163–4.
31. Balibar, "From Bachelard to Althusser," 220–1.
32. Ibid. 221.
33. Balibar, *Lieux et noms de la vérité*, 128–9; emphasis in the original.
34. Balibar, "Althusser's Object," 172.
35. Balibar, *Lieux et noms de la vérité*, 142.
36. Ibid. 132–3.
37. Regnault, cited in *Lieux et noms de la vérité*, 133.
38. Balibar, *Lieux et noms de la vérité*, 132–45.
39. Ludwig Wittgenstein, *On Certainty*, ed. G. E. M. Anscombe and G. H. von Wright (Oxford: Basil Blackwell, 1969), §97ff.
40. Quoted in Balibar, *Lieux et noms de la vérité*, 133.
41. Thomas Kuhn, *The Structure of Scientific Revolutions* (Chicago: University of Chicago Press, 1996), 111.
42. Balibar, "From Bachelard to Althusser," 216.

43. Ibid. 217; emphasis in the original.
44. Ibid.; emphasis in the original.
45. Louis Althusser and Etienne Balibar, *Reading Capital*, trans. Ben Brewster (London: New Left Books, 1970), 58.
46. Balibar, "Althusser's Object," 172.
47. Althusser and Balibar, *Reading Capital*, 34ff.
48. Louis Althusser, "Elements of Self-Criticism," in *Essays in Self-Criticism*, trans. Grahame Lock (London: New Left Books, 1976), 105.
49. Balibar, "Althusser's Object," 170-4.
50. Ibid. 164.
51. Ibid. 164.
52. Ibid. 175; emphasis in the original.
53. Ibid. 175; emphasis in the original.
54. Althusser, "Il marxismo oggi", cited in "Althusser's Object," 186-7, n. 39.
55. Thomas Nagel, *The View from Nowhere* (Oxford: Oxford University Press, 1986).
56. This description of the peculiar, unstable, status of Marxism's most crucial concepts owes a lot to Balibar's account of Althusser's own concepts (Etienne Balibar, "Tais-toi encore, Althusser!" in *Écrits pour Althusser* (Paris: Découverte, 1991), 71); I borrow here freely the phrase *"concepts non concepts"* from Balibar, who used it to a different aim and in a different context, referring to Althusser's "concept" of "practical concept" (78).
57. Louis Althusser, "Entretien," *Dialectiques*, 23 (1978): 5-12.
58. Althusser, "Marx in his Limits," in *Philosophy of the Encounter*, ed. François Matheron and Olivier Corpet (London: Verso, 2006), 60.
59. Althusser, "Entretien."
60. Althusser, "Il marxismo oggi," cited in "Althusser's Object," 186-7, n. 39.
61. Balibar, "Althusser's Object," 177.
62. Ibid. 177.
63. Ibid. 177; emphasis in the original.
64. Althusser, "Il marxismo oggi," cited in "Althusser's Object," 186-7 n. 39.
65. Balibar, "Althusser's Object," 174-8.
66. Louis Althusser, "On Marx and Freud," *Rethinking Marxism*, 4.1 (1991): 17-30; Balibar, "Tais-toi encore, Althusser " 81.
67. Balibar, "Althusser's Object," 177.
68. Althusser and Balibar, *Reading Capital*, 193.

Bibliography

Althusser, Louis. "Elements of Self-Criticism." In *Essays in Self-Criticism.* Trans. Grahame Lock. London: New Left Books, 1976. Pp. 105–50.

Althusser, Louis. "Entretien." *Dialectiques*, 23 (1978): 5–12.

Althusser, Louis. "On Marx and Freud." *Rethinking Marxism*, 4.1 (1991): 17–30.

Althusser, Louis. *Machiavelli and Us*. Trans. Gregory Elliott. London: Verso, 1999.

Althusser, Louis. "Marx in his Limits." In *Philosophy of the Encounter.* Ed. François Matheron and Olivier Corpet. London: Verso, 2006. Pp. 7–18.

Althusser, Louis and Etienne Balibar. *Reading Capital*. Trans. Ben Brewster. London: New Left Books, 1970.

Balibar, Etienne. "From Bachelard to Althusser: The Concept of 'Epistemological Break.'" *Economy and Society*, 7.3 (1978): 207–37.

Balibar, Etienne. "Tais-toi encore, Althusser!" In *Écrits pour Althusser*. Paris: Découverte, 1991. Pp. 59–89.

Balibar, Etienne. *Lieux et noms de la vérité*. Paris: Éditions de l'aube, 1994.

Balibar, Etienne. "Althusser's Object." *Social Text*, 39 (1994): 157–88.

Canguilhem, Georges. "Introduction: Rôle de l'épistémologie dans l'historiographie scientifique contemporaine." In *Idéologie et rationalité dans l'histoire des sciences de la vie*. Paris: Vrin, 2000. Pp. 11–29.

Canguilhem, Georges. "Introduction: L'objet de l'histoire des sciences." In *Études d'histoire et de philosophie des sciences*. Paris: Vrin, 2002.

Kuhn, Thomas. *The Structure of Scientific Revolutions*. Chicago: University of Chicago Press, 1996.

Lakatos, Imre. *Philosophical Papers. Vol. 1: The Methodology of Scientific Research Programmes*. Cambridge: Cambridge University Press, 1978.

Macherey, Pierre. "George Canguilhem's Philosophy of Science: Epistemology and History of Science." In *In a Materialist Way: Selected Essays by Pierre Macherey*. Ed. Warren Montag. London: Verso, 1998.

Marx, Karl. *Capital*. Trans. David Fernbach. London: Pelican, 1978.

Nagel, Thomas. *The View from Nowhere*. Oxford: Oxford University Press, 1986.

Wittgenstein, Ludwig. *On Certainty*. Ed. G. E. M. Anscombe and G. H. von Wright. Oxford: Basil Blackwell, 1969.

III Inequality, Violence and the Possibility of Citizenship

8

La Haine: Falling in Slow Motion
Hanan Elsayed

Race d'Abel, dors, bois et mange;
Dieu te sourit complaisamment.
Race de Caïn, dans la fange
Rampe et meurs misérablement.

Race of Abel, sleep, eat and drink;
God smiles on you complacently.
Race of Cain, crawl on your belly,
Die in the mire wretchedly.

Charles Baudelaire[1]

Convinced of the necessity of comparison and dialogue "as instruments for understanding the world we live in," Etienne Balibar in his essay, "Uprisings in the *Banlieues*," organizes his reflections in the "form of a series of 'files' attached to seven symptomatic words or expressions: names, violence, postcolony, religion, race and class, citizenship/the Republic, and politics/antipolitics."[2] To these words, which we all use "at home" and that thus require a theoretical "distantiation," he adds two terms that operate within and between these seven words or expressions and whose importance is derived from their indispensable role in making intelligible or at least interpreting the protests that occurred throughout France in November 2005: "uprisings" (*soulèvements*) and "*Banlieues*." The former makes visible the differences attached to the ways that the protests were characterized (riot, rebellion, violences and even *guérilla*), while the latter, very French term, "*banlieues*," evokes social and racial exclusion and signifies a kind of "frontier, a border-area and a frontline" separating an impoverished and marginalized world from an adjacent world that is both wealthy and powerful.[3] For Balibar, the combination of proximity and inequality in the case of the *banlieue* invites

> a political analogy (and not just a continuity of methods on the side of the administration and the forces of repression) with the way that, in the colonial territories, two populations with radically unequal rights found themselves brought together and set apart. But the institutional mechanisms and political effects are not the same.[4]

To the unity of proximity and inequality that characterizes the relation of these two worlds, I would add a third term that further complicates this already contradictory relation: inaccessibility, the way in which the *banlieue* reproduces the geographical division, typical of colonialism, between the European and indigenous zones is captured most powerfully in the inaccessibility of the first to the neighborhood of the second. The spatial character of this relation has made it particularly appropriable by cinema and literature, and it is in film and novel that the limits on the ability of the indigenous to circulate freely in the colonial city or even to enter the European neighborhoods are made visible.[5] In fact, it is perhaps only in our time that the ideal type of the relation between adjacent worlds characterized by proximity, inequality and inaccessibility, and further, in which the one is under the occupation of the other, has been brought to life: the wall erected to separate the West Bank from Israel.

In this essay I want to expand on some of Balibar's observations by exploring the function of language, not only in maintaining the spatial proximity-in-separation that defines the *banlieue*, but more generally in reproducing the form of subjection imposed, however unevenly, upon its inhabitants. I see the well-known film by director Mathieu Kassovitz, *La Haine* (1995, *Hate*), as offering a representation of the everyday racism, coercion and violence faced by the youth of the *banlieue* that carefully exposes the often overlooked and sometimes invisible spatial and discursive mechanisms that secure their subjection. In particular, the film captures the way in which the principle characters are interpellated in the broad sense that Louis Althusser conferred upon this term: interpellated by the police physically, which in French can refer to arrest, detention and even acts of violence, but also interpellated discursively through modes of address that take shape in the first contacts between the youth and the authorities, the demands for identification and the interrogations that follow. I argue that by representing these scenes of interpellation, the film forces us beyond the confines of Althusser's account, complicating it and allowing us to examine it as if it too were presented to us in slow motion. In this way, *La Haine* not only de-universalizes the subject of interpellation, showing its uneven and unequal operation, but it makes visible and audible the hatred this operation produces, the unpredictable side effect that threatens the organism whose equilibrium interpellation is supposed to maintain. The words "stigma" and "stigmatization" appear frequently in Balibar's essay and although he does not confer upon them the importance the seven key words take on, the way he uses them allows us to understand stigmatization as a form of interpellation, an identification of a given individual or more accurately a group of individuals in a way that literally marks or brands them with a distinguishing mark to separate them from others, a permanent scar to indicate that what they have done, or more typically today, what they are, is shameful. Thus, the stereotypical category of "*banlieue youth*" applies not to the totality of young people who live in the *banlieue*, but mainly to black and Arab youth,[6] just as the label of "immigrant" applies also to those who were born in France and who are French citizens:

> It culminates in the construction of a juridically and humanly monstrous social category: the hereditary status of immigrant – "once an immigrant, always an immigrant," generation after generation, whatever nationality is acquired. And hence "foreigners in their own country," since they do not have any other.[7]

Here again, "it is the citizens originally from the former colonies who are condemned to the absurd, but politically eloquent, appellation 'second or third generation immigrants' and to the discrimination that accompanies it."[8] This habitual designation/appellation (or indirect interpellation) frequently found in academic publications shows the extent to which France like so many other modern nations has attempted and in a certain sense succeeded in creating what Balibar calls a "fictive ethnicity."[9] Here, we may refer to the case of Mohamed Lamouri, a high-school student from Charleville-Mézières (a town in the north of France), who, while doing a one-month internship at a private company in

2010, was asked by his supervisor to identify himself on the phone as "Alexandre" when contacting customers. Mohamed refused and was immediately dismissed as a result. He filed a lawsuit on the grounds of discrimination, arguing that as a French citizen born and raised in France, he should be able to use his real and legal name as he sees fit without being compelled to disguise or change it, even temporarily. The fact that he won the lawsuit will not protect him from experiencing the same exclusion again, because of the stigmatization of non- "French" or non-European names (since in recent years names from neighboring countries to the north, such as "Evan," "Elliot," or "William," have gained noticeable popularity), points to a kind of double interpellation: for his employer, "Mohamed" needs to be effaced and replaced with an acceptable name given to, or imposed on, him by that employer – "Alexandre." Thus, the stigma represented by "Mohamed" is to be concealed for the duration of the work day's phone calls, after which, upon leaving the white world, it is uncovered, marking him and constituting his identity.[10]

Gérard Noiriel has shown that during the eighties immigration and "national identity" once again became major themes in the discourse of the right and the extreme right, due in part to their popularization by a media seeking a larger audience through an appeal to the "we" constituted by their public to the detriment of those who were not part of it.[11] In the same period the media established the connection between "young people" and "immigrants."[12] In addition, the discourse of class struggle and social conflicts was increasingly marginalized and discredited as disenchantment with the left increased, opening the way to a reconfiguration of this conflict as that of a French "us" against immigrants.[13] Balibar does not fail to point out the paradox proper to France:

> On the one hand, in a way that extends over centuries, France is an *immigration country*, whose population has grown through successive admissions, in the past from elsewhere in Europe, today from the whole world and especially the former colonies. On the other hand, France – whose political system has always drawn its legitimacy from the "Revolution of the Rights of Man" – thinks of itself as the country of universal values, where discrimination as such is unthinkable.[14]

Nowhere are these themes, oppositions and distinctions exhibited in a more comprehensive and visible form than in *La Haine*.

Mathieu Kassovitz stages the wanderings of three young men – Vinz (a Jew), Saïd (an Arab) and Hubert (an African) – over a period of twenty hours. Set on the day after the events of July 1995, following the killing of Makomé M'Bowolé, a seventeen-year-old boy of Congolese origin, by a policeman in a Paris police station in April 1993.[15] The film incorporates actual television footage of the protests. The first half of the film is set in the *banlieue*, which takes on the appearances of an occupied city, and follows the three friends as they attempt in vain to visit one of their companions, Abdel, who had been hospitalized after a brutal assault by the police. Here, *La Haine* alludes directly to the murder of Makomé, which provoked outrage and mass protest. The public announcement of Abdel's death later in the film moves his three friends to hatred and a desire for vengeance. The fact that *La Haine* was filmed in black and white serves to underscore the interweaving of real and fictional events and images, and produces the distantiation, to which Balibar refers, necessary to a critical reflection on social and political realities.[16] It also recalls the Manichean world of colonialism and anti-colonial struggle represented in a film like the *Battle of Algiers* whose director, Gillo Pontecorvo (like Kassovitz), was not part of the world he depicted.

La Haine, at its conclusion, offers as a kind of emblem two murals painted in black and white on the walls of the cité Noé à Chanteloup-les-Vignes, a housing project situated 30 kilometers outside of Paris, where much of the action takes place. Clearly visible in the background are the faces of two of France's greatest nineteenth-century poets, Charles Baudelaire and Arthur Rimbaud, themselves rebels and rioters (the first in the revolution of 1848 and the second in the Paris Commune of 1871), whose works, *Les Fleurs du Mal* (Flowers of Evil) and *Une Saison en enfer* (A Season in Hell), respectively, deeply resonate with the context of the film.[17] The bitter and penetrating face of Baudelaire and the youthful Rimbaud's oblique and despairing gaze represent a condensation of the anger, hatred and sense of exclusion that characterizes the lived experience of the *banlieue*. The presence of these poets in this space does not represent a "clash of cultures," as remarked by Susan Hayward.[18] Viewing them as emblems of high culture obscures their rebellious and anti-conformist side as well as their kinship to the marginalized, both of which nurture their unruly sensitivity. The looks on their faces say it all: Rimbaud's eyes, directed upward and away from the spectator only diverts our attention briefly from the agitation that his face barely masks, while Baudelaire, his face frozen on the wall, looks down with a brutal lucidity on the world of exile and subjection that passes before him, reminding us that his poetry crystallizes the experience of the oppressed and marginalized:

> Je pense à la négresse, amaigrie et phtisique,
> Piétinant dans la boue, et cherchant, l'œil hagard,
> Les cocotiers absents de la superbe Afrique
> Derrière la muraille immense du brouillard;
>
> À quiconque a perdu ce qui ne se retrouve
> Jamais, jamais! à ceux qui s'abreuvent de pleurs
> Et tètent la Douleur comme une bonne louve!
> Aux maigres orphelins séchant comme des fleurs!
>
> Ainsi dans la forêt où mon esprit s'exile
> Un veiux Souvenir sonne à plein souffle du cor!
> Je pense aux matelots oubliés dans une île,
> Aux captifs, aux vaincus! . . . à bien d'autres encor!
>
> I think upon the Negress, tubercular and wasted,
> Groveling in the mud, and seeking, with haggard eye,
> Beyond the massive wall of mist,
> Magnificent Africa's absent coconut palms;
>
> Of all who have lost what cannot ever be regained,
> Not ever! of those who drink their fill of tears
> And suckle of Sorrow like a good she-wolf!
> Of scrawny orphans desiccating like flowers!
>
> Thus in the forest of my spirit's exile
> An old Remembrance echoes full blast like a horn!
> I think upon sailors forgotten on isles,
> Of the captured, the defeated! . . . and of so many more![19]

In fact, *La Haine* stages the "Mal" or evil of the *banlieue* and the "enfer" or hell that is the lived experience of its principle characters by conferring upon these terms a very determinate form and content: the ever-present violence of the police, inseparable from the racism of which it is the concrete realization. Further, the presence of Arab and African police officers does nothing to limit either the racism or the violence that, despite their intentions, they are compelled to enact by the sheer weight of the institution. At one point, the character, Saïd, declares that an Arab will be dead within an hour in a police station and it is here that the film represents the differential effects of racist and stigmatizing interpellation. The three friends are indeed interpellated both by the police in the very specific sense of the French term and more generally, but in both cases interpellation separates and then hierarchizes them. Interpellation also varies according to place: in the privileged city center, a certain level of decorum is expected and even held up, through a kind of mimicry of colonialism, as what distinguishes the center from the periphery. And this decorum, whose primary existence is discursive, is displayed most clearly in the modes of address one person uses in speaking to another. Thus, during a short trip to Paris, Saïd is very surprised to be addressed with the formal "vous" by a policeman who, after giving him directions, tells him to "have a nice day, Monsieur," revealing the chasm that separates his world from that of Paris proper. It is as if this other form of police interpellation, one that exempts the individual addressed from stigmatization, was never meant for him and simply exposes by contrast the subjection that he until then accepted as universal.

After causing a disturbance trying to locate an acquaintance of Saïd in an upscale apartment building and during their brief visit, they discover upon leaving that they have been identified as outsiders and are accordingly interpellated as such by the plain-clothes police ubiquitous in the film: "Excuse us, gentleman, but it seems as if you have been making some trouble." Saïd notes how quickly the police arrive when certain internal borders are violated. While a policeman addresses Vinz using the formal mode of address when it is not clear that he is with Hubert and Saïd ("*Jeune homme, vous êtes ensemble?*"), he turns to Hubert after Vinz escapes and warns "Te fous pas de ma gueule" or "Don't you fuck with me." The use of the informal "*tu*" here marks the debasement of the young men, another element in the stigma imposed on them. As we follow them into the police station, we are conducted beyond a certain threshold of visibility. Up to that point, the film has allowed us to believe that there are good as well as bad cops (as in everything else), but now, outside of public spaces, we are forced to watch the two young men physically brutalized and humiliated with a stream of crude racist insults in the company of a rookie policeman who is observing the interrogation and whose revulsion allows us to understand the primary objective of his training: a total disidentification with the others, the "non-French," Arabs and Africans, whose very presence in France is seen as an insoluble problem. They torment the young men with boasts or threats of killing the outsiders, including the invocation of genocide: "Allez hop, au four, toute la racaille" (Go on, it's to the ovens with all the scum).

The film establishes the consubstantiality of discursive and corporeal violence in the production of the hatred that it both embodies and reflects upon. The three young men are not simply symbols of injustice, each serves as a reminder of the past and not so past forms of cruelty exercised on a mass scale by the colonizing nations (wars of conquest, slavery and finally genocide) first on those outside of Europe whose lives were considered disposable and later on those who, despite living within the borders of Europe, were identified as the internal enemy. The use of the informal "*tu*" reserved for certain adult citizens and not others is a powerful example of the unequal distribution of authority and power in a formally (that is, symbolically) egalitarian society. Indeed, the modern forms of address remain permeated with the relics and remainders of an authoritarian past that no longer exists, at least not in the same form. The use of the pronoun *vous* to address a single person as a mark of distinction or respect is clearly incompatible with the concept of the citizen who "comes after the subject" and whose existence presupposes at least symbolic equality, if not "equaliberty." The use of *vous*, as well as the demand that it be used, as a sign of privilege manifests itself as the politeness that one must show to certain persons (and its unspoken corollary: but not to others to whom one is permitted to be not as, or less, polite).

This past, despite the formal rights and equality assured by the republican constitution, remains imprinted at the level of discourse itself, the living legacy of colonial subjection and servitude, in modes of address such as the use of the informal "*tu*" as a marker of the inferiority of the person addressed. Frantz Fanon saw the interpellative function of the "*tu*" addressed to another adult outside the context of family or friends:

> Les médecins des salles de consultation le savent. Vingt malades européens se succèdent : "Asseyez-vous, monsieur ... Pourquoi venez-

vous?... De quoi souffrez-vous?... – Arrive un nègre ou un Arabe: "*Assieds-toi, mon brave... Qu'est-ce que tu as?... Où as-tu mal? – Quand ce n'est pas: "Quoi toi y en a ?..."*

Doctors in the examination rooms knew it. Twenty ailing Europeans followed one after the other: Sit down, Sir. What brings you here? What seems to be wrong? Let a single black man or Arab walk in: "Sit down, my man... what's the problem?... Where does it hurt? – When it isn't simply "what... wrong... you?"[20]

The use of "*tu,*" part of "the racism of standard language" in the colonial context, as Olivier Le Cour Grandmaison has argued, is closely linked to the idea of inferiority and subjection in non-egalitarian societies.[21] Historically, this mode of address is complemented by another that is no less offensive or degrading – *petit-nègre*, a "simplified French" to facilitate the transmission of commands by French officers to their West African conscripts.[22] *La Haine* invokes the colonial past concealed under the republican veneer of the present. It is in the presence of this past, its effectivity in the present, that allows us to understand the systemic nature of police violence in the *metropole*, where it appears that the antagonisms generated by all of France's imperial adventures and subsequent loss have taken up residence in and around Paris, as if the postcolonial were nothing more than a displacement of conflict.

La Haine, with its focus on the discursive forms of marginalization and stigmatization, thus both portrays and interrogates Althusser's concept of interpellation as developed in his text "Idéologie et Appareils idéologiques d'Etat" (1970). To capture the complexity of interpellation Althusser produces in the form of an allegory a scene in which an individual, addressed by an invisible Subjet, for whom the policeman is a stand-in, yells: "Hé, vous, là-bas!" or "Hey, you there!" The one who is interpellated turns toward the source of the voice and in doing so precipitates his own subjection: his attention is displaced and he deviates from his appointed path. By observing the requirements and conventions of the theater, Althusser presents in miniature and in temporal sequences the ideological interpellation he postulates as "eternal" and "omnipresent." "But in reality these things happen without any succession. The existence of ideology and the hailing or interpellation of individuals as subjects are one and the same thing."[23]

According to Althusser, "individuals are always-already interpellated by ideology as subjects."[24] As Warren Montag has noted, however, interpellation is not simply a call, but is closer to an order or command that always implies an "inequality of force."[25] In fact, it is the fruit of this inequality: in Althusser's scene, only the one who interpellates (or rather his stand-in) speaks; he masters the situation by "delegation" insofar as he decides the time, place and language of the staging, which must be meticulously calculated, but without "seeming to have done so." This last point is crucial, given that interpellation must appear instantaneous; the one who interpellates is not supposed to give an account of the subjectifying effect he produces. The invisibility (a divine attribute) of the Subject *per se* renders him an inaccessible figure whose inaccessibility obscures the very origin of interpellation.[26] The spatial distance and the insurmountable gap reflect the alterity necessary to the production of subjection.[27] In its verticality, emitted as if from a void, interpellation is the inverse of the language of acquiescence uttered from below before a Subject.

The discursive scene Althusser constructs is based on the command to halt that remains implicit in what appears to be the act of calling to or on someone: Hey, you there! ("Hé, vous, là-bas!"). It is directed at individuals who are as yet non-singularized and unidentifiable, "'abstract' with respect to the subjects which they always already are."[28] The call of authority inspires fear in those who did not anticipate it and they turn in response without knowing or intending to do so as if, as Pierre Macherey maintains, the matter at hand is urgent and demands an immediate reaction.[29] We are close to the idea of "reflex" here: the sudden turning around of the body of the interpellated individual is a defensive response to a threat of some kind. The ambiguity of the "vous" (that can indicate either that one is addressing more than one individual or that one has chosen the "respectful" form of address in speaking to a single individual) allows the individual interpellated to feel that he is the target: "the hail was 'really' addressed to him, and that 'it was *really him* who was hailed' (and not someone else)."[30]

But Althusser's allegorical scene presents interpellation as the universal condition of the transformation of the individual into a subject, that is, as an originally "free" agent equal to any other, even if, later, individual subjects are sorted into hierarchically organized positions. In contrast, *La Haine* displays the de-universalizing movements of interpellation, which is itself subject to the aleatory and unpredictable shifts and reversals that mark the social as a field of uninterrupted struggle. The police in the film precisely do not call out "Hey, you (*vous*) there," instantiating the sense of a universal personhood. On the contrary, by resorting to "Hey, you (*tu*) there," they have excluded *les banlieuesards* from the universal, reminded them of their subaltern racial and ethnic status rooted in colonial subjugation and placed them outside the realm of citizenship. The primary characters, for their part, constitute what Althusser calls "bad subjects," those who don't "work all by themselves," that is, who don't respond to the police officer's interpellation, especially when it stigmatizes the individual at whom it is aimed by addressing him as "*tu*." It is as if the interpellative excess that de-universalizes and hierarchizes, an excess that may be seen as the hatred that accompanies that excess of violence Balibar calls cruelty, produces the counter-hatred that engorges the world of the *banlieue*.

It thus appears that Althusser was not able to imagine a scene of subjection in which interpellation operated in the second-person singular, which would be explicitly degrading and could serve only to underscore the inequality that precedes interpellation and to resist its universalizing claims. *La Haine* suggests that in fact police interpellation is pronounced in the singular, merely confirming a subjection that pre-exists it. It is anticipated and originates in an authority that is both identified and hated, both an apparatus and a symbol of the "maintenance" or reproduction of a racialized order. As such, it is incapable of eliciting the acquiescence it seeks to produce and instead makes possible an interpellation of the interpellators, an expropriation of the hatred directed at those addressed as "*tu*," seizing it and turning it against the demand for subjection. But if hatred allows the characters to resist the mechanisms of subjection and renders them impervious to arrest, jail and brutality, it reproduces itself across dividing lines: *la haine attire la haine*, that is, hatred attracts or breeds hatred through a mimicry without limit. Kassovitz's scenario centers on the emergence of "the vicious circle of la Haine."[31]

Let us recall the title of chapter XIX of Niccolo Machiavelli's *The Prince*: "That One Should Avoid Being Despised and Hated." Machiavelli gives examples of historical figures who inspired the hatred and contempt of their subjects and were in consequence deposed, as well as those who inspired fear and were able to continue ruling.³² Fear not only prevents the people from plotting against the prince and disturbing the social order, but it implies a certain kind of respect and even esteem. Hatred, in contrast, may easily threaten the prince's rule: "as princes cannot help being hated by someone, they ought, in the first place, to avoid being hated by every one, and when they cannot compass this, they ought to endeavour with the utmost diligence to avoid the hatred of the most powerful."³³ Two questions arise here: (1) how does the prince inspire hatred (and conversely how does he avoid being hated)? and (2) who are the most powerful whose hatred he must avoid with the utmost diligence? The prince inspires hatred by despoiling his own people or by allowing them to fall into poverty and failing to relieve their sufferings, that is, by oppressing or abandoning them. From this we can deduce that the most powerful are not the wealthy or the nobility, but the people themselves, whose opposition no ruler can long withstand. Hatred is the passion of which this opposition is the expression and its power overcomes fear. Only those who possess something that can be lost or taken away, whether liberty, stability or privilege, will experience fear and neither Saïd nor Vinz nor Hubert have anything whose loss they would truly regret, not even their lives. They are those whose hatred has overpowered the fear they may have otherwise felt. The hatred that spurred the uprisings in the *banlieues* not only deflected stigmatizing interpellation but made visible the de-universalizing form that subjection takes: just as it recruits some individuals, so it rejects others, associating them discursively and corporeally with what Balibar refers to as "Jacques Rancière's now indispensible expression, 'the share of those who have no share.'"³⁴

The film opens with a gesture of defiance: four seconds of grainy news footage in which a single black man, his back to the camera, addresses a crowd of riot police standing not more than a hundred feet away. He shouts, "Murderers! It's easy for you to gun us down when all we got is rocks." What follows is a montage of television images of riots ignited by police brutality, but the images display the power of mass resistance: police lines forced back, demonstrators engaging police, the unimpeded looting of stores and finally a newscaster reporting that a "mob" of youth laid siege to a police station. In this way, we are forced to reflect on the way this violence or counter-violence, to use Balibar's expression, is represented or mediated:

But what should be taken from this "virtual violence" is that it transforms real, endemic social violence to which it responds, *into spectacle*, thereby at once making it *visible* in its intensity and *invisible* its everydayness. It expresses a desperate will to affirm not so much a "cause" or a "project" as an *existence* that is constantly forgotten or denied by the surrounding society (there is no recognized existence other than that which can be represented, reproduced by the media).[35]

Acts of resistance are irreducibly "double-edged, for they return against those who use them by imposing a certain identity on them."[36] This in turn reveals the possibility that these acts are destined to be a fleeting spectacle without any real transformation of the conditions that gave rise to them. Or, worse, that acts of resistance overflow their intended channels and inundate the *banlieue* itself, as for example when Hubert's gym is destroyed during the protest, and young people become bearers of their own exclusion and deprivation by destroying their own conditions of existence. This is perhaps best understood as the other, dark, side of the power of hatred: the ease with which it "breeds" and reproduces through a mimeticism that cannot be controlled or directed. As Balibar argues the ever-increasing scale of the mimicry of the other's violence shapes both the state apparatus and the forces that resist it:

> At the limit, police squads act like gangs fighting other gangs in an escalation of virile exhibitionism – the difference being that they are armed, sent by the state into "hostile territory," and that their own disproportionate violence (insults, beatings, shootings, arrests, detentions, threats) is inscribed within a more general process of intimidation, profiling, and harassment of legal and illegal immigrants. Here the incivility so often invoked as a social scourge is for the most part on the side of the state and its representatives.[37]

Thus, the film's final scene brings the opposing sides together in an act of mutual destruction. Vinz is captured by the police who have been pursuing the young men all night. The plain clothes police officer, whose appearance, speech and behavior renders him indistinguishable from any gang member, holds a pistol to Vinz's head, which suddenly goes off, killing Vinz. Hubert to whom Vinz had earlier given the gun, points it at the cop and the cop immediately points his own weapon at Hubert. The camera pans away from the pair and to Saïd who closes his eyes in horror as the sound of what seems to be a single gunshot is heard. The perfect synchronism of the two actions renders them indistinguishable and indissociable. To close the circle, we need only to recall that the gun Vinz gave to Hubert was a police weapon lost in the previous night's riot, as if weapons, actions and speech circulate freely between and among the opposing sides.

The movie stages a fall in slow motion that ends in a fatal crash. The voice-over tells us at the beginning: "It's a story about a guy falling from a fifty-story building. As he falls, he tries to reassure himself by repeating: so far so good, so far so good." The fall, that is neither natural nor normal since it is the consequence of a collision or some sort of disequilibrium, is a trivial matter to those who are not affected by it. Or so they think: against the background of the mutual destruction the voice tells us that the film is "about a society in free fall. To reassure itself, it repeats itself endlessly 'so far so good, so far so good, so far so good.'" If "it's not the fall that matters, it's the landing"; no one will survive the crash landing, neither those who have jumped from the fiftieth story, nor those unaware that they are falling. The film by refraining from representing the final scene of mutual destruction perhaps questions, or at least suspends, the idea of an inescapable destiny that can no longer be avoided. We are finally interpellated by the film's representation of the disequalizing interpellation of the *banlieuesards*, called up to participate in the movement to push catastrophe back and devise a different future.

Notes

1. Charles Baudelaire, "Abel et Caïn," in *The Flowers of Evil* ("Abel and Cain," trans. William Aggeler), FleursDuMal, <http://fleursdu-mal.org/poem/190> (accessed May 10, 2015).
2. Etienne Balibar, "Uprisings in the *Banlieues*," *Constellations* 14.1 (2007): 47–71, 47. "This does not replace fieldwork" adds Balibar.
3. Balibar, "Uprisings in the *Banlieues*," 50.
4. Balibar, "Uprisings in the *Banlieues*," 60.
5. See, for instance, *La Bataille d'Alger* by Gillo Pontecorvo and *Le Vieux nègre et la médaille* by Ferdinand Oyono (Paris: Julliard, 1956).
6. Balibar, "Uprisings in the *Banlieues*," 50.
7. Balibar, "Uprisings in the *Banlieues*," 58; Balibar writes: "The

functioning of the category of immigration as a substitute for the notion of race and a solvent of 'class consciousness' provides us with a first clue" (Etienne Balibar and Immanuel Wallerstein, *Race, Nation, Class Ambiguous Identities*, translation of Etienne Balibar by Chris Turner (London: Verso, 1991), 20).

8. Pierre Tevanian and Said Bouamama. "Un racisme post-colonial. Un passé qui ne passe pas," *Les Mots sont importants*, August 12, 2015, <http://www.lmsi.net/Un-racisme-post-colonial> (accessed March 1, 2016).
9. "No modern nation has an ethnic basis, meaning a permanent and homogeneous descent from prehistorical kinship groups or alliances" (Balibar, "Racism as Universalism," in *Masses, Classes and Ideas*, trans. James Swenson (London and New York: Routledge, 1994), 229).
10. See the following coverage, accessed November 20, 2015. <http://www.leparisien.fr/societe/mohamed-vire-parce-qu-il-ne-voulait-pas-s-appeler-alexandre-07-10-2010-1098765.php>.
11. Gérard Noiriel, *A quoi sert "l'identité nationale"* (Marseille: Agone, 2007), 57.
12. Noiriel, *A quoi sert "l'identité nationale,"* 60.
13. Noiriel, *A quoi sert "l'identité nationale,"* 67; I suppose that "immigrants" here includes citizens as well.
14. Balibar, "Uprisings in the *Banlieues*," 52.
15. See the following, accessed April 20, 2016. <https://paris-luttes.info/hommage-a-makome-mort-assassine-le?lang=fr>
16. "Black-and-white may give the film an historical *cinéma-vérité* aura, but at the same time it signals distance from 'normal' (colour) documentary and from the naturalistic *beur* films." Susan Hayward, "Designs on the *banlieue*: Mathieu Kassovitz's *La Haine* (1995)," in *French Film: Texts and Contexts*, ed. Susan Hayward and Ginette Vincendeau (London and New York: Routledge, 2000), 316.
17. The other murals show the poets Paul Valéry, Gérard de Nerval, Mallarmé and Victor Hugo. The latter's disappeared in 2005 when the building displaying his mural was demolished during renovation.
18. Hayward, "Designs on the *banlieue*," 319.
19. Baudelaire, "The Swan," trans. Kate Flores, in *The Anchor Anthology of French Poetry*, ed. Angel Flores (New York: Anchor Books, 2000), 33 (English translation of *Les Fleurs du Mal*).
20. Frantz Fanon, *Peau noire masques blancs* (Paris: Seuil, 1952), 45; the English translation is modified.

21. Voir Olivier Le Cour Grandmaison, "Violences symboliques et discriminations raciales dans l'empire français," *Historical Reflections*, 36.2 (2010): 24–38.
22. «To speak pidgin to a Negro makes him angry, because he himself is a pidgin-nigger-talker» (Frantz Fanon, *Black Skin, White Masks*, trans. Charles Lam Markmann (New York: Grove, 1967), 32).
23. Louis Althusser, *Positions* (Paris: Editions sociales, 1976), 127; trans. Ben Brewster, 175.
24. Althusser, *Positions*, 128; English translation, 176.
25. Warren Montag, *Althusser and His Contemporaries. Philosophy's Perpetual War* (Durham, NC: Duke University Press, 2013), 137; about the problem of translating "interpellation" as "hailing," see Warren Montag, "Between Interpellation and Immunization: Althusser, Balibar, Esposito," *Postmodern Culture*, 22.3 (2012), <http://www.pomoculture.org/2015/06/10/between-interpellation-and-immunization-althusser-balibar-esposito-2/> (accessed December 2, 2015).
26. "[I]t is the veiling effect that produces an effect of transcendence, the effect of *withdrawing the origin* of the interpellation, removing the possibility of identifying an author" (Balibar, "Althusser's Dramaturgy and the Critique of Ideology," *Differences*, 26.3 (2015): 1–22; 14; emphasis in the original.
27. "In order to be active within the reproduction as an 'ideological power,' the State must be in fact *absent* from the processes of reproduction." Balibar, "Althusser's Dramaturgy," 16; emphasis in the original.
28. Althusser, *Positions*, 128; English translation, 176.
29. Pierre Macherey, "Deux figures de l'interpellation: 'Hé, vous, là-bas!' (Althusser) – 'Tiens , un nègre!' (Fanon)," 15 February 2012, La philosophie au sens large, <http://philolarge.hypotheses.org/1201> (accessed November 15, 2015).
30. Althusser, *Positions*, 126; English translation, 175; emphasis in the original.
31. See Gilles Favier and Mathieu Kassovitz, *Jusqu'ici tout va bien . . .: Scénario et photographies autour du film* La Haine (Paris: Actes Sud, 1995), 7.
32. Balibar has already cited this reference in his essay "Althusser's Dramaturgy and the Critique of Ideology," 18.
33. Niccolò Machiavelli, *The Prince*, trans. W. K. Marriott, <http://www.gutenberg.org/files/1232/1232-h/1232-h.htm> (accessed March 12, 2016).
34. Balibar, "Uprisings in the *Banlieues*," 61.

35. Balibar, "Uprisings in the Banlieues," 52; emphasis in the original.
36. Balibar, "Uprisings in the Banlieues," 50.
37. Balibar, "Uprisings in the Banlieues," 50.

Bibliography

Anonymous. "Mohamed, viré parce qu'il ne voulait pas s'appeler Alexandre." *Le Parisien*. October 7, 2010. <http://www.leparisien.fr/societe/mohamed-vire-parce-qu-il-ne-voulait-pas-s-appeler-alexandre-07-10-2010-1098765.php> (accessed November 20, 2015).
Anonymous. "Hommage à Makomé mort assassiné le 6 avril 1993 dans un comico de Paris." *Paris-Luttes*. April 1, 2014. <https://paris-luttes.info/hommage-a-makome-mort-assassine-le?lang=fr> (accessed April 20, 2016).
Althusser, Louis. *Lenin and Philosophy and Other Essays*. Trans. Ben Brewster. New York and London: Monthly Review, 1971.
Althusser, Louis. *Positions*. Paris: Editions sociales, 1976.
Balibar, Etienne. "Racism as Universalism." In *Masses, Classes and Ideas*. Trans. James Swenson. London and New York: Routledge, 1994.
Balibar, Etienne. "Uprisings in the Banlieues." *Constellations* 14.1 (2007): 47–71.
Balibar, Etienne. "Althusser's Dramaturgy and the Critique of Ideology." *Differences*, 26.3 (2015): 1–22.
Balibar, Etienne, and Immanuel Wallerstein. *Race, nation, classe. Les identités ambiguës*. Paris: Découverte, 1988.
Balibar, Etienne, and Immanuel Wallerstein. *Race, Nation, Class: Ambiguous Identities*. Trans. Chris Turner. London: Verso, 1991.
La Bataille d'Alger, film. Dir. Gillo Pontecorvo. DVD. Irvington, NY: Rialto Pictures, 2004.
Battle of Algiers (La battaglia di Algeri). Dir. Gillo Pontecorvo. Italy and Algeria: Rizzoli, Rialto Pictures, 1966.
Baudelaire, Charles. "The Swan." Trans. Kate Flores. In *The Anchor Anthology of French Poetry*. Ed. Angel Flores. New York: Anchor Books, 2000.
Baudelaire, Charles. "Abel et Caïn," in *Les Fleurs du Mal* ("Abel and Cain." Trans. William Aggeler). Paris: Gallimard, 2007.
Baudelaire, Charles. "Le Cygne," in *Les Fleurs du Mal* ("The Swan." Trans. Kate Flores). Paris: Gallimard, 2007.
Baudelaire, Charles. *Les Fleurs du Mal*. Paris: Gallimard, 2007.
Fanon, Frantz. *Peau noire, masques blancs*. Paris: Seuil, 1952.

Fanon, Frantz. *Black Skin, White Masks*. Trans. Charles Lam Markmann. New York: Grove, 1967.
Favier, Gille and Mathieu Kassovitz. *Jusqu'ici tout va bien...: Scénario et photographies autour du film* La Haine. Paris: Actes Sud, 1995.
La Haine (Hate), film. Dir. Mathieu Kassovitz. Lazennec, 1995.
Hayward, Susan. "Designs on the *banlieue*: Mathieu Kassovitz's *La Haine* (1995)." In *French Film: Texts and Contexts*. Ed. Susan Hayward and Ginette Vincendeau. London and New York: Routledge, 2000. Pp. 310–27.
Le Cour Grandmaison, Olivier. "Violences symboliques et discriminations raciales dans l'empire français." *Historical Reflections*, 36.2 (2010): 24–38.
Macherey, Pierre. "Deux figures de l'interpellation: 'Hé, vous, là-bas!' (Althusser) – 'Tiens, un nègre!' (Fanon)." February 15, 2012. <http://philolarge.hypotheses.org/1201> (accessed November 15, 2016).
Machiavelli, Niccolò. *The Prince*. Trans. W. K. Marriott. <http://www.gutenberg.org/files/1232/1232-h/1232-h.htm> (accessed March 12, 2016).
Montag, Warren. *Althusser and His Contemporaries. Philosophy's Perpetual War*. Durham, NC: Duke University Press, 2013.
Montag, Warren. "Between Interpellation and Immunization: Althusser, Balibar, Esposito." *Postmodern Culture*, 22.3 (2012). <http://www.pomoculture.org/2015/06/10/between-interpellation-and-immunization-althusser-balibar-esposito-2/> (accessed December 2, 2015).
Noiriel, Gérard. *A quoi sert "l'identité nationale."* Marseille: Agone, 2007.
Oyono, Ferdinand. *Le Vieux nègre et la médaille*. Paris: Julliard, 1956.
Pierre Tevanian and Said Bouamama. "Un racisme post-colonial. Un passé qui ne passe pas," *Les Mots sont importants*, August 12, 2015, <http://www.lmsi.net/Un-racisme-post-colonial> (accessed March 1, 2016).

9

Morbid Perseverance: The Internal Border and White Supremacy
James Edward Ford III

There comes a moment when tenacity becomes morbid perseverance. Hope is then no longer an open door to the future but the illogical maintenance of a subjective attitude in organized contradiction with reality.

     Frantz Fanon, "Letter to the Resident Minister," 53[1]

To Reverend Clementa Pinckney, Cynthia Hurd, Sharonda Coleman-Singleton, Tywanza Sanders, Myra Thompson, Ethel Lee Lance, Susie Jackson, Daniel L. Simmons, Depayne Middleton Doctor and many thousands gone.

What lingers...

In 2008, acclaimed writer Charles Johnson published "The End of the Black American Narrative." He calls the titular storyline one "of group victimization" that has become obsolete.[2] For Johnson, "a people oppressed for so long have finally become as 'polymorphous' as the dance of Shiva". They are now "full-fledged Americans" with access to "plenty of good hard work" – phrases that Johnson quotes from W. E. B. Du Bois's "Criteria for Negro Art." "Criteria," he suggests, anticipates the triumphs of numerous middle-class and upper-class black Americans in the twenty-first century, whose stories herald the obsolescence of the Black American Narrative: "We have been mayors, police chiefs, best-selling authors, MacArthur fellows, Nobel laureates, Ivy League professors, billionaires, scientists, stockbrokers, engineers, theoretical physicists, toy makers, inventors, astronauts, chess grandmasters, dot-com millionaires, actors, Hollywood film directors, and talk show hosts."³ These results were achieved thanks to the "ancestors" who "fought daily for generations, with courage and dignity," and the "miracle they achieved" through transforming the nation.⁴

At stake in Johnson's argument, however questionable its claims and assumptions, is in fact a recalibration of what Etienne Balibar has called the "citizen subject" in the interdisciplinary context of intellectual history and black studies, such that racialization has been and continues to be the means by which a "nonequality" can "develop *on the basis of equality itself.*"⁵ Race becomes one of the primary ways of enacting and justifying exclusions from citizenship. It mars the formal relation between the citizen who is always also a subject (*subditus-subjectum*) and the sovereign (*sublimus/summa potestas*), beating that modern predicament back into the allegedly premodern relation between slave/servant (*servus*) and master (*dominus*). The emergence of a capitalism based increasingly on the labor of a supplemental, global underclass, however, generalizes enslavement or servitude in ways unfathomable to the Greek and Latin conceptions of *oikonomia/oeconomia*.⁶ While elsewhere this supplemental relation operated remotely between colonial territory and metropole, the U.S. developed it within national boundaries, with negative consequences for nonwhite populations generally and forcing the black population in particular to epitomize the *servus* indefinitely, even after this population officially obtained citizenship. Johnson's essay virtually proclaims the dissolution of that supplemental relation of servitude, making the Black American Narrative a quaint, unusable antique.

Seven years after the publication of Johnson's essay, near the end of President Obama's second and final presidential term, I find a stirring generativity in the conceptual and political space that Johnson would have readers abandon. I wager that lingering in the Black American Narrative will offer a compelling counter to Johnson's argument. Methodologically, lingering upsets the critic's desire for timeliness, appropriateness and neat periodization. Lingering conveys uncomfortable, often unacknowledged, intimacies between seemingly antithetical collectivities. Finally, lingering holds on to the possibility of the unexpected insight that may inform new political movement. Following this methodology reveals that Johnson's argument is both a misrepresentation and is misdirected. I place his argumentative wrong turns in the context of mass media investigations of racist reaction to Obama's presidency, which speak to the broad ideological reach of white supremacist views from the far right to the center (if not beyond). Doing so will show how effectively the Black American Narrative anticipates today's political reality. Then, I redirect Johnson's concerns with obsolete racial narratives to understand why the white supremacist narrative – the only truly obsolete racial narrative because it was *never* true – continues to complicate American race relations. Ample evidence suggests that Johnson's list of successes represents a series of defeats to those invested in white supremacy. Reactionary movements build momentum through a melancholic response to defeat, which triggers a cultural mechanism that Etienne Balibar, in a study of Fichtean nationalism, calls the drawing of an "internal border," which offers a place of *refuge* and the space for *moral rearmament*. There can be no racial reconciliation until this cultural mechanism is no longer effective or needed.

When Johnson calls the Black American Narrative a story of victimhood, he forgets that it is above all an indispensable *intellectual space* for studying the overdetermined processes and consequences of white supremacy across the political spectrum. One need only recount Frederick Douglass's account of how he began to "study" slavery to see how he, like virtually all other great contributors to this tradition, acknowledges victimization only to exceed its reach:

> I could not have been more than seven or eight ... when I began to make this subject [slavery] *my study*. It was with me in the woods and fields; along the shore of the river, and wherever my boyish wanderings led me; and though I was, at that time, quite ignorant of the existence of the free states, I distinctly remember being, even then, most strongly impressed with the idea of being a freeman some day. *This cheering was an inborn dream of my human nature – a constant menace to slavery – and one which all the powers of slavery were unable to silence or extinguish.*[7]

The black American Narrative is not determined by group victimization. It is the excess that exists *in spite* of group victimization – the immanent plotting of an "inborn dream."

As Hortense Spillers says, the idea of black culture only exists if it signals "critical edge" cutting against the grain of the American mainstream.[8] Black culture's visions of justice have consistently proven incompatible with mainstream American politics and culture, meaning that black culture is not merely another route to the American status quo. Hence the perplexity I feel when Johnson utilizes Du Bois and King to argue for the Black American Narrative's obsolescence. To do so betrays their understanding of black America's radical potential, and ignores their own biographies, which did not lead to mainstream acceptance in their lifetimes, but to stigmatization for being anti-patriotic, surveillance for being too radical, expatriation and the assassin's rifle. In this intellectual space one finds ample warning that a critical mass of Americans from the center to the far right would experience Johnson's success stories as a series of threats, and narratives of decline or even apocalypse. "Critical mass" designates a sizable, well-resourced, well-organized group within and beyond America's two major political parties, using its economic, political and social influence to ensure institutional discrimination and general hostility towards blackness. Significantly, much in the Black American Narrative demonstrates that anti-black racism increases with black successes that cannot be tokenized and that this increase has material consequences for the well-being of black Americans, other people of color and anti-racist whites. Unfortunately, Johnson's argument only works by understating this reality.

Johnson's argument hinges upon contrasting the Black American Narrative from the antebellum era until the 1960s with the progress of black Americans in the twenty-first century. Johnson acknowledges the "race riots, lynchings, and the destructions of towns and communities" that once "disrupted" black lives, but, tallying up economic and career successes in June 2008, Johnson finds the "narrative of group victimization" detached from the reality of the present, making it a defeatist ideology.

One may reply, nearly eight years later, that the 2008 Financial Crisis decimated the black middle class, that a politics of abandonment replaced "race riots" as the means of expeling blacks from the cities and repopulating them with upper-middle-class whites, that segregation in schools has been increasing in the twenty-first[t] century but through a privatization model with no mid-twentieth-century analog and that no analog exists for the Pentagon passing out military weapons produced for the War on Terror to local police departments across the country – and one could go on. But to respond in this way suggests that clarity only comes through hindsight. Instead, I will examine two passages each from Du Bois

The Internal Border and White Supremacy 257

and King that anticipate such reactions, even to the mainstream successes Johnson praises, including the election of a black president. Turning to these passages will reveal a different understanding of American whiteness' view of black success and demonstrate the oddity of using Du Bois and King to hail the Black American Narrative's obsolescence.

The first passage from Du Bois appears in *Black Reconstruction* (1935), where he merely posits the black worker's existence without granting that figure a political position. He considers how it is through the lens of "imperial white domination" – a form of whiteness that finds its coherence through treating blacks and other nonwhite populations as political, economic, emotional and cultural property – that the black worker is viewed.[9] Du Bois says that the black criminal "threatened society," but could be tolerated. Counter-intuitively, the black criminal validates the white supremacist's ideological position by confirming stereotypes of black inferiority and justifying violence against black bodies as justifiable punishment. But the "free Negro" invalidates not simply an individual white supremacist's ideological position but also white supremacy in its entirety: whether as the "educated property holder" or the "successful mechanic or even professional man," the free Negro counts as *"a contradiction, a threat and a menace."* This successful black worker *"more than threatened slavery. He contradicted and undermined it. He must not be. He must be suppressed, enslaved, colonized."*[10] Note Du Bois ventriloquizing white supremacy's logic towards the free Negro: "He *must not be.*" Again, Du Bois has not granted the free Negro a political viewpoint. The mere *potential* for free thinking, unfettered organization, and the power to bring radical dreams to fruition challenges the white supremacist's historical narrative, epistemology and existential coherence. Du Bois does not claim that this challenge yields reconciliation. The person invested in an "imperial white" perspective manages the anxiety posed by the free Negro through violence – "suppre[ssion], enslave[ment], coloniz[ation]." Also note that violence awaits both versions of the black. The black criminal is punished for fitting stereotypes; the free Negro *for not fitting* stereotypes. Violence towards blackness, whether "free" or "unfree," is nearly a precondition for the person invested in that imperial viewpoint.

In a second passage, this time from 1944, Du Bois doubts that racial prejudice will decrease even by the end of the twentieth century. He describes the last phase of his life's research and activism as "scientific investigation and organized action among negroes, in close co-operation, to secure the survival of the Negro race, *until the cultural development of America and the world is willing to recognize Negro freedom.*" Du Bois describes a multi-directional process of black culture's internal development in relation to nonblack collectives, fully recognizing that these collectives abide different, sometimes even opposed, timelines. Significantly, Du Bois, the black Diaspora's greatest exemplar of "centenary logic," does not conclude this essay with black culture's obsolescence or its culmination through the black middle class, but with the urgent need for its persistence. He says so because "the majority of men" act according to "social pressures, inherited customs and long-established, often sub-conscious, patterns of action. *Consequently, race prejudice in America will linger long and may even increase.*"[11] Combining Du Bois's hypothesis that racism "will linger and may even increase," with his argument that racists see successful blacks as objects to be "suppressed, enslaved, [and] colonized," reveals the discrepancy in Johnson using Du Bois to hail the Black American's obsolescence, to turn economic justice into middle-class consumerism or to reduce racial progress to black Americans abandoning their critical viewpoint when they are out-resourced and, quite literally, outgunned by a critical mass who may be increasingly racist.

Events during Obama's two terms confirm Du Bois's hypothesis that racism will not only linger but even increase in response to mainstream black successes that do not radically alter current structures of dominance. I find support in Evan Osnos's essay from August 2015, "The Fearful and the Frustrated" in *The New Yorker*, which discusses the far right's viewpoint on contemporary U.S. politics: "Ever since the Tea Party's peak, in 2010, and its fade, citizens on the American far right – Patriot militias, border vigilantes, white supremacists – have searched for a standard-bearer."[12] It would be convenient if the far right stayed on the political fringe. But the rise of the Tea Party, despite its specifically libertarian origin story, granted the broader range of far-right-wingers greater access to mainstream politics and opportunity to recruit from putatively mainstream conservative and even liberal traditions. They have become a constituency to which conservative politicians openly cater (rather than secretly support). Despite still significant differences between those whites who claim to be center, right and far right in the U.S polity, Osnos's essay suggests that they too often only differ in the degree of their racial anxiety towards the free Negro who surpasses societal expectations. Too often, the far right overtly states what their more politically correct counterparts quietly believe.

Before Obama's presidency, U.S. federal agencies and research centers concluded that domestic white supremacist groups posed the greatest threat to U.S. sovereignty. They have infiltrated the U.S. military and police forces across the nation to train for an inevitable U.S. race war. The number of hate groups rose from 602 groups in 2000 to 888 groups in 2007, which makes more than a 30 percent increase in the years just before Johnson publishes his article. By 2009, the year of Obama's first inauguration, the number rose to 926 and peaked in 2011 with 1,018 groups – an increase of more than 40 percent in eleven years, including old members becoming active again and new members turning to the far right in protest of changes in America's racial climate.[13] One of Osnos's interviewees suggested as much, noting the "unconscious vision" among "white people" "that their grandchildren might be a hated minority in their own country." A second interviewee embraced "white nationalism" despite his mainstream conservative upbringing. He fears that "all of the European peoples" are "dying out" from "mass immigration and multiculturalism." To Osnos, these statements indicate that "unlike previous generations of white nationalists," who were motivated by "nostalgia for slavery," this new crop is "inspired" "by their dread" of a future moment, when "non-Hispanic whites will no longer be the largest demographic group in America." Osnos falters in thinking that the older generations were strictly backward-looking. Nevertheless, one should take seriously the younger generation's fears of being overtaken demographically, which gives their view of the future a more apocalyptic tone. Osnos's interviewees "uniformly predict a violent future" with proclaiming that "[t]he American dream is dead, and the American nightmare is just beginning . . . I think that whites don't know the *terror* that's upon us."[14]

Mainstream centrists and conservatives may not share the specific apocalyptic visions of the far right, but I would argue that they share the same "terror," which they try to manage by tapping into the harshest stereotypes about black ignorance, animality and family dysfunction to attack President Obama and the First Family. Obviously, these stereotypes do not apply to the

President and his family and that's the point. These racist assaults are launched *out of anger at the fact that they do not fit the First Family*. They are punishments for not embodying the image of a dysfunctional family that could never occupy the White House. So many Americans have made disingenuous public apologies for these insults to stave off losing their livelihoods or social prestige, that the "non-apology for racism" has become its own media genre. Almost by definition, these non-apologists admit saying something overtly racist, then say they are not and have never been racist, and that their own racist words do not correspond to their actual views. Liberals or mainstream conservatives who are so profoundly confused about their racial outlook cannot provide support for Johnson's triumphalism.

Following Du Bois's logic, we can only conclude that the free Negro, even one who espouses a mainstream politics, stirs racial animosity and signals national decline, collective existential threat, sometimes even apocalypse. The terror derives from the fact that black America has *not* fully internalized a victimization narrative. It is this that allows the black to venture beyond the boundaries set by mass media stereotypes, unjust laws and institutional discrimination. The attempt to manage this terror has translated into verbal, economic, political and physical attacks against blacks and other nonwhite peoples.

Police killings of civilians have reached highs not seen in forty years – the very time period that Johnson says is gone for good. The juridical apparatus guarantees impunity to the police who kill unarmed and even subdued suspects, no matter how compelling the evidence against them, often resorting to illegal practices such as doctoring official reports, editing incriminating dashcam footage, turning off bodycams and altering online informational sites to mislead the public in order to prevent prosecution of police killings. Further, the mere investigation of police crimes is taken as an assault on law and order with the result that thousands, hundreds of thousands and sometimes millions of dollars are collected on behalf of wrongdoers through public fundraising sites. The breadth of this brutality, now well documented, has no place in Johnson's account of the Age of Obama, although it now in many ways defines it, through the pattern of mass traumatization, self-assertion among black folk and their allies, followed in turn by more racist hostility because, once again, the black will not accept the limits or borders imposed by the white supremacist narrative.

When we acknowledge the realities that Johnson's argument must ignore, we discover that any discussion of obsolete racial narratives compels us to pose the question of why and how the white supremacist narrative endures even today. Surely, he agrees to white supremacy's obsolescence and laments the psychological, physical and economic damage it wreaks upon black Americans, Asian Americans, Native Americans, mixed-race Americans and white Americans who reject that ideology. But the absence of any reference to this narrative suggests the possibility of reading Johnson's essay as an instance of transference. This allows us to postulate that Johnson relegates the Black American Narrative to the fate he would assign the white supremacist narrative, but does not dare to do, since he knows the latter's resiliency. Fatalism lurks in this post-racial optimism – willfully dropping one's weapons before a great antagonist only to herald this one-sided armistice as a complete victory, while one's antagonist remains poised to attack or is actively attacking. Radical change becomes unthinkable, acquiescence to American normality becomes the default goal and white supremacist (organized plans for) violence carries on basically unabated. One could still hope, like Johnson, that a postracial order has been achieved nonetheless. Such a hope, I argue, becomes "morbid perseverance," no longer offering "an open door to the future," since it cannot admit, let alone contend with, that future's greatest obstacles. Consequently, that hope becomes "the illogical maintenance of a subjective attitude in organized contradiction with reality."[15]

There are signs, in a recent essay on Trayvon Martin, that Johnson realizes the limits of his 2008 essay. He closes the essay on Martin by calling for the "systematic undoing of centuries of racial indoctrination" as "the necessary first step toward the epistemological humility and egoless listening we are morally obliged to bring to our encounters with all Others." Another word for this is "love," Johnson says.[16] I concur. But which mechanisms should be dismantled? I argue that one of these mechanisms is the "internal border," which gets triggered whenever the nation-state insufficiently supports the hegemonic national culture. This discrepancy between hegemonic culture and nation-state form results whenever so-called minority cultures begin to break out of the molds they have long inhabited, even as new migrant populations add further complexities. These new possibilities for inclusion can be read from the perspective of white supremacy as defeats. In response, the once-hegemonic national culture violently redraws lines of belonging *within* the nation to separate its supposedly true from its false members. While much great scholarship has addressed the specific forms of violence used to draw this line, I am more concerned with deducing the form of collective consciousness that needs such violence for its social, political and epistemological coherence. To do this, I look back from contemporary events to King's mid-twentieth-century account of backlash and, finally, to the post-Civil War moment to understand the collective consciousness opposing racial reconciliation.

On the beautiful soul and racialization

Rather than continue using Johnson's Black American Narrative to question his argument on its own terms, henceforward I will use the phrase *the black radical tradition*. The black radical tradition confronts the intellectual, aesthetic and political complexities that are too often sidestepped in the liberal and conservative intellectual traditions. This tradition seeks a more rigorous theorization of the reaction, which, so far, sounds synonymous with backlash. Backlash tends to designate a constituency's response to a putatively unfavorable turn of events. But the hatred for the free Negro is much fiercer than a reaction to a single unfavorable event. It bespeaks animosity towards a range of theoretical and practical *possibilities* to be suppressed, enslaved or colonized, as Du Bois noted. Were I to stop at merely proving that a powerful group reacts negatively to black success, I would also miss the more intractable issue at stake here. By returning to King's demand that his readers go beyond the insufficient term "white backlash" in his day, he provides a model for understanding the reactionary attitude at play in the twenty-first century.

Also, by returning to King I counter Johnson's liberal rendering of him as another supporter of the American mainstream. Johnson says that narratives "of individuals, not groups" will replace the Black American narrative and asks, "is this not exactly what King dreamed of when he hoped a day would come when men and women were judged not by the color of the skin, but instead by the individual deeds and actions, and the content of their character?" He answers by asserting "I believe this was what King dreamed and, whether we like it or not, that moment is now."[17] But in several of his later speeches and his classic *Where Do We Go from*

Here, King conceptualizes the opposition that Johnson too hastily ignores. This opposition does not nullify King's utopian vision (and, it must be said, this hyper-quoted statement from King does not encapsulate his utopian vision). But King would never consider his utopian vision fulfilled while the racism I have discussed effectively obstructs progress for millions of black people or anyone else. Any love that does not confront such obstructions cannot also carry out the demands of justice, and this sort of love King calls "sentimental and anemic."[18]

King wisely distinguishes between reaction and a reactionary attitude. He makes the latter his focus and somewhat akin to what Hegel called the "beautiful soul" in *The Phenomenology of Spirit*. With this figure, Hegel critiqued German intellectuals condemning the French Revolution by saying Germany's earlier intellectual and religions transformations made political upheaval unnecessary. Hegel posits their strongest argument to reveal its greatest weakness. The beautiful soul claims a purity that fears being tainted by the complexities of material change. In the U.S. context, at its boldest, Alabama Governor George C. Wallace's saying "segregation today, segregation tomorrow, and segregation forever" in his 1963 Inauguration Address epitomizes the beautiful soul's unwillingness to accept transformation of America's racialized power dynamics.[19] There, Wallace boldly located his Inauguration in the "Cradle of Confederacy," the "very Heart of the Great Anglo-Saxon Southland."

In its more timid, liberal forms, the beautiful soul logically and/or ethically admits the need for change, but practically allows the minimum amount of change necessary to halt more radical transformations. Despite these differences, a racial solidarity has taken shape at least from the far right to the center, something that Wallace anticipated in his speech, when he asked for the support of whites who had "moved north and west," along with whites born in "old New England" and "the great mid-West," that they, too, would also be "of the Southern spirit," "of the Southern philosophy," and "brothers" in the "fight."[20] The beautiful soul provides a model for examining this solidarity, even as the U.S. example emphasizes that Hegel's account can only address modern consciousness in general if it attends to racial difference.

The beautiful soul prefers the role of the spectator, whose "political judgment" "is an extension of the aesthetic judgment," and privileges sideline enthusiasm over full-bodied participation.[21] Such spectatorship allows the beautiful soul to pretend it remains at a safe distance from radical contingency and pretend to be at the center of the event, even orchestrating what occurs. The beautiful soul then demands that the world confirm this impossible outlook. This demand splits that subject into a double consciousness, espousing ideals it cannot bring into reality and, fundamentally, does not want to become reality. Having to bring the vision to reality would, once again, require an openness to change. Thus, the beautiful soul is a melancholic. Although recent scholarship has tended "to valorize melancholia ... for being somehow more 'ethical' than mourning – less vulgarly recuperative, more faithful to the dead because of its tenacity," philosopher Rebecca Comay calls this "far too easy; it ignores the inextricable link between melancholia and narcissism; and the secret gratification we garner in our grief."[22] Now, this tension between disinterested moral persona, unacknowledged but viscerally felt pleasure, and the demand that the world accommodate this contradictory structure must be further complicated by the complexities of race. King offers great insight here.

King confirms my assertion that the internal border violently draws a line of distinction between true and false members of the nation to thwart racial reconciliation. King traces this consciousness back to the nation's founding to understand the internal border's implementation. In the late 1960s, he says white Americans "shattered the hope that new attitudes were in the making."[23] Johnson says the Black American Narrative reached its zenith with the March on Washington and the Voting Rights Act, in 1963 and 1965 respectively. But as late as 1967 King theorizes a backlash building greater momentum that has already "shattered" certain hopes of transformation among the white majority. Perhaps the "post-Civil Rights era" racial conflicts Johnson calls misguided and pointless – an "antique" he says – are actively contending, however contradictorily and incompletely, with the ongoing backlash that King identified in 1967.[24] At any rate, King's own account testifies to a backlash outliving the endpoint Johnson assigns it, adding even more complications to his claim that, barely a generation later, narratives of racial struggle are obsolete.

Although I suggest that today's reactionary political formation begins to take shape in the late 1960s, he asserts that the reactionary view is much older. Hence King's disagreement with the "pat explanation" that "Negroes rioted," "the voice of Black Power was heard," and "the white backlash was born; the public became infuriated and sympathy evaporated." King counters with "the hard fact that *the change in mood had preceded* Watts and the Black Power slogan." He then displaces the origin once more, to the nation's founding. "*White backlash is nothing new*," he says. In the 1950s and 1960s, mainstream whiteness demonstrates "the same vacillations, the same search for rationalizations, the same lack of commitment that have *always* characterized white America on the question of race." It "*had always existed underneath and sometimes on the surface of American life.*" "Since the birth of our nation," King says, "white America has had a schizophrenic personality on the question of race," being "torn" between "a self in which she proudly professed the great principles of democracy and a self in which she sadly practiced the antithesis. This tragic duality has produced a strange indecisiveness and ambivalence toward the Negro."[25] For King, the twenty-first century instances of obstruction that I have catalogued and even the mid-twentieth-century opposition he faced each provide evidence of a history of whiteness's double-consciousness as old as the nation itself.

While Hegel argued that German culture, perhaps as far back as the Reformation, had already cultivated an allergy to the complicated, incomplete freedom accompanying the French Revolution, so King argues that the United States, since its very beginnings in the Age of Revolutions, has developed a "strange indecisiveness and ambivalence" towards black *autonomy*, meaning any set of ideas, affects and actions carried out by the black that do not fit expectations based on stereotypes – being a free Negro, as Du Bois said. In the United States, the beautiful soul directs its thinking, affiliating and political decision-making towards hindering any social transformation shaping and shaped by black autonomy.[26] Holding on, however openly or quietly, to Governor Wallace's desire for a past, present and future segregationist power structure and culture, the beautiful soul hopes to confine the black to unlivable conditions and impossibly narrow expectations. Crucially, any effective movement of the black beyond these limits, however momentary, may count as the beautiful soul's *defeat*. It is a chief delusion of dominance. After enjoying unfair privileges for extended periods, one thinks time a kind judge declaring one virtuous after all. One makes mere temporal endurance a stand-in for ethical fulfillment. The longstanding fact of one's hegemonic position, in itself, becomes the rightness of one's position. The beautiful soul knows that this is a delusion. Yet, the overturning of that hegemony, even when the beautiful soul knows this is just, and even if the new situation brings a new level of equity, will be felt as an injustice worthy of retaliation. Unless these emotional investments in an unjust status quo are shifted elsewhere to a different standard of ethical practice, this right change will become the basis for restoring the wrong. Another angle of Fanon's quotation comes to light. Morbid perseverance can effectively describe Charles Johnson's view that America was nearly overcome with Obama's election. It can also apply to those who feel defeated by any form of black progress and, then, seek to undue what they know is just. Thus, this sense of defeat requires greater elucidation.

Balibar's discussion of Fichte's *Addresses* will aid this effort immensely. The "internal border" I have mentioned previously in this essay is primarily a hegemonic racial group responding to a sense of spiritual and political defeat by violently redrawing the lines of belonging to the nation. To elucidate this mechanism's relation to defeat, I follow King's advice and look even further back, this time to the reaction against the Union's victory in the Civil War, the Emancipation Proclamation and the Reconstruction era.

Refuge and the internal border

As I have shown, in moments when changes in leadership, national symbolism and demographics suggest that the nation-state no longer coincides with the hegemonic national culture, a commonly unacknowledged solidarity between the far right, mainstream conservatives and the center comes to the foreground. Readers will have little problem associating this view with Alabama's Governor Wallace, who represents the most extreme, raw and politically incorrect version of this figure. He cannot even consider black progress hypothetically. Nor will readers be surprised by King noting a "reversion to barbaric white conduct marked by a succession of murders in the South" and in the North he found the "recrudescence of white hoodlumism" as the Civil Rights Movement progressed. But in King's account of white supremacy's "tragic duality," the beautiful soul wishes to espouse democratic ideals without bringing them to fruition. In such unpredictable conditions, even those who support black progress *in theory* must now publicly bridge the relationship between that theory and *practice*. So alongside the barbarity and hoodlumism King notes the "*cold systematic withdrawal of some erstwhile white allies.*"[27] Losing this untroubled moral high ground also means abandoning a secret narcissism, allowing one to adopt a condescending attitude towards the struggle without having to be engaged. Abandoning that ill-gotten psychological (and material) comfort for the risk and vulnerability of full-bodied engagement, where one's shortcomings would be on display (that is one cost of genuine alliance), is too much to lose for some liberal beautiful souls who agree with political change in theory alone, which undercuts theory altogether, if it logically excludes practice at the outset.

The beautiful soul utilizes several tactics to guard against, halt or reverse change while remaining above the fray. These tactics, as Balibar describes them, inform two movements of the defeated beautiful soul: *refuge* and *moral rearmament*. In my discussion of *refuge* and *moral rearmament*, I want to understand how the melancholic beautiful soul turns defeat, even a defeat it knows is just, into a new rational for restoring a destructive order. These tactics show up in rhetorical strategy as well as active political maneuvering. They all require violence and are key to protecting the narcissism of the beautiful soul's combination of condescension and apathy. The first tactic denies that change can happen, should happen or has happened, in order to sustain the current power dynamic, affective regime, terms of belonging and ways of knowing. Other tactics nuance this theme. The second only allows gradual change. King opposed this tactic in "Letter from Birmingham Jail," saying "for years now I have heard the word 'Wait!' . . . This 'wait' has almost always meant 'never.'"[28] The third tactic acknowledges the event, but denies the agent of change. The beautiful soul pretends to be the change it obstructed. If these tactics cannot work, the beautiful soul espouses the transformation, but deems the outcome so horrible it betrays the political cause. This fourth tactic admits change at a cost so high nothing should have changed. These tactics show up in the liberal and far-right responses to black self-emancipation and the national transformations resulting from four million freepersons becoming citizens.

If a turn to Fichte appears far-fetched, consider the U.S.'s foremost philosophical collective following the Civil War, the St Louis Hegelians. They first organized in St. Louis, Missouri before the Civil War and proclaimed German Idealism the pathway for understanding the historical role of the United States in the World. They reached a popular audience through their *Journal of Speculative Philosophy*. The Hegelians saw in Hegel "an optimist" "solv[ing] contradictions and enlarg[ing] the democratic self," filtered through Fichte's philosophies of history, education and the state, driven to fulfill the destiny of man.[29] Indeed, as good Fichteans, they made their greatest practical impact through teaching, designing and leading school systems. Most importantly, their emphasis on Fichte after the Civil War directly brings up the issue of defeat. Remember, no treaty between the Union and Confederacy ended the Civil War, since that would have formally recognized the secession. The Confederacy *unconditionally surrendered* to the Union, making the theme of defeat a sociopolitical reality for the post-Civil War South. The way the Hegelians theorize this enlarging democratic self after unconditional surrender, I argue, sets up a quite literal test case for understanding *refuge* and *moral rearmament* for the beautiful soul after the Civil War and even in the Age of Obama.

In Fichte's *Addresses*, the subject admits defeat and the inevitability of change just enough to refute it by an inward turn that one could call *refuge*. Balibar ventriloquizes this argument, saying,

> Doubtless we are defeated . . . but this is secondary and in truth is only *external*. A refuge always exists for national identity, which, as an essentially moral identity . . . never had anything but a secondary . . . connection with these states and borders, and this refuge is precisely the "self" of the Germans.

Balibar also notes that from this viewpoint, the Germans face no external border where they "run up against other peoples; it consists in the invisible reality of their inner world, where they can progress indefinitely while encountering only themselves."[30] The Hegelians in the U.S. South embraced this aspect of Fichte's philosophy, when A. Koerger translated the following portion of "Introduction to Fichte's System of Knowledge" in the Hegalians's *Journal*: "Attend to thyself; turn *thine* eye away from all that surrounds thee and into *thine* own inner self! Such is that task imposed upon the student by philosophy. We speak of nothing that is without thee, but merely of thyself."[31] The beautiful soul conflates the political as such with its own ego, to control or erase any confrontation with another. No outside standard can be considered, seeing that this would threaten the "purity" of the commitment to the nation, which consists of oneself and others who share this "invisible" bond.

Such a philosophical outlook leaves no place for the negativity simultaneously hindering and enabling the Hegelian subject. In his research on the St. Louis Hegelians, intellectual historian Shamoon Zamir illustrates this outlook's consequences for Hegel's master–slave dialectic. The Hegelians "falsely attribut[e] the myth of cowardly contract to Hegel, thereby providing philosophical alibis for the proslavery arguments of the 1890s."[32] By "cowardly contract," Zamir refers to the argument that agrees that slavery is a serious wrong, but believes that the right to private property is sacred, even if that property is a human being. The Hegelians would applaud any individual slave owners who emancipated their slaves. But overthrowing slavery, which necessarily meant overthrowing a form property, was actually worse than slavery itself. Here, one finds of the beautiful soul's fourth tactic for hindering change – acknowledge the wrongs of the present, only to claim that changing the situation proves to be worse than the previous order of things. But the Hegelians go further. They reference Aristotle's theory of the natural slave to claim that Emancipation did nothing for African Americans, and in so doing they use the beautiful soul's third tactic, of acknowledging change but denying the agent of change. By this logic, ending slavery only relieved the slave master of a status below his dignity, since owning slaves tainted his otherwise upright moral attitude. Of course, this argument yields the solipsistic conclusion that the civil war and emancipation were gifts that the slave owners gave to themselves, to free themselves from their own need for slavery, since they were already free a claim that enacts the third tactic, where the beautiful soul pretends to be agent of the change it attempted to obstruct.

The Hegelians racialized this bond among whites in ways that seem altogether far away from and surprisingly close to current liberal positions. As the most prolific Hegelian, Denton Snider says, in his book on the Civil War, "the Hero" epitomizing human freedom has appeared, an "Aryan Hero." That comments gives away its age by being so straightforwardly offensive. But then Snider admits "the World-Spirit has enjoined 'racial freedom' upon the United States" and utilizes the shockingly familiar rhetoric of multiracialism:

> The former slaves of the South having become freedmen and also citizens, have introduced a new world-historical problem whose working-out reaches far into the future. For the World's History as

> hitherto developed . . . has been confined to one race., we may call it *uniracial*. But at present, many indications show that the World's History is expanding its limits . . . hence we may call it *multiracial* . . . The supreme units of European History have mainly been tribes and nations of the same general ethnic character, of the same Race . . . But at present we the beginnings of a vast change; the ultimate political units of History are getting to be racial, rising above and including Nations . . . It would seem . . . that the Races are to constitute together the supreme processes of the World's History.[33]

Snider's observation of a multiracial future does not dispel anxiety; it increases it. It marks a greater need for racial distinctions by making particular claims on the nation. When Snider discusses "the Public opinion of other nations" against slavery, he quotes another pro-Confederate author saying "'what are they that should subject us to the question? *The Southern people are a nation*,' that is, taken by themselves apart from the North, and will not 'answer to the tribunal of any other nation.'"[34] This version of nation-building occurs within but cannot coincide with the U.S.'s external borders, cutting the nation in two (at least) to ensure that the so-called "true" members remain disencumbered by the racially "false" members.

Furthermore, Snider's own anti-black racism does not fade with his multiracial worldview. Snider maintains the Hegelians's argument that the slave owners freed themselves of slavery for their own benefit. The freed persons are merely an unhappy side effect of the slave owner's will. He adds that slavery's end has wrought "a revolution" of cultural expression in the South. He then adds,

> the best part of the old South will not be lost in the new order . . . The essentials of Southern character were native and inbred; *We refuse to believe that they depended for their existence upon negro slavery or upon the negro in any necessary way* . . . [T]he Southern gentleman and Southern lady are still alive, even under changed outward circumstances. It is natural for them to look back on their past with a fond regret, and to paint it in ideal colors; but ask them if they would wish to see it really restored.[35]

Rather than examine the evidence to consider how much the slaveowner depended upon the slave, Snider simply "refuses" other possibilities. The planter class could not have depended upon

The Internal Border and White Supremacy   271

slaves for their existence, he says, though their control over the South and inroads into national government and institutions depended upon what was their approximately four billion dollars in slave property.

He proclaims that the Southern aristocracy endures despite being decimated by losing the Civil War. Somehow, these Old South figures are alive and well though the social conditions that supported them are gone. But is it the case that they do not want the South "really restored"? How could this be when the passage hinges upon desiring the Old South's survival? Thus, the beautiful soul finds refuge in a contradictory array of bold-faced denials of reality.

Moral rearmament and the internal border

Feeling the pressure to admit these contradictions, the beautiful soul lashes out. Otherwise, by admitting the contradictions it internally accepts the defeat that is outwardly visible. As Snider says in unnecessarily lofty language, "permanent defeat of a cause is a negative judgment of the Tribunal of the Ages ... the lost case means the condemned cause, condemned at the forum of History, *but not necessarily at the forum of Conscience.*"[36] Snider, partly ventriloquizing and partly endorsing the Confederacy's position, strips the Confederate surrender in the Civil War of any moral force it obtained by taking up the claim of Emancipation. The conscience holds out to continue battles already lost. This requires a turn to Fichte's concept of "moral rearmament." Although Fichte will stress the physically nonviolent aspects of moral rearmament after defeat, Balibar notes that "this resistance is not incompatible with a call to arms, but it can be considered as ... preceding and conditioning military rearmament."[37]

This term can only have explanatory value in the U.S. context if one takes the potential for violence literally. Recall Snider referencing a pro-Confederate identifying the South as its own nation. Snider quotes the same Southerner again, saying, "we shall 'answer with weapons and in no other language than that of war and the knife,' should our slaveholding rights be challenged."[38] The economic, political and cultural loss associated with abolition weighs too heavily on this Southerner. Violence provides the answer, violence targeting those within the U.S.'s borders. This anonymous Southerner's statement forewarns of the merciless violence coming after the abolition of slavery and the strides for citizenship made by black Americans across the United States. Most importantly, those who enact this violence and those who support it – directly and indirectly – will not occupy society's fringes. Members of the far right, the mainstream right and the center will all share in the bloody carnival for political gain, economic gain and sheer sadistic enjoyment.

To make this final point, which combines my analysis of *refuge* with that of *moral rearmament*, I shift to Alfred Moore Waddell's white supremacy speech from October 24, 1898 and his "White Man's Declaration of Independence" published on November 9, 1898 in Wilmington, North Carolina. Waddell is widely considered the brains behind the overthrow of the local Reconstruction government in Wilmington, North Carolina. Waddell's approach became the model for overthrow at the state level. This ugly ordeal exemplifies how the "lost cause," though condemned by history, was not condemned "at the forum of conscience." They held on to an attitude captured in a transcription of Confederate President Jefferson Davis's speech by the *Wilmington Journal* while visiting the city in November 1863. As the Confederacy began losing the Civil War, Jefferson called the "ruin and devastation" of lost battles the ugly doings of "the vandal foe," the Northern "invader." Jefferson proclaimed that despite impending defeat, "with a resolute purpose and united effort we [Confederates] would regain all that we had lost, and accomplish all that we had proposed."[39] Waddell and his ilk saw themselves as fulfilling what Jefferson proclaimed thirty-five years earlier.

Some call it the 1898 Wilmington Race Riot, which seems to suggest a fair fight between white and black Wilmingtonians. Nothing could be further from the truth. The alternate name, the 1898 Wilmington Massacre, better captures the white-on-black violence, theft of property and terrorism that descended upon the city to establish Jim Crow Law definitively. Waddell's "Declaration" is the official political expression of rebellion against the Reconstruction agenda of establishing cross-racial equity. Few other documents surpass Waddell's "Declaration" and his speech in explicitly framing themselves as an instance of moral rearmament coupled with violent action in attempts of reversing unwanted political change. This lesson from Waddell's Declaration is clear: examine the beautiful soul's angelic white robe closely and one will find blood along the hem.

The Internal Border and White Supremacy 273

Waddell's "Declaration" finds refuge in a racial genealogy of political belonging and authority:

> Believing that the Constitution ... contemplated a government to be carried on by an enlightened people; believing that its framers did not anticipate the enfranchisement of an ignorant population of African origin, and believing that those men of ... North Carolina ... did not contemplate for their descendants subjection to an inferior race.[40]

Waddell joins Snider in wedding racial identity to genealogy, and genealogy to national belonging. Waddell's "we" includes the other signers and makes "white people" in general synonymous with "Anglo Saxon" as opposed to Americans "of African origin." The "Declaration" holds that this collective should not have to abide a set of race relations their fathers never experienced. Waddell's claim of "subjection" better known as "Negro Domination" is inaccurate but revealing, both conceptually and practically. Conceptually, the "Declaration's" signers defined freedom as the autonomy to subjugate black bodies. The white supremacist's inability to subjugate blacks counts as an affront to white freedom. Institutionally supported cross-racial equality, in this twisted logic, counts as a theft of white freedom. The white supremacist's inability to oppress others counts as being oppressed (and anticipates the call of reverse racism that will dominate liberal debates on restorative justice from the 1990s until the present). A freedom that does not actively subjugate others would be no freedom at all, for this collective.

Practically, Waddell and his followers' attitude was reminiscent of planter class and poor white workers, who despised the successful black worker even more than the criminal. Again, both versions of the black could face violence for any reason and no reason. But even the violent criminal gratified a white sense of superiority. The successful black worker *must not be*. Imagine Waddell standing in Wilmington where he would see such success stories in flesh and blood, based on black self-determination. Wilmington lived up to many of Emancipation's promises of creating a fairer context for economic, political and legal advance among black Americans. A 500-page report on the Wilmington Massacre notes that North Carolina boasted a growing "black business class" and Wilmington specifically set the standard. Statewide, blacks comprised nearly 10 percent of skilled labor. By 1897 in Wilmington, black skilled and semi-skilled workers comprised "32 percent of the total workforce" leaving the agrarian and service labor sectors behind.[41] Blacks became building contractors and state and federal government workers, and began developing loan and investment resources, which led to successful home ownership. In sum, many of the black success stories that Charles Johnson lists in the early 2000s were already around in the 1890s. This success made life "intolerable" for Waddell and his followers and they turned to the violent methods of suppression, enslavement and colonization to erase the successful black's existence from Wilmington.

Waddell justified this violence with a reference to the Constitution's "framers" that confirms King's claim that "backlash" inaccurately describes opposition to black autonomy. It reacts not against one or another single instance of black autonomy as the nation develops. It is a principled stand against black autonomy altogether at the nation's outset. Waddell's speech on October 24, 1898, part of the prelude to the Wilmington Massacre, adds supplementary evidence for King's theory:

> We are the sons of the men who won the first victory of the Revolution at Moore's Creek Bridge. We are the brothers of men who wrote with their swords from Bethel to Bentonville the most heroic chapter in American annals and we ourselves are men who, inspired by these memories intend to preserve at the cost of our lives if necessary the heritage that is ours. We maintained it against overwhelming armies of men of our own race, shall we surrender it to a ragged rabble of negroes led by a handful of white cowards. Let them understand once and for all that we will have no more of the intolerable conditions under which we live. We are resolved to change them, if we have to choke the current of the Cape Fear with carcasses.[42]

Waddell's privileged "Anglo-saxon" becomes the subject of history in his timeline from the American Revolution to the Civil War to 1890s Wilmington. The passage begins by utilizing the beautiful soul's fourth tactic against change. He makes white supremacist "Anglo-saxons" the sole agent of change in the founding of the United States. Being a great-great-great-grandson of Hugh Waddell, a general in the American Revolution, a great-grandson of Francis Nash, Brigadier General who died in the Battle of Germantown and a great-grandson of Supreme Court Justice Alfred Moore, Alfred Moore Waddell is quite literally a descendant of American Revolutionaries; his speech pulls his white listeners into this lineage.

But this inheritance and its authority should end with the Civil War. Waddell fought for the Confederacy, not the Union. Waddell and his pro-Confederate supporters fought to "preserve" racial "heritage" at the expense of the nation his forefathers founded. Defeat in the Civil War should have made this ideology a relic with no practical purchase. Yet, with a slight of hand, depending upon the very supernational racial solidarity that Snider noted, Waddell transforms his and his listener's rebellion against the nation into contributions to the "most heroic chapter in American annals." The role of black Americans in abolishing slavery, defeating the Confederacy and establishing Reconstruction governments disappears from view, save as "rabble" led by "white cowards." Waddell never explains how pro-Union cowards and rabble were able to win a war, but pro-Confederate traitors can count as preservationists by splitting the Union, failing to do so and then refusing to admit defeat at all costs. Thus, treason turns to national heroism. Racial solidarity alone turns this phantasmagoria into compelling thought. This is the egotism of *refuge* at full force, setting the stage for violence that, on its own terms, cannot be justifiable.[43]

That violence, Waddell warns, must come down to save future white generations from apocalypse: "The stand we now pledge ourselves is forced upon us suddenly by a crisis and our eyes are open to the fact that we must act now or leave our descendants to a fate too gloomy to be borne." The "Declaration" admits a terror similar to Osnos's interviewees in our present when thinking of a white minority America. Though the internal border grants him refuge, it does not grant peace. Waddell's October speech and "Declaration" call for literal violence to alter political, cultural and economic conditions. Just as the October speech decries "intolerable conditions," so Waddell and his colleagues

> declare that we will no longer be ruled, and will never be ruled again by men of African origin. *This condition* we have ... endured because we felt that the consequences of the War of Secession were such as to deprive us of the fair consideration of our countrymen. We believe that, after more than thirty years, this is no longer the case.

Thirty years: for almost a generation, North Carolina pro-Confederates planned to overthrow any and all traces of black progress after Emancipation, allowing no "foreign" influence to change their minds.[44]

Pro-Confederate newspapers claimed that only ten black people died in the Wilmington Massacre. It is hard to believe that only ten people died after pro-Confederate North Carolinian businessmen spent $1,200 purchasing a "rapid firing Colt gun capable of firing 420 .23 caliber bullets per minute" *in addition* to the Naval Reserve's "Hotchkiss gun that could fire 80 to 100 shots per minute with a range of five miles."[45] The six-man "Machine Gun Squad," led by William R. Kenan and Charles W. White, "hauled" the Colt machine gun through black and white areas of town, in addition to the rifles they carried with them. An African American attorney claimed that the Machine-Gun Squad killed at least 25 Africans Americans at an intersection and shot into a home killing a family of three. The Squad also aimed the machine gun at churches, threatening to shoot if the churches did not open their doors to be searched by white supremacist militias. Eventually, black militias formed to fight back, but clearly no black groups organized to overthrow the government or kick out journalists denouncing everyday instances of public torture, or threatened to shoot machine guns into churches. No one can accurately report the number of deaths, and suggesting that ten people died is an insult to the broader number who were killed, their surviving loved ones and the black Wilmingtonians who left town to hide in swamps and cemeteries, and anywhere else they could avoid being mobbed, to eventually leave town for good. This anti-black violence turned a majority-black city into a majority-white city in days.

Waddell and the other signers of the "Declaration" assumed, just like Snider, that "the ultimate political units of History are getting to be racial, rising above and including Nation." They guessed that the Federal government would accommodate their violent overthrow of the Reconstruction government as an ugly but practical means to their desired end – the hegemony of white supremacy. Significantly for the 1890s, for King's critique of white backlash and for my critique of Johnson's essay, Waddell and his colleagues judged rightly. Other white leaders in the U.S., even those who may be considered centrist for their day, shared this sense of solidarity and did not stop the change wrought by ballot stuffing combined with lynching, looting and exiling entire black communities. President Mckinley received urgent requests for federal intervention to save black and white citizens alike who supported the fusion government and, by extension, the new terms ... President Mckinley did nothing. The *1898 Wilmington Report* concludes, "[G]overnment at all levels failed to adequately respond to the violence or to reverse the political overthrow."[46] This mix of inaction and collaboration at all government levels, by whites across the political spectrum, reaffirms the racial covenant espied by Snider.

Even if the exact tactics of overthrow cannot be repeated today, the stubbornness with which Waddell stewed over Confederate defeat for more than thirty years, the patience he maintained to execute his plan, the confidence he kept in racial solidarity trumping legality at all levels of government and the fear he held for future generations who would not enjoy white hegemony – all these characteristics have analogs among white Americans in present-day United States. What is more, the equivocation in mainstream discussions and institutional operations with respect to anti-black racial violence can now be understood as more than honest mistakes, tragic coincidences, simply unexplainable phenomena or the works of a few lone evil people. Rather, this is *moral rearmament* playing out in an all-American way, which requires bloodshed. Add to this how so many enter the discussion to sabotage it, by deflecting to unrelated topics, reducing solutions to sharing good feelings, claiming that the problem has already been solved or that they perfectly understand the situation and so those who are most threatened need not speak up, and it is now clear that this is the narcissism of *refuge* at work, halting the justice that may emerge from wrongdoing that fits a pattern of racial solidarity even if it is unconscious at the level of the individual vigilante, the frightened police officer, the neglectful prosecutor, the obstinate juror, the unaware congressperson, the overburdened mayor, the angry far rightist or the guilty liberal.

Further investigation would attend to several topics. How does the internal border complicate forgiveness, seeing how white supremacy seeks to identify itself with blamelessness and nonwhite peoples with blameworthiness? How may forgiveness be channeled in ways that undo, rather than gird up, white supremacy and its supporting institutions?[47] How does the internal border complicate past and present versions of secular conversion narratives, where racists convert to anti-racism? How does this undermine how mixed-race identity has come to signify racial progress and erase racism's erotic operations? What would the end to this melancholy entail, theoretically and in practice? Whatever the answers may be, they will include ongoing struggle and a search for what King called "positive peace," that is, the presence of justice.[48] In this essay, I have asserted, in the strongest terms I can muster, that the black radical tradition remains a crucial intellectual resource for studying racial hatred's morbid perseverance in the citizen-subject.

Notes

1. Frantz Fanon, "Letter to the Resident Minister," in *Toward the African Revolution: Political Essays*, trans. Haakon Chevalier (New York: Grove Press, 1967), 53.
2. Charles Johnson, "The End of the Black American Narrative," *The American Scholar*, 77.3 (Summer, 2008): 32–42; 34.
3. Johnson, "The End," 37.
4. Johnson, "The End," 35.
5. Etienne Balibar, "Citizen Subject," in *Who Comes after the Subject?* Ed. Eduardo Cadava, Peter Connor and Jean-Luc Nancy (London: Routledge, 1991), 33–57; emphasis in the original.
6. James Ford, "From Being to Unrest, From Objectivity to Motion: The Slave in Karl Marx's *Capital*," *Rethinking Marxism*, 23.1 (Winter, 2010): 22–30.
7. Frederick Douglass, *My Bondage and My Freedom* (New York: Penguin, 2003), 41; emphasis in the original.
8. Hortense Spillers, "The Idea of Black Culture," *New Centennial Review*, 6.3 (Winter, 2006): 7–28; 26.
9. Saidiya Hartman, *Scenes of Subjection: Terror and Self-Making in Nineteenth Century America* (New York: Oxford University Press, 1997).
10. W. E. B. Du Bois, *Black Reconstruction* (New York: Free Press, 1998), 7; emphasis added.
11. W. E. B. Du Bois, "My Evolving Program for Negro Freedom," in *What the Negro Wants*, ed. Rayford W. Logan (Chapel Hill: University of North Carolina Press, 1944), 70; emphasis added.
12. Evan Osnos, "The Fearful and the Frustrated," *The New Yorker*, August 31, 2015, <http://www.newyorker.com/magazine/2015/08/31/the-fearful-and-the-frustrated> (accessed September 24, 2015).
13. Southern Poverty Law Center, "U.S. Hate Groups Top 1,000," February 24, 2011, < https://www.splcenter.org/news/2011/02/23/us-hate-groups-top-1000> (accessed September 20, 2015).

14. Osnos, "The Fearful and the Frustrated"; emphasis added.
15. Fanon, "Letter to the Resident Minister," 53.
16. Charles Johnson, "Every Twenty-Eight Hours: The Case of Trayvon Martin," in *Taming the Ox: Buddhist Stories and Reflections on Race, Politics, Culture, and Spiritual Practice* (Boston: Shambhala Publications, 2014), 94.
17. Johnson, "The End," 42.
18. Martin Luther King, Jr., *Where Do We Go from Here: Chaos or Community* (Boston: Beacon Press, 2010), 38.
19. George Wallace, "Inaugural Address of Governor George Wallace, which was delivered at the Capitol in Montgomery, Alabama," January 14, 1963, 2.
20. Wallace, "Inaugural Address," 3. < http://digital.archives.alabama.gov/cdm/ref/collection/voices/id/2952> (accessed September 26, 2015).
21. Rebecca Comay, *Mourning Sickness: Hegel and the French Revolution* (Stanford: Stanford University Press, 2013), 34.
22. Rebecca Comay and Joshua Nichols, "Missed Revolutions, Non-Revolutions, Revolutions to Come: On *Mourning Sickness*," *PhaenEx*, 7.1 (Spring/Summer, 2012): 309–46; 320.
23. See the following speech, Martin Luther King, Jr. "A New Sense of Direction," 1968, Carnegie Council for Ethics in International Affairs, <http://www.carnegiecouncil.org/publications/articles_papers_reports/4960.html/:pf_printable> (accessed September 27, 2015).
24. Johnson, "The End," 38.
25. King, *Where Do We Go from Here*, 72; emphasis in the original.
26. I am restricting my argument to discussion of how the Beautiful Soul in the United States grapples with progress among Black Americans. It would take further detailed studies to understand how this would play out in relation to Latino, Asian and Native Americans as well.
27. King, "A New Sense of Direction"; emphasis in the original.
28. Martin Luther King, Jr., *Why We Can't Wait* (Boston: Beacon Press, 2010), 87.
29. Shamoon Zamir, *Dark Voices: W.E.B. Du Bois and American Thought, 1888–1903* (Chicago: University of Chicago Press, 1995), 126.
30. Etienne Balibar, "Fichte and the Internal Border," in *Masses, Classes, Ideas: Studies on Politics and Philosophy before and after Marx* (London: Routledge, 1994), 67; emphasis in the original.
31. Fichte, Johann Gottlieb, "Introduction to Fichte's System of

Knowledge," trans. A. E. Kroeger, *The Journal of Speculative Philosophy*, 1.1 (1867): 23–36; 24; emphasis in the original.
32. Zamir, *Dark Voices*, 127.
33. Denton Snider, *The American Ten Years War* (St. Louis: Sigma Publishing, 1906), 328; emphasis in the original.
34. Snider, *American Ten Years War*, 278; emphasis in the original.
35. Snider, *American Ten Years War*, 298; emphasis in the original.
36. Snider, *American Ten Years War*, 427–8.
37. Balibar, "Internal Border," 66.
38. Snider, *American Ten Years War*, 278.
39. Jefferson Davis, "Jefferson Davis' Speech at Wilmington, N.C.," in *The Papers of Jefferson Davis*, Vol. 10, 48–54, <https://jeffersondavis.rice.edu/Content.aspx?id=98>
40. Alfred Moore Waddell, "White Declaration of Independence," in Lerae Umfleet, *1898 Wilmington Race Riot: Final Report*, North Carolina Department of Cultural Resources, 2006, 115.
41. Umfleet, *1898 Wilmington Report*, North Carolina Department of Cultural Resources, 2006, 47.
42. Alfred Moore Waddell, Speech, October 21, 1898, in in Lerae Umfleet, *1898 Wilmington Race Riot: Final Report*, North Carolina Department of Cultural Resources, 2006, 104.
43. More will have to be said about the how this egotism presumes a clearcut ethnic and racial separation between black and white Americans that is, was and will continue to be untenable. The "Declaration's" final demand bears this out for wanting to expel Alexander Manly, editor of the Wilmington *Daily Record*. Manly published an editorial rejecting the claim that all black men sought to rape white women. Manly acknowledges that every culture has its sexual assailants. But he points out that, in the U.S. South, this claim gets overstated in order to hide the many consensual sexual relationships occurring between black men and white women as well as black women and white men. This, Manly knew, because he was the product of such a bond, with a black woman domestic and one of the men in the family North Carolina Governor Manly. Perhaps Alexander was the son of Charles Manly himself. Significantly, Waddell's "Declaration" does not deny Alexander Manly's claims. Essentially, the "Declaration" condemns Manly for revealing the open secret of cross-racial sexual liaisons that white North Carolinians knew to hide. The tortured logic plays out by way of ousting a partially white man for telling the truth about white Americans, himself *being* the concrete evidence, only

to deny his whiteness since he is mixed, which then confirms that white Carolinians are not the pure Anglo-Saxons Waddell says they are and, most importantly, undoes the ability of restricting North Carolina's economic and political inheritance to whites. These are the twists and turns of the internal border's operation in the United States that require further perusal.

44. Waddell, "White Declaration of Independence," 115; emphasis in the original.
45. Waddell, *1898 Wilmington Report*, 145.
46. Waddell, *1898 Wilmington Report*, 2.
47. See Ashon Crawley, "Wednesday Night Prayer Meeting," *The Normal School: A Literary Magazine*, <http://thenormalschool.com/wednesday-night-prayer-meeting-by-ashon-crawley/> (accessed September 24, 2015).
48. King, *Why We Can't Wait*, 52.

Bibliography

Balibar, Etienne. "Citizen Subject." In *Who Comes After the Subject?* Ed. Eduardo Cadava, Peter Connor and Jean-Luc Nancy. London: Routledge, 1991. Pp. 33–57.

Balibar, Etienne. "Fichte and the Internal Border." In *Masses, Classes, Ideas: Studies on Politics and Philosophy before and after Marx*. London: Routledge, 1994. Pp. 61–84.

Balibar, Etienne. *Masses, Classes, and Ideas; Studies on Politics and Philosophy before and after Marx*. New York: Routledge, 1994.

Comay, Rebecca. *Mourning Sickness: Hegel and the French Revolution*. Stanford: Stanford University Press, 2013.

Comay, Rebecca and Joshua Nichols. "Missed Revolutions, Non-Revolutions, Revolutions to Come: On *Mourning Sickness*." *PhaenEx*, 7.1 (Spring/Summer, 2012): 339–46.

Crawley, Ashon. "Wednesday Night Prayer Meeting." *The Normal School: A Literary Magazine*. September 18, 2015. <http://thenormalschool.com/wednesday-night-prayer-meeting-by-ashon-crawley/> (accessed September 24, 2015).

Davis, Jefferson. "Jefferson Davis' Speech at Wilmington, N.C." *The Papers of Jefferson Davis*, Vol. 10, 48–54. <https://jeffersondavis.rice.edu/Content.aspx?id=98>.

Douglass, Frederick. *My Bondage and My Freedom*. New York: Penguin, 2003.

Du Bois, W. E. B. "My Evolving Program for Negro Freedom." In *What the Negro Wants*. Ed. Rayford W. Logan. Chapel Hill: University of North Carolina Press, 1944. P. 70.

Du Bois, W. E. B. *Black Reconstruction*. New York: Free Press, 1998.

Fanon, Frantz. "Letter to the Resident Minister." In *Toward the African Revolution: Political Essays*. Trans. Haakon Chevalier. New York: Grove Press, 1967. P. 53.

Fanon, Frantz. *Toward the African Revolution: Political Essays*. Trans. Haakon Chevalier. New York: Grove Press, 1967.

Fichte, Johann Gottlieb. "Introduction to Fichte's System of Knowledge." Trans. A. E. Kroeger. *The Journal of Speculative Philosophy*, 1.1 (1867): 23–36.

Ford, James. "From Being to Unrest, From Objectivity to Motion: The Slave in Karl Marx's *Capital*." *Rethinking Marxism*, 23.1. (Winter, 2010): 22–30.

Hartman, Saidiya. *Scenes of Subjection: Terror and Self-Making in Nineteenth Century America*. New York: Oxford University Press, 1997.

Johnson, Charles. "The End of the Black American Narrative." *The American Scholar*, 77.3 (Summer, 2008): 32–42.

Johnson, Charles. "Every Twenty-Eight Hours: The Case of Trayvon Martin." In *Taming the Ox: Buddhist Stories and Reflections on Race, Politics, Culture, and Spiritual Practice*. Boston: Shambhala Publications, 2014.

King, Jr., Martin Luther. "A New Sense of Direction." 1968, <http://www.carnegiecouncil.org/publications/articles_papers_reports/4960.html/:pf_printable> (accessed September 27, 2015).

King, Jr., Martin Luther. *Where Do We Go From Here: Chaos or Community*. Boston: Beacon Press, 2010.

King, Jr., Martin Luther. *Why We Can't Wait*. Boston: Beacon Press, 2010.

Osnos, Evan. "The Fearful and the Frustrated." *The New Yorker*. August 31, 2015. <http://www.newyorker.com/magazine/2015/08/31/the-fearful-and-the-frustrated> (accessed September 24, 2015).

Snider, Denton. *The American Ten Years War*. St. Louis: Sigma Publishing, 1906.

Southern Poverty Law Center. "U.S. Hate Groups Top 1,000." February 24, 2011. <https://www.splcenter.org/news/2011/02/23/us-hate-groups-top-1000> (accessed September 20, 2015).

Spillers, Hortense. "The Idea of Black Culture." *New Centennial Review*, 6.3 (2006): 7–28.

Waddell, Alfred Moore. "White Declaration of Independence." In Lerae Umfleet, *1898 Wilmington Race Riot: Final Report*. North Carolina Department of Cultural Resources, 2006.

Wallace, George. "Inaugural Address of Governor George Wallace, which was Delivered at the Capitol in Montgomery, Alabama." January 14, 1963.

Zamir, Shamoon. *Dark Voices: W.E.B. Du Bois and American Thought, 1888–1903*. Chicago: University of Chicago Press, 1995.

10

Just Like a Woman: Balibar on the Politics of Reproduction

Nancy Armstrong

In the selections of his work I will examine here, Balibar creates the conditions of possibility for thinking about women and novels outside the binaries that inevitably oppose women to men and fiction to political philosophy. To understand just how much is at stake in considering women and novels without their definitional opposites, one must begin by establishing what these particular categories of analysis share. Both are included under a dominant term – women, by way of the household, under political society, and novels, by way of realism, under political philosophy. The problem doubles as political philosophy acknowledges that women and novels play a role within modern political societies, only to designate that role as politically insignificant and/or off limits to political critique. Women and novels mark the point at which the private life of both household and personal experience begins. In practice, this means that if we want to think about women on an equal footing with men, we must think of them as if they were or should be men.[1] So, too, if we want to think of the narrative machinery of novels as comparable to that of political philosophy, we have to discount the very narrative operations that identify novels as works of fiction. In disavowing the political operations of these categories – that amounts to disavowing that their operations are indeed political – we inadvertently acknowledge that they serve as the "exclusive inclusion," the internal limit and foundation that a modern political society must suppress in order to be just that, a modern political society.[2] Among the growing number of political philosophers who are trying to imagine a world beyond capitalism, Balibar is, to my knowledge, the only one who openly acknowledges that to do so we must confront the roles of women and fiction under capitalism.

The riddle of reproduction

Given his intellectual debt to Louis Althusser and his collaboration with a group of graduates of the École Normale Supérieure in a project "on the French school system" during the period when Althusser was formulating his concept of ideology,[3] it seems fitting that Balibar should still be bent on solving the riddle of Althusser's claim that "the ultimate condition for production is *the reproduction of the conditions of production*."[4] Althusser of course responded to his own provocation with an influential theory of ideological state apparatuses that pays scant attention to the operations of "the family" as such an apparatus, much less to women and novels. His concept of ideology nevertheless provides the first step toward understanding why "familial ideology," as he calls it, is "something else" as well, something that puts the family itself outside the purview of political theory. As the site of the biological reproduction of human beings, Althusser explains, the figure of the family "is 'anchored' in a reality that is not purely ideological" and, in this respect, he admits, is not all that different from religion or education, the operations of which he seems more comfortable describing in detail. What is more, familial ideology is not, as he notes, losing its power even in "capitalist societies, in which [the family itself] is now 'disappearing.'"[5] At several points in the essays on the reproduction of capitalism collected by Jacques Bidet, Althusser holds familial ideology responsible for positioning biological life within any number of the oppositions that lend human bodies their complex individual identities. In each such instance, however, he stops well short of naming either woman as the agent of this process or citing novels as the most comprehensive theory of the kinship principles she performs for modern political societies.[6] Balibar turns the question of social reproduction back on itself in precisely this direction.

In making this claim, I don't mean to say that he turns either to "woman" or to fiction as useful categories of political analysis, for Balibar, too, stops short of so naming the reproductive machinery that Locke disavowed in proposing his model of a modern representative society.[7] Balibar's counter-intuitive readings of Locke's two major contributions to modern philosophy – theories of property and of consciousness, respectively – nevertheless set us on a path to understanding why the category, if not the name, of "woman" is so essential to the conceptual architecture of liberal democracy that it is virtually impossible to imagine a liberal society without one. Having called attention to how Balibar teases an alternative argument out of the *Second Treatise* of *The Two Treatises of Government*,[8] I turn next to the essay, "The Geneaological Scheme: Race or Culture?" in which he contends that very much the same structure of disavowal characterizes the novel's relationship to political philosophy. To consider what he calls the "genealogical scheme" of political philosophy, Balibar sets up "the novel" as the standard of comparison.[9] He proposes that in mediating between the family and the nation form, novels made it possible for national readerships to imagine the internal organization of their national communities as something like that of the traditional household and family. It is by thus refiguring the form of political inclusiveness that we call democracy in terms of kinship, Balibar observes, that novels produce what Benedict Anderson describes as an "imagined community."[10] To ask if democratic societies can be communities in the sense that families are, Balibar rephrases Anderson's influential concept of the modern nation-form as "*the concept of a structure capable of producing determinate 'community effects.'*"[11] We can use Althusser's claim – that the future of capitalism depends on the effectiveness of its ideological apparatuses – to push Balibar's translation of Anderson still further and think of the nation-form as "*the concept of a structure capable of [re]producing determinate 'community effects.'*" Consider what this says about the operations of familial ideology. To retain its character as such, a representative democracy must remain open to differences that, if left to their own devices, would generate forms of hybridity capable of eliminating the possibility of representation. To retain its character as such, by contrast, a family must practice a degree of endogamy, or what may be called the "reproduction of sameness."[12] To perform this role, "the family" must not only limit hybridity in specific ways but also reproduce those particular exclusions in successive generations.

To argue that this paradox also establishes the genealogy of political philosophy, Balibar makes the absolutely stunning point that the same kinship rules that political philosophy relegates to pre-modern theories of government ensure not only the continuity of modern political society in future generations but a continuous tradition of political critique as well. When it comes to including the purpose served by the family within an account of the rise of modern government, this double disavowal necessarily puts the philosopher who wants to address this problem at somewhat of a tactical disadvantage. Indeed, it puts him in much the same relation to the rules of his discourse as the great national novels of the nineteenth and twentieth centuries put the contemporary novelist who wants to imagine a community without the family as the form of community mediating between individual and nation. Neither philosopher nor novelist can blithely proceed to do so within the limits of their respective discourses or genres. To seize a tactical advantage from their current situation, both must be intimately familiar with the limits of the tradition in which they write and observe those limits in order to move beyond them. Balibar encounters this limit, it seems to me, whenever he invokes the element of the liberal subject that novels have traditionally figured as "woman." Because, in this respect, his field and mine represent what is currently "beyond" each other's, in trying to think beyond the limits of political philosophy, he gives me a way of thinking beyond the limits of novel theory as well.

In claiming that we share the same "limit," I have something rather specific in mind. To account for the origin of political society, we can say that Thomas Hobbes placed a caesura between the pre-modern concept of kinship and the modern concept of government. What had allowed Hobbes to narrate the rise of political society as a historical before-and-after story also made it possible for John Locke to designate a (quasi-sacral) private sphere as both spatially distinct and apart from a (secular-political) public sphere. As he described it in *The Second Treatise*, Locke's household retained the principle of kinship that sees power descending from the top down, while his model of government drew its authority from the bottom up, as Hobbes's did. By thus transforming a temporal break into a spatial divide, Locke smuggled traditional kinship rules back into political society in the form of a paternalistic household removed from but contained within a significantly updated model of Hobbes's political society. Locke, that is, included a household organized around and by the family within the political society from which the principle of kinship, by virtue of its primitive and patriarchal character, had to be excluded, along with the woman who embodied that principle.

So distinguished from earlier forms of government, his model of political society put the household and the family that organized it off limits to government intervention and political critique alike.[13]

Thus it was that Locke told two quite different origin stories in writing his *Two Treatises of Government* (1689) and *An Essay Concerning Human Understanding* (1690) – the first, a story of the individual's extension through labor into the world of property, and the second, an account of that individual's appropriation of sensory information from the world, as he transformed that information into a separate domain of personal experience. The schism between kinship rules and laws based on contractual exchange quickly reproduced itself within the rapidly expanding field of print culture during the eighteenth century.[14] In view of the fact that Locke himself was limited by the very contradiction he wrote into existence, it's hardly surprising that even the most radical accounts of modern political society fail to expose the role of the domestic sphere in the uneven distribution of vital resources and services.[15]

In the next two sections of this essay, I want to look at these moves in some detail, first, to see how Balibar dismantles the modern individual at its source in Locke's theory of property. Rather than answer the question of whether and how the individual can "own" himself, Balibar considers how, despite his adherence to the law of non-contradiction, Locke indeed made it possible for both opposing answers to the question of self-ownership to hold true. Thus reworked, as Balibar himself concludes, Locke's concept of "the individual" at once excludes and identifies itself with the concept of "woman." In a more recent article, Balibar pursues the implications of this argument across the caesura separating primitive kinship from modern democracy in the other direction, showing how what he calls a "myth" of genealogy operates within the political sphere to ensure that "the reproduction of the same" continues to limit those who participate directly in political society. In his view, the "imagined community" responsible for national identity depends on the reproduction of these limits in the form of a constituent exclusion, whether based on biological race or cultural ethnicity.

Many returns of the subject

In "'Possessive Individualism' Reversed," Balibar tracks a sequence of "reversals" "from Locke to Derrida." To launch this account, he transforms Locke's concept of property from an answer into a question, or as he puts it, into "a conflict, with an initial division at its core" (301). This "division" allows him to rework Locke's proposition that "every Man has a Property in his own Person" so as to counter the notion of "possessive individualism" that C. B. Macpherson derived from Locke's *Second Treatise*. This reading makes sense, Balibar contends, only so long as we concede the point that self-ownership is both the cause and the result of individual freedom. Balibar suggests that this concession forecloses the question of how an individual can simultaneously own himself and alienate his labor through an economic exchange. By failing to recognize that Locke used the concept of self-ownership in at least two ways, a reader like Macpherson has also failed to appreciate how Locke revises Hobbes. To make this point, Balibar produces a reading of "a Property in his own Person" that reveals "not one possessive individualism" in *The Second Treatise*, "but at least two, pushing in two directions."[16] But whether we assume, as Macpherson does, that liberal individualism is based on "constituted property," or go along with Balibar in holding "constituent property" responsible for the spread of liberal individualism, we are still taking up only one side in a very old argument that excludes the family from political consideration.

Rather than counter Macpherson's definition of "property" with a reading that reverses it, however, Balibar argues both sides of the debate that Locke inaugurated in an effort to produce a more adequate account than either reading on its own. Yes, he admits, we can always take the claim that "every Man has Property in his own Person" to mean that property is what entitles a man to self-ownership. That is to say, every man derives from the property he has acquired the freedom to associate with other people and the power to act politically. When thus understood as the precondition for citizenship, Locke's concept of property would necessarily limit the concept of "every man" to those few who already own property, excluding the rest of the population from direct political participation. Such a reading of Locke would be entirely reasonable, Balibar insists, only if we ignore the fact that Locke thought of property, not only as the particular property "constituted" by law, but also as property in an abstract and quasi-Spinozan sense, as the property "constituent" of every man's capacity to act and thus to own – in which case, we end up with an entirely different individual. To reverse Macpherson's reading of Locke's claim that "every man has a Property in his own Person," Balibar matches the notion of "constituted" property with a concept of property as contrastingly immanent in the individual, a self fully articulated in *An Essay Concerning Human Understanding*.

Published in French in 1998 and in an expanded version in English in 2013, *Identity and Difference* credits Locke with inventing the first truly "rationalist psychology." Here Balibar counters the traditional view of Locke as an out-and-out empiricist with the alternative Locke who inscribed the capacity for self-knowledge within an internal world of consciousness, putting that world beyond the purview of divine meddling.[17] Locke achieved this by attributing the individual's capacity for "reflection" to a source within the mind itself.[18] Counter to the traditional emphasis on his description of the mind's "passive" capacity to classify the information it receives as sensations from the external world, Balibar calls attention to Locke's investment in the mind's "active" process of reflection as the means by which it maintains its identity as a particular "self," or "consciousness." Just as the mind responds to the succession of encounters with the phenomenal world that bombard the individual with sensations, so, in Locke's view, is the mind always working to maintain its internal logic as the individual's experiences expand and diversify.[19] Balibar's reading of *An Essay Concerning Human Understanding* performs much the same logic that he observes in Locke.

To follow the process of subject formation as it unfolds sequentially from chapter I to chapter XXVII of Book II of *An Essay Concerning Human Understanding*, is to see how the individual mind takes in and arranges information from the world of objects. One could easily come away from such a reading with the idea of Locke as an empiricist plain and simple. But once we have read Locke's argument retrospectively, as Balibar does, from the later perspective achieved in chapter XXVII, "Of Identity and Diversity," added in the 1694 edition, we too will have become aware, from chapter I on, that the mind is ever registering and regulating the operations that increase and diversify its internal archive. Otherwise, as Locke sees it, the mind would quickly cease to exist as a coherent whole, and the individual would cease to be himself. By reading the *Essay* through the lens of the penultimate chapter, Balibar indicates how seriously the traditional emphasis on the empirical Locke has misrepresented his rightful place in the European philosophical tradition.[20] In *Identity and*

Difference, Balibar is clearly not only out to disrupt what that tradition has done with Locke, but also to use him to pursue another argument that governs how he handles Macpherson. As Stella Sandford explains this argument in her introduction to *Identity and Difference*, Balibar's Locke "assumes that individuals preexist society and that the individual is defined as, by nature, a property owner."[21] His pursuit in the political philosophical tradition of a self prior to property ultimately requires Balibar to think with the category "woman" and with novels as well.

In order to give such a concept of the self a chance to animate a reading of Locke's *Second Treatise,* Balibar goes after Macpherson for failing to see that Locke, in formulating his double concept of property, was already conceptualizing the two operations of human consciousness he developed a decade later in *An Essay Concerning Human Understanding.*[22] Thus, where Macpherson insists on an absolute, "constituted," notion of property, Balibar shows that Locke in fact oscillated between two notions of the individual corresponding to the two operations of the mind that organize the inner world of consciousness. Where Macpherson collapses Locke into Hobbes, Balibar argues that Locke introduced a second "constitutive" concept of property that was both immanent in the individual and responsible for his *"exercise of liberty."*[23] Once we understand the exercise of freedom, as Balibar does, as an expression of property that is already there in the individual, it follows that "a free man, including a man who is free in the city, a free citizen, must always be considered *somehow a proprietor or an 'owner' of something.*"[24] Armed with an alternative definition of "every Man has Property in his own Person," he spells out what Locke meant by the claim that "each man has an exclusive disposition over his own person [it is his *own*], just as he has an exclusive disposition of [or *owns*] his Life, his Liberty, his Estates," a string of concepts that, in Balibar's view, "ultimately ... means the same" as self-ownership.[25] To understand property as a capacity or force that every man already has in himself may seem to fly in the face of Macpherson's notion of "constituted" property, Balibar cautions, only if we assume that if one proposition is true the other must be false. To keep his counter reading from becoming a simple reversal of Macpherson's and another partial reading of *The Second Treatise,* Balibar goes on to show how both readings can be true. Macpherson's reading of Locke is not, it turns out, a straw man for a Spinozan reading of the individual's property in himself but rather the means for Balibar to demonstrate that each reading has its own logic, both of which are necessary to grasp the whole Locke.

That said, the question ceases to be which notion of property to choose and becomes a matter of how the two interact with each other. Accordingly, Balibar explains how "labor" does for the public individual in Locke's *Second Treatise* much the same thing that "consciousness" does for the private individual in *An Essay Concerning Human Understanding*. As Balibar uses the concept, "labor" is the process where the places of the subject, *self* and *own*, are continually exchanged. Or, to put it another way, what is mine/my ownership can always become alienated if I *myself* remain my *own* self. Conversely, the self can remain an identical self if the own/owned/ownership steadily returns from its alienation.[26]

A second reading of this passage shows Balibar's prose performing exactly the labor it describes, as it reproduces the slippage he has teased from Locke's *Second Treatise*. The progression from "*self* and *own*" to "*myself*" and "my *own* self," objectifies the subject as its "own" while subjectivizing the object as its "self." The prose simultaneously doubles back across the line between noun and verb in the progression from "mine/my ownership" to "own/owned/ownership." In the very act of making difference, the slash-marks bring self as subject into such close proximity with self as object that Macpherson's "possessive individual" appears entirely self-possessed.

This noun-verb-noun palindrome is Balibar's means of "returning" the very subject that objectifies itself in property to a community that reverses its self-alienation. To become an owner in Macpherson's sense, the individual must indeed remove himself from the world given to men in common.[27] By putting himself into objects, however, Locke's subject also "*[puts] in common* his productions, thus building the worldly community."[28] In this way, "labor" serves as a social medium linking the immanent capacity of the subject to produce with the objectification of his labor in the things he actually produces for exchange: while the individual "is privatizing nature and himself on the one hand, he is also socializing it and himself on the other."[29] "Labor" thus refigures the individual's oscillation between object and subject as a work-in-progress, wherein warring concepts of property form the inner and outer perspectives of a moebius strip. Still and all, once he has achieved this resolution, Balibar seems no more convinced than I am that, to this point, he hasn't simply added to the long history of reversals that reproduce the inner and outer limits of his discourse. Having tracked these limits across the historical span of political philosophy from Rousseau through Marx to Derrida, Balibar indeed seems to want out of the repetition compulsion to which his critique of Macpherson's lopsided account of modern individualism has confined his "own" thinking.

The point of no return

That the essay "'Possessive Individualism' Reversed" ends on a note of promise is owing to the fact that Balibar happens across the possibility of a wholly different tactic in the form of Derrida's attempt to get "beyond affirmation and negation by retrieving a more fundamental notion [of property] which is neither appropriation nor ex-propriation but simply 'propriation.'"[30] The curious passage from *Spurs* to which Balibar is referring here seems to throw his entire argument with Macpherson off its mark by suggesting a way of formulating a different difference, not one that supplements the empiricist Locke, nor even a patched together resolution of the two, but a difference that challenges the very difference between his reading and Macpherson's. Like the subject that he pursued in *Identity and Difference,* Balibar spots in this passage from Derrida the possibilities of a subject that is neither first nor second temporally, neither private nor public spatially, but something altogether different, something we can consider a true alternative.[31] In view of this discovery, and with little more than one page of a sixteen-page essay left to go, Balibar derails a line of argument that has fastened its hope to the immanent aspects of the human subject. He interpolates the lengthy passage from *Spurs* where Derrida "departs from the Heideggerian denegation of sexual difference" within his quarrel with Macpherson just as it seems to have come to rest.[32]

Insofar as Derrida's elevation of "the woman" seems to parallel what Balibar does with the Spinozan self in Locke, we have to ask what he gains by introducing sexual difference into a philosophical argument that has, to this point, steered well clear of it. Balibar clearly relishes the disruption created when Derrida refuses to let the so-called marriage contract fall in line with the exchange regulated by the social contract. Does he spot in Derrida's use of "woman" the possibility of a self that lacks a property in her own person that she can give in exchange, a self, in other words, that cannot be alienated from itself? It was, after all, in an effort to end the sequence of "reversals" that used the economy of gift giving to critique the logic of exchange that Derrida resorted to "woman" as the means of disabling that logic. According to the sexual contract, we may say that the woman gives herself, the man takes that self by way of replenishing his capacity for labor and he returns her gift in the form of the legal protection of his property. If it is true that no exchange ever brings equal returns, then this one is notoriously asymmetrical.

Rather than "marry" opposing terms by subordinating "woman" to "man," Derrida turns to the undervalued term "woman." If it is her very nature to give, he reasons, then in giving herself woman not only retains her self, but also, by the very act of doing so, nullifies the difference between giving and taking.[33] From this, it follows that the figure of exchange – that doubles and reverses give and take, appropriation and expropriation – does not unify the forces distinguished as male and female so much as install the twin principles of difference and disequilibrium in a social field of interconnected singularities. Though hardly worked out in detail, here Derrida's use of "woman" implies that prior to its division into subject and object, the self is something entirely different from the compromise formation that results from attempts to return man to women in a symbolic state of unity, which is actually political subordination. As Balibar explains in his article on "the genealogical scheme," however, getting back to a relationship that is neither giving nor taking is nowhere on the horizon of possibility.[34]

Here, he focuses on the form of community peculiar both to modern political societies and to political philosophy as a discipline or discourse. Both, he observes, must have a mechanism, at once institutional and imaginary, something "that binds successive generations with one another, carrying identities and norms."[35] Whether we refer to it as "family," "community" or "ethnicity," the term comes bundled with "household," which designates the site of consumption, maintains the archive of kinship practices and ensures that certain exclusions will remain consistent over generations and through repeated dislocations. The family in this sense operates in much the same way that "self-reflection" does in Balibar's reading of the crucial chapter XXVII, Book II, of Locke's *An Essay Concerning Human Understanding*. In order for a group to retain an identity over time and with demographic diversification, its reproductive machinery, or marriage rules, will have to remain relatively constant. To explain how the paradox that a woman retains a self by giving her self away makes sense on a national scale, Balibar turns to the anthropological concept of "kinship." This move takes him directly into the territory of fiction and, by way of the example of William Faulkner's *Absalom, Absalom,* into "the great Western novel[s] [of] the nineteenth and twentieth centuries."[36] With Benedict Anderson's concept of "imagined communities" clearly in mind, Balibar uses Faulkner's novel to suggest what a reading of that particular novel would look like if we were to stress the undervalued term "kinship" over and against the ways in which the novel extends the community to include a diverse national readership. Balibar's encapsulation of Faulkner's novel shows how it exposes the pseudo-endogamous operations of kinship that in more conventional novels have to be pseudo-endogamous rather than either endogamous or exogamous, strictly speaking. Oscillating between incest and miscegenation as the inner and outer limits of their collective identity, the Sutpen family undergoes the same conflation of endogamy and exogamy that no less spectacularly brought down Edgar Allan Poe's House of Usher and the many other national novels in which siblings appear to one another in the form of strangers and vice versa. American novelists from James Fenimore Cooper to Faulkner found the family's failure to reproduce itself an especially effective means of suggesting what limits would have to be observed in order to avoid incest on the one hand, and miscegeny on the other.

Insofar as variation within such limits is required in order for sexual relations to organize a household, generational change is both absolutely essential to and terribly risky for any national community that hopes to sustain its identity over time. *Homo nationalis* reappears in each new generation as a stranger whose difference is cloaked as sameness, making it likely that he will destroy the legacy that extends to future generations through the daughter.[37] The uncanniness of this familiar stranger calls attention to the family's need for a daughter who desires the sameness that will keep the family's character intact. If the family is to reproduce itself, this daughter must, at the same time, be attracted to difference. As Balibar's reading of *Absalom, Absalom* demonstrates, novels require a new head of household to be both different and the same. Whether novels succeed or fail in doing so, to be recognized as novels, they have to negotiate this double bind.

Before a liberal government could afford to open itself up to the risk of democracy, Rousseau observed, it would have to educate the populace. So, too, if a community hoped to maintain its identity at the edges of empire, in lieu of trading them among other elite households, that community had to educate the desires of its daughters.[38] It was in persuading the literate classes not only to see but also to feel courtship in these terms that the novel provided a reproductive mechanism in its own right. This is why we find the novels whose production coincided with successive waves of European colonialism reproducing "the stranger" in explicitly racial terms. At the far reaches of empire, novels reproduced the difference between the universal concept of property and that based on legal entitlement as a natural partition between those whom colonial women could desire and with whom sexual relations would obliterate the national heritage. Yet, to observe the kinship practices of that nation, desire a "stranger" that woman must. By building this element of risk and potential for the scandalous surprises that accompanied it into colonial romances, novels intensified the affective investment of national readerships in certain kinship practices. So it was that, as Balibar aptly puts it, "reproduction was always governed not by the *application* but by the *transgression* of its own law."[39] At the same time, he hastens to add, the "pseudo-endogamy" that continues to operate in Western culture is a far cry from "random or generalized hybridization."[40] So long as the family continues to mediate the relationship between the individual and the nation, individuals will find themselves already marked as suited for certain social exchanges and barred from others, the former therefore defined in relation to the latter, so that marriage will reproduce kinship practices specific to their positions within the national community.

On this basis, we can hold the same kinship rules responsible for the division within modern nations between the universal definition of property in oneself and the property specific to those eligible for citizenship. More than any operation of liberal government, the reproduction of this discrepancy is probably the one most responsible for the question that Balibar invariably poses at some point in all his recent work. This question receives perhaps its clearest articulation in his brief preface to the English translation of a collection of Althusser's essays, *On the Reproduction of*

Capitalism, where Balibar invites us to consider how Althusser, were he alive today, would define what is "outside" ideology and assess the possibility of thinking from that position. Balibar resists the impulse to address this question with Althusser's formulation of "the bad subject" as the one who "resists interpellation." Instead he locates "*excessive power*" in the act of complete submission to the position that "confers her 'form' on her."[41] I would rephrase this claim to say that by becoming that role and allowing it to choreograph her, "woman" (who after all naturally embodies submission) acquires a sense of the political power inherent in her performance as such. Let us see.

What comes after the family

In an essay titled "Althusser's Dramaturgy and the Critique of Ideology," Balibar contends that Althusser's analysis of "theatre as politics" offers a way of thinking about "politics as theater."[42] To afford such insight into the dramaturgy of ideology, an encounter between the philosopher and dramatic work requires both a description of the processes or procedures of *subjection* and *subjectivation* that form the essence of ideology *and* a "performative" gesture allowing for a subject to become located, as interpellating interpellator, within the ideological mechanism itself in order to reveal its coherence and insecurity.[43]

The experience of what it would mean to be outside ideology is brought on by an encounter, Althusser cautions, specific to works of art under specific circumstances. In order for a novel to afford that insight, it would have to force one into identifications so self-annihilating as to release her from any and all positions within the system of familial relations. One consequently sees the practices to which identification the novel has subjected her from the perspective of an Austen or Flaubert. In *Clarissa*, by contrast, Samuel Richardson eliminates the position of "the interpellating interpellator," abandoning both male and female readers in a state, some felt, of abject submission from which they felt suicide was the only way out.

As from the quote above, so from Balibar's snapshot of Faulkner's novel, it follows that how we perform such an identity makes all the difference between a community that can reproduce itself down through generations and one that violates the limits ensuring such continuity.[44] In such extreme cases as Mary Shelley's *Frankenstein* or Franz Kafka's *The Metamorphosis*, failure to reproduce kinship practices calls into question the limit on who or what can belong to the human community. In Brontë's *Wuthering Heights*, the protagonist Catherine Earnshaw knows better than to marry the marginally human Heathcliff whom her father brought into the family "as dark almost as if it came from the devil."[45] When her sister-in-law refuses to heed Catherine's advice, no one is surprised that her radical act of exogamy ruptures the continuity of daily social life in Brontë's novel. Only when a stranger emerges who is an Earnshaw by blood beneath his apparent savagery, can the family "return" from a state of primitive patriarchy to a family that maintains community within the field of characters through young Earnshaw's marriage to Catherine's well-domesticated daughter. That novels routinely, if less spectacularly than Faulkner's and Brontë's, disrupt the family in order to restore it in updated terms implies that novels cannot imagine community without the family. Until rather recently, it seemed rather obvious that Georg Lukács was using a figure of speech in characterizing the protagonist of the European novel as "homeless."[46] "Homelessness" applies only too literally to contemporary protagonists, not by virtue of their lack of fellow travelers, but because they neither desire a home nor see the future in terms of reproducing one. Kinship no longer appears to organize the novel.

Beginning perhaps with J. M Coetzee's Michael K, the new protagonist is consistently incapable of supporting the binaries grounded in sexual difference: Michael K, because he's too different to have an interest in or be interesting to either men or women, save as a curiosity; Kazuo Ishiguro's sterilized clone Kathy H, who being virtually interchangeable with other members of her cohort, is too different from everyone else; W. G. Sebald's Austerlitz, because he, like the narrator of Tom McCarthy's *Remainder*, has no past, thus nothing to reproduce; and any number of David Mitchell's narrators who rely on reproductive technologies to hang on to the lives from which they have been irrevocably severed. For lack of a woman who can reproduce it, the lost community fails to materialize. By dispersing whatever qualifies as personal or material property, in other words, these novels refuse to cohere around a central subject, arguably placing their readers outside the imagined community and beyond reach of the novel's vaunted power of interpellation. Rather than identify with a protagonist, as even Shelley's manufactured man and Kafka's once human cockroach require us to do, the contemporary novel forces us to recognize the parts of our selves distributed across the entire field of characters that only coalesce as what Jane Elliott characterizes as a "microeconomy."[47] If, as Balibar suggests, the family serves both novels and political societies as the mechanism for reproducing the difference between who is inside and who or what outside of community as such, then this gesture could be said to turn inside out the "inclusive exclusion" that sustains modern political societies.

By dispersing the contents of the private sphere across a social field without restriction as to their use or protection, the contemporary novel raises the possibility of imagining community without kinship. When restated, this is the same question that Balibar opens up at the conclusion of the essays I have been considering, namely, how to imagine an affirmative way of existing "outside" the privileges and protections of property. This question strikes me as one that novelists and political philosophers have to address in order to challenge the limits of their respective genres. For if, as Balibar suggests, the family operates as the inclusive exclusion that supports the laws protecting property rights, then the family marks the formal limit of both novels and political philosophy, the limit, that is, at which property law would begin to encroach on kinship principles and vice versa. To understand the politics of kinship practices, novels as well as political philosophy would have to understand politics as exactly that, a performance that generates family feeling among members of a group out of a felt need to exclude certain others. This, at a moment when the family has clearly ceased to provide anything like an adequate means of distributing resources, labor, services and information to a national population. A political analysis of the implications of this discrepancy rests, in my view, on better understanding of the political power distinctive to women and novels.

Notes

1. The introduction to Wendy Brown's *States of Injury: Power and Freedom in Late Modernity* (Princeton: Princeton University Press, 1995) explains why: "It would thus appear that it is freedom's relationship to identity, its promise to address a social injury or marking that is itself constitutive of identity – that yields the paradox in which the first imaginings of freedom are always constrained by and even require the very structure of oppression that freedom

emerges to oppose" (7). "Consequently," she concludes, "efforts by women to assume" autonomy comparable to that of men "are often maligned as selfish, irresponsible, or often, more to the point, simply unfeminine" (158). In this respect, self-subordination is constitutive of feminine identity.

2. In *Homo Sacer: Sovereign Power and Bare Life*, trans. David Heller-Roazen (Palo Alto: Stanford University Press, 1998), Giorgio Agamben uses the concept "exclusive inclusion" to describe the figure of *Homo Sacer* as the necessary symmetrical opposite to what he calls the sovereign exception. This figure personifies the discrepancy between the community to which all human beings belong and the community of citizens protected by the law (177). I find it rather astonishing that an argument with as much influence on political theory as Agamben's would go to such rhetorical, philological, philosophical and historical lengths to ensure that both the sovereign's body and the bodies subjugated and disenfranchised by the law – those "who can be killed but not sacrificed" – be imagined as the bodies of men. Doubly disenfranchised, women are nowhere to be found in this argument. Although I've never considered myself the site at which *biòs* meets *zoë*, birth meets death, and, I suppose, man comes out of woman – or what might be called the original "zone of indistinction" between inside and outside, exclusion and inclusion (184) – I nevertheless feel the omnipresence of this doubly abjected figure when reading Agamben's theorization of sovereignty.

3. In his "Translator's Note" to the English edition, Louis Althusser, *On the Reproduction of Capitalism: Ideology and Ideological State Apparatuses*, trans. G. M. Goshgarian (London: Verso, 2014), G. M. Goshgarian attests that the English edition contains Althusser's unfinished manuscripts from the late 1960s and the 1970s and that Jacques Bidet assembled, edited and published in French under the title *Sur la reproduction* (Presses Universitaires de France, 1995). Balibar's "Foreword" to the English edition provides a sense of the personal and political turbulence that made it impossible for Althusser to turn these insights and observations into a continuous argument (xiii).

4. It is worth noting that the figure of the family nevertheless shapes Althusser's argument to the effect that reproduction takes priority over production, as suggested by the sentence that provides the basis for making that claim: "As Marx said, even a child knows that if a social formation did not *reproduce* the conditions of production

while producing, it would not last a year" (*On the Reproduction of Capitalism*, 47; emphasis in the original).
5. Ibid. 77.
6. The term "reproduction" itself encapsulates and suppresses the conflict between lineal descent or genealogy and the horizontal expansion of a group. In 1782, according to the *OED* entry under "Reproduction," John Wesley roundly condemned Comte de Buffon's *Natural History* for having substituted "for the plain word *Generation*, a quaint word of his own, *Reproduction*, in order to level man not only with the beasts that perish, but with nettles or onions."
7. I draw here on Joan Scott's phrase "gender as a category of historical analysis," with which she famously took Gareth Stedman Jones to task for treating "language simply as a vehicle for communicating ideas rather than as a system of meaning or a process of signification." "On Language, Gender, and Working-Class History," *International Labor and Working-Class History*, 31 (Spring, 1987), 6. Scott argues that because he assumed that the language of gender is a political language, he failed to recognize that "the idea of working class not only implied antitheses (capitalists, aristocrats), but also inclusions (wage-earners, the unrepresented) and exclusions (those who held no property in their labor, women and children)" (6). By successfully expanding the definition of property to certain members of the working class, Scott concludes, the Chartists secured the franchise for themselves and subordinated other members of the working class on the basis of gender, thereby reproducing within working-class culture the same kinship principles distinguishing the class of owners from the rest of the population.
8. Etienne Balibar, "'Possessive Individualism' Reversed: From Locke to Balibar," *Constellations*, 9.3 (2002): 299–317.
9. Etienne Balibar, "The Genealogical Scheme: Race or Culture?" *Trans-Scripts: An Interdisciplinary Journal in the Humanities and Social Sciences*, 1 (2011): 1–9.
10. In his "Introduction" to the revised edition of *Imagined Communities: Reflections on the Rise and Spread of Nationalism* (London: Verso, 2006), Benedict Anderson argues, "In contrast to the immense influence that has exerted on the modern world, plausible theory about the form 'community' takes is conspicuously meager" (3). In accepting Anderson's claim that "all historical communities are primarily 'imagined communities,'" Balibar is concerned, as Anderson is not, with the relationship between imagined communities and existing

"structures of domination and exploitation" that make it difficult to distinguish revolutionary violence from the forms of violence that give rise to revolt. Etienne Balibar, *We, the People of Europe?: Reflections on Transnational Citizenship*, trans. James Swenson (Princeton: Princeton University Press, 2004), 130–1.

11. In *We, the People of Europe*, 20–1, Balibar translates the difference between Anderson's "imagined community" and "structures of domination and exploitation" into a political force in its own right, claiming that "the *nation-form is not itself a community*, it is not even the ideal type of a community, but *the concept of a structure capable of producing determinate 'community effects.'*" Thus "[t]he nation-form cannot be defined simply as an abstraction of the national community," because it designates certain "constraints that are exerted together" in order to provide "*a way for economic forces to determine symbolic effects and vice versa*" (emphasis in the original).

12. In "Cloning Cultures: The Social Injustices of Sameness," *Ethnic and Racial Studies*, 25.6 (2002): 1,071; emphasis in the original. Philomena Essed and David Theo Goldberg address the political consequences of reproducing sameness: "a critical account of systems of preference for sameness – from kinship to nation, from aesthetics to production and consuming" – reveals such preference "as contributing to the reproduction of systems of social distinction and privilege" (pp. 20–1).

13. In "Of Paternal Power," chapter IV of John Locke, *The Second Treatise of Government* (Cambridge: Cambridge University Press, 1960), John Locke claims that what he means by "Paternal Power" actually includes "the Mother" and should be thought of as "Parental Power," on the grounds "that Fundamental Authority from whence [children] would derive their Government of a single Person only, was not plac'd in one, but in two Persons jointly" (IV, 53). This phrase performs the *léger de main* that slips the name of "the Mother" in under the father that at once acknowledges her presence and makes it disappear.

14. In Friedrich A. Kittler, *Discourse Networks 1800/1900*, trans. Michael Metteer with Chris Cullens (Palo Alto: Stanford University Press, 1990), Friedrich A. Kittler's description of "the discourse network of 1800" argues that "the originary [vernacular] text . . . occupies the same position in the field of writing that the Mother's voice, as the natural origin, occupies in the field of speaking and reading." That, as Kittler says, "the construct of the originary text,

which has no basis in the real, can be possible only through a parasitic relation to the Mother's Mouth" is arguably demonstrated *ad infinitum* by those authors – Daniel Defoe and Samuel Richardson among them – who constituted in print the interior worlds of both household and feminine subject, as they ventriloquized the voice of a woman (86).

15. Also at work on the problem of "the reproduction of relations of production" during the early 1970s, Henri Lefebvre argued that any theory that hoped to forecast the end of capitalism would have to "sift the various ideas, ideologies, representations and images in order to find out how they have contributed to the renewal of existing relations, either by stimulating reproduction directly, or by obscuring it. Nothing can escape this." *The Survival of Capitalism: Reproduction of the Relations of Production*, trans. Frank Bryant (New York: St. Martin's Press, 1976), 11. Lefebvre ultimately dismisses "the family" as the means for addressing this question on the grounds that the family, on its own, is "insufficient to maintain private property," (74). In *Anti-Oedipus: Capitalism and Schizophrenia*, trans. Robert Hurley, Mark Seem and Helen R. Lane (Minneapolis: University of Minnesota Press, 1983), Gilles Deleuze and Felix Guattari reject the subordination of reproduction to production (or *vice versa*) in favor of the perpetual interaction between two modes of production, the vertical flow we call lineage and the horizontal expansion of alliances (145–53).

16. "Possessive Individualism," 301.

17. Often dismissed as simply an argument against sovereignty, Locke's argument against "innate ideas" takes issue with "the 'false' idea that certain notions may owe their universality to a divine insemination in the human mind." Locke must do so, Balibar contends, in order to make "consciousness" the basis for defining human being as both particular and universal. Bringing out this aspect of Locke's theory of consciousness allows Balibar to argue for "a dissociation of two parts of the Cartesian heritage," in which Locke inaugurates the unrecognized part Etienne Balibar, *Identity and Difference, John Locke and the Invention of Consciousness*, trans. Warren Montag (Durham, NC: Duke University Press, 2013), 47.

18. In "Of Paternal Power," chapter IV of *The Second Treatise* (Cambridge: Cambridge University Press, 1960), John Locke claims that what he means by "Paternal Power" actually includes "the Mother" and should be thought of as "Parental Power," on the grounds "that Fundamental Authority from whence [children] would

derive their Government of a single Person only, was not plac'd in one, but in two Persons jointly" (IV, 53). This phrase performs the *léger de main* that slips the name of "the Mother" in under the father that at once acknowledges her presence and makes it disappear.

19. "I do not say there is no Soul in a Man, because he is not sensible of it in his sleep; But I do say, he cannot think at any time waking or sleeping, without being sensible of it." Book II, I. 10. 25–7. Locke maintains this line of argument through Book II to chapter XXVII, which credits the self with remaining identical to itself over the course of time and with new experiences: "*Self* is that conscious thinking thing ... which is sensible, or conscious of pleasure and pain, capable of Happiness or Misery, and so is concern'd for it *self*, as far as that consciousness extends." *An Essay Concerning Human Understanding* (Oxford: Oxford University Press, 1975), Book II, XXVII, 17, 14–18; emphasis in the original.

20. In her "Introduction" to *Identity and Difference*, Stella Sandford explains how Balibar set out to make Locke "le grand protagoniste" in an alternative genealogy of the philosophy of mind by crediting him with "the invention of the (European) philosophical concepts of consciousness and of the self in the second half of the seventeenth century" (xiii). By so rethinking the English Locke as a European philosopher, Balibar suggests "the construction of a very different, multi-branching Franco-Germanic lineage from chapter XXVII of Locke's *Essay*, one that moves in the stream of 'continental' philosophy of the subject, starting with Kant, through Hegel and Marx to the twentieth-century philosophies of the subject, notably in France" (xii–xiii).

21. Ibid. xli.

22. In a talk delivered at Duke University in February 2015, "Locke: Property and Life," Warren Montag observes, "Indeed, it is possible to argue that the doctrine of property developed in the first five chapters of the Second Treatise of Government paradoxically depends upon even as it logically precedes the concept of personal identity Locke elucidates in Ch 27 of *ECHU*" (ms, 5).

23. Balibar, "Possessive Individualism," 302; emphasis in the original.

24. Ibid. 302; emphasis in the original.

25. Ibid. 302.

26. Ibid. 304.

27. If, as Roberto Esposito contends, we think of "*communitas*" as that "relation, which in binding its members to an obligation of reciprocal donation, jeopardizes individual identity," then we have to

understand "*immunitas*" (or self-removal) as a "defense against the expropriating features of *communitas*." Property affords an immunity that spares the individual from contact with people who are constantly exposed to risk. In keeping these people out, property initially "restores borders that were jeopardized by the common." *Bíos: Biopolitics and Philosophy*, trans. Timothy Campbell (Minneapolis: University of Minnesota Press, 2008), 50.

28. Ibid. 305; emphasis in the original.
29. Ibid. 304–5.
30. Ibid. 314. Quoted from Jacques Derrida, *Spurs: Nietsche's Styles*, trans. Barbara Harlow (Chicago: University of Chicago Press, 1979), 109–11.
31. Ibid. 314. Seizing on Derrida's notion of a different difference that is fundamentally "undeconstructible," Balibar challenges himself to think beyond his previous resolution to the problem "that self-ownership must necessarily be at the same time a process of alienation and a manifestation of the inalienable, or an expenditure of the subject into the economy of properties, *and* a retreat of the subject into the inalienable." The difference he imagines will involve "the subject's escape: something like a 'property without property,' a 'self without a self,' or a 'self that is not his or her/its own" (emphasis in the original). In the next section of this paper, I suggest a link between his concept of the self as "something else" and the figure of the migrant.
32. Ibid. 314.
33. In the first chapter of a book in progress, Timothy Campbell invites us to consider "form" as the expression of the moment that interrupts the over-determined pathways of ideology that operate in terms of exchange. He argues that such a notion of form holds open an interlude with no explanation for it or what may close it, putting exchange itself on hold long enough so that we can examine it. Campbell proposes "parataxis" – from *para*, meaning "beside," and *tassien*, meaning "assemble" – as a way of imagining conjunction without subordination.
34. Balibar, "The Genealogical Scheme," 1–9.
35. Ibid. 3.
36. Ibid. 5.
37. "*Homo nationalis*" is the figure that results, according to Balibar, when all the categories that compose an individual's identity are shaped by the limits and peculiarities of "national being," including attempts "to adopt an opposite point of view, an 'internationalist'

or cosmopolitan worldview." "We, the People of Europe?" 12. Putting this observation together with Essed and Goldberg's claim – "Kinship and connectivity tend to be extended outwards from the narrower circle of 'organic' or 'nuclear' family to wider circles of claimed community, ultimately to embrace the metaphorics of 'national family,' 'family of nations,' or indeed to some idealized, naturalized, and stereotypically streamlined 'human family'" (Essed and Goldberg, "Cloning Cultures," 1,073) – we gain a sense of how familial ideology indeed operates at various levels of modern life.

38. I have elsewhere argued at length that the rise of the domestic novel in England was also the rise of novel criticism and that the apparent opposition between the two modes of discourse was in fact a collaboration that spelled out, naturalized and periodically updated the kinship principles that sustain modern liberal societies, giving each a distinctive national character. See Nancy Armstrong, *Desire and Domestic Fiction: A Political History of the Novel* (Oxford: Oxford University Press, 1987).
39. "Genealogical Scheme," 8; emphasis in the original.
40. Ibid. 8.
41. "Preface," *The Reproduction of Capitalism*, xxvii.
42. Etienne Balibar, "Althusser's Dramaturgy and the Critique of Ideology," *Differences: A Journal of Feminist Cultural Studies*, 26.3 (2015), 19.
43. Ibid. 3.
44. Anne Garréta and Colson Whitehead are two of any number of contemporary novelists to experiment with characters unmarked as to gender like the lovers in Garréta's *Sphinx*, or as to race, in Whitehead's *Zone One*. It's worth noting in the first instance that race quickly takes over for sexual difference in *Sphinx* and that gender seems at first to do the same for race in *Zone One* – that is, until the difference between normal individuals and zombie multitude reveals itself as the division between inside and outside.
45. Emily Brontë, *Wuthering Heights* (New York: W. W. Norton, 1990), 28.
46. In *The Theory of the Novel: A Historico-philosophical Essay on the Forms of Great Epic Literature*, trans. Anna Bostock (London: The Merlin Press, 1988), Georg Lukács famously declares: "the transcendental structure of the form-giving subject and the world of created forms has been destroyed, and the ultimate basis of artistic creation has become homeless ... the novel form is, like no other, an expression of this transcendental homelessness" (39–40).

47. In "The Microeconomic Mode," forthcoming in the journal *Novel: A Forum on Fiction*, Jane Elliott identifies texts in this mode as "characterized by a combination of abstraction and extremity, a fusion" that cuts across media as well as the demarcation between high and low culture. "Abstraction," she writes, "results from a focus on delimited or capsule worlds in which option and decision, action and effect, have been extracted from everyday contexts and thus made unusually legible – for example, the life raft, the desert island, the medical experiment, the prison cell. Extremity registers in forms of painful, grotesque or endangered embodiment, including deprivation, torture, mutilation, self-mutilation and various threats to life itself. The combination of the two results in situations in which individuals make agonized choices among unwelcome options, options that present intense physical or life-threatening consequences for themselves or their loved ones" (manuscript, 1).

Bibliography

Agamben, Giorgio. *Homo Sacer: Sovereign Power and Bare Life*, trans. David Heller-Roazen. Palo Alto: Stanford University Press, 1998.

Althusser, Louis. *On the Reproduction of Capitalism: Ideology and Ideological State Apparatuses*. Trans. G. M. Goshgarian. London: Verso, 2014.

Anderson, Benedict. *Imagined Communities: Reflections on the Rise and Spread of Nationalism*. London: Verso, 2006.

Armstrong, Nancy. *Desire and Domestic Fiction: A Political History of the Novel*. Oxford: Oxford University Press, 1987.

Balibar, Etienne. "'Possessive Individualism' Reversed: From Locke to Balibar." *Constellations*, 9.3 (2002): 299–317.

Balibar, Etienne. *We, the People of Europe: Reflections on Transnational Citizenship*. Trans. James Swenson. Princeton: Princeton University Press, 2004.

Balibar, Etienne. "The Genealogical Scheme: Race or Culture?" *TransScripts: An Interdisciplinary Journal in the Humanities and Social Sciences*, 1 (2011): 1–9.

Balibar, Etienne. *Identity and Difference, John Locke and the Invention of Consciousness*. Trans. Warren Montag. Durham, NC: Duke University Press, 2013.

Balibar, Etienne. "Althusser's Dramaturgy and the Critique of Ideology." *Differences: A Journal of Feminist Cultural Studies*, 26.3 (2015): 1–22.

Brontë, Emily. *Wuthering Heights*. New York: W. W. Norton, 1990.

Brown, Wendy. *States of Injury: Power and Freedom in Late Modernity.* Princeton: Princeton University Press, 1995.
Deleuze, Gilles and Felix Guattari. *Anti-Oedipus: Capitalism and Schizophrenia.* Trans. Robert Hurley, Mark Seem and Helen R. Lane. Minneapolis: University of Minnesota Press, 1983.
Derrida, Jacques. *Spurs: Nietsche's Styles.* Trans. Barbara Harlow. Chicago: University of Chicago Press, 1979.
Elliott, Jane. "The Microeconomic Mode." *Novel: A Forum on Fiction* (forthcoming).
Esposito, Roberto. *Bíos: Biopolitics and Philosophy.* Trans. Timothy Campbell. Minneapolis: University of Minnesota Press, 2008.
Essed, Philomena and David Theo Goldberg. "Cloning Cultures: The social Injustices of Sameness." *Ethnic and Racial Studies*, 25.6 (2002): 1,066–82.
Garréta, Anne. *Sphinx.* Trans. Emma Ramadan. Dallas: Deep Vellum Publishing, 2015.
Kittler, Friedrich A. *Discourse Networks 1800/1900.* Trans. Michael Metteer and Chris Cullens. Palo Alto: Stanford University Press, 1990.
Lefebvre, Henri. *The Survival of Capitalism: Reproduction of the Relations of Production.* Trans. Frank Bryant. New York: St Martin's Press, 1976.
Locke, John. *The Second Treatise of Government.* Cambridge: Cambridge University Press, 1960.
Locke, John. *An Essay Concerning Human Understanding.* Oxford: Oxford University Press, 1975.
Lukács, Georg. *The Theory of the Novel: A Historico-philosophical Essay on the Forms of Great Epic Literature.* Trans. Anna Bostock. London: Merlin, 1988.
Montag, Warren. "Locke: Property and Life." Paper presented at Duke University. Feburary, 2015.
Scott, Joan W. "On Language, Gender, and Working-Class History." *International Labor and Working-Class History*, 31 (Spring, 1987): 1–13.
Whitehead, Colson. *Zone One.* New York: Anchor, 2011.

11

Another "Neo-Racism": Balibar and the Everywhere War
Mike Hill

> Yes, we are at war. Or rather, henceforth, we are all *in* war. But *which war* are we talking about? It is not an easy war to define because it is formed of various types which have been pushed together over time and which today appear inextricable.[1]
>
> Balibar, "In War"

Being in war

The italicized words in this passage from Balibar's own *hommage aux victimes du 13 novembre* 2015 in Paris, will govern my attempts to answer the question they pose, at least provisionally. It must be provisionally because, if Balibar is correct and *whichever* war we are *in* marches sometimes visibly, sometimes invisibly, down an evidently permanent path, I must be thinking and writing this chapter on war, *in* "war." "But," and this is crucial, "*which war?*" Yes, *which*, as if to suggest that there are not only many wars afoot at the current historical moment but also various "types" of war, applications and intensities that while commonly violent are applied in unprecedented, or at least unexpected, ways. Beyond the specificity of these wars, the word that in the epigram also conjures the problem of the many, not only as in a multiplicity of wars but also the problem – always upfront in Balibar's large and wide-ranging œuvre – of the *many* itself, a mode of political action and (or better, *as*) a mode of thought. Balibar's longstanding pre-occupation, often in concert with Spinoza, with mass agency, collective organization, repression and most of all, mass resistance, is intertwined just beneath the surface of this short epigram within the difference between being "in" rather than simply "at" war.

Thus, we can say from the onset that the difference with being *in* war is apposite to the current "conjuncture," a term in the Althusserian tradition that means precisely the set of relations I just mentioned between the agency of *many*, relations of force, equality and class division, and knowledge. On that latter term, Balibar insists, the "state of war" today involves "an epistemological discussion of the category of war," which reveals the "insufficiency of ideal type of dichotomies": war and peace, civilian and combatant, beginning and ends, state and non-state actors, information about and information as violence.[2] I will open up on all of these below.

For now, simply note that our conjuncture, the wars within it, and therefore, the wars we are necessarily *in*, exist under conditions of what Balibar describes (after Wendy Brown) as "the neo-liberal mode of governance," which tends – but *not*, we must allow, if we are to follow Balibar as I will try to do all the way through, *irreversibly* – towards the "de-democratization of democracy."[3] What makes the current tendency toward "de-democratization" so difficult to sort is also what moves democracy, or what Balibar more concretely calls civil society, more and more proximate to so many manifestations of violence. It is, again, a problem – especially for those once presumed to be *outside* war, that is, especially for civil society's traditionally *civilianized* actors – of finding ourselves so suddenly "in" war. Ultimately, this reckoning amounts to nothing less politically profound than the move toward a precipice where "the category of citizenship [itself is about to be] annihilated."[4] Balibar continues, "I see [this annihilation] as the destructive character inherent in the antinomies of citizenship" (C 4). Moreover, as the latest manifestation of a contradiction between citizenship and violence that was always already there, "the neo-liberal reaction to the crisis of the social-national state . . . [now] consist[s] in the promotion of individualism and 'rational' self-interest, along with the privatization of public sector functions."[5] The point beyond this less arguable one about a collapse between the relatively autonomous zones of state authority and the free market is that this so-called "promotion" of "self-interest" is also more or less suicidal. It eventuates in the "annihilation of citizenship" but does so, paradoxically, in the citizen's own name.

Underscoring this paradox, Balibar writes, "extreme violence" designates a condition in which "no *symmetric* counter-power or counter violence can be opposed that does not disseminate or worsen it (think of the case of the 'War on Terror'), pushing politics toward its own self-destruction."[6] This observation is akin to the paradoxical loop between life and death as manifest in what twenty-first century military strategists call the Revolution in Military Affairs (RMA). The rise of *asymmetrical* (or "net-centric") warfare portends a new war-reality that operates preemptively, and without epistemological as well as political precedent, "compressing the kill-chain," as they say, such enemies are killed almost before they become enemies; such that war exists without fronts and on the broadest possible scale; and such that civil, democratic and even anti-violent activity are absorbed (or almost) within the all-encompassing horizon of an "everywhere war."[7]

At the very least, war in its most capacious sense means that if my own attempt to describe *which* war, as Balibar says, while *in* war, is to follow the lines of inquiry his work makes clear, it is an attempt that must be doubly accountable: I must address different kinds of war than the "ideal" or "dichotomous" ones, analyze at least *some* of the colliding new "types" and, above all, I must be attuned to the immanent relation between war and what it is I am trying to do while coming to terms with it. I must in other words think precisely about *words*, or at least about communication, technology and modes of representation that are themselves – it turns out – a more or less ambivalent extension of the current war machine. You may not be interested in war, to paraphrase Trotsky, but it is interested in you.

Let me be more concrete. I want in this chapter to bring Balibar's work on citizenship, war, multitudes and neo-liberalism to bear on some of the key manifestations of how we are *in* war today. The *we* I have in mind is precisely the *we* who until now might well have presumed ourselves and our activities at a comfortable enough distance from war. That such a distance is no longer affordable is evident, among so many other ways, in the confusing climate of planetary terror, which ought to include the rise of the national-security state, mass surveillance, the simultaneous designation of every citizen as always also a political suspect, if not also a target or war. More to the specific case studies about being "in" war that I wish to examine below – and here let me accentuate the issue of *being*, its legal but also its ontological status – is the U.S. military's various experiments in soft power, the "softening" of war, its much debated "cultural" turn. I take such a turn, after Balibar, to be an application of violence in the innovative, neo-liberal, sense.

"Soft" violence means that war has moved into the very fabric of civil society and its attendant components: identity, community and communication, especially, as we will see, insofar as these topics are brought together under the common heading of race.

Balibar says about race that it designates "the illusion of a style of thinking ... Whoever classifies thinks, and whoever thinks exists."[8] But the word worth thinking about further, before getting to "race," is "illusion." The designation of a person in racially objectified form points out a paradox that is the same one as the violence within civil society, which is predicated on the desire for unity through division, usually at the level of some sort of violence, whether it be "hard" violence or "soft." The "illusion" of category – that is not to challenge its functionality in different ways, at different times – betrays an attachment both to what the community-as-unity model makes absent and, what is harder to surmise, the occulted force of that absence precisely as heterogeneity (read: multitude). Althusser put this succinctly, and ironically, as the "omnipotence of genus," the presumption of equivalencies within categories under conditions of what is in fact inequality.[9] "There is external differentiation" in community vis-à-vis race," Balibar writes to the same point, "but also internal differentiation, since unity is posited only to be realized as an infinite variety of forms."[10] Moreover, there is a "specificity of contemporary racism" that subtends "the growth of urban poverty, [and] the dismantling of the welfare state," which must also include the introduction – or *re*-introduction, if you read Balibar on Hobbes – of violence to civility.

As I want to show further below, the "open spectrum" of "a number of racisms" oscillates uniquely today under the heading of war (specifically, insurgency) between what Balibar designates as racism's "biological" and "cultural" modes. I say uniquely, because the "neo-racism" of our time has been adjusted in war. The oscillation "around the spectrum of possible racisms" leads toward *another* "neo-racism," one being developed this time as a war application where the category at stake is the farther-reaching one not just of the citizen and its sub-categories but also of the larger category – perhaps again about to split – of the human being per se. Something on the order of a new bio-militarism is at hand. And this other neo-racism threatens to divide humanity along new lines, ones that make parts of humanity disposable, not at all human, as if they were the living dead. To site Balibar's more recent thinking along these lines, our zombie moment hinges on the "ultra-objectification" of the person as well as of "the people," what he also calls "ultra-subjective cruelty": "the elimination of the humanity and the human in man."[11]

As I will detail below, war applications on this order are exemplified internally by developments in national security strategy, as well as externally in the latest developments within counterinsurgency doctrine (COIN), not least, the COIN tactic known as the US Army's Human Terrain Systems (HTS) program. Alongside the pre-occupation with "soft" power and, effectively, the weaponization of culture, I want also to offer details that swing war *at the same time* in a biological direction. Here I have in mind war-neuroscience, Brain Machine Interface (BMI), which should exhibit more concretely – indeed quite literally – a pronounced *hardening* of the simultaneously *soft* relationship between war and thought, between violence and representation. There is a flip-flop between the subjective and objective sides of war, in other words, and this, I would argue, is what makes our neo-racism new. Regarding BMI, we may recall Balibar's loaded summary of orthodox Cartesianism as (wrongly) celebrating "pure self reference," and in doing so begin to surmise that such an epoch has well and truly passed. Once we may have supposed an escape from corporeality, where the rough-and-tumble life of conflict, inequality and social unrest could be trumped by superior self-consciousness, writ in Descartes time (for now, never mind Spinoza's different take!) as the "[immortal] soul's perfect knowledge of itself."[12] It is here that politics reaches an *anthropological* limit, one inherited precisely from the seventeenth century, and not just from Descartes but, as we will see, more importantly from Hobbes. Thinking along Cartesian lines, which is to say, *thinking* itself, has for a long time been linked to the status of *being*, our relationship to other *beings*, all in order to transcend the world of things, if not also to transcend war.

No longer.

Zombie humanism

[There are] no longer any limits to the process of differentiation. The triumph of humanitarianism and the violence specific to it are humanisms tomb. So much for universalism.

Balibar[13]

So much indeed, and precisely *so much*. What is being put on the table in this epigram is not only the (overdue) disappearance of the long tradition of liberalism – humanitarian universalism *absent* real equality – but also, and again, the proliferation of "differentiation," or what I called above, after Balibar (and Spinoza) the perpetual problem of the *many*. The question then is how to follow the many as subject to *another* neo-racism. How does racial violence work through inclusion rather than exclusion, the proliferation of difference rather than its suppression, to repeat, the "annihilation of the citizen," if not also the end of the human being per se, in the name of the protection rights and civility? How did we get from the violence that cordons off difference, or that uses categorical impermeability to make community *immune* from its others, to one that deploys "a situation of indistinction" not only within and between racial categories but also "between production of [civil] institution and the production of violence."[14] In other words, how is humanism's own racism, something that perhaps used to be more secretive, becoming visible now that humanism is itself being entombed? *Zombie humanism*: Balibar places this concept on the table in his most important work to date on contemporary war and violence. And it is this ghoulish standard that I want to apply to the "cultural" turn in COIN doctrine and its "biological" counterpart in war-neuroscience today.

The US National Security Strategy (NSS), composed in the wake of September 11, 2001, helps to begin to explain what is at stake in zombie humanism, which is both the elimination of any pretense whatsoever, even the fictional kind, of human identity as generically whole, at the same time that it gives up humanity's political correlate of absolute peace. The NSS insists that warfare in the past has maintained at least an official investment in the eighteenth-century separation between civil society – that social arena within which Habermas distinguishes the "human being *per se*" – and the various matters of state.[15] Civil society under this earlier condition marks the establishment not simply of *civilization* but of *civilian-ization*, to recall one of Paul Virilio's provocative terms.[16] By contrast, contemporary and future wars are being said to exceed traditional lines of opposition. In the figurative language of the NSS, twenty-first century wars will involve "shadowy networks . . . [that] reach into every corner of the globe." [17] Thus connected, the net-centric dynamic of mapping local "cultures" begins already to extend outward beyond whatever ideological node is at hand in order to subsume the planet at large: not just *inter*-national war (between states) but also *intra*-national war (within them). This war – the everywhere-and-forever war – we are told will be "different from any other war in history." This means, "fighting on many fronts . . . against a particularly elusive enemy." Future wars will be "seen . . . [and] unseen . . .[,] and will continue over an extended period of time."[18]

Balibar is clear on what is essentially a return to a Hobbesian historical moment, with twists and turns that are unique to present-day technological applications and are consistent with planetary capitalism's demands. Under the new reach of violence, which comes full circle back to civil society itself, we face "the exhaustion of the very word 'democracy,' the dominant use of which now seems obsolete or perverse."[19] At stake in that word "perverse" is a contemporary "flipside of the construction of the people, namely the violence of war of all against all, [which] now takes center stage in the form of conflicts between hegemonic equivalences that rend apart the possibility of naming a people."[20] The presumed exclusion of violence from civility, according to the "dominant" re-writing of whatever fragile social contract the state may once have had with its citizens, is rendered null. But it is rendered null *perversely*, which is to say again, in the preservation of civilization's own name. Beyond that, this re-connection with Hobbesian violence advances, again perversely, along the lines of what one could call Spinoza 2.0: the state "refus[es] . . . [the] transcendence" of violence, and oddly embraces it *within* the boundaries of "political right."[21] War now is a reciprocal social action, "one that characterizes the existence of a body politic . . . [and] causes the dissolution of different types of regimes."[22] Or to cite Balibar citing Spinoza from the *Tracatus Politicus*: "'no body politic can exist without being subject to the latent threat of war ("sedition") . . . This is the cause of causes . . . *Its own citizens (cives) are always the greater threat to the body politic than any external enemy's* (hostes)."[23] The point of this in the current context is that the latency identified by Spinoza and for a long time left that way is today activated in the name of security. The "external" is "internalized" as so *many* points of division within what is no longer presumed to be either unified or peaceful. This is as much as to say that "the true 'mass era' is perhaps upon us."[24] But how does *this* war – with sufficient capaciousness to include civil society activities, its new multiples of people under the expanded rubric of planetary violence – connect with the neo-racism of our day?

As I have suggested, what the doctrinal literature calls a Revolution in Military Affairs (RMA) construes warfare differently than before. And this difference is what former US Defense Secretary Robert Gates has expressed by recruiting the very concept of "culture and people" as an instrument of geo-political conflict. The RMA depends upon mobilizing "multiple" sources of enmity according to a newly expanded logic of "network[ed]" conflictual grids. In the lexicon of the RMA, that term "multiple" signifies a turn to *quantitative* reasoning that, I would suggest, subsumes – or proposes to subsume – the *qualitative* aspects of cultural analysis that are invisible unless they can be known by numbers through machines. We will see in a moment how this process of quantification is both a technological and a political problem, which link to Balibar's notion of "ultra-objective" violence. For now, let me offer more description of the war strategies currently at hand.

The paradox inherent in civic violence and its path toward contemporary neo-racism are offered up as an official tactic of asymmetric warfare in the US Army's newly revised *Counterinsurgency Field Manual (CFM)*.[25] Drawn from the lessons of Napoleonic Spain, French Algiers, British Malaysia and other examples of empire's eventual failure, the *Manual* is both a tactical bluebook for combatting urban insurgency and a sustained effort in critical race studies as war by other means. With its high dose of up-to-the-minute social network theory, this is a *post*-post-colonial studies text: its purpose is to wage low-intensity conflict within what it loosely calls the "global civil societies" of our "host countries," and make "culture" a decisive "[a]rea [of war] Operation" (or "AO"). Counterinsurgency operations are designed to focus on "those paramilitary, political, economic, psychological, and civic actions ... [that are necessary] to defeat insurgency,"[26] and to place those AOs within the charge of US war tactics. COIN operations are thus designed to manipulate "identity-focused insurgencies"[27] as "soft[ly]" re-instrumentalized mechanisms of population control that – unlike past orders of liberal govermentality – do not presume to separate civil society practices with the strategies of war.

Notably, the new COIN *Manual* presumes that the soldier-ethnographer's work in redrawing global systems of "racial" belonging "may not conform to *historical* facts ... or may drastically simplify [them]."²⁸ This aspect of the Army's Human Terrain System (HTS) program, which is the practical offshoot of the new *CFM*, highlights a temporal dimension to "identity-focused" tactics of counter-insurgency. History itself is placed at the service of war. And in that manner, culturally embedded violence is a keystone of so-called "global civil society" where new technologies allow strategists to "create divisions between movement leaders and the mass base."²⁹ Commanders can thus "seek ... cleavages between groups ... crosscutting ties between [them]; reinforcing or widening seams between [them]."³⁰ And as the HTS literature points out, the "cultural analyst" *cum* advance guard soldier should accordingly "gather, store, manipulate, and provide cultural data from hundreds of categories ... [that also] reaches back ... to US academic sources" (*Mra* 3). The "dynamics of identity politics and group loyalties" in this context are assumed to be "fluid, opaque, and variable across localities that counterinsurgents cannot afford to neglect [as part of] its legitimacy building tool kit" (*GIC* 132). What's being deployed here is an explicitly *non-normative* conception of identity politics. Here, the kinds of things that a good deal of domestic multiculturalism has celebrated over the last decade or so, like "hybridity," or difference, or trans-cultural affiliation, are being used for military ends. Again, this is just to pose my central questions: to what extent is this war an adherent of neo-racism? And may we ask of neo-racism the same question Balibar invites us to ask of contemporary war: which one? In short, is the Zombie humanist still white?

This last question is not as daft as it may sound. Elsewhere I have asked a question about what it means to think of U.S. hegemony under the conditions of multi-racialism and its demographic correlate – not even a generation away – of a coming white minority.³¹ At the center of my interests there was the U.S. census 2000, which for the first time sense the advent of self-enumeration in the 1960s, allows for a "check all that applies" option on the issue of race and ethnicity.³² Even limiting one's choice to just two combinations, this new law stands to increase the tabulation from 5 to 128 possibilities.³³ Categorical speculation on this order is something the National Association for the Advancement of Colored People (NAACP) finds understandably disquieting.³⁴ As the NAACP is quick to point out, the relatively recent fine-tuning of identity-based claims for civil rights works on behalf of reversing half a century's worth of racial jurisprudence. The undoing of the OMB official five effectively opens up a way to undermine all forms of juridical redress involving race by complicating racial identity to a point of multiplicity that is also a point of categorical collapse.

To point out this paradox is to confirm Balibar's investigation into the unique way in which racialized domination "progresses in the contemporary world"[35] and how it can in turn be connected to what he identifies as "the negative repercussions of post-national integration."[36] The emergent post-white racial imaginary confirms Balibar's neo-racism, with a contemporary twist: the prospect of "becoming-minority" that he borrows from Deleuze in order to affirm the potential for a re-invigoration of mass struggle on the side of racial and economic justice outside the limits of liberal consensus leans in the adjoining of war and demography in the opposite direction. The economic order that a governmental embrace of so-called multitudes as "a rival to identity politics" – and I am adding to Balibar's point:such an embrace would amount to a cynical appropriation of them – "reflects the development of a quasi-apartheid social structure."[37] To sum up, "the rights of the different individuals involved add up, or, even better, multiply . . . to the extent [that] they neutralize each other, or even lead to a cycle of mutual destruction."[38] It is telling both in Balibar's use of the word "destruction" – that is the logical end of a citizen's right to be recognized under conditions that reinforce the security of "a fabulously wealthy minority"[39] – and in the fact that this last set of citations are taken from Balibar's book on Spinoza, not the one on race, that violence is positioned as historically immanent to, and not at Hobbes would have it, contracted out of, social existence. "*The rulers and the ruled, sovereign and citizen, all belong to the multitude*",[40] Balibar writes. And elsewhere, neo-liberal governmentality: "neutralizes as completely as possible the element of conflictuality that was essential to classical liberalism . . ., depriv[ing] it preemptively of any meaning." This, Balibar continues, "creates a social context in which actions of individuals and groups (even when these actions are violent) fall under the jurisdiction of a single criterion: quantifiable unity."[41]

I will have more to say below about the importance of that term *quantifiable*, how it is dependent upon a whole new techno-informational regime that is apposite to what we have already seen in the making of "humanity" and "culture" into "terrain." But to sum up here, let me simply emphasize that the U.S. census since

2000, on the inside of the state, and the Army's HTS program, on its outside, use identity politics to blank out identity. This is true insofar as self- and state- recognition are no longer sutured to liberal juridical norms. And this is equally true to the extent that the inside and the outside of civil society, the so-called peace *out there* and *this* war *in here*, are no longer divided as completely as they were once assumed to be. Such a paradox, that identity rights terminate identity's claim to justice, that citizens are suspects or that they are even unwitting combatants today, is logically consistent with a political ethos that engages the nation in autogenic forms of "culture" war.

Thus, about white Zombie humanism, and to get a little bit more critically at this issue of the war *in* "culture," here is one more example from the neo-race war front. The Canadian military has also tarried with an HTS approach to war, and in 2008 deployed what they called – without irony – " *white situation awareness teams*." These teams are given the objective of "map[ping] out the movers and shakers of [Kandahar] and how they relate to one another."[42] I say *without irony* because the "whiteness" being evoked here occurs in a context where – in keeping with what I have proposed about the dependence of fluid demography as a "perverse" application of neo-liberal governmentality – color takes on a more *functional* than descriptive quality. Just below I will return to the apparent retreat from subjectivity allowed by the turn toward biology, as we shift topics from HTS to military neuroscience. But further on the unmooring of whiteness from its place within traditional race and ethnic divisions, note that in military parlance, "Red" means foe, "Blue" means friend and "White," as evident here, simply means civilians of whatever racial or ethnic identity. So the mapping of "white Afghans" in this sense treats "whiteness" as a local and temporary condition of demographic-military inactivity in the form of an eternal and minutely negotiable battlefield-census. "Whiteness" as such is produced in a context of insurgency where friend and foe slip in and out of designation, and where battles are won and lost at the level of information management, you could say, by "greening" the data, as much as they are through kinetic means. As the Afghan "*whitens*" – fails to become white, or travels, day-to-day, in and out of "whiteness" – such knowledge can be recorded, transmitted, stored and manipulated immediately and in real time, or at least as soon as computational analysis can quantify the data.

I am already thinking back to the self-admonition I raised by way of an introduction about a second need for accountability attached to writing *in* war (the first, recall, was to determine *which* war: the everywhere war), as Balibar's work would seem to demand. That second accountability had precisely to do with the transmission and production of knowledge. How does war not only find its way into so-called culture, but, once it's there, how does it become operational as problem of representation? This is why I tried to flag those words from Balibar regarding the link between *multitudes* and *quantitative* analysis. I want to elaborate now on how quantification lends itself to the end of politics understood as an exclusively anthropological problem. This raises the issue Balibar refers to as our unique brand of "cruelty" – the *unmanning* of man – what I have tried to exemplify describing how the *human* becomes *terrain*.

It is entirely possible now – allowable, even effectively encouraged – to think of people in a perversely anti-Cartesian way, not as thinkers and owners of "things," but the reverse, people as "things." As Balibar says (after Bertrand Ogilvie), ours is an age of "'disposable humans' or 'non-persons' . . . [who are] permanently exposed to elimination of one form or another."[43] "In the process of depersonalization," he writes, "the possibility of political *action* that is neutralized or destroyed by being demoted from the collective into the individual level . . . represents the extreme limit for democracy."[44] The word "individual" here has an ambivalent bent and should be read in line with the massification of minorities that Deleuze describes, but in ways that keep the masses *from*, rather leading them *to*, political innovation. Think here about "white Afghans" and U.S. census takers. The *terrain*-ing of the human is part and parcel of neo-liberalism's heartless oscillation between "both its '*subjective*' and its '*objective*' sides,"[45] with a measure of fluidity that is calculated to be just right for keeping populations under control. "The very distinction between 'subject' and 'object' vacillates in the limit experience of cruelty."[46] In this way, the anti-political *political* effectiveness of *terrain*-ing both cellularizes social life – literally, as we will see with BMI – and anesthetizes political potential. Thus the kind of "ultra-objective violence" that Balibar has in mind turns "whole populations [into] 'superfluous' or 'excessive'" – we could add, disposable – *matter*, "reduc[ing] human beings to the condition of a thing."[47] In this grim, forbidding sense, as I have already suggested, the dawn of the mass epoch this time is also the dawn of dead.

But how does the production of human-as-terrain happen, or better, since we have given some examples, by what means comes Zombie humanism? By communicative means, which is to say, at least in their war applications, according to *quantitative* machines. Our new capacities for human elimination – moral as well as physical – "begin . . . by suppressing their individuality and treating them as quantities of residual 'pieces.'"[48] But piecing humans out for neo-liberal re-assemblage, or worse, dividing the species itself between those many who are left to die, and we few who are supposed to go on living, requires, just like neo-racism requires, occasional recalibrations of "sociopolitical techniques."[49] The "techniques" that Balibar is referring to here, it should not be surprising, are those of "'differentialist culturalism'," namely, "demography."[50] Nor should it require much explaining that the technology necessary for calculating newly massive populations of racialized data in the modern age of census taking was IBM's Electronic Numerical Integrator and Computer (ENIAC), the same means used to maximize kill-ratios in World War II.[51] That making live and letting die were always moveable feasts does not take a lot of research to reveal. What is more difficult to surmise, however – because we are *in* them – is how the technologies of violence and civility change over time, and to what ends they are directed. (I insist that they can be directed to multiple ends: computers by themselves don't kill people, yet.)

Thus, we see the importance of the embedded nature of politics and representation in Balibar's work, the essential need to link communicative *means* to power. In whatever racialized "topography," according to whatever "system of reference . . . for classifying and interpreting" difference that may be at work at whichever historical moment (and they differ, vastly), "a mediation is required."[52] Media, means, technology, communication: thinking again through Spinoza, Balibar hovers over the point that an "individual is a function of communication, and that communication develops most not between predetermined social types but between singularities, between practical experiences."[53] There is an insurgent gesture in this citation that we must at least acknowledge. It is there in the terms "singularity" and "practical," which at least potentially function to undercut "predetermined social types" in the assembly wars over "piecing" (peacing?) out the human as a matter of war. "The incontrovertible modalities of violence . . . [may] suffice to invalidate the 'hegemonic' scheme of politics,"[54] as Balibar more affirmatively suggests. With a variation this time on a Hegelian scheme, he argues that "the masses . . .[,] the exploited classes . . . are transformed . . . into a popular movement." This for Balibar is the only kind of "civility" worth having. But this potential, as we have seen, is just what neo-racism neutralizes insofar as it redraws or makes fluid the distinctions between "types."[55] This for Balibar is the kind of "civility" worth having. As much as other forms of inequality, Balibar is invested in "the inequality of knowledge, which is at once a difference between the mass and the elite."[56] The reason is explained in the later clause: the history of the production of knowledge, while designating masses from the elite in the political sense, is also a struggle over how to do the designating itself. Whom to categorize? By whom? Toward what kind of equality? – as a foundational epistemological concern. Race is an analytic in other words, and its effects are dependent upon certain technical and communicative applications.

This is why Balibar can speak about "the withering of the public sphere . . . under the triumphant impact of communication," where communication (*contra* Habermas) withdraws from or even cancels out – more accurately, reverses – civil society's collective power over things.[57] To emphasize: "racism is a genuine mode of thought . . ., [a] mode of connecting not only with words but with objects"; further, "racism embodies a very insistent desire for knowledge . . . It is a way of asking *who* you are in a certain social world, *why* there are some compulsory places in this world to which you must adapt yourself" and, not least, "why we are violent."[58] It is important to take at full scale Balibar's qualification about a "certain" social world, as if to suggest *avant la lettre* that such a world is subject to change. To get to the change I am after, and the one I have been following Balibar in order to surmise, we must add to the questions of who and why, one other question – that is crucial in a "social world" based on the expanded agency of things – and that is the question of how many?

So we have at least established that "the new visibility of extreme violence [emerges] particularly in the techniques of media."[59] In this quote Balibar is referring to "modern techniques of media coverage and broadcasting and the transformation of images . . . 'virtual reality' . . . [the] transformation of extreme violence into show."[60] We all know what he is talking about in the if-it-bleeds-it-leads mentality that is no longer the exception but the rule of war as media power. (Think here of ISIS's slick web productions and the hanging of Saddam Hussein playing on Fox news in infinite loop.) I would like to get at something similar in the example of war neuroscience, which is attached to the notion of the *virtually* real, specifically, in the way that switch we have been following between subjective and objective realms parallels this paradox of *virtuality*. The extremely mysterious making of images into the reality is directly related to a new and – if one may still speak this way – symptomatically relevant connection between violence and representation. This interface puts us squarely at the next step in human *terrain*-ing, and follows to the letter the neoliberal oscillation between "culturalism" and "biologism "that we have already covered. More than that, war's digital turn marks a stealthy come-back, post-Weimar republic, "of the biological theme."[61] Here, paradoxically, mechanically – or we should say, electro-mechanically – as well as biologically, mind becomes a *literal* extension of media. This is already part of our contemporary war arsenal. It is an egregious sign not only of the war that we are *in* but also of the war that is in us.

As a key co-participant in the U.S. government's multibillion-dollar Brain Research through Advancing Innovative Neurotechnologies® (BRAIN) initiative, the Defense Advanced Research Projects Agency (DARPA) is keenly interested in the military applications of what is called *neuronal* census work. About the idea of living in an age of global "banlieues," Balibar remarks on "a type of revolt, perhaps of struggle, that is being generalized transnationally – a 'revolt of the excluded' – if not a 'molecular civil war,' that forms the horizon of the 'great migration'."[62] The curious fact about the widening of war on a planetary scale to encompass the extremities of poverty and revolt the world over is the simultaneous micro-scaling of violence even as it continues to increase on the "geo-political" scale. We are no longer just counting people as a war application, but "piec[ing]" them out to their molecular, chemical and electrical levels. One military neuroscientist calls brain mapping "the greatest scientific and philosophical challenge ever taken."[63] Because the agency's "*only* charter is radical innovation" science and philosophy are pushed here to limits that no one can cross in institutionalized humanities settings.[64] DARPA's Systems of Neuromorphic Adaptive Plastic Scalable Electronics

(SyNAPSE) program, rather than beginning with biological neural systems and then linking them to machines, attempts to make a brain out of mechanical parts. The goal of this neuro-simulation project consists of putting together 1.6 billion neurons and 8.87 trillion synapses, which matches the scale of a cat cortex and is 4.5 percent of a human cortex. This project involves a highly sophisticated mapping tool called *BrainCam*: "a framework that record[s] the firing of all neurons and convert[s] them to a movie for convenient visualization – similar in concept to an EEG [electroencephalogram] trace." The *BrainCam* movie reveals thought-as-data: "simulations . . . [that are] reproduced alpha waves (8 to 13Hz) and gamma waves (>30Hz) as often seen in the mammalian cortex" (CSB). The ability to manufacture neuro-mechanical infrastructure – specifically, the *visual* cortex – such as that produced by SyNAPSE, portends a range of bio-synthetic forms of intelligence already coming to military markets.

In the common language of geological mapping we have seen used by HTS, neurons are "targeted" as "populations." "Biology" in DARPA's own terms is an "application."[65] "Nodal positions" are monitored on the order of insurgent elements, charted as "terrain" or "signal systems," that can be manipulated in the form of short-term memory downloads that the soldier-patient may not even know she has.[66] Memory has itself become a military frontier in the same way COIN makes human beings into "terrain." Self- and community-awareness in the form of what the soldier-patient can willfully recall from a battle is sidelined by ways of seeking memory as math. According to the application of what the biomilitary researchers call Cognitive Augmentation (AugCog): "the target of memory enhancement is not long-term memory . . . but rather working memory, which encompasses processes used for both storage and manipulation."[67]

What is enabling the prospect of increasing working memory is the ability to visualize it on screen as an "electrophysiological event . . . where changes in the visual field held by an unconscious mind . . . [can be translated by] information processing."[68] In other words, you saw where that improvised explosive device (IED), sniper or target was before you shot or were shot. But you simply did not know that you saw it and, by letting the machine remember for you, we can access those unknowns to deal with similar situations at a later time. As Jonathan Moreno has revealed, "by programming neurons to respond to light, neural activity can be controlled . . . optogenentic[ally]."⁶⁹ What is being manipulated in the course of BMI is an area of the brain where the sub-disciplines of computational and affective neuroscience interact. Memory, especially traumatic memory, is where a good deal of military medical research is happening.⁷⁰

This is exactly counter to the practice of self-enumeration up to the *schizogenic* census 2000, which not only challenged the difference between self and other but also deliberately jettisoned the assumption that racial categories would maintain at least a functional sense of communal fidelity over time. Neither are so when brain meets machine. What the latest neuroscience makes clear is that the brain, like we used to say about the unconscious, knows more than you do. On the problem of scale, neuro-scientific complexity extends beyond the new demographics preferred by HTS – not tens of thousands of diverse cultures here but 100 million nerve cells differently wired together by a million billion connections. Just one cubic meter of brain tissue contains hundreds of thousands of nerve cells. As the last frontier of the last frontier, the scale of the brain, though microscopic, far exceeds the global communications network, which has only five billion mobile phones.

Note here in returning to the paradox of the virtual, the crucial role of machine intelligence in the making of the human into thing, *real* knowledge – defined in the discourse of AugCog as *quantitative* data over the *qualitative* kind that registers in a woefully incomplete way as mere self-perception – is only assessable in on screen. As the literature on BMI makes clear, what the researchers call "brain reading" does not need the self-awareness of the brain that is being read.⁷¹ Like the non-normative understandings of race that emerged in the US Census 2000 debates, and that were applied on a global scale by HTS forms of net-centric population intelligence, military neuroscience is seizing on the opportunity of turning subjectivity into an electro-kinetic affair. Indeed, the epoch of cognitive avionics is already upon us. The wireless linking between a pilot's brain and the enhanced video-vision of drones is now an operational option. Innovations in non-invasive BMI have set the stage for telepathic helmets, already in proto-type.⁷² These helmets "read" and visually transmit a soldier's brain activity and transmit it to a data cloud, commander, small unit, Unmanned Aerial Vehicle (UAV) or unmanned ground vehicle.

Consider on this final point regarding war and this *other* neo-racism, the problem not of whiteness, post-whiteness or even of "white Afghans," but at this stage in the processes of human *thing*-ification, the problem of "white matter." "White matter" is composed of bundles of axons, and not the more famous neurons and synapses of grey matter. The tightly packed axon suites themselves, are seen literally, not figuratively, as "composed of millions of communication cables, each containing a long, individual wire, or axon, coated with a white, fatty substance called myelin" (WM 56). If the wire in question is not *white* enough, that is, if *myelination* occurs irregularly in certain brain regions or is malformed along the axon wire, then high-level cognition is adversely affected (examples range from autism and schizophrenia, to compulsive lying).

"Whiteness" is in this sense performing a supremely *integrative* function, but on a scale and at a velocity that is not conceivable without one network (the brain's) plugging in bio-electronically to another (the machine's). In "grey matter," "memories are stored." In the more difficult to map "white matter," "electric signals ... jump swiftly down the axon, node to node."[73] Apposite to non-linear modalities of war, scientists working as part of the BRAIN initiative have followed a net-centric method of "non-linear" data analysis to map the brain because it is organized in the same way.[74] They call repeatedly for a brain "census," and one that allows for "finer categories [of] enumeration" than mere human-body census taking has been able to produce, the fine-tuning of US Census 2000 notwithstanding.[75] An important moment of progress in the mapping of the brain has been the ability to simply name "cells" and calculate "circuits." This is put notably as a mathematical problem of the "quantitative sciences": "machine learning," literally, the adding to the brain's networks the necessary forms of computer interface that, in turn, do more effective adding than we humans can achieve. "Algorithms" in turn become "prosthetics."[76] In the refreshingly frank language of the neuroscientists, what they are after is a "parts list."[77] But this parts list is tremendously large, so large the scientists say that it changes the very status of the human. The census-work being done here, like the fluid demography we have seen in HTS (only with the brain, non-metaphorically fluid), involves "quantities of information" that detail "thousands of millions [of] parts," and at "petabytes of scale."[78]

We should say then that "whiteness" in the Afghani as well as the *myelinated* sense is no longer a subject position but instead a *fluid* substance (literally), one ready for the net-centric forms of topology we have already discussed in the new COIN. "Whiteness" has also, again quite literally, become a medium, not the memory itself, which is the work of grey matter but a key electro-chemical component of a massive data infrastructure that organizes categorical and temporal value.

So to say again, after Balibar, we are *in* war, and in coming to terms with *which* war – there are many – we must also come to terms with that war that is going on within us. But even here, it is not enough to point out that war is occurring *within* the physiology of the human being per se. Rather, the fulcrum of biomilitarism as a matter of *terrain*-ing people is encapsulated by: (a) not only the way that human corporeality itself, rather like the disappearance of the enemy into the fabric of the Homeland under terror, is dissolving into violence, but also (b) the way that non-subjective elements of human existence (thought, memory, affect) are being given agency through the translation of thoughts into things. Repeatedly in Balibar we see this process linked to the rise of the liberal state gone awry by going toward its logical end: a neo-liberal order within which citizens' rights are canceled out by the means of a more accurate and technically sophisticated – if also fluid – remapping of traditional racial typologies from whiteness, to post-whiteness, to "white Afghans," and finally to the even more nettlesome problem of "white matter." To appeal once again to Spinoza, "when the state has grown so 'mad' that it threatens to deprive its citizens of the minimum viable measure of individuality, below which they will effectively be dead to themselves, it always in the end provokes the outrage of the multitude, and this outrage destroys it."[79] Our final question about Zombie humanism – what Balibar refers to as "Marx's nightmare"[80] – must therefore be whether or not there is anything left on the side of equality and liberty that may be left in its wake. Let us at least pose the question.

Notes

1. Etienne Balibar, "In War," *Open Democracy*, November 17, 2015 <https://www.opendemocracy.net/can-europe-make-it/etienne-balibar/in-war> (accessed May 10, 2016); emphasis in the original.
2. Etienne Balibar, "What's in a War?" *Ratio Juris*, 21.3 (September 2008): 366.

3. Etienne Balibar, *Citizenship* (Cambridge, MA: Polity, 2015), 4; emphasis in the original.
4. Balibar, *Citizenship*, 4.
5. Balibar, *Citizenship*, 5.
6. Etienne Balibar, *Violence and Civility* (New York: Columbia University Press, 2015), 2; emphasis in the original.
7. On the "everywhere war," see Derek Gregory, "The Everywhere War," *The Geographical Journal*, 177.3 (September 2011): 238–50.
8. Etienne Balibar and Immanuel Wallerstein, *Race, Nation, Class: Ambiguous Identities* (London: Verso, 1991), 221.
9. Louis Althusser, "Marx in His Limits," in *Philosophy of the Encounter: Later Writings, 1978–87*, ed. Francois Matheron and Oliver Corpet (London: Verso, 2006), 65.
10. Balibar, *Race, Nation, Class*, 221.
11. Balibar, *Violence and Civility*, 54.
12. Etienne Balibar, *Identity and Difference, John Locke and the Invention of Consciousness* (London: Verso, 2013), 34.
13. Balibar, *Violence and Civility*, 15.
14. Balibar, *Violence and Civility*, 16.
15. Jurgen Habermas, *The Structural Transformation of the Public Sphere*, trans. Thomas Burger (Cambridge, MA: MIT Press, 1989), 29.
16. See Paul Virilio, *Pure War* (New York: Semiotexte, 1997).
17. *The National Security Strategy of the United States of America* (2002), 5.
18. *The National Security Strategy of the United States of America* (2002), 7.
19. Etienne Balibar, *Equaliberty: Political Essays* (Durham, NC: Duke University Press, 2014).
20. Balibar, *Equaliberty*, 193.
21. Etienne Balibar, *Spinoza and Politics* (London: Verso, 1998), x.
22. Balibar, *Spinoza and Politics*, 67.
23. *Spinoza, Political Treatise*, trans. Samuel Shirley (Indianapolis: Hackett Publishing, 2000), vi. Hereafter referred to with book and page number in text as TP; Balibar *Spinoza and Politics*, 68.
24. Balibar, *Race, Nation, Class*, 37.
25. *Counterinsurgency Field Manual* (Chicago: University of Chicago Press, 2007).
26. *Counterinsurgency Field Manual*, xxiii.
27. *Counterinsurgency Field Manual*, 24.

28. *Counterinsurgency Field Manual*, 93.
29. *Counterinsurgency Field Manual*, 181.
30. *Counterinsurgency Field Manual*, 87.
31. See Mike Hill, chapter 1, "Incalculable Community: Multiracialism, US Census 2000, and the Crisis of the Liberal State," in *After Whiteness: Unmaking an American Majority* (New York: New York University Press, 2004), 21–74.
32. In the 1850 Census where the term "mulatto" was used, and in 1890 populations could be identified as "quadroon" and "octoroon." The new decision is not substantially different from the interagency recommendations issued in the 1977 mandates of OMB 15. For the Census 2000 standards, see *Federal Register* 62.131 (July 9, 1997).
33. See William O'Hare, "Managing Multiple-Race Data," in *American Demographics* (April 1998), 44.
34. In a letter presented at the congressional hearings in 1993, the nation's top civil rights leaders expressed "extreme concern that [the] new [multiracial] category will inadvertently cause confusion and inconsistent reporting." See *Hearings before the Subcommittee on Census, Statistics, and Postal Personnel . . .*, Serial no. 103-7 (Washington, DC: US Government Printing Office: April 14, 1993; June 30, 1993; July 29, 1993; November 3, 1993), 224. An editorial by Charles Byrd in *The Interracial Voice* (September 5, 2000) "The Political Realignment: A Jihad against 'Race' Consciousness," blames the NAACP directly for maintaining "the one drop rule" and discouraging multiracial Census reclassification. *Interracial Voice* can be found online.
35. Balibar, *Race, Nation, Class*. 9.
36. Etienne Balibar, *We the People of Europe?* (Princeton: Princeton University Press, 2004), 116.
37. Balibar, *We the People*, 116.
38. Balibar, *Spinoza and Politics*, 62.
39. Balibar, *Spinoza and Politics*, xvii
40. Balibar, *Spinoza and Politics*, 70; emphasis in the original.
41. Balibar, *Citizenship*, 103.
42. Editorial, "Mapping 'White' Afghans Aim to End Civilian Deaths," *National Post*, November 8, 2008, <http://www.canada.com/calgaryherald/story.html?id=a6df4358-ceco-4555-9efa-d7e66b4a31bc> (accessed May 10, 2016); emphasis added.
43. Balibar, *Equaliberty*. 86.
44. Balibar, *Equaliberty*, 87; emphasis in the original.
45. Balibar, *Equaliberty*, 105; emphasis in the original.

46. Balibar, *Violence and Civility*, 70.
47. Balibar, *Violence and Civility*, 69.
48. Balibar, *Violence and Civility*, 69.
49. Balibar, *Race, Nation, Class*, 69.
50. Balibar, *Race, Nation, Class*, 55.
51. NIAC, see Hill, chapter 1, *AW*.
52. Balibar, *Equaliberty*, 52.
53. Balibar, *Equaliberty*, 61.
54. Balibar, *Violence and Civility*, 35.
55. Balibar, *Violence and Civility*, 39.
56. Balibar, *Violence and Civility*, 69.
57. Etienne Balibar, *Masses, Classes, Ideas: Studies on Politics and Philosophy before Marx* (New York: Routledge, 1994), xii.
58. Balibar, *Masses, Classes, Ideas*, 200; emphasis in the original.
59. Balibar, *We the People of Europe*, 125.
60. Balibar, *We the People of Europe*, 125.
61. Balibar, *Race, Nation, Class*, 26.
62. Balibar, "Uprisings in the *Banlieues*," *Constellations*, 14.1 (2007): 49.
63. *Opportunities in Neuroscience for Army Applications* (Washington, DC: National Research Council, 2009), vii. Hereafter with page number in text as *ONA*.
64. Cited in Jonathan D. Moreno, *Mind Wars: Brain Science and the Military in the Twenty-first Century* (New York: Bellevue Literary Press, 2006), 27; emphasis in the original.
65. Moreno, *Mind Wars*, 26–7.
66. Howard Caygill, "Physiological Memory Systems" in *Memory: History, Theories, Debates*, ed. Susannah Radstone and Bill Schwarz (New York: Fordham University Press, 2010), 227–34.
67. Rod Flower et al., *Brain Waves Module III: Neuroscience, Conflict, and Security* (London: The Royal Society, 2011), 8.
68. *Opportunities in Neuroscience for Army Applications*, 15.
69. Moreno, *Mind Wars*, 33.
70. *Opportunities in Neuroscience for Army Applications*, 24; 27.
71. Rod Flower et al., *Brain Waves Module I: Neuroscience, Conflict, and Security* (London: The Royal Society, 2011), 8.
72. See Jordan Pearson, "Brain Controlled Flight is a Thing Now." *Motherboard*, May 28, 2014, <http://motherboard.vice.com/read/brain-controlled-flight-is-a-thing-now> (accessed May 10, 2016).
73. WM, 56.
74. Flower et al., *Brain Waves Module I*, 6.
75. Flower et al., *Brain Waves Module I*, 20.

76. Flower et al., *Brain Waves Module I*, 38.
77. Flower et al., *Brain Waves Module I*, 14.
78. Flower et al., *Brain Waves Module I*, 14; 32.
79. Spinoza, *TP* III ix; Balibar, *Spinoza and Politics*, 68.
80. Balibar, *Citizenship*, 108.

Bibliography

Althusser, Louis, "Marx in His Limits." In *Philosophy of the Encounter: Later Writings, 1978–87*. Ed. Francois Matheron and Oliver Corpet. London: Verso, 2006.

Balibar, Etienne. *Masses, Classes, Ideas: Studies on Politics and Philosophy before Marx*. New York: Routledge, 1994.

Balibar, Etienne. *Spinoza and Politics*. London: Verso, 1998.

Balibar, Etienne. *We the People of Europe?* Princeton: Princeton University Press, 2004.

Balibar, Etienne. "Uprisings in the *Banlieues*." *Constellations*, 14.1 (2007): 47–71.

Balibar, Etienne. "What's in a War?" *Ratio Juris*, 21.3 (September 2008): 365–86.

Balibar, Etienne. *Identity and Difference, John Locke and the Invention of Consciousness*. London: Verso, 2013.

Balibar, Etienne. *Equaliberty: Political Essays*. Durham, NC: Duke University Press, 2014.

Balibar, Etienne. *Citizenship*. Cambridge, MA: Polity, 2015.

Balibar, Etienne. "In War." *Open Democracy*. November 17, 2015.

Balibar, Etienne. *Violence and Civility*. New York: Columbia University Press, 2015.

Balibar, Etienne and Immanuel Wallerstein. *Race, Nation, Class: Ambiguous Identities*. London: Verso, 1991.

Byrd, Charles. "The Political Realignment: A Jihad against 'Race' Consciousness." *The Interracial Voice*. September 5, 2000.

Caygill, Howard. "Physiological Memory Systems." In *Memory: History, Theories, Debates*. Ed. Susannah Radstone and Bill Schwarz. New York: Fordham University Press, 2010. Pp. 227–34.

Counterinsurgency Field Manual. Chicago: University of Chicago Press, 2007.

Editorial, "Mapping 'White' Afghans Aim to End Civilian Deaths," *National Post*, November 8, 2008, <http://www.canada.com/calgaryherald/story.html?id=a6df4358-ceco-4555-9efa-d7e66b4a31bc> (accessed May 10, 2016).

Federal Register 62.131 (July 9, 1997).
Flower, Rod et al. *Brain Waves Module I: Neuroscience, Conflict, and Security*. London: The Royal Society, 2011.
Flower, Rod et al. *Brain Waves Module III: Neuroscience, Conflict, and Security*. London: The Royal Society, 2011.
Gregory, Derek. "The Everywhere War." *The Geographical Journal*, 177.3 (September 2011): 238–50.
Habermas, Jurgen. *The Structural Transformation of the Public Sphere*. Trans. Thomas Burger. Cambridge, MA: MIT Press, 1989.
Hearings before the Subcommittee on Census, Statistics, and Postal Personnel . . ., Serial no. 103-07 (Washington, DC: US Government Printing Office: April 14, 1993; June 30, 1993; July 29, 1993; November 3, 1993).
Hill, Mike. "Of Multitudes and Moral Sympathy: E. P. Thompson, Althusser, and Adam Smith." In *Masses, Classes, and the Public Sphere*. Ed. Mike Hill and Warren Montag. London: Verso, 2000. Pp. 202–25.
Hill, Mike. "Incalculable Community: Multiracialism, US Census 2000, and the Crisis of the Liberal State." In *After Whiteness: Unmaking an American Majority*. New York: New York University Press, 2004. Pp. 21–74.
Moreno, Jonathan D. *Mind Wars: Brain Science and the Military in the Twenty-first Century*. New York: Bellevue Literary Press, 2006.
O'Hare, William. "Managing Multiple-Race Data." *American Demographics*, 4.2 (April 1998): 42–4.
Opportunities in Neuroscience for Army Applications. Washington, DC: National Research Council, 2009.
Pearson, Jordan. "Brain Controlled Flight is a Thing Now." *Motherboard*. May 28, 2014.
Spinoza, Political Treatise, trans. Samuel Shirley. Indianapolis: Hackett Publishing, 2000.
Virilio, Paul. *Pure War*. New York: Semiotexte, 1997.

Notes on Contributors

Warren Montag is Professor of English at Occidental College, Los Angeles. His publications include *The Other Adam Smith* (with Mike Hill) (Stanford University Press, 2014; Chinese translation forthcoming), *Althusser and his Contemporaries: Philosophy's Perpetual War* (Duke University Press, 2013; Spanish translation forthcoming) and *Selected Essays* (Brill, forthcoming).

Hanan Elsayed is Assistant Professor of French and Arabic at Occidental College, Los Angeles. She is the author of *L'Histoire sacrée de l'Islam dans la fiction maghrébine* (Paris: Karthala, 2016). Her essays include "Early Islamic Historiography: The Background and Sources of *Loin de Médine*" in *Approaches to Teaching the Works of Assia Djebar* (PMLA, 2017).

Nancy Armstrong is Gilbert, Louis and Edward Lehrman Professor at Duke University, Durham, North Caroline. She is editor of the journal *Novel: A Forum on Fiction*, and her books include *How Novels Think: The Limits of Individualism, 1719–1900* (Columbia University Press, 2005), and "Network Novel: Community in the Age of Democratic Writing" (University of Pennsylvania Press, forthcoming).

James Ford currently teaches in the English Department at Occidental College, Los Angeles. His first book, *Thinking through Crisis: Depression-Era Black Literature, Theory, and Politics*, is forthcoming from Fordham University Press.

Giorgos Fourtounis is Assistant Professor of Philosophy at Panteion University of Social and Political Sciences, Attica, Greece. He is co-author (with A. Baltas) of *Louis Althusser and the End of Classical Marxism: The Precarious Immortality of a "Null" Philosophy* (Athens 1994, in Greek). He has translated and edited George Canguilhem's *Le normal et le pathologique* (Athens, 2007) and is currently working on a monograph on Althusser.

Mike Hill is Associate Professor of English at the State University of New York at Albany. He is currently completing a book on twenty-first century warfare for the University of Minnesota Press. His most recent book, co-authored with Warren Montag, is *The Other Adam Smith* (Stanford University Press, 2015).

Vittorio Morfino is a Senior Researcher in the history of philosophy at the University of Milano-Bicocca, Milan, Italy. His publications include *Plural Temporality. Transindividuality and the Aleatory between Spinoza and Althusser* (Leiden, 2014) and *Genealogia di un pregiudizio. L'immagine di Spinoza in Germania da Leibniz a Marx* (Hildesheim, 2016).

Mohamed Moulfi is Professor of Philosophy at the Université d'Oran 2, Algeria. He is the author of *Engels, Falsafa wa Oloum* (Beirut: Rawafed, 2015). His recent essays include «Lectures machiavéliennes d'Althusser» in *The Radical Machiavelli: Politics, Philosophy and Language* (Leiden, 2015) and «Au-delà de l'autre, nous» in *L'IvrEscQ* (Alger, 2015).

Jason Read is Associate Professor of Philosophy at the University of Southern Maine, U.S.A. He is the author of *The Micro-Politics of Capital: Marx and the Prehistory of the Present* (SUNY, 2003) and *The Politics of Transindividuality* (Brill, 2015/Haymarket, 2016).

Index

Page numbers with 'n' are notes.

"Abel et Caïn" (Baudelaire), 235
Absalom, Absalom (Faulkner), 295, 297
"absolute method," 212
absolutism, 49, 65
"abstract universalism," 187
abstraction, 3, 114, 136, 198n23, 307n47
  ideological, 212
  and the nation-form, 302n12
accountability, and war, 320
active/passive citizenship, 8–9
Ad Ethicam (Leibniz), 133
Addresses to the German Nation (Fichte), 268
Agamben, Giorgio, 86n49, 103, 170, 300n2
"age of extremes," 42
agency, 2, 4, 5, 219, 309, 310, 322; *see also* consciousness
al-'asabiyya, 19–20, 22
al-shūrā, 16
Alfarabi (Al-Farabi), 13
alienation, 66, 70, 71, 88n62, 97, 292
alter ego, 136–7, 141, 148, 152, 153
Althusser, Louis, 1, 160, 182, 185, 203, 219, 220
  double inscription, 227
  and epistemological break, 228–9
  epistemology, 209
  essential section, 183
  on Hegelian topography, 224
  "Idéologie et Appareils idéologiques d'Etat," 243
  and ideology, 285
  interpellation, 243
  Machiavelli and Us, 212
  on Marxist theory, 225–6
  Montesquieu. La politique et l'histoire, 23
  On the Reproduction of Capitalism, 296–7
  on race, 312
  self-criticism, 182, 222, 223
  theoreticism, 220
"Althusser's Dramaturgy and the Critique of Ideology" (Balibar), 297
Anderson, Benedict, 286, 301n10
annexation of property, 169, 171
annihilation, of citizenship, 310, 314
anthropological differences, 10, 25, 182, 183, 184, 185, 191, 192–4
anti-clericalism, 95–8
anti-Semitism, 38, 44–6, 77n3, 77n4
appresentation, 136–7, 148
appropriation, 168–9, 173, 294
Arabic, 13–23
Arendt, Hannah, 183, 188
Aristotle, 14, 269
Aron, Raymond, 77n4
Assman, Jan, 102
associations, public/private, 7, 63, 65, 67, 69, 95, 97, 99–101, 103
asymmetrical warfare, 311, 316
AugCog (Cognitive Augmentation), 324, 325
authority, 60, 82n32, 95, 176

335

autonomization, 48, 122–3
Averroes (Ibn Rushd), 13, 14
Avicenna (Ibn Sina), 13

Bachelard, Gaston, 204–5, 209
backlash, 26, 264–5, 274
"bad subjects," 245, 297
Balibar, Etienne
   "Althusser's Dramaturgy and the Critique of Ideology," 297
   Citizen Subject, 159, 185
   "Geneaological Scheme: Race or Culture?," 286
   Identity and Difference, John Locke and the Invention of Consciousness, 159, 165–6, 290–1
   "In War," 309
   "Mortal God and his Faithful Subjects: Hobbes, Schmitt and the Antinomies of Secularism," 24, 94–105
   "'Possessive Individualism' Reversed," 288–9, 293
   Spinoza: From Individuality to Transindividuality, 144–7
   Spinoza and Politics, 318
   "Uprisings in the *Banlieues*," 26, 235
   see also "Schmitt's Hobbes, Hobbes's Schmitt"
"Balibar-effect," 1–2
banlieues, 235–48, 323
Battle of Algiers (film) (Pontecorvo), 239
Baudelaire, Charles, 239
   "Abel et Caïn," 235
   Fleurs du Mal, Les (Flowers of Evil), 239
   Swan, The, 240
Beaud, Olivier, 78n12
beautiful soul, 263–9, 271, 272, 274
Behemoth, 50, 52
Behemoth (Hobbes), 97, 98
Bellarmine, Robert, 82n32, 103
Bidet, Jacques, 285
Black American Narrative, 253–8, 261, 262, 264
Black Reconstruction (Du Bois), 257
BMI (Brain Machine Interface), 313, 320, 325
Bodéi, Remo, 183
Bodin, Jean, 51

Bonaventure, 14
"bourgeois" democracy, 40
Bourguet, Louis, 132
Brain Machine Interface (BMI), 313, 320, 325
brain mapping, 323
"brain reading," 325
Brain Research through Advancing Innovative Neurotechnologies® (BRAIN), 323–4
BrainCam, 324
Bredekamp, Horst, 88n6, 89n65, 98
Breuer, Stefan, 79n16
Brontë, Emily, *Wuthering Heights*, 298
Brown, Wendy, 299n1

Canguilhem, George, 208, 209, 211
Capital (Marx), 114, 126
Capitalism, 254, 284–5, 286, 303n15
Cartesian Meditations (Husserl), 134–8, 140–1
Catholicism, and Schmitt, 43
census, U.S., 317, 321
children of pride, 5, 56, 83n34, 170
Church
   and Hobbes, 53, 65, 67, 69, 71
   and translation, 13, 29n26
   see also secularism
citizen, defined, 5, 6
Citizen Subject (Balibar), 159, 185
"citizen subjects," 2, 4
Citton, Yves, 127
civil equality, 71
civil law, 9, 69, 75–6
civil liberty, 69
civil society, 8, 59, 310, 314, 319, 322
   and communication, 322
   and the family, 125
   global, 317
   Hegel on, 125, 126
   and liberalism, 62
   Marx on, 126
   and natural law, 59, 99
   and Schmitt, 49, 101
   spiritual authority, 95
   and violence in, 27, 312, 315–16
   and war, 27, 310, 312, 314, 315, 316, 317, 319
civilian-ization, 314
Clarissa (Richardson), 297
Coetzee, J. M., 298

Cognitive Augmentation (AugCog), 324, 325
COIN *see* counterinsurgency doctrine (COIN)
Cold War, 118, 119, 120
Cole, G. H. D., 63
collective organization, 65, 309
collectivity, 57, 66, 111, 114, 117–18, 124–5
Colliot-Thélène, C., 184
colonialism, 24, 176, 236, 239, 243, 296
Comay, Rebecca, 264
commensurability, 216; *see also* incommensurability
commodity fetishism, 117, 127
commons, 169, 174, 176
communication, 321, 322
communitarianism, 103
communitas, 304–5n27
communities, 41, 59, 64, 100, 125, 196, 286
  family as, 294
  imagined, 288, 302n11
Comte, Auguste, 103
Concept of the Political, The (Schmitt), 47–8, 54, 63
concrete order, 44, 62, 71
Condemnations, 14
conscience, 161, 162
consciousness, 11, 12–13
  Husserl on, 135, 152
  Locke on, 25, 157–69, 171
constituent power, 43, 46, 62, 71, 72, 74
Constitutional Theory (Schmitt), 46, 62, 72
"constitutionalization," and "institutional mediations," 189
content/form, 157, 194, 220, 221, 222–7
contract, cowardly, 269
Cooper, James Fenimore, 295
cooperation, 114–15
cosmopolitanism, 186, 195
cosmopolitics, 195
counter-revolution, 24, 38, 40–1, 43, 45, 64, 72, 104
counter-violence, 53–61
counterinsurgency doctrine (COIN), 313, 314, 316–17, 327
Counterinsurgency Field Manual (US Army), 316–17

Crisis of Parliamentary Democracy, The (Schmitt), 46
Cristofolini, Paolo, 151
"Criteria for Negro Art" (Du Bois), 253
critique, 212, 213
  Marxist, 215, 222, 223, 224

Davis, Jefferson, 272
De cive (Hobbes), 52, 54, 56, 88n63
De Libera, Alain, 14
decisionism, 48, 60, 75, 80n18, 86n48
Declaration of the Rights of Man and of the Citizen (Rousseau), 7–8, 120
Defense Advanced Research Projects Agency (DARPA), 323–4
Deleuze, Gilles, 305n15, 320
democracy, 38, 41–2, 62, 265, 286, 296, 315, 320
  "bourgeois," 40
  and "de-democratization," 310
  and liberalism, 62
  social, 87n53
demography, 321
depersonalization, 320
Derrida, Jacques, 294–5
  Spurs, 293
Descartes, René, 4–5, 134
dictatorships, 40, 59, 90n66
difference, 122, 123
  anthropological, 10, 25, 182, 183, 184, 185, 191, 192–4
differentiation, 1, 7, 312, 313–14
discontinuity, 209, 211, 214
divine law, 57
double position/inscription, 227, 228
doubt, universal, 134
Douglass, Frederick, 255
dramaturgy, and ideology, 297
Du Bois, W. E. B., 26, 256–8
  Black Reconstruction, 257
  "Criteria for Negro Art," 253

effects, primary, 151–2
ego, 134–8, 152–3
  alter, 136–7, 141, 148, 152–3
Electronic Numerical Integrator and Computer (ENIAC), 321
emancipation, 188–9, 192, 269–71, 272, 273, 275, 276
empathy, 148
"empiricism," 220

"End of the Black American Narrative, The" (Johnson), 253–4
enemies, 70
  friend–enemy distinction, 63–4
  internal, 10, 24, 45, 69, 95, 98, 104, 242
Enlightenment, 73, 96, 188, 189, 196, 273
ensembles, 114, 123
entelechy, 149
epistemological break, 203–29
epistemology, 26
equaliberty, 25, 118–28, 183, 187, 189, 190, 191–2
equality, 7, 9–10, 71–2
"*Es denkt*" (It thinks), 14
Esposito, Roberto, 5, 97, 170, 304n27
Essay Concerning Human Understanding, An (Locke), 11, 157, 159–60, 168, 288, 289, 294
"Essay on the Poor Law" (Locke), 174–5, 177
Essed, Philomena, 302n12
essences, 113, 114, 220, 224, 225
Ethics (Spinoza), 112, 144–5, 148, 150, 151, 157
exception, 9
  and anthropological difference, 194
  state of, 37, 40, 65, 71, 86n49, 103, 245
exclusion, 9, 41, 123
  Arabic texts, 13, 14, 23
  gendered, 8, 122, 123
  Locke on, 168–9, 178
  racial, 235, 238, 239, 247, 254, 288
  Schmitt on, 46
  and universalism, 26, 189, 191, 193
  violence, 127, 314, 315
  see also inclusion
exclusive inclusion, 299, 300n2
expropriation, 169, 170, 245, 294
extremity, 59, 307n47

facet of exception, 40–1
familial ideology, 285
family see kinship/family
Fanon, Frantz, 253, 266
Faulkner, William, *Absalom, Absalom*, 295, 297
Fayard, Jean-Pierre, 79n16

fear, 55–6, 57, 61, 71, 100, 246
Fearful and the Frustrated, The (Osno), 258–9
Fichte, Johann Gottlieb, 266, 267–8, 271
  Addresses to the German Nation, 268
Filmer, Robert, 173, 175, 177
Fleurs du Mal, Les (Flowers of Evil) (Baudelaire), 239
form/content, 157, 194, 220, 221, 222–7
Foucault, Michel, 7, 193
France, 94–5, 98, 120, 235–48, 323
Frankenstein (Shelley), 297
free Negro, 257, 259, 260, 262, 265
freedom of inquiry, 38–40
friend–enemy distinction, 63–4

Garréta, Anne, 306n44
Gates, Robert, 316
general will, 6, 46, 61, 62, 89
Geviert, das (Heidegger), 51
Gierke, Otto von, 87n53
Gleichartigkeit, 101
Gleichheit, 24, 46, 80n22, 101
globalization, 195
Glossarium (Schmitt), 77n3
God
  and conscience, 162
  Hobbes on, 51, 52–3, 56, 59–60
  and Islam, 16–17
  Locke on, 3, 158, 163, 165, 170, 174, 175–8
  and metaphysical intersubjectivity, 139–41
  and St. Paul, 161
  and secularism, 94–105
  and sovereignty, 59–60
Goldberg, David Theo, 302n12
group feeling, 19, 22

Habermas, Jurgen, 46, 314
Hadith, 15–16, 17
Haine, La (Kassovitz), 26, 235–48
harmony, metaphysical, 138–41, 147, 150, 152
Hayward, Susan, 239
Hegel, G. W. F., 44, 127, 133, 265
  concrete universal, 187
  cowardly contract, 269
  Doctrine of Essence, 133
  and epistemological break, 223–4

Phenomenology of Spirit, 124, 263–4
Philosophy of Right, 125
and Spinozism, 157
see also St. Louis Hegelians
Heidegger, Martin, 4, 38
  Geviert, das, 51
historicity, 11, 225
  and equaliberty, 192
  and science, 206, 208, 217, 215, 222, 224
  and science/Marxist theory, 205, 208–9, 218–19, 223–7
History and Philosophy of Science (HPS), 206–7, 208
history of science, 206
Hobbes, Thomas, 5–6, 14, 23–5, 287
  Behemoth, 97, 98
  De cive, 53, 54, 56, 88n63
  individualism, 99–103
  Leviathan, 48–53, 54, 56–7
  and Nazism, 47–8
  separation of Church and State, 94
  systems, 99–100, 103
  see also "Schmitt's Hobbes, Hobbes's Schmitt" (Balibar)
Hobsbawm, Eric, 42
Hoffmann, Hasso, 80n22
homelessness, 298
Human Terrain System (HTS) (US Army), 313, 317, 319, 320, 324, 325
humanism, 48, 83n32, 313
  Zombie, 313–27, 314
humans, 8
  as terrain, 320–1, 327
  as things, 320, 325–6
Husserl, Edmund, 139, 152, 197n10
  Cartesian Meditations, 134–8, 140
hybridity, 286, 317

Ibn Khaldun, 17–18
  al-Muqaddimah (Prolegomena), 18–21, 22
identity, 164–5
  group, 294–5
  and insurrection, 316–17
  Locke on, 158, 163, 168
  national, 288
  racial, 273, 317–18
  and refuge, 268
Identity and Difference, John Locke and the Invention of Consciousness (Balibar), 159, 165–6, 290–1
identity politics, 317–19
ideological state apparatuses (ISAs), 3–4
"Idéologie et Appareils idéologiques d'Etat" (Althusser), 243
ideology, 210, 211–12, 213, 214–15, 219
  and Althusser, 285
  dramaturgy, 297
  -form, 227–8
  and interpellation, 2, 3, 4, 236–8, 241–5
  practical, 219, 220
imagination, 146, 152
imagined communities, 288, 302n11
imitation, 147–8, 152, 167
immanence, of science, 221
immunitas, 304n27
impotence (*impuissance*), 48
"In War" (Balibar), 309
inaccessibility, 6, 18, 60, 158, 164, 236, 244
inclusion, 3, 8, 45, 145, 189, 261, 301
  exclusive, 299, 300n2
  see also exclusion
incommensurability, 206–9, 211, 213–14, 216–17
indirect powers, 48, 62, 69
Individu et communauté chez Spinoza (Matheron), 112
individual, Locke's, 288
individualism, 62, 99–102, 289, 292
individuality, 65, 189
individuation, 141–3, 211–12
individuation psychique et collective, L' (Simondon), 112, 141–3
inequality, and proximity, 236
ingenium, 112–14
"institutional mediations," and "constitutionalization," 189
Institutionalism, 60
insurgencies, 10, 121, 316–17, 319
intensive emancipatory principle, 188–9
intensive universality, 188
internal borders, 10, 241, 253–78
interpellation, 2, 3, 4, 236–8, 241–5, 297
intersubjectivity, 134–8, 139–41, 147, 152
invisibility, 244, 247, 268

irreversibility, 213–14
Ishiguro, Kazuo, 298
Islam, 13, 15–23, 105
ius circa sacra, 95

Al-Jabiri, Mohamad Ali, 16
Jacobi, F. H., 132
Jameson, Frederic, 129n34
Jaume, Lucien, 88n58
Johnson, Charles, 256–8, 261, 262, 264, 266
  "End of the Black American Narrative, The," 253–4
Jones, Gareth Stedman, 301n7
Journal of Speculative Philosophy, 268
Jus Publicum Europaeum, 40, 48
justice, Ibn Khaldun on, 20

Kafka, Franz, *Metamorphosis*, 298
Kant, Immanuel, 5, 44, 159, 187
Kassovitz, Mathieu, *Haine, La*, 26, 235–48
Katechon, 60, 94, 97
Kelsen, Hans, 61, 63, 75
Kenan, William R., 276
King, Martin Luther, 26, 257, 262–5, 274, 278
  "Letter from Birmingham Jail," 267
  Where Do We Go From Here (speech), 263
kinship/family, 287–8, 294–5, 296–9
Kittler, Friedrich A., 302n14
knowing the enemy, 38–9
Koerger, A., 268
Kuhn, Thomas, 207, 208, 216

labour/labor, 115, 122, 226, 292–3
"laïcité," 102–5
Langland, William, *Piers Ploughman*, 169
language, and racism, 241–6
Laski, Harold, 63
Le Cour Grandmaison, Olivier, 243
Lefebvre, Henri, 303n15
Lefort, Claude, 191
Leibniz, G. W., 14
  Ad Ethicam, 133
  Monadology, 139, 149
  see also Leibniz–Spinoza alternative
Leibniz–Spinoza alternative
  metaphysical intersubjectivity, 139–41

monad and mode, 147–50
monadology and Spinoza, 132–3
Simondon and the transindividual, 141–3
Spinoza and the transindividual, 143–7
Spinoza's passions, 150–2
transcendental intersubjectivity, 134–8
Lessay, Franck, 86n47
"Letter from Birmingham Jail" (King), 267
Levellers, 89n65
Leviathan (Hobbes), 48–53, 54, 56–9, 65–72, 95–8
Leviathan in der Staatslehre des Thomas Hobbes, Der (Schmitt), 45, 46–9, 54
Lewis, Bernard, 30n35
liberalism, 46, 99
  failure of, 54
  Hobbes on, 65
  neo-, 27, 311, 320
  and racism, 314, 318
  Schmitt on, 55, 62
liberty *see* civil liberty; equaliberty
Locke, John
  consciousness, 11, 14, 157–78, 290
  Essay Concerning Human Understanding, An, 11, 157, 159–60, 168, 288, 289, 294
  "Essay on the Poor Law," 174–5, 177
  ius circa sacra, 95
  and the sovereign, 5–6
  theories, 285–6, 289
  Two Treatises of Government, 157, 158, 168, 169, 171–2, 173–8, 286, 288, 289, 291–2
Lucretius, 153
Lukács, George, 298

Macherey, Pierre, 207–8
Machiavelli, Niccolo, *Prince, The*, 245–6
Machiavelli and Us (Althusser), 212
"Machine Gun Squad," 276
Mckinley, William, 276–7
Macpherson, C. B., 82n31, 289, 291–3
"man/citizens," 188
Manent, Pierre, 86n47
Manley, Alexander, 280n43

"man's own mind, a," 167
marginalization, 27, 238, 239, 240, 243
Martin, Traybon, 261
Marx, Karl/Marxism, 182, 187
  Capital, 114, 126
  critique, 212
  and the epistemological break, 203, 204–6, 209–10, 218–19, 224–6, 228
  "On the Jewish Question," 120
  reproduction, 300n4
  Theses on Feuerbach, 114, 116
  and transindividuality, 112–18, 124
Marx's nightmare, 327
massacres, Wilmington Race Riot, 272–8
materialist epistemology, 206
Matheron, Alexandre, 113
  Individu et commauté chez Spinoza, 112
M'Bowolé, Makomé, 239
media, 322–3
melancholia, 264
memory, 324–5
Merleau-Ponty, Maurice, 197n10
Metamorphosis (Kafka), 298
metaphysical intersubjectivity, 139–41, 152
metastable equilibrium, 142, 143
modernities, 25
  first, 187–90
  second, 190–1
monad/monadology, 152–3
  metaphysical intersubjectivity, 139–41
  and mode, 147–50
  and Spinozism, 132–3
  transcendental intersubjectivity, 134–6
Monadology (Leibniz), 139, 149
monads, and harmony, 138–41, 147, 150, 152
"monopsychism," 14
Montag, Warren, 147, 152, 244, 304n22
Montesquieu. La politique et l'histoire (Althusser), 23
moral rearmament, 255, 267, 268, 271–8, 277
Moreno, Jonathan, 325
"mortal god," 50, 59, 85, 143, 90n70, 96, 102

"Mortal God and his Faithful Subjects: Hobbes, Schmitt and the Antinomies of Secularism" (Balibar), 24, 94–105
Muʿāwiya Ibn Abī Sufyān, 18
Muhammad, Prophet, 15–16, 17
"mulatto," 329n32
multitudes, 311, 312, 320
al-Muqaddimah (Prolegomena) (Ibn Khaldun), 18–21
mutatis mutandis, 197n10
Muwāten, 21–2
myth totality, and Leviathan, 50–3

nation (the)
  and citizenship, 9–10, 22
  and equaliberty, 118
  and internal borders, 261
nation-form, 286, 302n11
National Association for the Advancement of Colored People (NAACP), 317
National Security Strategy (US), 314–15
nationalism, "ultra-," 42
nationalist myth, 40, 44
natural law, 5, 47, 55, 57, 75, 76, 99
  and property, 170–1, 173
Nazism, 23–4
  "Schmitt's Hobbes, Hobbes's Schmitt," 40, 41–6, 75
necessity, and sovereign, 170
negativity, 55–7, 97
"Negro Domination," 273
neo-racism, 27, 309–27
"non-apology for racism," 260
novels, 284, 295–9
novelty, 209

Obama, Barack, 259–60
obedience, 6–7
  and Hobbes, 55, 61, 75, 83n35, 96
  and Islam, 16, 19
  St. Paul on, 162
  and religion, 69
  and Schmitt, 68–9
obligation
  and Hobbes, 56, 59, 71, 99
  in Islam, 16
  and Locke, 173, 177
  and Schmitt, 61
obviousnesses, 134–5, 136, 160, 210, 212, 213, 215

oikonomia/oeconomia, 254
On Certainty (Wittgenstein), 215
"On the Jewish Question" (Marx), 120
On the Reproduction of Capitalism (Althusser), 296–7
Osno, Evan, Fearful and the Frustrated, The, 258–9
overdetermination, 219, 227, 228

paideia, 192
parallelism, 157, 168, 178
Parlementarianism and Democracy (Schmitt), 62
participation, 21, 22, 117, 119, 121–2, 163, 182, 188, 263, 289
particular see universal/particular opposition
passions, theory of, 150–2
passivity, 8–9, 145
Paul, St., 161–2
personality of the state, 95
phenomenology, 134–5, 195
Phenomenology of Spirit (Hegel), 124
philosophical anthropology, 24, 113, 114, 116, 193
philosophy
  of history, 45, 184
  history of, 159
  of science, 203–29
Philosophy of Right (Hegel), 125
Piers Ploughman (Langland), 169
Pluralism, 61–72, 74, 99–102
Poe, Edgar Allan, 295
police, and killings of civilians, 260
Polin, Raymond, 89n65
political anthropology, 111
political philosophy, 26–7, 182–96; see also Hobbes; Locke; Schmitt
Political Philosophy of Hobbes (Strauss), 55
political power, 56, 59, 188
  and equaliberty, 25
  fear of, 55
  Locke on, 172
  and the Muslim empire, 18
  and women, 297, 299
political society, 175, 176, 284, 287–8
political theology, 24, 43, 45, 47–8, 71
Political Theology (Schmitt), 47–8, 62–3, 65, 75, 84n39, 102

Political Treatise (Spinoza), 151
Politics as Vocation (Weber), 76
Pontecorvo, Charles, Battle of Algiers (film), 239
positive law, 40, 57, 172, 173, 188
positivism, 96
  legal, 44, 48, 60, 61, 73, 75–6, 100
possessive individualism, 288–9, 292
"'Possessive Individualism' Reversed" (Balibar), 288–9, 293
post-Kuhnian Science Studies, 208–9
Potestas indirecta, 82n32, 87n52, 103
practice, theory of, 219–23, 266
praxis, 191, 219, 220
preserve/preservation, in the Second Treatise, 172–3
preventative counter-violence, 58, 60, 69, 104
primary affects, 151–2
Prince, The (Machiavelli), 245–6
private property, 8, 88n58, 88n59, 160, 269, 303n15
proletarian myth, 40
property, 291–2
  Locke on, 25, 167–78, 285–6, 288, 289
  and novels, 296, 299
  private, 8, 88n58, 88n59, 160, 269, 303n15
  rights of, 20
  see also self-ownership
proximity, and inequality, 236
public enemies, 69, 98, 103, 104
public law, systems, 66–9
public spaces, 94, 192, 241

racialization, 254, 262–6
racism, 4
  "biological," 45
  neo-, 27, 309–27
  and novels, 296
  and the Paris banlieus, 235–48
  and white supremacy, 253–78
  see also anti-Semitism
ra'iyya/ra'āyā, 15–16, 19, 21
rationalism, 212–13, 214, 216, 289
reason, Spinoza's concept of, 146–7
recurrence, epistemological, 210, 212–14, 217
refuge, 255, 266–71, 271
regeneration, 145, 148
Regnault, François, 209, 213, 214, 216

religion, as superstition, 117
reproduction, politics of, 284–99
resistance, 73–7, 246, 309
responsibility, and property, 157, 168–9
resurrection, 167, 168
reversals, 288–93, 294
revolution, 7, 42, 50, 58, 62, 74, 126–7, 263, 265
 American, 274
 counter-, 24, 38, 40–1, 43, 45, 64, 72, 104
 and equaliberty, 121
 French, 8, 120
 in Military Affairs (RMA), 311, 316
 permanent insurrection/revolution/counter-revolution, 7–8, 24, 87n56, 104
 scientific, 207, 216–17
 social-democratic, 190–1
 see also violence
Revolution in Military Affairs (RMA), 311, 316
Reynaud, Phillipe, 77n4
Richardson, Samuel, *Clarissa*, 297
right of resistance, 48, 60, 61
rights
 and equaliberty, 118, 120
 of property, 176–8
 of resistance, 48, 60, 61
 social, 190, 191, 198n31
 symbolic/formal and actual, 8
 to rights, 188
Rimbaud, Arthur, *Saison en enfer, Une* (A Season in Hell), 239
Rosenthal, Franz, 19, 31n48
Rousseau, Jean-Jacques, 5, 6, 296
 Declaration of the Rights of Man and of the Citizen, 7–8
 and total alienation, 97

St. Louis Hegelians, 267–71
Saison en enfer, Une (A Season in Hell) (Rimbaud), 239
Sandford, Stella, 291, 304–20
Schelsky, Helmut, 48
Schmitt, Carl, 23–4, 37–42, 42–6
 Concept of the Political, The, 47–8, 54, 63
 Constitutional Theory, 46, 62, 72
 Crisis of Parliamentary Democracy, The, 46

Glossarium, 77n3
and *Katechon*, 97
Leviathan in der Staatslehre des Thomas Hobbes, Der, 45, 46–9, 54
and necessity, 170
Parlementarianism and Democracy, 62
and pluralism, 61–5, 68, 100
Political Theology, 47–8, 62–3, 65, 75, 84n39, 102
and sovereignty, 60, 66
Theory of the Constitution, 46, 75
see also "Schmitt's Hobbes, Hobbes's Schmitt" (Balibar)
"Schmitt's Hobbes, Hobbes's Schmitt" (Balibar), 37–77
 concepts or positions, 42–6
 Hobbes: from "total alienation" to "subject systems," 65–73
 Hobbes, Schmitt's "resistance"?, 73–7
 Leviathan: logos and mythos, 46–9
 mythic totality, 50–3
 Schmitt's struggle against *pluralism*, 61–6
 to read, to study Schmitt?, 37–42
 violence and counter-violence, 53–61
Schutz, Alfred, 10
science, philosophy of see philosophy of science
Science Wars, 203, 208
scientificity, 26, 28, 205, 209, 217–18
Scott, Joan, 187, 301n7
secularism, 24, 31, 70, 73, 94–105, 186, 187
self-consciousness, 165, 168
self-criticism, 182, 222, 223
self-ownership, 288, 289, 290, 292
self-preservation, 172–3
self-subjection, 166
Sen, A., 191
separation of Church and State, 94
seven symptomatic words, 235
Shelley, Mary, *Frankenstein*, 297
shepherd–flock concept, 16
Simmel, Georg, 10
Simondon, Gilbert, 111, 141–3, 144
 individuation psychique et collective, L', 112, 141
Skinner, Quentin, 98

slavery
  and colonization, 242
  emancipation, 26, 188–9, 192, 269–71, 272, 273, 275, 276
  theory of the natural slave, 269
  and white supremacy, 255, 257, 259, 269–70
sleepwalking, 163, 165
Snider, Denton, 269–71, 275
social citizenship, 121, 191, 192
social contract, 6, 7, 293, 315
social justice/rights, 190, 191, 198n31
social science, and Marxism, 205
social state, 41, 190–1
society, civil *see* civil society
soft power, 311, 313
soft violence, 27, 312
sovereign/sovereignty, 5–7
  divine, 4
  and Hobbs, 59–60
  and Islam, 17–20
  and mythic totality, 50–3
  and necessity, 170
  and property, 170–2, 173–4
  and race, 254
  system, 67–8
  and white supremacists, 259
space, public/private, 192
Spillers, Hortense, 255
Spinoza: From Individuality to Transindividuality (Balibar), 144–7
Spinoza, Benedictus de, 95, 327
  Ethics, 112, 144–5, 148, 150, 151, 157
  Political Treatise, 151
  Tractatus Theologico-Politicus, 102, 115, 315
  and transindividuality, 112–18, 124, 143–7
  see also Leibniz–Spinoza alternative
Spinoza and Politics (Balibar), 318
spirit, 129n34
Spurs (Derrida), 293
Stahl, F. J., 49, 83n33
state of nature, 5–6, 24, 54–5, 57–9, 70, 104
  and Locke, 171, 173, 174, 175
stigmatization, 26, 50, 237, 238, 241, 243, 245–6, 256
Strauss, Leo, 48
  Political Philosophy of Hobbes, 55
  and Schmitt, 53–7

"Straussian" strategy, 73
structural causality, 113, 219
subjection, 2, 4–5, 11, 95, 159, 166, 245
subjectivation, 99, 297
subjectivity, 2–3, 11, 12, 189, 190
subjects, 11, 159
  bad, 245, 297
  definition, 2–3
  in Islam, 17–19
  and race, 254
  and translation, 12, 15
Subjekt, 5, 15
Subjektion, 5
submission, 2, 7, 19, 176, 297
substances, and Leibniz–Spinoza, 133
superstition, religion as, 117
Swan, The (Baudelaire), 240
syneidēsis, 161–2
systems, subject, 63, 65–72, 75, 95, 99–101, 103, 113
Systems of Neuromorphic Adaptive Plastic Scalable Electronics (SyNAPSE), 324

al-Tahtawi, Rifa'a Rafi', 21
Tea Party, 58
temporality, objective, 138
terror, 50, 53, 55, 57–8, 69, 98, 170, 256; *see also* fear
theocracy, 117
theoretical ideologies, 220, 221
theoretical practice, theory of, 222–3
Theory of the Constitution (Schmitt), 46, 75
theory-form, 220, 221, 223, 225, 227
Theses on Feuerbach (Marx), 114, 116
things, human beings as, 320, 325–6
topography, 164, 166, 178
  and practices, 219, 224, 225, 226, 227
Tort, Patrick, 185
totality, 47, 48, 50–3, 64
Tractatus Theologico-Politicus (Spinoza), 102, 115, 315
transcendental intersubjectivity, 134–8, 141, 152
transindividual intellect, 14
transindividuality, 25, 111–18, 123–8, 143–7, 152, 161

translation, 11–15
Two Treatises of Government (Locke), 157, 158, 168, 169, 171–2, 173–8, 286, 288, 289, 291–2
tyranny, 59

"ultra-nationalism," 42
universal/particular opposition, 186–7, 195, 196
universalism, 8, 25, 26, 62, 182–96
unthought, 214–15, 216, 221, 228
uprisings, 235, 246–7
"Uprisings in the *Banlieues*" (Balibar), 26, 235

victimization, group, 255, 256
Vienne, Council of, 29n26
violence, 20–1, 53–61, 310–14, 322
  and the *banlieues*, 247
  legitimate, 98
  racial, 257, 267, 271–8, 314
  and war, 27, 310–18, 320
Virilio, Paul, 314

Waddell, Alfred Moore, 272–6
  "White Man's Declaration of Independence," 272–3, 274, 275, 276
Wallace, George C., 263, 266

war, 27, 309–27
war-neuroscience, 313, 314, 323
Weber, Max, 58, 98
  Politics as Vocation, 76
welfare state, 190–1
Wesley, John, 301n6
Where Do We Go From Here (speech) (King), 263
White, Charles W., 276
"White Man's Declaration of Independence" (Waddell), 272–3, 274, 275, 276
white supremacy, 253–78
Whitehead, Colin, 306n44
"whiteness," 319, 326–7
wickedness of men, 54–5, 56–7
Wilmington Race Riot, 272–8
Wittgenstein, Ludwig, *On Certainty*, 215
Wolf, Frieder Otto, 86n47
women
  Derrida on, 294–5
  and novels, 26–7, 284, 296–9
  as passive citizens, 8–9
writing, materiality of, 11–12
Wuthering Heights (Brontë), 298

Zamir, Shamoon, 269
Zarka, Yves-Charles, 88n58
Zombie humanism, 313–27

EU representative:
Easy Access System Europe
Mustamäe tee 50, 10621 Tallinn, Estonia
Gpsr.requests@easproject.com

www.ingramcontent.com/pod-product-compliance
Lightning Source LLC
Chambersburg PA
CBHW061705300426
44115CB00014B/2574